Alfonso Rodriguez

The practice of Christian and religious perfection

Vol. 3

Alfonso Rodriguez

The practice of Christian and religious perfection
Vol. 3

ISBN/EAN: 9783337202101

Printed in Europe, USA, Canada, Australia, Japan

Cover: Foto ©Lupo / pixelio.de

More available books at **www.hansebooks.com**

THE PRACTICE
OF
CHRISTIAN AND RELIGIOUS
PERFECTION.

WRITTEN IN SPANISH

BY V. F. ALPHONSUS RODRIGUEZ,

OF THE SOCIETY OF JESUS.

TRANSLATED FROM THE FRENCH COPY OF

M. L'ABBE REGNIER DES MARAIS,

OF THE ROYAL ACADEMY OF PARIS.

IN THREE VOLUMES.

VOL. III.

DUBLIN:
JAMES DUFFY, 7 WELLINGTON QUAY:
AND
LONDON: 22 PATERNOSTER ROW.
1861.

CONTENTS.

The author to the reader, ... vii

THE FIRST TREATISE.

On the end for which the Society of Jesus was instituted—The means which are conducive to this end, and which regard all religious in general

CHAPTER
I. Of the end and institution of the Society of Jesus, . . 9
II. What a glorious enterprise it is to labour for souls—how precious and meritorious this labour is, . . . 13
III. That this pious enterprise regards the whole society in general, and even those who are not priests have a part in it 17
IV. That to labour profitably for the salvation of souls, it is necessary first to be well grounded in virtue, . . 23
V. That the care of the advancement of our neighbour ought not to render us negligent in what regards our own, but on the contrary it ought to oblige us more seriously to apply ourselves to it, ... 30
VI. That we ought to take care not to fall into another extreme, which is entirely to withdraw ourselves from conversing with our neighbour upon pretence of applying ourselves to the care of our own salvation, ... 37
VII. Some remedies against the timidity of those who dare not engage in the employments of charity, lest they should thereby lose their own soul, ... 44
VIII. Of the means to produce fruit in souls—of sanctity of life, which is the first means, ... 49
IX. Of prayer, which is the second means to produce fruit in souls, 57
X. The third means of producing fruit in our neighbour is a great zeal for their salvation, ... 63
XI. The same subject continued, ... 66
XII. Three things which contribute very much to give us this zeal, 69
XIII. What zeal is pleasing and what is displeasing to God, 71
XIV. Another means of succeeding in our ministry is to regard only what belongs to the soul, without letting ourselves be influenced by outward appearances, . . . 78
XV. Another means to produce fruit in souls is not to confide in ourselves, but to put our whole confidence in God, . 81
XVI. That confidence in God is another very efficacious means to obtain favours from him, ... 88
XVII. The want of confidence is very displeasing to God, . . 92
XVIII. That we ought not to be discouraged though we perceive we produce very little or no fruit in souls, . . . 94

THE SECOND TREATISE.

On the three principal vows of religion—the advantages of a religious state.

CONTENTS.

CHAPTER	PAGE
IV. Why the oblation we make of ourselves to God in religion, by means of vows, is styled by the saints a second baptism and a martyrdom, ...	109
V. That the obligation we contract by the vows of religion, so far from diminishing our liberty, renders it more perfect,	111
VI. The great advantages of religion—the obligation we have to God for having called us to it, ...	114
VII. A continuation of the same subject, ...	122
VIII. The renewing of vows, which is a custom practised among us.—The fruit which may be reaped from it, . .	123
IX. A continuation of the same subject, ...	127

THE THIRD TREATISE.

The vow of poverty.

I. That the vow of poverty is the foundation of evangelical perfection, ...	132
II. Of the greatness of the reward which God bestows upon the poor in spirit, ...	135
III. That God rewards the poor in spirit, not only in the other life, but in this also, ...	137
IV. In what true poverty consists, ...	140
V. Of the fault of some religious who in religion place their affection upon trifles, having left considerable estates in the world, ...	146
VI. Of the three different degrees of poverty, . .	148
VII. Means to acquire and preserve poverty of spirit, .	150
VIII. Another efficacious help to obtain and preserve this poverty of spirit, ...	154
IX. What has been said in the preceding chapter is confirmed by several examples, ...	158
X. The obligation of the vow of poverty, . .	160
XI. How far it is against the vow of poverty to give or receive without permission, anything, though even it should not belong to the house, ...	164
XII. A solution of some difficulties which relate to the vow of poverty, ...	167
XIII. An objection is answered, and thereby this subject is more clearly elucidated, ...	173
XIV. That the vow of poverty obliges under pain of mortal sin, .	175
XV. Whether a religious can without leave of his superior receive money, in order to do works of charity with it; and what those cases are, wherein he would sin against his vow of poverty by doing so, ...	177
XVI. Some examples in confirmation of what has been said, .	182

THE FOURTH TREATISE.

On chastity.

I. Of the excellency of chastity, and the degrees by which we ought to raise ourselves to perfection in this virtue, .	186
II. That to live chaste we must necessarily mortify ourselves, and keep a strict watch over our senses, particularly our eyes, ...	189
III. That we ought to be very nice and careful, even in the least	

CONTENTS.

CHAPTER	PAGE
IV. That the least offence against chastity is to be told in confession,	194
V. Of the nature of love: how violent and dangerous a passion it is: how much we ought to dread it,	197
VI. Certain remedies against temptations to impurity,	200
VII. That penance and mortification of our flesh is a very good remedy against all temptations to impurity,	204
VIII. Several other remedies against temptations to impurity,	209
IX. That the fear of God is the most sovereign remedy against temptations to impurity,	211
X. The advantages which flow from the fear of God,	218
XI. The preceding doctrine confirmed by examples,	222

THE FIFTH TREATISE.

On obedience.

I. Excellency of the virtue of obedience,	225
II. Of the necessity of obedience,	230
III. Of the first degree of obedience,	233
IV. Of the second degree of obedience,	238
V. Of the third degree of obedience,	242
VI. Blind obedience,	245
VII. Obedience in spiritual matters,	251
VIII. What has been said in this treatise confirmed by several examples,	257
IX. Whence proceeds the opposition we find in our judgment to the orders of obedience,	262
X. The explanation of St. Paul's three arguments for obedience,	269
XI. That to look on your superior as on Jesus Christ himself, is an excellent means to obtain obedience in perfection,	275
XII. That to acquire this virtue we must obey our superior as Christ himself,	280
XIII. Of other advantages which arise from obeying the superior as we would Christ himself,	283
XIV. That God looks on disobedience and disrespect to a superior as an injury done to himself,	285
XV. That obedience does not hinder us from representing our difficulties to the superior—the manner of doing it,	288
XVI. Of too much solicitude for the things which relate to the body, and how necessary it is to avoid all singularity in this point,	294
XVII. An objection answered,	299
XVIII. The preceding doctrine confirmed by several examples,	304

THE SIXTH TREATISE.

On the observance of rules.

I. Of the favours God has bestowed on religious by guarding and fortifying them with rules,	307
II. That our perfection consists in the observance of our rules,	310
III. That though our rules do not oblige under pain of sin, yet we ought observe them exactly,	312
IV. The levity of the matter commanded by the rule, is no excuse for our violating it. This circumstance, on the con-	

CHAPTER	PAGE
V. How dangerous a thing it is to contemn our rules, though but in small things,	316
VI. The great advantages derived from an exact observance of rules, even in the least things,	319
VII. The preceding doctrines confirmed by examples,	322
VIII. Some other causes of the non-observance of rules. The remedy that may be applied thereunto,	326
IX. Some other means, which may contribute to an exact observance of our rules,	330

THE SEVENTH TREATISE.

On the fidelity which all ought to have in laying open the bottom of their heart and conscience to their superiors and ghostly fathers.

I. How necessary it is to make ourselves known to superiors exactly as we are,	336
II. That great comfort and repose of mind is produced by keeping nothing hid from our superior or ghostly father—of several other advantages derived from this practice,	342
III. To lay open our hearts to our superior, or ghostly father, is a most excellent remedy against temptations,	347
IV. That we ought not neglect to discover our temptations to our ghostly father, under pretence that we already know the remedies he will counsel us to make use of,	351
V. That we must never omit discovering anything to our ghostly father, under pretence that it is inconsiderable,	353
VI. A solution of the difficulties which might hinder us from giving an exact account of our interior,	356
VII. An answer to the principal difficulty which usually hinders us from freely discovering ourselves to our superior,	359
VIII. Another answer to the aforesaid difficulty,	365
IX. That we are under great obligations to God for having rendered this account of conscience amongst us so easy : the cause of this facility,	368
X. In what manner we are to render an account of conscience,	372
XI. An answer to several difficulties resulting from what has been said in the preceding chapters,	378

THE EIGHTH TREATISE.

On fraternal correction.

I. That correction is a mark of charity : how useful it is,	384
II. That it is pride which hinders us from receiving corrections so well as we ought,	388
III. Of the inconveniencies resulting from not receiving correction in good part,	390
IV. Of how great importance it is to receive correction well,	392
V. What has been said in the foregoing chapter confirmed by examples,	396
VI. Of the rule that obliges us presently to discover to our superior the faults of our brethren,	399
VII. Some important admonitions concerning this matter,	407

THE AUTHOR TO THE READER.

THE matters I have treated of in the first and second volumes regard a religious life in general, but these I now treat of regard it in particular; and therefore I have entitled this third volume, *Practice of Christian and Religious Perfection.* Things are so disposed in it, that they do not only suit all other religious orders as well as our own, but also that they may be very profitable to all secular persons who aspire to perfection. For, though the first treatise, for example, speaks of the end and institution of our Society in particular, yet it omits not to treat of several general matters, such as good example, zeal for the salvation of souls, diffidence in ourselves, and confidence in God, fraternal correction, manifestation of conscience to our confessor and spiritual father, all which are subjects interesting to every one. And generally, all the virtues I treat of in this last volume, are proper to all sorts of persons; because every one may either embrace and practise them in desire, if the obligation of their state hinders them from observing them in effect, or they may make use of them to resist and overcome the contrary inclinations which nature causes in them. I hope, by the mercy of God, that the reading of this work will excite religious more and more to the practice of perfection according to the duty of their profession, and will inspire seculars with a desire of imitating them, as far as the state of each one will permit; so that the one and the other will hereby daily increase their fervour in God's service.

THE PRACTICE

OF

CHRISTIAN AND RELIGIOUS PERFECTION.

THE FIRST TREATISE.

ON THE END FOR WHICH THE SOCIETY OF JESUS WAS INSTITUTED.
THE MEANS WHICH ARE CONDUCIVE TO THIS END; AND WHICH
REGARD RELIGIOUS IN GENERAL.

CHAPTER I.

Of the end and Institution of the Society of Jesus.

"ATTEND to thyself and doctrine", says St. Paul to Timothy; "be earnest in them. For in doing this thou shalt save both thyself and them that hear thee"—I. *Tim.*, iv. 16. The end and institution of the society consist in these two things, of which the apostle speaks. Our constitutions and the apostolical bulls expressly declare, "that the end of this society, is that all those who compose it may, with the grace of God, labour not only for their own salvation and perfection, but also seriously apply themselves to the salvation and perfection of their neighbour"— *Cap.* i. *Exam.* §. 1. It is not sufficient to apply ourselves after an ordinary manner, but we must, according to the Latin words, *impenso incumbere*, "earnestly apply ourselves", that is, we must apply ourselves with zeal and ardour to attain this end. Now it is to be observed, that as our constitutions oblige us to labour not only for our own salvation, but for our perfection; even so they will have us labour not only for the salvation of others, but also for their greater perfection and greater advancement in virtue. Hence, Father Aquaviva, in his instructions to confessors, counsels them to be less zealous in attracting a greater number of penitents, than in perfecting their present number daily more and more. In a word, the same care we have for our own advancement and perfection, we ought also to have for the advancement and perfection of our neighbour.

In effect, it is particularly for this that we have been instituted. For St. Ignatius, on the one hand, perceiving that the Church was furnished with many religious orders, which continually applied themselves to the divine worship and their own spiritual advancement; and considering, on the other, that it was afflicted with an infinity of heresies, disorders, and scandals, "that the harvest was great, and that the workmen were but few"— *Mat.*, ix. 37,—was inspired by God to institute our society, to be, as he himself said, like a kind of flying-camp, that should be ready at the least alarm, and always be in a condition to fight the enemy, and to afford help and succour wherever it should be wanting. And for this reason he would not have us subject to the keeping of choir, or to other spiritual practices, which might interfere with our giving succour to souls. If you should see, says St. Chrysostom, a blind man on the point of falling into a ditch, you would endeavour to save him; how then can we behold our brethren casting themselves headlong into the abyss of Hell, and not stretch out a hand to draw them back?

We see that even the ancient fathers of the desert, though particularly called by God to solitude, quitted the repose of their cells in times of persecution, and went into towns to oppugn heretics, to instruct the faithful, and encourage them to suffer constantly for the love of Jesus Christ. Thus great St. Anthony did in the days of Constantine. The same was done by the holy old man Acepsimus, who had lived three-score years in the desert without having had any communication with man; and this is what others have done at other times. We have an illustrious example hereof in the reign of the emperor Valence, in the person of a holy man called Aphraates. This emperor having driven all Catholics, not only out of their churches in towns, but also out of many others in the country, to which they retired to say their prayers and to offer holy sacrifices of praise to God, this holy old man left his cell to protect and defend the flock of Jesus Christ. One day as he went to the place where they were assembled, the emperor, to whom they had discovered him, caused him to be called to him, and asked him whither he went. The saint replied, that he went to offer his prayers to God for the preservation of the empire; and the emperor having told him, he would do much better to go and offer them in his cell, according to the custom of hermits; it is true, courageously replied the holy man, it is there I should offer them, if you did not hinder me from doing so, and it is this I ever did, while the flock of Jesus Christ were permitted peacefully to enjoy their pastors. But now, when they are deprived of them, and in danger of being lost, all things must be renounced for their preservation and defence from the wolves. If a virgin lived in great retirement and modesty, and saw the house of her father on fire, what ought she do? Ought she out of delicacy and modesty remain with folded arms, at the hazard of letting the house be burnt, and of being burnt in it herself? Or ought she not rather run and cry out for help, and use her endeavours to put out the fire? Now seeing that the house of God our Father is at present on fire, and that you yourself, sir, have set it on fire, it is to extinguish this fire, that we, who lived before in retirement, bring help from all places to it.

St. Chrysostom, speaking of the care we ought to have for the salvation of our neighbour, makes use of another very just comparison. If, when we are out at sea, says he, we discover a vessel afar off, in danger of being wrecked, we feel ourselves presently touched with compassion, and how favourable soever the wind is for our own course, we turn and steer towards the place where the vessel is in distress. We approach it, we take in our sails, we cast anchor, we throw out ropes and planks on all sides, and in fine, we do all things imaginable, to endeavour to save those we perceive in danger. It is thus we ought to behave while we navigate the sea of this world. The tempests which continually rise upon it, and the banks and shelves which it is full of, cause every day disastrous shipwrecks. When, then, we see our neighbour in this condition, we must presently quit all our affairs, and run to his succour, since the danger in which he is, admits of no delay.

Now, it was precisely for this end, and by a particular providence, that God raised our society in those deplorable days, when the Church stood so much in need of assistance. Ecclesiastical historians remark, that upon the very day that Pelagius was born in England, St. Austin was born in Africa; God so uniting the remedy to the disease, that when the one should endeavour to spread abroad the darkness of his heresy over the whole Earth, the other should be ready to dissipate it by his light, and to triumph over error by his doctrine. He that writes the life of St. Ignatius, also observes, that in the same year that Luther began to unmask himself, and to declare open war against the Church and against truth, God permitted that St. Ignatius should be wounded in the defence of Pampilona, and that he should be attracted by this means to his service, in order to put him at the head of a new militia, which he designed to raise for the defence of his Church. It is in this manner that divine Providence, which continually watches for the salvation of the faithful, never fails to send them extraordinary succours, when they stand in need of them.

The same author, enlarging upon this matter, shows also, that at the same time when the Albigenses and other heretics molested the peace of the Church, and when the field of our Lord was so filled with brambles and thorns, that the good seed was almost choked, God raised St. Dominick and St. Francis to oppose heresy with all vigour, to fight against vice and error by the purity of their lives and doctrine, and in imitation of the ancient fathers, to illumine the world by their light, and to sanctify it by their example. It was also by the infinite providence of God, that when the eastern church was oppressed by infidels, he formed several military religious orders to defend it with sword in hand. And finally, it is the same providence that has lately established so many religious orders, and our society in particular, the institution whereof is the subject of the present discourse. For in the beginning of the heresy of Luther, which destroyed the obedience that is due to the pope—which denied the truth of the Blessed Sacrament of the altar—and which wished to abolish the sacrament of penance—God raised our society, which makes a singular profession of obedience to the pope, which engages its religious thereunto by a particular vow, and which applies itself particularly to instruct all persons in the truths of faith concerning the sacraments of penance and the eucharist, to preach the frequent use of them, and to render men worthy of receiving them by a reformation of their lives. And just as a good general, when the battle is begun, observes from a rising ground the state of the combat, in order to send reinforcements wherever they are wanted—to send a squadron here and a battalion there—so Jesus Christ, who is the general of the Christian army, beholds from the heavens above the state of his Church in the different combats it has to sustain; and according to its necessities, he sends from time to time new reinforcements of doctors and heads of orders to succour it ; and herein the providence and mercy of our Saviour is very great, never to permit any distemper without applying a remedy to it in due time. Now this is properly the end for which our society has been instituted, as the bull of its confirmation says—it is to defend the faith against heretics, it is to carry it to infidels, it is to preserve it amongst Catholics, by our doctrine and example, for which God has called us.

CHAPTER II.

What a glorious enterprise it is to labour for the salvation of souls—how precious and meritorious this labour is.

THE salvation of souls is an end so noble and sublime, that it is for it God descended from Heaven and became man; and for it he chose his apostles, vouchsafing that, of catchers of fish, they should become fishers of men. St. Denis says, "that to co-operate with God in the salvation of souls, is the most divine of all employments"—*De Cœles. Hier.*, c. 3. And St. Chrysostom assures us that there is "nothing more pleasing to God than the salvation of souls; neither is there anything that he takes more to heart"—*Hom.* ii. *and* 40 *sup. Genes.* "It is his will", says the apostle, "that all men should be saved, and come to the knowledge of the truth"—I. *Tim.*, ii. 4. And does not God himself tell us by the prophet Ezechiel, saying: "Is the death of a sinner my will? is it not rather my will that he be converted and live?"—*Ezech.*, xviii. 23. In fine, God desires the salvation of all men, and therefore we can do nothing more pleasing to him than to labour for their salvation. Hence, "though your riches should be ever so great", says St. Chrysostom, "and though you should give all you have to the poor, yet you would do far more by converting one soul than by doing all this". St. Gregory says it is a greater miracle to convert a sinner than to raise the dead to life; and in effect the salvation of a sinner is a far greater work of God than the creation of the world. To be convinced of this, we need but consider what the one and the other cost him. The creation of the world cost him only a word; "he said, and all things were made: he commanded, and all things were created"—*Ps.*, cxlviii. 5. But the salvation of men cost him much more than words; it cost him his blood and his life. Does not Jesus Christ himself sufficiently declare to us of how great merit it is in the sight of God to employ ourselves in the salvation of souls, when he says in St. John, "It is for this reason that my Father loves me, because I lay down my life?"— *John*, x. 17. The saints remark very justly, that "he says not his Father loves him because by him all things were created", but only that his Father loves him because he lays down his life. And why does he give his life, but in order to save men? And hence we see that there is nothing more pleasing to God than to labour for the salvation of souls. St. Thomas explains in the same sense what our Saviour says in the same place: "As my Father knows me, so I know my Father, and I give my life for my flock"—*John*, x. 15. Jesus Christ, says the doctor, would not only express by these words that, as his Father knows him by a full and perfect knowledge, so he knows also his Father in the same manner; for he had already said it, as we see by these other words: "No one knows the Son but the Father, nor does any one know the Father but the Son"—*Mat.*, xi. 27. But as it is the duty of a good son to do what he feels to be most pleasing to his father,—and if asked why he did so, he could answer, because he knows his father very well, and knows what he likes best,—even so our Saviour having said that a good pastor gives his life for his sheep, and wishing to anticipate the question that might have been put him, why he gave so precious a life for so vile a thing? he answers it beforehand, by saying: "I know my Father very well, and I lay down my life for my sheep"; as if he would say: I know my Father's sentiments; I know very well that his sheep are very dear unto him, and it is this makes me cheerfully give my life for them. We ought to act on the same principle; this knowledge of the bounty of God to man, and of the love he has for those that labour for the salvation of souls, ought engage us to employ ourselves therein with all our strength. St. Chrysostom observes on this subject, that Jesus Christ having thrice demanded of St. Peter if he loved him, he gave no other answer to all the assurances that St. Peter gave him of this, but only, "Feed my sheep"—*John*, xxi. 17; as if he would have said: It is true you love me indeed, but you cannot testify this your love better, than by labouring with me for the salvation of the souls I have redeemed with my blood.

We may also judge of the excellency of this employment, and

how pleasing it is to God, by the greatness of the price that is annexed thereunto; and this is first seen in our Saviour himself, and by the glorious recompense that followed his death. "For it is for this", says the apostle, "that God exalted him, and gave him a name above all other names, that at the name of Jesus every knee shall bend in Heaven, Earth, and Hell, and all tongues shall confess that Jesus Christ is in the glory of his Father"—*Philip*, ii. 9, etc. King David gives us to understand the same, when he says of the Messias, "that upon his way he will drink of the water of the torrent, and for this reason his head shall be exalted"—*Ps.*, cix. 7. This is the sense of these words also of the prophet Isaias: "If he gives his life for sinners, he will see a long posterity"—*Isa.*, liii. 10; that is to say, that for all he will have suffered for men, he will be glorified eternally by his Father. "He", says St. James, "who shall bring back a sinner from his evil ways, shall save his soul from death, and shall cover a multitude of sins"—*James*, v. 20. And St. Gregory says hereupon, that if the saving a man from corporal death, who must die sooner or later, be an action worthy to be recompensed, what recompense does he not deserve who delivers a soul from everlasting death, and is the cause that it eternally enjoys God in glory? The Scripture likewise is not content to say, "that those who shall teach wisdom to men", as Jesus Christ did, "shall have life everlasting"—*Ecclus.*, xxiv. 31; it says moreover, "that those who show the way of justice to many, shall shine like stars for all eternity"—*Dan.*, xii. 3. God himself assures us by the mouth of Jeremias, that, "if we separate what is precious from what is vile, we shall be like his mouth"—*Jerem.*, xv. 19. That is to say, if we disengage souls from the servitude of sin, who are so precious and dear to him, he will love us tenderly. This is a way of speaking we sometimes make use of; for example, that we love a person as our own life and as our own eyes. God makes use of the same phrase, somewhat after the same manner, saying, we shall be as his own mouth; and by that he gives us sufficiently to understand how precious a soul is in his sight, and how dear those that labour for the salvation of souls become to him.

It is related of St. Catherine of Sienna, that when she saw a preacher go through the streets, she presently ran out to kiss the ground upon which he had walked. One day being asked why she did so, she answered that God had clearly let her see how great the beauty was of a soul in grace, and therefore she had so great a veneration for those who were employed in the conversion of souls, that she could do no less than give some mark hereof by kissing the ground which they had walked upon.

Now it is to the dignity of this employment that God has called us. The end of our institute is to coöperate with him in the most sublime and excellent function in the world, which is the salvation of souls. Hence we may truly say with the apostle, that "we are God's assistants, and that men ought to look upon us as ministers of Jesus Christ, and as dispensers of the mysteries of God"—I. *Cor.*, iii. 9. Can anything therefore be imagined more dignified than an employment which the Son of God himself came upon Earth to exercise, for which he sacrificed both his blood and his life, and by which we are called children of God, according to the words of the evangelist, "blessed are the peace-makers; for they shall be called the children of God"?—*Matt.*, v. 9. For the gospel, by this word peace-maker, according to St. Jerom and Theophilact, not only understands those who, after having overcome their own passions, enjoy peace within themselves, or those who procure peace and union between men, but likewise all such as procure peace between God and men, by converting sinners and reconciling them to God. Happy then are these peace-makers! They shall with justice be called children of God; because it is an employment which the Son of God himself exercised, "reconciling all things to his Father, and pacifying, by the blood he shed upon the cross, whatsoever is upon Earth, and whatsoever also is in Heaven"—*Col.*, i. 20. It was for this reason that the angels sung at his nativity, "Glory be to God on high, and peace upon Earth to men of good will"—*Luke*, ii. 14.

From all this, we ought to derive three things for our spiritual profit. The first is a great love and esteem for our ministry; because it is so sublime, so pleasing to God, and so profitable to our neighbour. The second is a very great confusion on seeing ourselves called to so sublime a ministry, weak as we are, and at the same time considering how difficult it is to render a good account of ourselves, we are, notwithstanding, charged with the salvation and perfection of others. This was the counsel which St. Francis Xaverius, a most apostolical man, of consummate virtue, and arrived to a very great height of perfection, gave to the fathers of Portugal, in a letter he wrote to them. I advise you, my brethren, says he, that when you think of the greatness of the ministry which you exercise, and of the esteem men make of you, that you think of nothing else but of humbling and confounding yourselves before God, according to the words of the prophet, "when I was exalted I humbled myself, and filled myself with confusion"—*Ps.*, lxxxvii. 16. One of the first fathers of our society, and one of the most eminent for his piety and learning, said, that when he considered the excellency of the end for which the society was instituted, and cast his eyes upon himself, he was so confounded to find how incapable and unworthy he was of so sublime a ministry, that he not only found no vanity in being called to it, but on the contrary, made it a new subject of his confusion and debasement. It is thus we ought to do, and by this means neither the consideration of the excellency of our employment, nor the esteem that men shall have of us, nor the honours they shall give us, will ever be of prejudice to us. The third thing which the consideration of our ministry ought to produce in us, is a serious application to our spiritual advancement; for, as I shall show hereafter, we ought to have laboured very solidly for our own perfection, and be very well advanced towards our own salvation, to be able profitably to labour for the salvation and perfection of others.

CHAPTER III.

That this pious enterprise regards the whole Society in general, and that even those who are not priests have a part in it.

WHEREAS those who are not engaged in the society but in quality of brothers, may perhaps think that the end of which we have spoken, regards only those who are priests and intrusted with the direction of souls—and lest these thoughts should discourage them, I shall here make it appear, for their comfort, that they have also their share in this holy enterprise. And when they shall well understand, that their functions, whatever they be, do all relate thereunto, this consideration will excite them to apply themselves to their duty with new fervour. We make altogether but one body, and the end of all this body is, what I have already said, which is, not only to labour for our own salvation and perfection, but to labour also for the salvation and perfection of others. Now to attain this end, it is necessary that the different members of this body should have different employments. There must be some of these religious to preach; there must be some to hear confessions; there must be some to instruct others; and there must be some also to serve others in their temporal necessities. It is thus, that, in an army well disciplined, there must be some troops to fight, and others to guard the baggage. The one, however, has as great a share in the victory as the other, and as a great a share also in the spoils and recompense. "For the part of him who goes to fight, and of him who remains with the baggage, ought to be equal, and equally divided between them"—I. *Kings*, xxx. 24. This is what David said at his return from the expedition against the Amalecites; and the Scripture remarks that this was ever after observed by the people of Israel as an inviolable law. And no doubt this was extremely just. For all the troops of an army compose but one and the same body; and those that guard the baggage contribute no less to the victory, than those that fight; because these could not fight, if the others did not remain with the baggage. It is the same amongst us religious. We all make but one body of Christian soldiers, who propose to ourselves the conquest of souls. There would be none able to preach, or hear confession, or teach, or study, if there were not some to take care of temporals; so that he who takes care of them, helps to preach, to hear confessions, and to gain souls to God, and therefore has his part in the victory and merit. St. Austin says, that St. Paul, by keeping the clothes of those that stoned St. Stephen, did worse than they. "For it was he", says the saint, " that stoned him by the hands of all the rest. He guarded their clothes, and did more hurt by this help he gave than if he had stoned the saint with his own hands"—*Serm.* xiv. *de Sanctis*. If this may be said of bad actions, we may with greater reason say the same of good ones, God being more inclined to recompense than to punish.

Father Avila, writing to two priests who were upon the point of entering into the society, tells them that though by their character they were already workmen in our Lord's vineyard, and that the society into which they intended to enter made particular profession of labouring for the salvation of souls; yet they ought not to propose this to themselves on their entering into it, nor be troubled after their admission, if they were not employed in this ministry. The reason he gave them for it, was that which I have just now spoken of, viz., that everything which persons do in the society, even in the lowest and most vile functions, was the same as if they were immediately employed in the gaining of souls to God. Because the institution of the society, relating entirely to the salvation of souls, and the progress which can be made in it depending extremely upon the preservation and increase of the society, whatever can contribute thereto, at the same time contributes to the conversion of souls, and ought consequently be embraced with a great deal of joy. Since therefore we are all members of the same society, we all contribute, every one in his function, to the fruit that is produced by means of the whole society, and we participate in the merit of all the conversions and all the good works it performs. It is this which our holy founder expressly tells us in his constitutions, speaking of those who assist in the temporal employments of the society; so that each one ought to have a great deal of satisfaction and comfort in his employment, and ought to look upon it as a great and special grace of God to be a member of a body that labours so profitably for God's glory, the salvation of the neighbour, and the conversion of souls. In fine, as I have said before, even the meanest and most vile functions of the society do all of them contribute to the conversion of souls; because their conversion being the end which the society proposes to itself, it is contributing to the same end with her to serve her even in any manner whatsoever.

To prove this more clearly, if amongst us only those who preach, who hear confessions and who are most engaged in the direction of souls, had all the merit and all the glory of the fruit which the society produces in souls, superiors would have most reason to complain of their employments, because effectively it would be they who would be less able to attend to duties of this kind. For the functions which are inseparably annexed to the offices of general, provincial, and others of the like nature, so take up their whole time that they have none left to devote to the help and salvation of their neighbour. Notwithstanding it is very certain that a superior who performs his duty well, and who takes care that all who labour under his charge do theirs well, renders more service to his neighbour than if he were continually employed in preaching and hearing confessions: just as an architect who directs a building renders more service than all those others who labour in it, and as a general of an army does more good by the judicious orders he gives than if he should charge the enemy as a common soldier. He does even more than all the rest, by the care he takes to make all the arrangements, and it is for this that, ordinarily speaking, all the honour of the victory is attributed to him. Now, as for the reason I have alleged, superiors have their share of the fruit which preachers and confessors produce in souls; even so, all who serve the society in any capacity whatsoever have their share in it, because in assisting the preachers and confessors with things which would divert them from their functions, they enable them wholly to apply themselves thereunto, which otherwise would be utterly impossible.

It is this, properly speaking, that makes us all be one body and members of the same body. Now as the members of the body have functions and properties different from one another, and what each member does it is not for itself alone it does it, but för the whole body: the feet, for example, do not walk for themselves only; the hands do not work for themselves alone; nor does the mouth eat for itself only; and so of the rest: just so all the mystical members of an order ought unanimously cooperate for the general good of the order, in the different functions that belong to them. This metaphor is taken from the apostle, who makes use of it to show that all the faithful make but one body in Jesus Christ, and that each of them ought to be content in the rank in which God has placed him. "The body", says he, "is one, and has many members, notwithstanding all the members are but one body. Wherefore if the foot says that it is not of the body, because it is not the hand, is it not therefore of the body? And if the ear says it is not of the body, because it is not the eye, does it for this reason cease to be of the body? If all the body were an eye, where would the sense of hearing be? and if it were all an ear, what would become of the sense of smelling? Since, therefore, God has placed each member in the body after such a manner as he thought fit, and that the eye cannot say to the hand, I want not your help; nor the head, in like manner, say to the feet, I have no need of ye: so God has placed in his Church, in the first place, apostles; in the second, prophets; in the third place, doctors. And to the one he has given power and the virtue of commanding, to others he has given the grace of healing, and to others the understanding of languages". It is necessary, therefore, that there should be divers functions and different degrees in the Church of God, "but it is always one and the same Spirit that works all these things, distributing them to each one as he pleases"—I. *Cor.*, xii. 12, etc., etc. It is the same in a religious body. There cannot be therein all eye, all tongue, nor all ears; all cannot be superiors, preachers, and confessors; there must be some religious in it, to serve the others in temporal functions; "and the eye cannot say to the hand, I want not your help; nor the head say to the feet, I do not want ye"; because the whole body of the society stands in need of the different functions of its members, to attain the end it proposes; and therefore the fruit which the whole society produces in souls is the work of all the individuals together.

But it is not only in this manner that all the religious of the society can contribute to the salvation of souls; for, without speaking of the example of a holy life, which is one of the things most conducive hereunto, as I shall hereafter treat of, they can likewise assist very much by holy conversation with their neighbour, which is one of the means whereby we produce the most fruit in souls. Hence amongst all of this nature that St. Ignatius speaks of in the seventh part of his constitutions, he particularises this as one of the most proper and most general means which all the religious, and even the lay brothers themselves, ought to make use of in occasions. He even makes mention expressly of lay brothers; and to make us better comprehend the importance of this means, and to excite us still more to practise it, he has made it a particular rule. Let all the religious, says he, each one according to his state, apply themselves in all occasions to render themselves useful to their neighbour by pious discourse, exhorting those of the world to good works, but, above all, to confession. So that it is not only the preachers or confessors who ought to endeavour to contribute to the salvation of their neighbour by their discourses; in proposing to one one sort of devotion, to another, another sort; counselling this man to swear no more; the other to make a good confession; the third, who is already more advanced than the rest, to make examen every night, and so of other devotions; but this obligation attaches to all the religious in general, and to the lay brothers as well as to the rest. In effect there have been many of them amongst us, who by this means have done much spiritual good, and who, perhaps, have gained more souls to God than many preachers and confessors have done.

We may likewise promote the conversion of souls by prayer, which is one of the means most conducive thereunto, as I shall afterwards speak of; and this means is, in like manner, in the power of every man. Very often a preacher, or a confessor, or one who assists a dying person, imagines the fruit he produces in souls to be his own work, when perhaps it is the work of the brother who accompanies him, who shall have put himself in prayer for this end, or of some other brother, who has mortified his body with this intention, and who has offered up his sighs before God. How many preachers and confessors imagine themselves to have brought forth many spiritual children, whom at the day of judgment they will not find to be theirs? They are at present their reputed fathers: "It is believed that this infant is the son of Joseph"—*Luke*, iii. 23. It is believed that this preacher, or this confessor, has brought forth such a one in Jesus Christ; it will be seen that he was the child of some poor, ignorant, and good religious brother. "She that was barren had many children, and she who had many children was deprived of them"—I. *Kings*, ii. v. This director, who seemed to have a great number of them, will find himself, perhaps, to have none at all. "Rejoice, therefore, thou that art barren, who bringest forth no children; cry out with joy, thou that bringest forth none, because she that was cast off and deserted shall have more children than she who has a husband"—*Isai.*, liv. 1. Rejoice ye, therefore, my brethren, whose ignorance and simplicity seem to render ye incapable of having spiritual children. Perhaps ye all have a great many more than the most renowned preachers and confessors shall have, and then, surprised with astonishment to see yourself to have so many children, "each of you will say within yourself, who has given me these children, I who am barren and deserted? and who has bred them up for me?"—*Isai.*, xlix. 21. You will say, I am neither preacher nor confessor, I have no knowledge, nor have any talent: whence then do these children come? Would you know from whence? They come from your prayers, from your sighs, from your tears, and from your groans. "For God hears the desire of the poor. Our Lord does the will of those that fear him, and he hears their prayers"—*Ps.*, ix. 41. Behold what it is that gives these children to those who never seemed to have any. St. Francis Xaverius said, that preachers and confessors ought to make use of these helps for two reasons: one, that the labour being divided between themselves and their brethren, they will take away the occasion of esteeming themselves more than them; and the other, that they may always keep alive the spirit of union and charity.

One advantage which the brothers have in thus contributing to the salvation of souls, is, that they are in greater security than preachers, confessors, or divines. For preachers and divines are continually exposed to the attacks of vanity and pride; and as to confessors, the direction of souls is so difficult and delicate a matter, that being liable to be deceived in it, they ought always to be filled with fear. Moreover, offices and employments of this kind are accompanied with so many cares and difficulties, that oftentimes, to satisfy what their duty requires therein, they forget their duty to themselves and their own spiritual advancement. But with respect to lay brothers, as their state defends them from vain glory, and delivers them from these cares and fears, the merit of what they do towards the conversion of souls comes whole and entire to themselves, without being the least corrupted by anything. So that without having any part with us in the danger, they participate in the profit and merit; and oftentimes even gain the better part. God grant that it does not sometimes happen that vain-glory be not all the preacher's part, and that all the merit and fruit which he should have got comes not to the brother, his companion, for this would be a very bad division. God grant us, then, of his mercy, that we may enjoy all the fruit of our labour, by doing everything always with a view to his greater honour and glory.

CHAPTER IV.

That to labour profitably for the salvation of souls, it is necessary first to be well grounded in virtue.

THE two things I just now spoke of, viz., to labour for our own salvation, and to labour for the salvation of our neighbour, are equally the end of the society, and they are so linked together by our constitutions, that they reciprocally help and lend the hand to each other. Hence the means which the society makes use of for the spiritual advancement of its children are very different from those made use of by other orders, who by their institute are not so much engaged in assisting their neighbour. St. Ignatius used to say, that if he had consulted the individual good of the society, he would have made many regulations in it which he did not, that it may be more at liberty to apply itself to the service of the neighbour. He likewise said, that if he consulted but his own interest, he would have run about the streets as a fool, in order to show more clearly the contempt he had of the world, and also to give the world a greater occasion of contemning him. But the zeal he had for his neighbour repressed these motions in him, and the fear he had of scandalizing and wounding the neighbour, by wounding gravity and civility, caused him to abstain from all the humiliations which might be contrary thereunto. He says, moreover, that if he had followed his own inclination, and regarded the profit he derived from the singing used in the church, he would have established the use of it in the society; but he did not do it, because God had made him understand that he would have the society serve him in other exercises of piety. Since, therefore, the society does not propose to itself its own spiritual advancement alone, but also the advancement of the neighbour, its object is that the means which it has given us for our spiritual advancement may render us more fit to labour for that of our neighbour, and that the functions of charity in which we shall be employed for our neighbour, may promote our own particular advancement. We ought, then, make account that our progress in virtue and perfection consists in acquitting ourselves well of our functions, and, on the one hand, view the help given our neighbour as a proper means for our particular advancement, and, on the other, regard the graces and helps which God bestows upon us for that end as a means to become more profitable to our neighbour. But if we do not apply ourselves to this, we deserve that God should stop the course of his graces; because it is with a view to this he bestows them so abundantly upon us, and it is to this the grace of our vocation is attached. For it was not for the particular advantage of Joseph that God raised him to so high a state of glory and power in Egypt, but for the advantage of all his brethren, and to save them and all their families in the time of famine, as he himself acknowledged, when he said to them: "It is to save you that God sent me hither before you"—*Gen.*, xlv. 5; so it is not for our particular profit that God calls us to the society, and pours down his graces upon us in so great abundance. No; it is for the profit of our neighbour; it is that our light may shine before men, and not that we should hide it under a bushel. But let us speak of these two things separately, though they always are connected one with the other.

As to the first, which regards the advancement of each one in particular, it is certain that, to be in a state to labour profitably for the advancement of our neighbour, we ought first of all have laboured for our own; and it is this the apostle recommends to us, in the first place, as the foundation of all the rest, when he says: "Attend to thyself". Each one ought first of all to attend to himself, and seriously apply himself to his particular advancement. For God, who is the author of grace as well as of nature, who "reacheth from end to end mightily, and disposeth all things sweetly"—*Wisdom*, viii. 1,—keeps the same order in the works of grace that he does in those of nature, wherein (to speak philosophically) "every like produces its like". Since then in natural things, we see that, besides the general causes of their production, there ought to be also a near and immediate cause, and of the same species, to give to each being that particular form which it ought to have—that there ought to be fire, for example, to produce another fire, and light, to produce another light; so, in spiritual things, it is God's pleasure that, to produce patience, charity, and humility in a heart, the preacher or confessor, who is the immediate cause he makes use of, should be humble, patient, and charitable. Moreover, as in natural things we see, for example, that a plant produces no seed for the multiplication of its own species till it be grown great, so in things of grace God will have us be great in virtue and spirituality, to bring forth spiritual children, and to be able to say with the apostle: "By means of the gospel I have begotten you in Jesus Christ"— I. *Cor.*, iv. 15.

It is for this reason that the first thing in which the society employs those it receives, is to labour for their own advancement, that in the beginning they may lay a solid foundation. This is also the reason why it appoints such different times of probation; first, it causes them to make two years of noviceship before their studies; afterwards at the end of their studies, they are put again into the fire to give them a new heat and temper by causing them to make another year of probation, in order that if, by application to study, they should perhaps have relented anything from their first fervour, they may regain new strength before they begin to treat with their neighbour; and that they should not treat of spiritual things with others till they were previously well grounded in spirituality themselves. Moreover, even after all this, it seems that we are never to cease almost to be novices; our profession is deferred so long, that almost our whole life, as it were, passes in a noviceship and probation before the society admits and acknowledges us to be true and fit workmen in the vineyard of our Lord. It does this, because the matter in question is the conferring upon us what is of the greatest importance in the world; and therefore it is necessary to have a good trial of us beforehand, to see what we are and what we are capable of. The thing in question is, to charge us, not only with the conversion, but with the perfection also, of our neighbour; and therefore it is necessary we should first have laboured very well for our own. Hence it is easily seen how much those are deceived who seem to think these probations too long or even useless, and who, from the first ray of light they receive in prayer—from the least spark of piety they feel in their heart—would on a sudden thrust themselves into the offices of preaching and hearing confessions. St. Ephraim deplores this abuse, and says it is a sentiment that springs, not from the spirit of God, but from the spirit of presumption and pride. "They would begin", says he, "to teach before they know anything themselves. They would intrude themselves to give laws and rules to others, before they have learned the law or rules themselves; they would take upon them to give their opinion in everything, before they have begun to spell; and before they are capable of receiving correction, they take upon them to correct others"—*Serm. de Vit. Monach.*

St. Gregory, speaking of those who are guilty of this fault, treats this subject perfectly well, and to render things more sensible, he makes use of some familiar comparisons. "Such persons as these", says he, "ought to be admonished to consider, that little birds, who fly before their wings are fully feathered, fall upon the ground instead of flying in the air. Likewise when a wall is fresh and new made, if the roof is put upon it, it rather destroys than makes a building: moreover, women who are brought to bed before their time, rather increase the number of graves than augment families"—3 ^{1}p. *Pastor. Adm.* 26. The employments that regard the health of our neighbour require a great fund of virtue and mortification. If without this you engage herein, you will have more reason to fear than to hope, and you will rather imbibe the spirit and sentiments of the world, than the world will imbibe yours. The same St. Gregory therefore observes, that though Jesus Christ, the eternal wisdom of the Father, was infinitely wise from the first moment of his conception, yet he began not to teach others till he was thirty years of age, and till he had prepared himself for it by his retreat in the desert, by forty days' fast, and many other austerities. "It is not that he stood in need", says this great saint, "of any preparation; but he would teach us by his own example how great preparation and perfection is required for so great a ministry. Also when he was twelve years of age, when he stayed in Jerusalem, and his parents went there to seek him, they found him in the temple in the midst of the doctors, disputing with them. And hence", continues this father, "those that are still weak and infants in virtue ought to learn not to meddle with the teaching of others, nor intrude themselves before their time into so sublime a ministry, since Jesus Christ himself would, at the age of twelve years, be instructed by those whose master he himself was, and was contented to hear and to ask them questions, though it was he who inspired them with all the light and knowledge they had to answer him. It was also for this reason", says the same saint, "that Jesus Christ having commanded his apostles to go and preach the gospel throughout the whole world, and having then the power to give them grace necessary for this end, yet he would not do it, nor permit them, in the weak and imperfect state they were, to go and preach his word, but commanded them, saying: Go into the town, and remain there till ye shall be replenished with the virtue of the Holy Ghost". And this he did to let us see that we ought to be very well grounded in humility, mortification, and all other virtues, in order that the employments which engage us to treat with our neighbour may be profitable for their salvation, without being prejudicial to our own.

St. Bernard upon this subject makes use of these words of the Canticles: "Our sister is little, and as yet has not any breasts"— *Cant.*, viii. 8; and applying them to the state of the Church before the descent of the Holy Ghost, he says: The Church was then very little, and at that time had neither breasts nor milk to nourish its spiritual children; but when the Holy Ghost descended upon the apostles, he replenished them with milk and with his gifts and graces. "All were filled with the Holy Ghost", says the Scripture, "and they began to announce in different languages the wonderful works of God"—*Acts*, ii. 4,—and to work conversions without number. If you would therefore produce fruit in souls, and raise spiritual children to God, you ought to have your breasts full of milk—one of them ought to be filled with the milk of all the virtues, and the other with the milk of pure and wholesome doctrine.

St. Jerom, explaining these words, "when the clouds shall be filled, they shall pour down rain upon the earth in abundance" —*Eccl.*, xi. 3,—says that the preachers of the word of God are clouds, and that as the clouds water the earth when they are full of rain, so when preachers are full of the wholesome water of evangelical doctrine, they water the hearts of men. It is for this reason that, when God threatened his vineyard by the prophet Isaias, he said that "he would command the clouds to give no more rain upon it"—*Isa.*, v. 6. By this, says this holy father, he would give us to understand that one of the greatest chastisements with which he is wont to punish the sins of men, is to hinder the rain of his divine word from falling upon them, and not to send them preachers, or not to permit that they produce any fruit. When, therefore, these clouds shall be full of the celestial rain of grace, they may then, says the saint, shower down their waters upon the earth, and these words of Moses may be applied to them: "Let the earth hear the words of my mouth, let my doctrine be poured down like rain, let my discourse fall like dew; let it be like rain upon the grass, and as drops of water upon the meadows"—*Deut.*, xxxii. 1. It is then they will be able to render the earth fruitful—then they will be able to soften and temper the dryness of men's hearts, and render them capable of producing the fruits of justice and salvation. But if these clouds have no water, what will happen? Would you know? Behold what St. Jude, in his canonical epistle, says: "They are clouds without water, which the winds drive every way"—*Jude*, xii. So that, as the clouds which are not full of water are easily carried by the wind from one side to the other, because of their great lightness; even so, if a preacher be not full of the spirit of humility and mortification, if he be not filled with all sorts of virtue, he will infallibly be carried from one side to the other with the wind of vain-glory and self-love; and this quality of an evangelical preacher, this quality of the cloud, which is raised above the earth, will serve him for nothing else than to make him be the more easily turned and tossed up and down by all sorts of winds.

St. Austin, speaking of riches, says: "It is hard to be rich without being proud, because it is the ordinary effect of riches to engender pride". "Everything", says this father, "has a particular worm that eats it. All sorts of fruit, all sorts of grain, all sorts of wood, have a particular worm; and the worm of an apple, that of a pear, that of a bean, that of a grain of corn, are each of them different one from the other: the worm of riches is pride". If, therefore, the rich be so exposed to pride, because their riches attract to them the esteem of men, how much more are they exposed who are elevated above the earth, like clouds, to water and render it fruitful by the rain of their word, who are looked upon as saints of our Lord, and whose functions and ministry render them venerable to all the world! We owe more respect to priests and spiritual fathers, says St. Chrysostom, than to kings and princes. Nay, we owe more, and have a greater obligation to them, than to our own fathers. For these begot us for the world and to live in the world, but those begot us for heaven, and to live eternally with God. There is nothing so great amongst men, nor attracts a greater respect from them, than to have the reputation of sanctity. All the honours they give upon other motives are usually only exterior, and are very often accompanied with the contempt of him that renders them; but the honours given a man upon account of his being esteemed a saint, are always filled with sincere and profound veneration. Now, as vain-glory is the worm that sticks ordinarily to good actions, and the greater and more holy they are, the greater fear there is of its corrupting them, there ought, without doubt, be a greater foundation of humility, to sustain the weight of the reputation and honours which they attract. Hence St. Chrysostom, speaking of the dignity of priesthood, and the dangers that accompany it, puts vain-glory at the head of them, and says it is a far more dangerous rock than all those whereof the poets have given such frightful descriptions.

CHAPTER V.

That the care of the advancement of our neighbour, ought not to render us negligent in what regards our own, but on the contrary it ought to oblige us more seriously to apply ourselves to it.

" RECOVER thy neighbour according to thy power, and take heed to thyself, that thou fall not"—*Ecclus.*, xxix. 27. This is properly the end of the institute of the society; this is the high road whereon all of us ought to walk. Now we can go off this road two ways, viz., leaving it to the right, by entirely withdrawing ourselves from conversing with our neighbour, to think only upon our own advancement; or to the left, by so entirely giving ourselves to the help of our neighbour as to become forgetful of ourselves. Both these extremes are vicious; and in order that between one and the other we may keep the middle, in which perfection consists, and that we may not turn either to the right or the left, I shall speak of each separately. First, then, to speak of the more dangerous one, which is the giving of ourselves so entirely to the help of our neighbour, as to become forgetful of ourselves. This is an inconvenience which our Saviour himself sufficiently admonishes us of, when he says, " What does it profit a man to gain the world, if he loseth his own soul? And what can a man give in exchange for his soul?"— *Mat.*, xvi. 26. For this loss no compensation can be made; and therefore reason and well ordered charity require, that we should not neglect our own salvation for anything whatsoever in this world, and that we never ought to relent in the care of our own advancement. The Psalmist observes this order very well, when he begs of God, saying, "Teach me goodness, discipline, and knowledge"—*Ps.*, cxviii. 66. For he puts goodness in the first place, as what is more particularly necessary for him, and more for his advantage than the others. We ought not therefore forget ourselves, or neglect our own salvation, upon pretence of labouring for the salvation of our neighbour. This would be a very great abuse; and Seneca himself, speaking of those who have greater care of the amendment of others than of their own, compares them to wells which impart clear water to others, and keep the mud to themselves. Pope Nicholas also in one of his decrees, makes use of a comparison very apposite to our subject;

he asks whether priests of an ill life can validly administer the sacraments. And after having decided that they can, because they do prejudice to none but themselves, he says that they are like lighted torches, which give light to others, but at the same time consume themselves.

St. Bernard, writing upon these words of the Canticles, "your name is like oil spread abroad"—*Cant.*, i. 2,—treats this matter perfectly well. He says that the Holy Ghost works two things in us: the one, by which he first establishes us in virtue for our own advancement, he calls "infusion"; the other, by which he communicates to us his gifts and graces, for the profit and advantage of our neighbour, he calls "effusion", or pouring forth, because it is a grace that is given us to bestow upon others. Now this "infusion", he says, ought to precede the "effusion". We ought first be well filled with virtue, before we can fill others therewith. And hereupon he makes a comparison, which exp'ains his thoughts very well. He says, there is this difference between a channel, or pipe that serves to conduct the water from a fountain, and the basin that receives it, that the channel receives and renders the water at the same time, without retaining anything of it; whereas the basin first fills itself, and afterwards the superfluous water runs over, which it cannot do without still keeping itself full. "You will do very wisely then", says he, "to become like the basin, and not like the channel"—*Bern. Serm.* lxxviii. *sup. Cant.*; and that you may contemn this counsel, continues the saint, as coming from myself, know that it is not I, but the Holy Ghost that gives it: "A fool uttereth all his mind; a wise man deferreth, and keeps it till afterwards"—*Prov.*, xxix. 11. The one retains nothing, no more than a channel does; the other, on the contrary, is like a basin, that lets nothing run over till it be first full itself. "But alas!" says this father, "the misery is, that we have now-a-days a great many channels and pipes in the Church, but very few basins"—*Serm.* xviii. *sup. Cant.*, *num.* 5. There are many people who are channels out of which the water of the divine word passes to water the hearts of the faithful, and to cause them to bring forth the fruits of grace and benediction, but they remain dry themselves. They have so much charity, continues this saint, that they wish to give away before they have gathered together. They wish to lead and help others, and know not at all how to help themselves. There is a great deal of folly and no charity at all in this, because there is no degree of charity above that which the wise man advises us to have for ourselves, when he says, " Take pity on your own soul by rendering it pleasing to God"—*Ecclus.*, xxx. 24. Behold here the first thing we ought to do, behold what we ought to begin with: as to what regards the help and advancement of our neighbour, it ought only to follow *this*. " For if I have but a little oil left for my own use, as the widow of Serapta had, do you think I will deprive myself of it for you? I will keep it, and will not give it, but at the prophet's command. But if one of those who perhaps think better of me than they see me deserve, or hear me spoken of, do with instance press me for it" —*In Cant. serm.* xviii., *num.* 5,—I will answer them with the wise virgins : " Lest there should not be enough for me and thee, go rather to those that sell it, and buy some for thyself"—*Mat.*, xxv. 9. " For it is not just", says the apostle, "that others should be eased and you burdened; but by an equality"—II. *Cor.*, viii. 13. This is all that true charity requires of you, which commands you to "love your neighbour as yourself"—*Mat.*, xxii. 39. Behold here the equality of which St. Paul speaks. But he does not require of you that you love your neighbour better than yourself, that you prefer him to yourself, and that you neglect the care of your own advancement to labour for that of others. " Let my soul", says the prophet, " be filled with exquisite and delicious meat ; and then, O Lord, my mouth shall sing hymns of joy and thanksgiving"—*Ps.*, lxii. 6. Our heart therefore ought first be filled, that it may be " from the abundance of the heart that the mouth speaks"; and it is for this reason that the apostle says, " that we ought very carefully observe what we hear, lest at any time we should let it slip"—*Heb.*, ii. 1. We ought carefully preserve in us what the grace of God has poured into us ; we ought to let it flow from us as from a vessel that is full, and not let it leak, as out of a cracked vessel that can retain nothing. So that the care of the advancement of our neighbour's salvation ought to be so far from rendering us negligent in what concerns our own, that it is this which ought to oblige us to apply ourselves more earnestly thereunto. For a great fund of humility, mortification, and all other virtues is required, as I have already said, to be in the world, and not to partake of the sentiments of the world, and to hinder the world, instead of conforming itself to our spirit, from perhaps making us conform ourselves unto its spirit. " He that handles pitch", says the Scripture, "will have his hands defiled therewith"—*Eccl.*, xiii. 1. And they ought to be well rubbed over first with oil, if he wishes the pitch not to stick to them. It is the same with us in regard of those of the world. We ought to be well filled and penetrated with the unction of grace and prayer, that worldly conversation may not stick to us and defile us. But if we take not this precaution, we shall have reason to fear that it may communicate its vices and maxims to us, and that these may draw us along with them into its irregularities and disorders, to verify the saying of Osee, "Such as the people are, such is the priest"—*Osee*, iv. 9.

One of the chief instructions that St. Ignatius gave to those whom charity engaged to converse with their neighbour, was to persuade them that those they had to treat with were not perfect, but that they went, as says St. Paul, "into the middle of a wicked and perverse generation"—*Philip.*, ii. 15. And this warning teaches us to be extremely upon our guard, lest the scandals and disorders we see amongst them should corrupt our minds and hearts. The physicians and such as assist the sick are accustomed, when the diseases are very contagious, to take preservatives, and to carry perfumes about them, to prevent the effects of the contagion and of the bad air which is breathed by sick persons. Now the sick we treat, and have greatest conversation with in the world, are attacked with contagious diseases, which are easily caught, if we bring not with us the preservatives of prayer, mortification, and all the virtues. It is requisite that a confessor, who is continually obliged to apply his hands to wounds full of filth and rottenness, should have a good stomach to prevent the bad odour of the many sins that confessions are filled with, from turning his stomach and exciting bad thoughts and motions that may corrupt his purity.

Some say very justly that we ought to be like certain rivers, which enter into the sea without losing any of the sweetness of their water and without mixing with that of the sea. St. Chrysostom, in order to show us what priests ought to be, whose ministry and zeal for souls oblige them to converse with all sorts of people in the world, says, they should be in the midst of the world, as the three children were in the midst of the fiery furnace of Babylon. For in effect we are in the world in the midst of flames, and these flames are far more ardent than those of that furnace were. The flames of ambition, of impurity, of envy, of detraction, raise themselves furiously round about us and encompass us on all sides; and because the fire penetrates wheresoever it finds entrance, and spoils and blackens all it meets with, the priest of God, adds the father, ought to take care lest this smoke approach so far as to touch him. Now to prevent the flames not only from burning us, but even to hinder the smoke they send forth from blackening us, what precautions ought we not take, and with what circumspection ought we not carry ourselves? St. Austin, explaining these words of our Saviour in the Gospel, "You are the world"—*Mat.*, v. 14,—says, "That light contracts no uncleanness by passing through foul places"—*Aug. Tract.* iv., *sup. Joan.;* but, on the contrary, that it purifies them and chases away their bad smell, without receiving any impression thereof in itself. It is in this manner that our light ought to make manifest the sins of the world, and penetrate their filth without contracting any corruption from them. It is thus that it ought to purify the heart of sinners and drive away the bad exhalations of vice. But to do this, we ought to have a great application to our spiritual exercises, to prayer, examens, spiritual reading, penance, and mortification. Above all, we must never neglect our prayer, which each of us is obliged daily to make for our spiritual progress. This is a thing of which we cannot take too much care, because the Devil, who perceives that he cannot hinder us from labouring for the advancement of our neighbour, as we are particularly obliged thereunto by our institution, endeavours to make us apply ourselves so to it that we come at length to forget the care of our own and to neglect the means necessary for it. The rivers that overflow their channels ordinarily enrich the grounds they overflow, but they carry also a great deal of mud along with them. Behold here what the Devil aims at when he moves us to employ ourselves too much in the commerce with worldly people, and not to keep such measures therein as we ought to do; and since this kind of temptation is very frequent, we ought to be extremely upon our guard. And what ought chiefly oblige us to do so is, that the care of our own advancement is, as I shall show hereafter, the best means we have of helping our neighbour and producing much fruit in souls. So that the greater affairs we have in that way, the more we ought to give ourselves to prayer, to obtain of God a blessing upon our ministry, and to make it succeed. It was thus the saints arranged matters. We read of St. Dominick, that he divided his time in the following manner: he gave the day to the service of his neighbour, and the night to prayer. Behold here what made him bring forth such great fruit; it was because he consulted at night with God what he ought to do the day following; and before he put his hand to the work, he had already obtained success by his prayers. Jesus Christ himself has also given us an example of this practice, by withdrawing himself to mountains and retired places, and there passing whole nights in prayer. He employed the day in preaching to the people, in healing the sick, and in casting out devils; and as the gospel says, "he passed the whole night in prayer to God". He did this, as St. Ambrose very well takes notice, not because he stood in need of the help of prayer, but that he might hereby give us an example of what we ought to do.

But if prayer be so necessary for those who are exteriorly employed in the ordinary functions of charity, it is also more particularly necessary for those who are employed in missions. The rules we have concerning missions state this expressly. Here is one of them: "Let them take care not to fail in their exercises of prayer and examen of conscience, which they are wont to have in colleges and in other houses of the society". And it is without doubt with a great deal of reason that the rule expressly has these terms, "let them take care"; for in effect it is needful that they take very great care of themselves, and that they do not neglect these exercises when they are thus employed abroad. It is indeed very easy to perform them in our houses, where our employments are more regular, where we are advertised and called by the sound of bell to these exercises, and where the example of others excites us to do as they do. But when we are employed abroad in laborious functions, with which we are sometimes as it were overcharged,—when we are neither advertised by the sound of bell nor excited by the example of our brethren, but, on the contrary, meet with many things that distract and hinder us,—we ought to pay a continual attention to ourselves, that we may not frequently neglect these spiritual duties. It is also very certain that missions require persons of tried virtue, and therefore St. Francis Borgia was wont to say that he was never content with the missions he furnished but when they cost him a great deal of trouble. It was in effect, because he could not without a great deal of difficulty send such persons as were required, and such as he wished to select for these employments. In fine, with a great deal of reason, many more things are required for employments abroad than for those at home; and hence it happens that amongst us those only who have made four vows are destined for missions; for it is supposed that these are already sufficiently tried and advanced in virtue. Moreover, besides all this, it is necessary that they should not stay too long abroad without returning to their houses to recruit themselves, for fear that the interior spirit of piety should be extinguished in them by their continual exterior labours abroad.

But if the duties which relate to the salvation of souls ought never to make us neglect our ordinary exercises, that regard our own spiritual advancement, because it is not just that the interest of our neighbour should make us forget what we owe to ourselves, what consequence, therefore, ought we not draw from hence for all the employments and occupations that regard only temporal affairs? This remark applies no less to people in the world than to those in religion, and each one may make an application thereof to himself, conformably to the state it has pleased God to put him in. But let the state be what it will, and how good soever his functions may be of themselves, very great care ought to be taken to prevent exterior things from making a Christian neglect his own salvation, or causing a religious to dispense with those practices of piety which regard his advancement and perfection. It is not reasonable to prefer the less to the greater, and what regards our spiritual advancement ought always have the preference. This is the order that God would have us keep; it is this the superiors require of us. We ought to take care, for example, not to quit our spiritual exercises, or to make them in haste or by halves, in order to apply ourselves entirely to our studies. For what will it profit a religious to become learned, if he does not in the first place satisfy the duties of his profession? But what ought still oblige us faithfully to acquit ourselves herein is, that these spiritual exercises are so far from hindering us from making any progress in learning, that, on the contrary, they serve to obtain from God all the light and knowledge we shall stand in need of to succeed in them.

Albertus the Great was wont to say, that in divine sciences a greater advancement was made by piety and prayer than by study; and he alleged in proof of this the words of the wise man: "I desired to have a right knowledge of things, and God gave it me; I invoked the Lord, and he filled me with the spirit of his wisdom"—*Wisd.*, vii. 7. It is also by this means that St. Thomas, who studied under him, became so learned and enlightened; and it was this that made him say that, for all he knew, he was more indebted to prayer than to his own labour or studies. We read also of St. Bonaventure, that when he taught divinity at Paris, with a great deal of reputation, and when by his works he attracted to himself the esteem and admiration of all the world, St. Thomas of Aquin, going one day to see him, begged of him to show him those books he made use of for his studies; whereupon St. Bonaventure led him to his cell, and showed him some very common books that lay upon his table; and when St. Thomas told him he had a particular desire to see those other books from which he acquired so many wonderful things, the saint then showing him his oratory, upon which he had a crucifix, Behold, father, says he, all my books, and behold the chief book from which I derive all I teach and all I write; and it is by casting myself at the feet of this crucifix —it is by supplicating light in my doubts—it is by assisting at mass, that I have made greater progress in sciences, and that I have gained more true knowledge than by the reading of any books whatsover.

CHAPTER VI,

That we ought to take care not to fall into another extreme, which is entirely to withdraw ourselves from conversing with our neighbour, upon pretence of applying ourselves to the care of our own salvation.

BUT if treating with our neighbour, as you may object, be filled with so many dangers, I will not expose myself to it, but live in retirement, to think only upon my own salvation; for I am more strictly bound to take care of myself than of others, and it is not just I should expose myself to lose my own soul to save the souls of others. This is another extreme, and another mode of going out of the way of our institutions. But the gospel furnishes us with a very just answer to this objection in the parable of the talents. It tells us that a man having a long voyage to make, divided his money amongst his servants, to take care of it; to one of them he gave five talents, to another two, and to a third one. The two first increased their money twofold, and were praised and recompensed by their master at his return: but the third, who had received one talent, buried it, and when he was called to account for it by his master, "he said: Lord, I know that thou art a hard man; thou reapest where thou hast not sown, and gatherest where thou hast not strewed; and being afraid, I went and hid thy talent in the earth: behold here thou hast that which is thine. And his lord answering, said to him: Wicked and slothful servant, thou knewest that I reap where I sow not, and gather where I have not strewed; thou oughtest therefore to have committed my money to the bankers, and at my coming I should have received my own with usury. Take ye away therefore the talent from him, and give it him that hath ten talents: for to every one that hath shall be given, and he shall abound; but from him that hath not, that also which he seemeth to have shall be taken away; and the unprofitable servant cast ye out into the exterior darkness. There shall be weeping and gnashing of teeth"—*Mat.*, xxv. 24, 30. St. Austin explains this parable much to our purpose, and says, that it is proposed to us by Jesus Christ, for the instruction of those who, being able profitably to serve the Church and their neighbour in the dispensation of the word of God and in the help of souls, refuse to charge themselves therewith, under pretence that they have no wish to answer to God for the sins of their neighbour. Let them learn wisdom from this example, says the father; for at bottom, we perceive no cause of the damnation of this servant, but that he made no profit of the talent he had received, for he had neither lost it nor made an ill use of it; but on the contrary he had carefully hid it under ground, for fear of being robbed of it. Wherefore, says St. Ambrose, let us take care that we have not an account to render to God for our unprofitable silence. For there are two sorts of silence, a silence very profitable and efficacious, as the silence of Susanna, who held her peace before men whilst she elevated her heart to God, and did far more by this than if she had spoken in her own defence. The other is unprofitable and vain, as when we may contribute to the salvation of our neighbour by our discourse, and we fail to do so. Now, as we shall render one day an account to God for our unprofitable words, so we shall render an account for our unprofitable silence. Moreover, he will require of us a very exact and severe account hereof, by reason of the talent of his word which he has confided to us, and of the charge he has given to us to help souls. For he will not content himself with requiring an account of our own advancement, as he will require of those who ought not to labour in anything else; but he will require an account also of us of what we have done for the advancement of our neighbour; and if he finds that we have buried the talent, he will take it from us and punish us as bad servants. We have therefore two things to propose to ourselves at the same time—our own perfection, and that of our neighbour; and we are obliged to labour for both: so that the care of one ought not to hinder us from taking care of the other. The example also of the Son of God teaches us what method we ought to observe herein. The Gospel takes notice that having put himself in prayer in the garden of Olives, he rose three times from it, to go to visit his disciples, and presently returned to it again. See here what we ought to do. We ought to pass from prayer to employments of charity, and from employments of charity presently to return back to prayer.

St. Bernard treats perfectly well this matter in applying to this subject these words of the bridegroom to the spouse: "Arise, make haste, my beloved, my dove, my fair one, and come"—*Cant.*, ii. 10. "Who can doubt", says he, "but that he calls her to the conquest of souls?" But how comes it to pass, adds the father, that he would have her rise in such haste? Had he not forbidden her to rise a little before? "Ye daughters of Jerusalem, I conjure ye by the goats and hinds of the country, that ye trouble not the repose of my beloved, and that ye do not wake her till she will wake herself"—*Cant.*, ii. 7. How comes it then to pass that she must not only rise, but that she must also make haste? He had a little before forbidden them to wake her, and almost at the same moment he would have her get up, and that quickly too. What does this sudden change in the mind of the bridegroom signify? Can you think that it is perhaps out of levity and changeableness it happens? and that now he will not have what he just before desired? It is no such thing. He only wishes to show us, that he would have us continually pass from the repose and sweet sleep of prayer and meditation, to the employments of charity and to the ministry of the salvation of souls. For the love of God cannot remain idle; it is a fire that by its continual activity, would put the whole world in a flame; and upon this consideration he would not only have her quit the repose and sweetness of contemplation, but to press and hasten herself, so that he may let us see his zeal and ardour for the salvation of souls. Do we not perceive, says St. Bernard, that the spouse had scarce taken any repose on the breast of her bridegroom? "His left hand was under my head", says she, "and his right hand embraced me"—*Cant.*, ii. 6; but presently he awakes her, and commands her to employ herself in more profitable things. I say more profitable, continues this father, because it was more profitable and more meritorious in the sight of God, to labour for the salvation of souls, and for her own salvation also at the same time, than to labour solely for her own. But this is not the first time that the bridegroom had thus treated his spouse. She had a long while had a desire to enjoy the repose and sweetness of contemplation in the embraces and kisses of her bridegroom. "Let him give me the kisses of his mouth"; and he answers her, "that her breasts are more delicious than wine"—*Cant.*, i. 1; whereby he gives us to understand that she ought to have children, and that she ought to think of breeding them up and nourishing them. Remember, therefore, that you are a father, that you have children, that you ought to nourish them, and that you ought to quit your repose and tranquillity to take care of them. The holy Scripture gives us a figure of this in the person of Jacob. When he expected with impatience to possess Rachel, who was fair but barren, they gave him Lia, who was blear-eyed, but was proper to have children. The same happens here also: when the spouse sighs for the embraces of her bridegroom, he represents to her that she ought to be a mother, and that she ought to have children, and that "her breasts are more delicious than wine". This signifies in effect, that the fruit which one brings forth in souls by the offices of charity, is more pleasing to God than the holy ebriety of contemplation. It is true Lia is not so fair as Rachel, but she is more likely to have children, and this quality is far more to be esteemed than the beauty of Rachel. It is the same in the active and contemplative life: the contemplative life is in truth more perfect than the active; but when the active life, that regards the employments of charity and the help of souls, is joined with the contemplative, it is without doubt far more perfect than the contemplative life alone. It is in this sense that St. Chrysostom interprets these words of St. Paul: "For I desired to be an anathema, and to be separated from Jesus Christ, for the sake of my brethren, who according to the flesh are my kinsmen"—*Rom.*, ix. 3. The apostle, says he, wished to be separated for some time from the conversation of Jesus Christ, and whatsoever sweetness he felt in the acts of the love of God which he continually produced, yet he wished to interrupt them, to apply himself the more to the salvation of souls: and it was in this manner that he wished to become anathema for the love of the neighbour. Now all the doctors agree that in this St. Paul made an act of charity sovereignly perfect; and consequently we see that the zeal of souls, which seems in a manner to separate us from God, unites us more closely to him. Hence we ought to feel convinced that the care we shall take in the advancement of our neighbour will not at all hurt our own, but, on the contrary, will help it, and be a means of our making greater progress in virtue and perfection. Clement Alexandrinus makes use of some comparisons to elucidate this truth. The more water, says he, that we draw out of wells, the clearer and the more wholesome it is to drink; but when we draw out none at all, it grows muddy and corrupts. The more we use a knife, the brighter it becomes; but if we make no use of it, it presently grows rusty. The flame diminishes not by communicating itself, but it rather becomes greater and more violent. Do we not likewise perceive, adds he, in human sciences, that he who teaches others learns himself by teaching them, and renders himself more able and learned? It is the same in the science of God; it is by practice and communication that we become more profound and enlightened. The word of God is a two-edged sword, that cuts no less on the side that is next him who makes use of it, than on the side next those for whom it is used. That which I say to others does often regard myself, and perhaps I have as much need of it as they; and if I do not practise what I teach them, I presently feel my conscience reproach me, and cry out: "Unhappy they who practise not what they teach". The sins that are discovered to me in confession are an admonition to me to keep myself upon my guard, and a subject to give God thanks that he has not permitted me to fall into the like faults, and to beg of him that he would always uphold me by his all-powerful hand. Likewise we learn by assisting others at their death to have death always present before our eyes, and to put ourselves in such a state that we may never be surprised by it. We learn by visiting prisons and hospitals, and by labouring to reconcile enemies, how many miseries and disorders there are in the world, and thereby we come to have a greater esteem of the happiness of our vocation. In a word, the offices in which charity employs us are so far from being an occasion of remissness, that, on the contrary, they help us to stand more carefully upon our guard, and to excite ourselves more and more to virtue and perfection.

Add to what I have said, the graces which God pours down upon such as exert themselves in employments of charity. For if he has promised so great recompenses to works of mercy which regard only the necessities of the body, how will he reward the works of charity that regard the necessities of the soul, and consequently are as far above the others as the soul is above the body? St. Chrysostom says, that these words of the gospel are addressed to those that do these works: "Give and it shall be given to you"—*Luke*, vi. 38; and these others of the *Proverbs*, "the soul that blesseth, shall be made fat; and he that inebriates, shall be inebriated"—*Prov.*, xi. 25. Those that feed others with spiritual food, and inebriate them with the love of Heavenly things, God will feed them also with consolation, and inebriate them with his love. Some compare them to the almoners, to whom princes give great sums to distribute, according to the alms they give. But this comparison is not very just; because if an almoner be faithful, he keeps nothing for himself of what is given him, and is not enriched by giving to others; whereas those that exercise spiritual works of charity enrich no less themselves than their brethren. St. Peter Chrysologus, who compares them to nurses of kings' children, is more in the right. "As", says he, "care is taken that the nurses of kings' children be fed with more delicate meats than ordinary, that thereby their milk may be better; so the King of kings takes care that the ministers of his word should always be nourished with the best meat of his table, that they may nourish his children with so much the better milk".

But we above all others have a particular obligation to apply ourselves to works of charity towards our neighbour, since God has made it a means of our advancement, engaging us to it even by our vocation. It is thus the bull of our institution speaks of it, wherein Julius III., after having stated the end which our society proposes to itself, and the offices which it is obliged to exercise towards our neighbour: "Let it take care", says he, "first of all, to have God before its eyes, and always to behold what it is engaged to by its institute, which is a sort of path that leads directly to him". So that as the spiritual advancement of some religious orders consists in an exact observance of recollection and enclosure, of singing the divine office and of keeping certain fasts, and undergoing such other austerities as they are particularly obliged to; just so, our advancement and spiritual progress consist in acquitting ourselves well of our duties and charities towards our neighbour; because it is to this that we are called, as the others are to solitude and retirement. We may say then to those towards whom we exercise these charities, what St. Paul said to the Philippians and Thessalonians, "Ye are my joy and my crown"—*Phil.*, iv. 1. "Ye are our glory and our joy"—I. *Thessal.*, ii. 20. "For it is certain", says St. Ambrose, upon these words òf the apostle, "that the progress of scholars is a joy and advancement to their master". We ought, therefore, to make account that our perfection and merit consist in acquitting ourselves well of these duties, so that the spirit of prayer and retreat ought to be a very laudable thing amongst us; yet such a spirit of prayer and retreat as would withdraw us from the help of souls and other offices of charity, would be a kind of temptation. Had you been in the world, or had God called you to another religious order that made it not its particular profession to apply itself to the salvation of souls, the inclination you should have to entertain yourself continually with God in retirement, and to think only of your own perfection, might perhaps come from the Spirit of God. But here it can be nothing else but an illusion of the Devil, who transforms himself into an angel of light to deceive you, and to endeavour to withdraw you from your vocation, under the pretence of labouring for your own advancement, and of avoiding those dangers that are met with in treating with your neighbour. We ought to give ourselves to prayer, according to the spirit of our vocation, that is to say, with a view of obtaining new lights and new strength for the help of souls ; so that we may be able to say with Job, "If I go to bed to sleep, I will say, when shall I rise again? And in the morning, I shall be impatient until the evening approaches"—*Job*, vii. 4. In fine, we ought to look upon prayer as a necessary preparation for the acquitting ourselves of our duties of charity; and the better you shall find yourself disposed for these employments when you leave your prayer, the more you may assure yourself of your having made your prayer well; and the more the love of God will thereby have increased in your heart, the more zeal and fervour ought you have on leaving it for gaining souls to God, and procuring that God should be loved and glorified by all the world.

We read of a holy religious, of the order of St. Francis, that after he had for many years very profitably laboured in the conversion of the Indians, he had a great desire of retiring from the world in order to prepare himself to die well; and in effect he for this end retired into a monastery of his own order in Spain, where he lived in a very austere recollection. However, as often as he went to prayer, he seemed as if he saw Jesus Christ crucified tenderly making this complaint to him, "Why hast thou left me thus upon the cross, whilst thou searchest thy own repose and quiet?" And he was so touched with this vision, that he returned again to the harvest he had left, and therein served God again for a very long time.

CHAPTER VII.

Some remedies against timidity of those who dare not engage in the employments of charity lest they should thereby lose their own soul.

To cure ourselves entirely of the fear we may have of losing our own souls whilst we labour for the salvation of others, and to encourage herein the most scrupulous and fearful persons, we must in the first place suppose one thing, which is very true. It is that, in what way soever God has been pleased to call and place us, our salvation is much more secure in *that*, than in all those we imagine to be more secure. Let obedience send us to preach in public places; or send us to the confessional, to confess the most wicked and impure wretches in the world; we shall hereby be in greater security, than if, to avoid these employments and the dangers they expose us to, we should of our own choice embrace retirement. For perhaps in the solitude of retreat we might give way to an hundred bad thoughts, whereas in the employments we exercise by obedience, God, who has placed us in them, takes care of us, "and covers us with the buckler of his good will"—*Ps.*, v. 13. Do not imagine, says St. Basil, that to become chaste, and to be delivered from temptations of impurity, nothing more is necessary than to live in solitude—solitude contributes nothing hereunto. St. Jerom himself confesses that in the desert, where he lived only upon herbs, and where he practised continual penance, his imagination often carried him into the midst of the dances of the Roman ladies, and that neither his fasts nor his austerities, nor his decline of life, were able to hinder his flesh from rebelling, or to deliver him from its rude combats. Abbot Elias, on the contrary, for forty years together, governed three hundred religious in one monastery, without ever being attacked with so much as one temptation against purity, and, as Palladius relates, without ever feeling his imagination troubled with the least bad thought. The flames did not so much as touch the clothes of the three Hebrews who were cast into the fiery furnace of Babylon, yet in an instant they destroyed those that cast them in and who seemed to be far enough from receiving any hurt. This shows that God can easily free from flames those that expose themselves to them for love of him.* Nay more, he was not content to free the Hebrew children from the flames, but he caused that the furnace should even become a place of delights to them, where they employed themselves in blessing God and singing forth his praises. The same thing happens to those whom zeal for God's glory and for the salvation of souls causes to enter into the burning furnace of the Babylon of the world. There they sing the praises of God in the midst of flames, and bless him for having called them to religion, whilst the same flames devour the people of the world; and the commerce with the world, which is the ruin of so many persons, serves only to give them a greater knowledge and a greater contempt of its vanity, and to give them a greater esteem of the advantages they enjoy in religion. "To them that love God, all things work together unto good"—*Rom.*, viii. 28. All things succeed well in their ministry. It is the love of God and obedience that engage them therein, and oil and honey run out of the rock to feed them. In a word, when we have a heart touched with a lively desire of serving God,—when we are not called to the exercise of our functions by ourselves, but are called unto them by God,—we must not lose courage, but, on the contrary, hope that God, who has called us thereunto, will render us useful and profitable for his glory and our own salvation.

But, omitting many other reasons which might persuade us to

what we now speak of, I will only at present insist upon one that ought entirely to convince us, and to be a subject of confidence and consolation to us, either in our ministry for the salvation of souls, or in other offices belonging to the vocation of our society. It is "that the works of God are perfect"—*Deut.*, xxxii. 4. He makes nothing useless: and as, in the order of nature, he never gives a natural cause the power of producing an effect but he likewise gives it the means to reduce to act the power that is given to it, without which this power would be absolutely vain and useless, in like manner, in the order of grace, which is more perfect than that of nature, he never calls any person to any state or for any end without giving him the means and necessary helps to attain it. This being so, it is not to be doubted but that when God institutes a religious order for any end, he gives it at the same time such grace as is necessary for those who are called to this order to attain this end. This grace is called the grace of religion, which is common to all orders, that they may arrive to that state of perfection for which they were instituted. But there is a difference in the graces, according to the difference of the particular end for which each order was instituted, and according to the difference of the means which are proper to attain it. The one, for example, receives a particular grace to lead a holy life in solitude, in retirement, and in continual abstinence. Others receive another grace to celebrate the divine office, and so of the rest. But our society is a religious order, instituted in the Church by the authority of the pope for the help of souls; and God, who has particularly instituted it for this end, has given it also such means as are proper to attain it, which, as the bull of our institute says, are, to preach, to hear confessions, to teach, to give rules for spiritual exercises, to labour in reconciling enemies, and to visit prisons and hospitals; so that, as it is called by God for the help of souls, it is also called to those functions that regard their help or service; and this deserves to be well taken notice of, and ought to be a great subject of comfort to us, that the offices which we exercise towards our neighbour are no less of our institute than the end for which we perform them. In effect, it belongs to our institute to preach, to hear confessions, to teach both divine and human sciences; and not only these kinds of spiritual employments are of our institute, but also all corporal works of charity, viz., to visit prisons and hospitals, and the like, as the bull of our establishment testifies.

But to come now to the conclusion: it follows from all that I have said, that our society receives a particular grace from God to attain the end for which it was instituted, which is the help of souls, and to attain it by such means as are proper to our vocation, and which he himself has given us for this effect, and this is that grace which it has pleased God particularly to grant to the society. We ought, then, have a great confidence in God in all those offices of charity which we perform for the help of souls, and assure ourselves that he will particularly concur with us to render them efficacious, as by his infinite mercy we daily experience. For to what, think you, ought we to attribute the fruit that a preacher of the society produces, who oftentimes, though he comes fresh from his studies, even fills a whole town with the spirit of true conversion and penance, and causes such reconciliations as no one before was able to compass; who abolishes such public scandals as neither the magistrates nor ecclesiastical superiors were ever able to correct before? Does this proceed from his learning, from his eloquence, from his abilities? Not at all; it comes from the particular grace of the vocation of the society, which was instituted for this effect, and which God for this reason, out of a particular love, favours with his grace in all the means he has given to compass this end. In proof of this, do we not at other times perceive that some preachers who preached with a great deal of reputation and fruit whilst they were in our society, and who believed they should have the same success when they were out of it, yet had none at all as soon as they quitted it? This shows it was the grace of the vocation of our society that gave them wings to raise themselves as they did, and that, being by their desertion deprived of them, they necessarily fell. We read in the first chapter of Machabees what is very much to our purpose. Some of the chief men among the Jews, speaking of the wonders the Machabees had wrought, and of the great victories they had obtained against the gentiles, wished to establish a reputation for themselves, saying, "Let us also make ourselves a name"—I. *Mach.*, v. 57. For this effect they gathered all their troops together, and went against the enemy, but the success answered not their hopes, for their enemies came upon them, defeated them, and killed above two thousand. And hereupon the Scripture takes notice, "that they were not of the race of those men who had been chosen by God to save the people of Israel"—I. *Mach.*, v. 62. Now the reason of their defeat was that they presumed too much upon themselves, and that they called themselves to a thing to which God had not called them.

Hence, then, none of us ought to attribute to ourselves the glory of the fruit which God produces by our means. It is to God to whom we must entirely render it; it is to the choice that he has been pleased to make of us, "to be ministers of the spirit of the New Testament"—II. *Cor.*, iii. 6; it is to the religion to which he has been pleased to call us. These particular graces which he gives you to gain souls to him, and to work your own salvation by labouring for theirs, he gives you, because you are a member of a religion which he has instituted for this end. This is what we ought to imprint deeply in our mind, because, as it serves, on the one hand, to repress our vanity, so it serves on the other to give us confidence and courage. St. Bernard upon these words of the spouse, "come, arise, make haste, my beloved, my dove, my fair one, come"— *Cant.*, ii. 10: the bridegroom, says he, desiring to have his spouse quit the sweet sleep of contemplation to go to the employments of charity, says not to her, *go*, but he says, *come;* and this ought extremely to encourage us, because he makes us hereby to understand that the command he gives us does not separate us far from him, but on the contrary causes us to approach nearer to him, and that it is a means to draw us nearer to himself. It is not, therefore, to separate us from himself, that he employs us in works of charity; it is only to unite us the more to himself. It is by this path we go to him; he guides us in it himself, and always accompanies us. We have no reason to fear anything in order to ourselves; but, on the contrary, we have reason to fill ourselves with confidence and courage, and to hope by these means that we shall make great progress in our salvation. For this end, let us imagine that God says the same words to us, that Absalom said to his servants: "Fear nothing, it is I that command you, take courage and be men of resolution"—II. *Kings*, xiii. 28. For, in effect, what subject of apprehension can I have, if thou, O Lord, commandest me to apply myself to the help of my neighbour, and if thou engagest me hereby to a commerce with the people of the world? How dangerous soever it may be, I am there in greater security, if I be there by thy order, than if, by my own choice, I were shut up between four walls; "and when I shall walk in the midst of the shades of night, I will fear nothing, because thou art with me"—*Ps.*, xxii. 4.

By this, we may see how much some religious deceive themselves, who, hearkening only to their own sentiments, are disgusted with their employment, and imagine if they had been given any other, or had been sent to any other house, they should have laboured there more profitably for their own salvation and for the service of God. It is a great abuse to think we should work out our own salvation better in those employments we choose ourselves, than in those in which the hand of God has placed us; and would to God that experience had not too clearly let us know how dangerous this illusion is. We have seen several religious who were uneasy in the employments that God and obedience had given them, and who sought others with a great deal of earnestness, imagining they could produce in them more fruit for themselves and for their neighbour, and who at length found means to induce their superiors to accord what they desired; but we have also seen them so unhappy from the change, that they themselves were convinced it was a just punishment from God. Wherefore we ought to take very great care not to desire anything of ourselves, nor to hearken to our own inclination in the choice either of place or employments in which we are to be put. All that we have to do herein is, entirely to renounce our own will, and to abandon ourselves to that of God, and to permit ourselves to be led to him by the way of obedience. For, without doubt, we shall never anywhere be in greater security of our salvation, than where God has been pleased to put us.

CHAPTER VIII.

Of the means to produce fruit in souls.—Of sanctity of life, which is the first means.

I SHALL speak at present of some general means which may help us to produce fruit in souls, and which are set down in the seventh part of our constitutions; and I shall not touch on the other particular means which are mentioned in the fourth part, and which properly regard such religious as are already priests. But though what I propose here to speak of, seems chiefly to regard the salvation and spiritual advancement of our neighbour, yet it fails not also to regard our own advancement and salvation. For these two things, as I have already said in the beginning of this treatise, are so linked together, that what serves for the spiritual advancement of our neighbour serves also for our own; and what serves for our own, serves also for that of our neighbour: so that what I shall say on this subject may be of equal profit to all persons. The first means that St. Ignatius recommends to us to make use of for the advancement of souls, is that of good example and sanctity of life. "In the first place", says he, "the good example which we give by leading a most holy and Christian life, has great power over the minds of men; wherefore we ought to take care to edify our neighbour as much or more by our actions than by our words"—4 *P. Constit. c.* 8. In effect the most efficacious and most proper means to produce much fruit in souls, is to lead a holy and irreproachable life, and to be such ourselves as we would have others to be; for, as a tree, the larger it grows, the more fruit and profit it brings to its master; so the more progress a preacher or a confessor makes in virtue, the more he renders himself profitable to those of whom God has given him the care and direction.

Now the importance and necessity of this means is easily perceived, inasmuch as it is certain that example has more power over men than all the words in the world; and it was for this reason that the Saviour of souls taught us the way to Heaven by his actions, before he taught it us by his words. Jesus Christ, says St. Luke, "began to do and to teach"—*Acts*, i. 1. He vouchsafed to practise for thirty years together what he was to teach in three. St. John Baptist, says St. Jerom, made choice of a retreat in the desert to make known the kingdom of God, and calls himself "the voice of him that cries in the desert"—*John*, i. 23. But how comes it to pass, says this father, that the preacher and precursor of Jesus Christ made choice of the desert to preach in? for the desert seems a place more proper for being neither seen nor heard in than a place wherein to instruct others. It is, answers the saint, because he knew very well that example moves more than words, and therefore he would, by the example of the austerity of his life, move men to bring forth fruits worthy of penance, and to imitate what he practised. "He was", says the gospel, "a shining light that burned and enlightened"—*John*, v. 35: he burned within himself with the love of God, and he enlightened others by the example of his holy and penitential life.

It is a saying of Seneca, which is repeated by all people, "that the way to virtue is shorter by example than by precept;

because men more easily believe what they see than what they hear". St. Bernard gives us another reason for it; "Example", says he, "is a very efficacious and a very proper lesson to persuade, because it shows that what it teaches is feasible, and this is what has most influence on us". Man's weakness is so great, says St. Austin, that one is very hardly moved to do what is good, unless he sees others do it; and hence it extremely imports preachers of the gospel to be holy men, that their auditors may have in them a model to imitate. The apostle knew very well this truth, and how great the power of example was, when he said to the Corinthians, "be ye imitators of me, as I am of Jesus Christ"—I. Cor., iv. 16.

Add to this, that when the life of a preacher is conformable to his doctrine, what he says has more weight, because they perceive he himself is the first who is convinced of it; whereas when his actions do not correspond to his words, these can never make any impression.

St. Basil and St. Chrysostom, speaking of those who preach only by their words, say that they are not true preachers, but only comedians, who act their parts upon the stage, and who possess nothing of what they represent. You represent humility very well in the exterior; you represent also very well the vanity of the things of the world, and the contempt that ought to be had of them; but if you are not really humble, if you do not truly contemn whatsoever may any way separate you from God, you are not a preacher of the gospel, you are a comedian who only acts your part. St. Basil compares them also to painters, who, though they are ugly themselves, yet fail not to make and paint very beautiful pictures; so these, says he, paint humility in its true shape and colours, but they themselves are filled with vanity and pride; they make beautiful pictures of patience, but impatience and anger transport them every moment; they make beautiful pictures of modesty, recollection, and silence, but they are continually dissipated and distracted by a thousand-frivolous objects. St. Austin compares them to finger-posts, which are set to show the road, and which always remain in the same place. And this, says he, is what the scribes and pharisees did; they showed the sages the way to Bethlehem, but they themselves went not thither with them. St. Jerom, writing upon these words of the Proverbs: "The slothful man hides his hand under his arm-pit, and it is a pain to him to raise it to his mouth"—

Prov., xxvi. 15,—says that the slothful of whom the wise man speaks, is a figure of a preacher that practises not what he says, and whose actions agree not with his words. St. Gregory Nazianzen says that those who preach not by their actions as well as by their words, draw souls to them with one hand, and drive them away with the other; they build with one hand, and pull down with the other, as the scribes and pharisees did, whom the Son of God severely reprehends in the gospel. Woe be to those who practise not what they preach; they touch not the heart, they produce no fruit at all by their discourse: "But he who does and teaches, he", says our Saviour, "shall be called great in the kingdom of Heaven"—*Matt.*, v. 19. It is only apostolical preachers, who practise what they teach, that touch and move the heart, and produce great fruit in souls. It is only the sanctity of their lives, attracting to them the veneration of all the world, that makes them be considered rather as angels than as men, and hence all they say is received as coming from Heaven, and consequently makes a deeper and more lively impression upon the heart. Thus the apostle orders the labourers in our Lord's vineyard to lead an irreproachable life; to be irreprehensible in their words and actions, and to be an example of all sorts of virtue to the whole world, that by this means their doctrine may more deeply penetrate the hearts of men, and destroy whatsoever it finds there contrary to Jesus Christ.

We must begin, then, with sanctity of life, in order to render ourselves useful in saving souls. First, because good example has great influence; and secondly, because if we wish to be fit instruments in bringing forth much fruit in our neighbour, we must beforehand have brought forth much fruit in ourselves, and have made great progress in virtue. St. Ignatius, in the tenth part of his constitutions, speaking of the means of attaining the end for which the society was instituted, which is the help of souls, says, that the means which dispose us for this effect in regard to God, and whereby we put ourselves into his hands that he may do with us what he pleases—such as piety and all other Christian virtues—are means far more proper than those which dispose us in regard to the world, such as sciences and other natural means, and therefore it is upon the first that we ought chiefly insist. Let all, says he, give themselves to spiritual things and solid virtue, and rely chiefly thereupon, because these are the interior gifts of grace which give force and efficacy to sciences and natural talents, and render them useful for the end we have proposed to ourselves. The reason of this is very plain, it is that if indeed we have only human views, human prudence and other human means may suffice for success; but the conversion and sanctification of souls, which is the end we propose to ourselves, being a divine and supernatural end, which has no proportion or relation to any human means we can make use of, and which can only be the work of God, it is certain that we cannot compass this end but by divine and supernatural means. He who said in the beginning of the creation of the world, "Let there be light, and there was light"—*Gen.*, i. 3; "whose words are like fire, and who has the words of everlasting life"—*Jer.*, xxiii. 29; he only can give such efficacy to our words and discourses as is able to give new life to souls. Hence the more we shall be united to him, the fitter instruments we shall become to convert and sanctify them, because then we shall be in a better state to draw his graces unto us, and consequently to communicate them to others.

St. Denis, speaking of the sanctity and perfection which priests and ministers of the Gospel ought to have, whom God has chosen to be the dispensers both of his blood and of his word, says, "that they ought to be saints to sanctify others; perfect, that they may render others so; and enlightened, that they may illuminate the faithful by their light". They ought to be inflamed with the love of God, that they may inflame others, because, as St. Gregory says, "he who burns not cannot set another on fire"; which is conformable to the words that St. Thomas of Villanova was wont to repeat very often: How is it possible that from a congealed heart inflamed words should proceed? Would you have your words inflame your neighbour? Endeavour that they proceed from a heart inflamed with divine love, and then it will happen that you shall communicate to all the world that fire which the Son of God came to bring upon Earth. "I came to set the Earth on fire, and what do I desire but that it should burn?"—*Luke*, xii. 49. Then it will happen that one word of yours shall have greater effect than all that you could be able to say at another time.

Plato, speaking of the virtue of the loadstone, makes a comparison in which he exceeded the bounds of his knowledge. He says that, as iron touched with the loadstone attracts iron to it, so a man touched by God draws other men to him; but if your words be not those of a man touched by God, how can they be able to draw other men to God? And how can you be able to inflame others with the love of God, if you be not first inflamed yourself? Does not rhetoric itself teach us that there is not a better means to excite any passion in the heart of others than first to excite it in our own? For how can an orator draw tears from his audience, if he sheds not a tear himself? It is the same here. How can you inspire the contempt of the world into your auditors, if you do not truly contemn it yourself? How can you move them to mortification and penance, if you are not yourself moved thereunto? And how can you render them humble, if you are not so yourself? We can never communicate that to another which we have not in ourselves, according to the common saying, " nobody gives what he has not". How can you inspire into others those sentiments you have not yourself? Preachers who have nothing else but words are like pieces of cannon which are discharged without a bullet, the whole effect of which ends in making a great deal of noise with their words: "but this is only as it were to beat the air"—I. *Cor.*, ix. 26. For in reality they touch the heart of no one, because they have not that within themselves with which they ought to touch others, and they have not the spirit of God, which alone can give weight and force to what they say.

The talent of preaching consists not in knowing how to use the arts of eloquence, and to speak of things that are very spiritual and very high; for it was not in this manner the vessel of election preached, whom God made choice of for the conversion of the gentiles. "And I, brethren, when I came to you, came not in loftiness of speech or of wisdom, declaring to you the testimony of Christ. For I judged not myself to know any thing among you, but Jesus Christ, and him crucified. And I was with you in weakness, and in fear, and in much trembling: and my speech and my preaching was not in the persuasive words of human wisdom, but in the showing of the spirit and power: that your faith might not stand on the wisdom of men, but on the power of God. For Christ sent me not to baptize, but to preach the Gospel: not with wisdom of speech, lest the cross of Christ should be made void"—I. *Cor.*, ii. 1—5; i. 17. Ecclesiastical history praises very much the ancient fathers, who, contemning the vain ornaments of eloquence, contented themselves to give holy instructions to the people, and to apply such remedies to the spiritual maladies of their hearers as would be most proper for them. We ought to do the same in our sermons; "because we preach not ourselves", says the apostle, "but Jesus Christ our Lord"—II. *Cor.*, iv. 5. And without doubt such preachers as wish to display their erudition and eloquence, will for two reasons produce very little fruit. First, for the reason I have already spoken of, which is, that those few of their hearers who have sense, know very well that he who preaches in this manner admires himself in all that he says, and seeks more to make his eloquence appear, and to gain their applause, than to instruct and procure their salvation. In the second place, because this very eloquence and selection of words will hinder what they say from producing fruit; and thus the more care will appear to be taken in selecting their language, the less persuasive will it be. Besides, do not even professors of rhetoric say, that the sense languishes in a discourse wherein too much care is bestowed on the words? By this, they mean that too great application to the choice of words cools the imagination and renders it less lively for the production of things; and hereby they would have us likewise understand that affectation in words diverts the auditors from that attention they ought to have to the truths that are said, and causes them, instead of attending to what a preacher says, to think of the manner in which he says it. If masters of rhetoric look upon this affectation as a great fault in an orator, with how far greater reason ought it not to be blamed in a preacher of the gospel, who ought to think only of the spiritual profit of his auditors? "It is for profit", says the apostle, "that the manifestation of the spirit of God is given to every one"—I. *Cor.*, xii. 7; and therefore a preacher ought never regard any thing else but the profit and advantage of souls. "Preach", says St. Jerom, "after such a manner that the church may reëcho with the sighs and sobs of the audience, rather than with their acclamations, and that their tears may become your praises"—*Ep.* ii. *ad Nep.* A man is not a good preacher because he is applauded, nor because on leaving the church the people say of him: "No man ever spoke like him—what fine things he said—how elegantly he said them". No; but he preaches well, who excites in his audience a sincere compunction—who makes them weep for their sins, and who makes them change their lives. The talents of a preacher consist chiefly in touching the heart; in showing his hearers the vanities of the world; in making them comprehend the misery of their disorders, and in moving them to turn to God with all their hearts. It is not to preach, said Father Avila, to be an hour speaking of God in public. It is not to do this alone that a man ascends the pulpit; but it is to convert his auditors, and to change into angels those who were before devils; behold here in what consists the talent of a good preacher. Another servant of God said, that when we go from a sermon with our eyes cast upon the ground, without speaking to any one, it is a sign the sermon was good and profitable, because it is a mark that each one found in it what was adapted and advantageous to himself.

We read in the life of St. Francis of Borgia, that when he preached in Biscay, the greatest part of his audience heard not what he said; and this happened because the multitude of people was so great, that very few could come near the pulpit, as also because very few understood Castilian. Yet it was a wonderful thing to see the attention with which they listened to him, and the tears which they shed at his sermons; and when some were asked why they wept at his sermon, since they understood not what he said, they answered that they wept, because they beheld so great a person that was become so great a saint, and because they felt within themselves a divine inspiration that made them understand the sense of what the preacher spoke. At another time, when he was at Lisbon, he was no sooner arrived in town, than the Cardinal Don Henry, who was afterwards king of Portugal, sent to beg of him to preach: and the saint having excused himself, because he was extremely tired from his journey; I do not ask him to preach, says the cardinal, but only to go into the pulpit, and show himself to the people, that they may see him who has renounced all for God. Behold here in effect what produces fruit in souls, and what preaches most eloquently to the people—example and sanctity of life; and therefore it is to this that confessors, preachers, and all those whose employments have any relation to their neighbour, ought chiefly to apply themselves, in order that God may make choice of them to be fit instruments for the salvation of souls.

CHAPTER IX.

Of prayer, which is the second means to produce fruit in souls.

THE second means St. Ignatius assigned to render us useful to our neighbour, is prayer. "Our neighbour is also helped", says he, "by the fervour of prayer"—7 *P. Const.*, c. 4. For, since the affair of converting souls is purely supernatural, we do it better by fervent prayers, by tears and sighs of heart, than by eloquence and force of words. The prayer of Moses had a greater share in the victory the Israelites gained against Amalec, than all the lances and swords they made use of against them. So long as Moses was able to keep his hands lifted up towards Heaven, the advantage was on the side of the Israelites, but as soon as he let them fall down they began to give way to their enemies; so that during the fight it was necessary to have two men to sustain him, the one on the one side, and the other on the other, that his hands might always be lifted up, and that the Israelites might gain a complete victory. It was in this manner the people of God defeated their enemies by prayer; and it was this the Midianites meant, when, astonished at the great victories the Israelites had gained, they said: "This people will destroy all those that live around them, like the ox which is accustomed to bite the grass to the very roots"—*Numb.*, xxii. 4. They intended hereby, say Origen and St. Austin, that as the ox feeds upon the grass with its mouth, and bites it to the very root, so the people of God destroyed their enemies with their mouth, that is to say, by virtue of their prayers. Now, if even in war, where the success seems to depend upon human forces, God accords the victory to the merit of prayer, what shall it be in this spiritual warfare which we have undertaken for the conversion of souls, and where our forces are so far short of the end we propose to ourselves? It is then by our prayers and by sighs we must endeavour to gain the victory; it is by them we must endeavour to appease the wrath of God, and to obtain his grace for the conversion of our brethren.

St. Austin, writing upon these words which God said to Moses, "let me alone, that my fury may be inflamed against them, and that I may destroy them"—*Exod.*, xxxii. 10,—takes occasion to speak of the merit of prayer, and to let us see how efficacious and powerful a means it is to obtain anything of God. God intends to destroy the children of Israel because they had adored a golden calf; Moses intercedes for them, and says to God, "Why is thy anger inflamed against this people, whom thou hast brought out of Egypt by the force and power of thy hand? Give not, I beseech thee, an occasion to the Egyptians to say, he has brought them well hither to destroy them in the mountains and to erase them from the earth! Let thy anger cease, and permit thyself to be appeased for this sin of thy people. Remember Abraham, Isaac, and Jacob, thy servants, to whom thou hast sworn by thyself, that thou wouldst multiply their seed as the stars of Heaven, and that thou wouldst give them and their posterity all this land thou spokest of"—*Exod.*, xxxii. 11, 12. "Let me alone", says our Lord, "I will destroy them". But what dost thou mean by this, O Lord? says St. Austin; why dost thou say, "let me alone"? Who hinders thee, or who is able to do so? Who can tie thy hands? "Who can resist thy will?"—*Rom.*, ix. 19. How comes it to pass then that thou sayest, "let me alone"? You will see from whence it proceeds, continues this father. It is certainly because the force of prayer hinders the effect of his anger: and it is this he would have us to understand by these words, "let me alone", which are not words of command; because, had they been so, Moses would have done very ill to disobey them. Nor are they words of petition, because God does not beg of his creatures; but they only show that the prayers of the just are capable of appeasing God's wrath. St. Jerom says the same thing upon these words of our Lord to Jeremias, "Do not thou therefore pray for this people, nor elevate thy voice and prayers for them, and do not resist me"—*Jer.*, vii. 16. God, says this father, makes us hereby to understand that the prayers of the saints are able to resist his anger; and he more expressly declares this to us by the words of David, "and he had resolved to destroy them, if Moses had not stood before him in the breach to avert his anger, and to hinder him from destroying them"—*Ps.*, cv. 23. When God had his hand already lifted up to strike and destroy his people, Moses withheld him by his prayers, "and the Lord was appeased", says the Scripture, "so that he did not that evil with which he had threatened his people"—*Exod.*, xxxii. 14.

The same thing happened in the sedition which had been raised against Moses and Aaron on account of the death of Core, Nathan, and Abiron, which the people of Israel imputed to them.

God was so angry hereat, that he intended to destroy all the people, and had already killed more than fourteen thousand by fire, when Aaron advancing by the order of Moses into the middle of the dead and dying, with a thurible in his hand, and having offered incense and prayers to God for the people, the plague ceased. Hence the wise man, speaking of this plague and of the manner that it came to cease, calls prayer a buckler. " But thy anger, O Lord, lasted not long; for a man without reproach made haste to pray for the people, offering thee his prayer, which was the sole buckler he had to resist thee, and joining incense to his prayers, he stopped thy anger and put an end to that desolation"—*Wisd.*, xviii. 20, 21. Another version has, "making haste to fight for the people"; so that to pray is in effect to fight, and it is by fighting in this manner that Aaron disarmed God's anger. " O how admirable a buckler is prayer", says St. Ambrose ; " it repels all the darts which our adversaries shoot against us".

But what is more than all this is, that when God has his hand lifted up to punish us, he wishes that some one would seize his hand, and hinder him from striking. A father who exceedingly loves his son, is not inclined to chastise him as often as he deserves it, but on the contrary wishes to find some one that will prevent him, and sometimes even makes a sign to one of his friends to do it. It is the same with God. He is a father that tenderly cherishes us, and lets us see he does so, because he has given even the last drop of his blood for us. When, therefore, there is question of chastising us, he does not wish to do it in effect. His wish is that his friends should ward off his blows; he seeks out some one that will do so; and when he finds none that will do it, he is troubled and complains severely. " I sought", says he, " amongst them a man that might put a hedge between us, and would take part with the earth against me, that I might not destroy it, and I was able to find none"—*Ezech.*, xxii. 30. " You have not come up", says he in another place, "nor opposed a wall against me for the defence of the house of Israel"—*Ezech.*, xiii. 5. On this St. Jerom says, that as the walls and ramparts of a city serve to repel the attacks of the enemy, " so do the prayers of saints serve to repulse the effects of God's threats". Isaias complains also, that there is no one who makes an effort to stop and appease him : " There is no one", says he, " O Lord, who calls upon thy name, who raises himself against thee, and holds thee back"—*Isai.*, lxiv. 7. There is no Jacob to be found to wrestle with the angel of the Lord, and say to him, "I will not let thee go till thou hast blessed me"—*Gen.*, xxxii. 26. All this shows us how exceedingly meritorious the prayers of the just are in the sight of God; because they have power to hold back his hand, and to disarm his wrath. It likewise confirms what I have said in the preceding chapter, that we ought to be in favour with God to be profitable to our neighbour, and that it is the best means we can make use of for this effect. For it is of very great importance that he who negotiates with any one for the pardon of another, should be very much in favour with him whom he entreats, otherwise he would rather irritate than appease him. In a word, sanctity of life is of so great advantage for the help of souls, that if we should do nothing else for our neighbour than labour to become saints, we should always do very much for him.

What God said to Abraham relative to the destruction of Sodom proves this truth very well. The abominations of Sodom and Gomorrah were come to such a height, that God resolved to destroy these two cities. He discovers his intention to Abraham on the way to Sodom, "and Abraham being already near the city, said to him: Alas! O Lord, wilt thou destroy the just with the wicked? If there are fifty just persons in the city, shall they perish with the rest? Or rather if there be found fifty just persons, wilt thou not pardon the rest for their sakes? Take heed of doing such a thing as to destroy the just with the wicked, and to cause the just to be treated like them; this is not to act like thyself, who dost render justice to all the world: thou wilt not therefore treat them after this manner. If I find fifty just persons in Sodom, answers our Lord, I will pardon the whole city for love of them. Since I have begun once to speak, I will speak again, O Lord", says Abraham, "though I be but dust and ashes. If there should want five of fifty, wouldst thou destroy the city for want of these five? No, answers our Lord, I will not destroy it, if I find five-and-forty. Abraham replies again, But if there should be only forty found, what wouldst thou do? I will pardon the whole city for the sake of these forty, answers our Lord. I beseech thee, O Lord, adds Abraham, be not displeased if I speak once more: what if thirty only should be found?" Where by the way take notice that Abraham in the beginning diminished only five at a time; but finding the Spirit of God disposed to grant him what he asked, afterwards diminishes ten at a time.

"I will not destroy it, answers our Lord, if I find thirty. Since I have once begun to speak to my Lord, pursues Abraham, I will go on: what if there be found only twenty? I will not destroy it, says the Lord, for the love of these twenty. I humbly beseech thee, O Lord, says Abraham, not to be angry if I speak only once more: what if perchance only ten should be found? Well, says our Lord, for the love of these ten I will not destroy it"—*Gen.*, xviii. 23, etc. Now there were not ten just persons found; and, in consequence, God destroyed it by fire, with four other cities; and this makes us clearly see how profitable the sanctity of life in just persons is to the rest of mankind. For what an advantage would it not have been to these miserable wretches, to have had ten virtuous men amongst them!

At another time God intending to chastise the city of Jerusalem, by reason of the enormity of its crimes, and to deliver it into the hands of the Chaldeans, that they might destroy it and put all its inhabitants to the sword: "Go", says he, "through all the streets of Jerusalem, see, consider, and search in every corner thereof, whether thou canst find a man that can do justice and that will keep his word, and I will pardon the city"—*Jerem.*, v. 1. Who is there, says St. Jerom upon this passage, but must needs admire the esteem God has for a just man? He says not here as he did at another time to Abraham, that he would pardon the city if he could find ten just men in it; but he says, if even one can be found amongst such an infinite number of sinners, he will pardon them all for the love of this one. The love of God for a just man ought to be very great and tender, since in consideration of him he will show mercy to so many sinners. This shows us how great an esteem we ought to have for good and virtuous men, and how very serviceable they are to the commonwealth they live in, though they do nothing else than live virtuously. And here one of the reasons which the saints and divines allege, to prove that religious persons ought, to be maintained at the public expense, though they should render no exterior service to the public, but should remain retired in their cells, is, that even in this retreat in their cells, they render a very great service to the state. For it is through love of a small number of virtuous persons that God bears with so many wicked men in the world; it is because of the good seed that for some time he lets the cockle grow up, "lest", says he, "while you gather the cockle you should also root up the wheat. Let them both grow till the harvest"—*Mat.*, xiii. 29.

With respect to the destruction of Sodom, we are likewise to observe that the Scripture adds, that "when God overthrew the cities of this country, he remembered Abraham, and delivered Lot from the ruin of the cities in which he lived"—*Gen.*, xix. 29. Yet there is no mention made that Abraham prayed for Lot; how therefore comes it to pass that God delivered Lot for the love of Abraham? It was because he loved Abraham so tenderly, that he took care of all related to him, without waiting to be prayed to do so. Lot was the nephew of Abraham, and for this reason God presses him to save himself: "Make haste, go to the city for which thou hast spoken", says the angel of God, " and save thyself there, for I can do nothing until thou art entered into it"—*Gen.*, xix. 22. O bounty, O infinite mercy of God! How tender a love hast thou for a just man, and what is there that thou dost not do for him? Thou tiest the hands of thy ministers of vengeance, and wilt not permit them to do anything till he be in security. Wherefore, my brethren, take care to be just; take care to gain God's favour; and for this end do everything in your power, and be assured that God will take care of whatsoever belongs to you. He will be mindful of your parents, of your friends, and of all your relations, though you should not so much as think to pray for them; and the more he sees that the care you take to give yourselves entirely to him hinders you from thinking of them, and of asking anything for them, the more he will pour down his benedictions and graces upon them. For the voice of actions urges God more to hearken to them, than the voice of words; and if the crimes of the wicked cry to God for vengeance, according to the words of Scripture, " the voice of thy brother's blood cries out to me from the earth"—*Gen.*, iv. 10,—ought we not believe that the piety and good works of virtuous persons cry out for mercy more efficaciously to God, who is so ready to do us good, and "to whom it belongs to pardon and to have mercy"? Behold therefore a very holy means to obtain of God whatsoever our parents and friends stand in need of.

CHAPTER X.

The third means of producing fruit in our neighbour is a great zeal for their salvation.

"THE zeal for thy house has eaten me up", says the Royal Prophet, "and the reproaches of those that upbraided thee have fallen upon me"—*Ps.*, lxviii. 10. Behold here another means very efficacious for producing fruit in our neighbour, and our holy founder places it amongst those which are most conducive to the preservation and progress of our society, and to the attainment of the end for which it was instituted, which is the help of souls. "One of these means", says he, "is a sincere zeal for the salvation of souls, having in view the glory of him who has created and redeemed them, with an entire disengagement from all other things"—x. *P. Const.*, §. 2. "My dear brother", says St. Austin, writing to Count Boniface, "are our hearts made of steel, that they do not tremble? Or have we lost all sense, that we are not awakened at these terrible words: Go, you cursed, into everlasting fire"—*Mat.*, xxv. 41. "Why do we not say with the Prophet Jeremias: who will give a fountain of water to my head, and a fountain of tears to my eyes, that I may weep day and night for the children of the daughter of my people who are destroyed"—*Jerem.*, ix. 1. There is sufficient subject to weep continually, when we think of the number of those that die every day, not only the temporal death of the body, but the eternal death of the soul. For in what can we better employ our tears, than in weeping with St. Paul for so great a loss? "Who is there", says he, "that is weak, whose weakness I do not feel?"—II. *Cor.*, xi. 29. Let us learn then of the apostle, says St. Austin upon these words, to have an ardent zeal for the salvation of souls; or rather let us learn of God himself, who has so tenderly loved them, that "he has not spared his own Son, but has delivered him up for us all"—*Rom.*, viii. 32. These words, "for us all", show that we ought to extend our charity to the whole world, and not neglect the salvation of any one, because there is no one but has cost the Son of God even the last drop of his blood.

Zeal for the salvation of souls, or, to style it better, zeal for the glory and honour of God, is a desire to see God so loved, honoured, and served by all the world, that those who are inflamed with this beautiful fire wish to communicate it to the whole world, and they employ themselves therein as much as they are able, without ever ceasing. But if they perceive that God is offended without their being able to hinder it, then they weep and lament, and the fervour of their zeal even devours and consumes them within. It was such a zeal as this with which the saints of the old law found themselves inflamed. "I found my heart and my bones", says Jeremiah, " secretly inflamed, as with a fire that even devoured me; and I fainted away, not being able to resist it; because I heard the blasphemies of many people"—*Jerem.*, xx. 9, 10. "I was inflamed with zeal for the God of armies", says Elias, "because the children of Israel have broken their covenant"—III. *Kings*, xix. 10. "A fainting hath taken hold of me", says the Royal Prophet, "because sinners hath forsaken the law; and my zeal hath made me pine away, because my enemies forgot thy commandments"—*Ps.*, cxviii. 53. These great saints were thus afflicted on seeing with what licentiousness the wicked violated the law of God; and the sorrow of their mind passing into the humours of their body and into their blood, made the whole exterior man feel it. "I beheld the wicked", says David, "I pined away, because they kept not thy commandments"—*Ps.*, cxviii. 158. "Mine eyes became fountains of water, because they observed not thy law"—*ib.*, v. 136. As whatsoever is put into an alembic is dissolved into water by the operation of fire, so was David dissolved into tears by the violence of his zeal, when he perceived they offended the infinite majesty of God. We ought to have similar zeal, so that on the one hand we should make it our chief business and our greatest joy to see the glory of God continually increase, to see his holy will as perfectly fulfilled on Earth as it is in Heaven; and on the other hand, that nothing ought to give us more pain than to be witness to the contrary. "This is true zeal", says St. Austin, "he is truly eaten up with the zeal of God's house, who would wish to be able to prevent all the evils he sees committed, and who is troubled extremely, and grieves very much when he is not able to do so". It was for this motive that Samuel wept over Saul, after God had forsaken him. "Samuel", says the Scripture, "wept over Saul because the Lord hath repented that he had established him King of Israel"—I. *Kings*, xv. 35.

Moreover, there is nothing more pleasing to God, or even so pleasing to him, as zeal for his glory and for the salvation of souls; and it is thus the saints and doctors of the Church speak of it: "We cannot offer any sacrifice to God", says St. Gregory, "which is equal to that of the zeal of souls". "There is no service", says St. Chrysostom, "more agreeable to him than this". "And there is nothing", says Richardus, "that pleases God so much as the zeal and gaining of souls". The reason of this is, because there is nothing so pleasing to God as charity; for, as St. Paul says "charity is the greatest of virtues, and the bond of perfection"—1. *Cor.*, xii. 13. Now the zeal of which I speak is nothing else than an ardent charity, which makes us not only love God with all our heart and to serve him with all our power, but to wish that all the world love and serve him in the same manner, and that his name be glorified throughout the whole world, and that his kingdom be everywhere extended. It is an exceeding great love of God that makes us feel inconceivable joy at whatsoever contributes to his glory, and be penetrated with sorrow at all the sins that are committed. Yes! a child of good education takes nothing more to heart than the glory and advancement of his father: as his only joy and comfort is to see his father advanced, and as all the offences committed against his father are felt by him as sensibly, nay sometimes more sensibly, than if, they were committed against himself; even so, all those who have a true zeal for the glory of God, wish so ardently to see him praised and honoured by all the world, that they place all their joy therein, and nothing gives them greater pain than to witness the contempt which is daily offered to God. And hence it is not to be doubted, but that the zeal I speak of, is a most perfect act of the love of God.

It is likewise a most excellent act of the love of our neighbour; for as the love of God consists in being rejoiced at whatever conduces to his glory, and in being afflicted at whatever offends him, in like manner the love of our neighbour consists in rejoicing at his good, and in being afflicted at his real misfortunes, which are sins, and in preventing them as much as is in our power. The saints say, therefore, that to know whether we love our neighbour, we must examine ourselves whether we are afflicted for his faults, and rejoiced at his good works and spiritual advancement. Because in effect the true mark that you love your brother is, that you rejoice as much at his good as you do at your own, and that you lament his misfortunes as you do those which happen to yourself. This is truly to love our neighbour as ourselves, and it was this the apostle practised when he said: "Who is weak amongst you, and I am not weak with him? Who suffers amongst you without my suffering also?" "Who is he", says the gloss on this passage, "that becomes feeble in faith or in any other virtue, without my becoming feeble with him; that is to say, without my being afflicted for him as I would be for myself? And who is in adversity—who is scandalized or in trouble, and I feel not myself burnt up with tenderness and compassion?"— II. *Cor.*, xi. 29. St. Chrysostom says, that zeal for the salvation of souls is of so great a value, that if we should give all our goods to the poor, if we should pass our whole life in the exercise of all sorts of austerities, this were nothing in comparison of it. For inasmuch as the soul exceeds the body, by so much those who supply the necessities of the soul by confession, by preaching, and by practising other spiritual works of mercy, exceed those who supply the necessities of the body by their alms. Would you not be happy, says this father, to expend large sums of money in corporal works of mercy? He who labours for the salvation of souls does a great deal more; and the zeal of souls is of far greater merit in God's sight than to work miracles. For what miracles and prodigies did not Moses do when the children of Israel went out of Egypt? yet all that was nothing in respect of that ardent zeal he testified when, interceding for them to God, he said: "Either pardon them this their fault, or if thou wilt not do so, blot me out of thy book of life, which thou hast written"—*Exod.*, xxxii. 32. Behold here, continues this doctor, the greatest wonder that Moses ever wrought.

CHAPTER XI.

The same subject continued.

THE zeal I speak of is a very efficacious means to produce fruit in our neighbour for other reasons: first, because it is a fire, as I have before said; for as fire fails not to convert all things into itself when the matter is well disposed, or else disposes it when it is not, in like manner, when we shall be well inflamed with this fire, with this zeal of the love of God, we shall not fail to communicate it to others, and to convert them in some measure into ourselves, making them as much inflamed as we ourselves are, according to the words of the apostle : "I wish all that hear me this day may become like myself"—*Acts*, xxvi. 29. But if we find they are not as yet sufficiently disposed, we must labour incessantly to make them so. Charity cannot be idle; it is a fire which is never in repose; it is in constant activity; "It works great effects wherever it is, and where it does not work great ones, it is certain that it is not great"—*Greg., Hom.* iii. *in Evang.*

In the second place, this zeal is very conducive to the salvation of the neighbour, because it makes us apply ourselves to it with ardour. So far from dragging us by force, which indeed would be shameful, it moves us of itself to seek all occasions of doing good. When zealous, we are always ready to embrace those that present themselves, and would always be very glad to do more than we do. Now this is without doubt a very great point of perfection; for it is certain that, when we give our mind to anything, we act quite differently, and succeed far better. Zeal being the animating principle, if we have it not, we languish, and consequently it is of great importance to be abundantly possessed of it.

In the third place, zeal makes us seek, and even makes us find, the means of helping souls; for a good will is very inventive, and succeeds admirably in finding out means to obtain what it desires. "Wherever this good will is found", says St. Bonaventure, "the effects necessarily follow, as far as opportunity permits". Be not afraid that he who has an ardent zeal will ever want matter or means for the salvation of his neighbour: if he finds not an opportunity in his cell, he will go and seek it abroad; and if he finds it not where he seeks it, he will go to the hospitals and prisons, where he will not fail to find it. The zealous labourers in the vineyard of our Lord find always something to do. Hence the Holy Ghost calls them sometimes hunters, as in these words: "I will send them many hunters, who shall hunt them from the mountains and from all the hills, and out of the hollow places of the rocks"—*Jerem.*, xvi. 16. He sometimes calls them fishers also: "I will make ye fishers of men"—*Matt.*, iv. 19. It is because neither fishers nor hunters wait till the fish or the game come to put themselves into their hands; but they cast their nets, lay their snares, and day and night make every effort to take them. The Devil labours continually for the ruin of souls; is it not, therefore, just that we should continually labour for their salvation?

In the fourth place, when we have zeal all things become easy. We surmount all difficulties, and feel no pain in anything. It seems that St. Denis would attribute to this zeal the firmness and constancy with which our Saviour supported all the pains of his passion. He says that he was assisted in this combat by the aversion he had for sin, and applies to this subject the words of the prophet Isaias: "I have trod the wine-press alone, and amongst all the gentiles there was not so much as one man with me. I have trod them under foot in my fury, I have broken them in pieces in my anger, and my indignation has assisted me" —*Is.*, lxiii. 3, 5.

In the last place, when we are thoroughly penetrated with this zeal, we become thereby far more fervent in prayer, because in this case we cease not to pray till we have obtained of God what we beg of him. It is in this manner that many saints have often interposed themselves between God and men to appease his wrath, and have not ceased their intercession till they had disarmed him. We read in the life of St. Ignatius, that knowing a young man of Paris to be carrying on sinful commerce with a woman, and having very often without success endeavoured to withdraw him from it, he at last resolved one day to go out of town, and await him in a place near which the young man must necessarily pass to go to her. This was a great pond of water; the saint went into it, up to the neck, in a very cold season, and when he saw him passing by, he began to cry out with all his strength: Go, miserable wretch; go and enjoy your unhappy courtships, whilst I will do penance to stop the wrath of God, which is ready to fall upon you! God has already his arm lifted up to strike you! Hell is open to devour you! do you not fear the chastisements that are prepared for you? This extraordinary example of zeal and charity surprised this young man so much that he stopped on a sudden, and, powerfully touched by God, full of confusion and astonishment, he returned back, and for ever renounced that infamous engagement, from which he could not before free himself.

CHAPTER XII.

Three things which contribute very much to give us this zeal.

BESIDES what I have already said, there are chiefly three things which may excite this zeal in us, and urge us to do all in our power for the salvation of our neighbour. The first and chief is, to consider that "it is for these Jesus Christ died", and how tenderly must he have loved them, since he gave his blood and life for their purchase! The earth sprinkled with the blood of God shows us the price of a soul, and the esteem and love Jesus has for her. It is this should fill us with zeal and fervour in those offices which regard the salvation of souls. It is this should make us eagerly seek out occasions of doing them service, that we may be enabled to say with the apostle, "the charity of Jesus Christ urgeth us"—II. *Cor.*, v. 14. Now, can we feel difficulty in shedding our blood for him for whom the Son of God has shed his? And can we refuse to sacrifice our life for the love of a God who has sacrificed his for us? What! I see a soul ready to perish, I see it ready to fall into Hell, I think that God died to redeem it, that it is in my power to save it, and I will not do it, even at the loss of my life!—this is what charity cannot permit. The zeal of souls ought engage our hearts every moment; it ought always to be our greatest care, as it was the sole care of the apostle, who, "in his labours, in his chains, and in his sufferings, having death often before his eyes, was less touched with the things without, than with the care and solicitude he always felt within for the churches under his care"—II. *Cor.*, ii. 23, 28.

St. Austin writing upon this passage of St. John, "Jesus therefore being weary from his journey, sat down upon a fountain"—*John*, iv. 6,—quotes also this other passage of St. Matthew, "How often would I have gathered your children together, as a hen gathers her chickens under her wings, and you would not"—*Mat.*, xxiii. 37. And he says, that it is with reason our Saviour compares himself to a hen that has chickens. For we cannot know when other birds have little ones, but when they cover them in the nest; but when a hen has chickens, she becomes so lean, her wings hang so low, her feathers are so erect, and in fine she is so changed, that that alone shows she is a mother. This is a true image, adds the father, of the state our Saviour was in, when going to the conquest of souls, and overwhelmed with labour and weariness, he sat down upon the fountain of Jacob; and it is in this manner that the zeal of souls, and the earnest desire of bringing up spiritual children for Heaven, ought as it were so devour us as to weaken our constitution and make us forget our own wants. For though our Saviour was harassed from the journey, and was very hungry, yet he refused to eat, preferring the care of the salvation of souls to that of his own nourishment. Hence, when his disciples pressed him to eat, he said to them, "I have food to eat that you know not of. Lift up your eyes, and behold the country, which is already white for the harvest" —*John*, iv. 32, 35. The food of which our Saviour intended to speak, was that change he was going to make in the heart of the Samaritans; it was the salvation and conversion of souls, and it is this also we ought to make our food.

Father Avila makes use of another consideration which is very proper to excite in us a zeal for the salvation of souls. It is, that though, generally speaking, it is very true that as to the graces God bestows upon us, he gives them out of pure love, and without desiring any return from us, yet in another sense it may be said, he gives us nothing for which he seems not to desire a return, not for himself, "because he is master of all things, and stands in need of nothing"—II. *Mach.*, xiv. 35,—but for our neighbour, who stands in need of our compassion and assistance. God acts herein, says he, like a man who, having done great services to another, and lent him a considerable sum of money, should afterwards say to him, I do not desire that what I have lent to you should redound to my own profit, for I am rich enough without it; but I transfer it to such a person, who wants it; pay him what you owe me, and you shall thereby cancel your debt to me. We have an infinity of obligations to God. He has created us, he has redeemed us by his blood, and has had the goodness not to punish us for our sins, in expectation of our doing penance; he daily heaps his graces upon us, and in fine, it is to him we owe all things. But since he stands in need of nothing, he transfers to our brethren the right he has to all we owe him, and gives us a full discharge thereof, upon condition that we serve them in all things possible for us to do. Let us therefore consider them, on the one hand, as the adoptive children of God, and as brethren of Jesus Christ, who has given the last drop of his blood for them; and on the other, as assignees to whom God has transferred all the claims he has on us for so many benefits conferred; and by this means we shall feel ourselves inflamed with zeal for our neighbour's salvation.

Another thing which will contribute very much to this, is to consider that one of the best means we have to satisfy God for all the offences we have committed against him, is to procure that others cease to offend him for the future, and that they serve him with all their heart. This is the doctrine of St. James, who says, "that he who makes a sinner forsake the errors of his life, will save the soul of the sinner, and cover a multitude of his own sins"—*James*, v. 20. And St. Austin takes notice of this truth, upon occasion of the cure of the possessed person in the gospel. The holy text says, that this man seeing himself cured, wished to follow Jesus Christ in acknowledgment of the benefit he had received; but our Saviour, not willing to permit him, said to him: "Return home and recount the wonders that God has wrought in thee; and he went about the town preaching the wonders that Jesus had wrought in him"—*Luke*, viii. 39. What God requires of you in acknowledgment of the grace he has done you, in drawing you from the contagion of the world and the occasion of sin, is, that you help to draw your neighbour also out of sin, and that you urge him to serve God with all his heart.

CHAPTER XIII.

What zeal is pleasing, and what is displeasing to God.

THERE are false virtues as well as true ones; the wise man tells us that "there are some who falsely humble themselves, and whose interior is full of deceit"—*Ecclus.*, xix. 23. They appear humble, and are not so; they wear old clothes, they walk with their heads and eyes cast down upon the earth, they speak in a low voice, they sigh every moment, they call themselves sinners and miserable creatures at every word; but say anything to them that may give them the least pain,—they are presently troubled, fall into a passion, and discover what they took so much care to conceal—they show that the exterior they put on was a mere disguise and perfect hypocrisy. Now as there is a kind of humility that appears good, but is not, there is also a sort of zeal that appears laudable, yet is not so, because it is indiscreet and not well ordered. It is of this the apostle warns us when he says: "I bear witness that they have the zeal of God, but they have it not with discretion"—*Rom.*, x. 2. Such was the zeal which our Saviour condemned in St. James and St. John, who felt great indignation because the Samaritans would not receive him; for on being so irritated as to say to our Saviour, "Lord, shall we beg that fire may descend from Heaven to consume them?" He answers them, "You know not what spirit inspires you. The Son of God came not to destroy souls, but to save them"—*Luke*, ix. 54. Since there is, therefore, a good and a bad zeal, and that it is dangerous lest the resemblance they have one to the other should cause us to confound them, it will not be amiss here to point out the good zeal which is pleasing to God, and the bad zeal which is void of prudence and discretion, that when we know them both very well, we may embrace the one with fervour, and avoid the other with care. St. Denis, treating of this subject, says, we must deal with sinners as we do with those that are blind. Now we are not severe on a blind man for going where he should not, because he knows not whither he goes, and we are never angry with him, but, on the contrary, we feel for him, and even lead him by the hand. Sinners are truly blind, according to the words of Sophonias, "they shall walk like blind men, because they have sinned against our Lord"—*Sophon.*, i. 17. We ought not, then, presently be angry with them, or desire their punishment or destruction, but we ought to have great compassion for them, after the example of the good pastor, who went to seek after his strayed sheep, called it to him, and when he found it, took it upon his shoulders and carried it back in this manner to the fold, and after the example of the father of a family, who received his prodigal child with the bowels of a true father. This is a zeal which is good and according to God; but the zeal that moves us to anger against sinners is not a good zeal, nor does it please God, because it is not conformable to his infinite goodness.

The same saint relates a thing to our purpose which happened to St. Carpus, whom God favoured with a great many revelations, and who never offered the sacrifice of the altar without being beforehand warned to do so by a particular revelation, and he states that it was St. Carpus himself who told him this story. A new convert permitting himself to be perverted by an infidel,

St. Carpus was so afflicted that the day he heard of it he fell sick on account of it. His sickness, however, hindered him not from rising, as he was wont, at midnight to make his prayer. The indignation he felt against this infidel who had seduced the new convert, and against the new convert who had abandoned Jesus Christ, transported him in such a manner that he made a lively complaint of it to God, saying: It is not just, O Lord, that the wicked should live; how long will you suffer them to do so? Why do you not send fire from Heaven to destroy them? And as soon as he had ended these words, it seemed to him upon a sudden that the house in which he was, trembled and opened asunder, and that out of the middle of the cleft that was made in it there arose a prodigious fire, which ascended even to Heaven. Just over the fire he saw Jesus Christ sitting upon his throne of glory, encompassed with an infinity of angels, and casting afterwards his eyes down upon the earth, he perceived a precipice which reached to the very bottom of Hell, at the bare sight whereof he was filled with horror. The two men against whom he had conceived an indignation were upon the brink of this precipice, who trembled for fear, and from time to time there arose from the bottom of this abyss serpents and snakes, which terrified them sometimes by their hissing, sometimes by winding themselves about their legs and biting them, endeavouring to make them fall in. There also came black men out, who endeavoured to do the same, either by dragging them to them or by pushing them. It seemed to the saint as if he found himself not only pleased to see these two men in this danger, but even displeased that they did not effectively fall in, and he was almost ready to go plunge them in himself. With this thought he lifted up his eyes to Heaven, as it were to beg of God that he would finally destroy them, and then he saw that Jesus Christ, taking compassion on them, descended from his throne into this abyss, and drew them out of the danger in which they were, placing them amongst the angels, and then turning himself towards him, he said, "Now stretch forth thy hand to strike me; I am ready to suffer again for sinners. Do you not think it better to be in my company and in that of angels, than in the company of serpents and devils?" Afterwards the vision disappeared, and the man of God reaped this fruit from it, that he corrected the indignation to which his zeal had moved him, comprehending, as. we also ought to do, that this kind of zeal was not pleasing to God. God wills not the death of sinners, because they have cost him very dear. They are his "Benjamins, his sons of sorrow", whom he has brought forth upon the cross, and who have cost him the last drop of his blood! He wills not their death, therefore; he only wills that they be converted, and live eternally.

The prophet Jonas had announced to the Ninivites, on God's part, that their city should be destroyed in three days; and perceiving that his predictions had no effect, he took it very impatiently that God did not destroy it, as he had threatened to do. In this disposition, he leaves the city, and having made himself a booth, he sat under it in the shadow; and then on a sudden, God caused an ivy tree to grow up, which raising itself above the head of the prophet, gave him a shade, and defended him from the scorching sun. But the next day the ivy by God's order withered; and when the prophet, scorched by the sun which shone upon his head, lamented the loss of the ivy, "thinkest thou", says the Lord, "that thou hast reason to be afflicted? Thou art angry that the ivy is withered, yet thou didst not plant it or dress it, or cause it to grow; and yet thou wouldst not have me pardon so great a city as Ninive, in which there are sixty thousand children who are not yet come to the use of reason".—*Jonas,* iv. 4, 10. There is a thing very remarkable and very much to our purpose, which the emperor Constantine said in the council of Nice, to a bishop called Acacius, who would not admit to penance those who had erred, and who came to abjure their error in the council. O Acacius, says he, pray take a ladder and mount alone to Heaven, if you can! A holy person on a like occasion said to another, who testified too great severity, if that sheep you will not receive into your fold had cost you as much blood as it has cost Jesus Christ, you would bring it back on your shoulders, and not leave it abroad with hazard of its being devoured by wolves.

The holy Scripture in the person of Moses, gives us an admirable model of the zeal which the servants of God ought to have. St. Austin observes very justly in his questions upon Exodus, that Moses being ascended to the top of the mountain of Sinai to receive the law God wished to give his people, received it in two tables of stone which God had made, and which he had engraved on both sides with his own hand; and having found at his return that the Israelites adored a golden calf which they had made, he felt so great indignation that he cast down the tables he carried, and broke them in pieces. Consider, says St. Austin, how great the indignation of Moses must needs be against this sin of the people, because he broke the tables of the law which he had a little before received from God, and which were written by God's own hand, and were given him with so much pomp and magnificence, after having been forty days and forty nights fasting, and conversing with God face to face. But how great soever his anger was, he returned presently to God, and prayed most fervently for the children of Israel, and begged of him to pardon them, or to blot himself out of the book of life. Behold here, says this father, what ought to be the zeal of the true ministers of God. They ought, on the one hand, be so zealous for God's glory, that the offences committed against him should even pierce their hearts, and fill them with indignation against sin; and, on the other, they ought to have so great a compassion and tenderness for sinners, that they should presently go and intercede with their God for them, in order to appease his wrath and to obtain their pardon, as Moses did.

St. Paul gives us in himself a like example, when he says in his epistle to the Romans: "I assure you in Jesus Christ that what I say is true, and that I lie not, and my own conscience and the Holy Ghost are my witnesses, that I have an extreme sadness and continual affliction of heart; for I even wished to be myself anathema, or separated from Jesus Christ, for the sake of my brethren the Israelites, my kinsmen according to the flesh"—*Rom.*, ix. 1, 3. The apostle, on the one hand, was sensibly afflicted for the sins of those of his nation, because he had a very great horror of sin; and on the other, he had so great a love and compassion for them, that he wished to be destroyed himself in order to save them. Many different explanations are given of what I have now said, both of Moses and the apostle. St. Jerom says, that it ought to be understood of a corporal death; and that what he desired was, that he might die in time, to save his brethren for eternity; and for this effect he proves that the word anathema is often taken in Scripture only for the separation of the soul from the body. But omitting for the present many other explanations that are given of these two passages, I will speak only of that which St. Bernard gives, and which is both very just and moving. He says, that Moses, in the place I mentioned, speaks to God with the love of a father, or rather with the bowels of a mother; and that nothing was able to give him any comfort, if his children were excluded from having part with him. Suppose, says he, for example, that a rich man should invite a mother to a feast, and say to her: You shall come to my house to make good cheer; but as for your child you carry in your arms, you shall leave him behind you, because he will do nothing but cry and trouble us. Can you believe that this woman would purchase his feast at so dear a rate? Or would she not rather fast than forsake her infant in this manner? And would she not answer him who invited her,— Either I will have none of your feast, or else I will bring my child with me? Behold here, pursues the saint, the very spirit with which Moses spoke to God. He would not enter into the joy of his Lord, if the children of Israel, whom he loved with the tenderness of a mother, were excluded from it.

Now this tenderness of a mother, and these bowels full of charity and compassion for souls that are under the tyranny of the Devil, is what is very pleasing in God's sight. It is this he requires of our zeal, and this which most particularly belongs to a workman of our Lord; and it is for this reason that St. Paul exhorts us "to put on the bowels of mercy, as the elect and favourites of God"—*Coloss.*, iii. 12. The apostle would hereby render us conformable and like to God, who is all goodness and mercy, and to this high priest, of whom he says, "for our parts, we have not a priest that cannot have compassion on our infirmities"—*Heb.*, iv. 15;—and he would have us, in imitation of our Master, compassionate the weakness of our neighbour. St. Ambrose, in his second book of penance, asked nothing else of God than this charitable and tender compassion for the sins of his neighbour; and he obtained it to so great a degree, that Paulinus says of him in his life, that he wept with those that confessed to him, and even discovered to them the bad state of his own conscience, to encourage them to do the same. Penitents are sooner by this means drawn to God, than by an indiscreet and rigorous zeal: for as nothing moves us more to love than to see ourselves beloved, so the affection which a confessor shows his penitent by a charitable compassion of his weakness, gains his heart; and then whatsoever is said to him in this state, makes a deep impression upon him, and whatsoever correction is given him is received with submission and as coming from a father. Hence St. Basil would have all our actions be full of tenderness, "like those of a nurse that cherishes her infant in her bosom"; and that our manner be such, that those we reprehend may be persuaded, that all we say comes from a pure motive of charity, and from a desire of obtaining their everlasting happiness. This is knowing how "to pour wine and oil into wounds"—*Luke*, x. 34,—as the Samaritan in the gospel did, and as those do who mix sweetness and compassion with reprehension, which is of itself displeasing, and who, by this means, cure the wounds of the soul much better than by treating sinners rudely and harshly. For, ordinarily speaking, you will gain very little upon them by this means, but will rather render them the more obdurate and less capable of counsel, and you will not only cause them to fly from yourself, but make them shun all of your order likewise, because they will suppose all of them to have the same spirit of harshness and severity that you show towards them. St. Bernard, pointing out the mode of reprehending, alleges the example of Joseph, "who could not forbear weeping" —*Gen.*, xlv. 1,—at the time that he reproached his brethren; and thus he showed that it was not with anger and indignation he did it, but that it was with a heart full of tenderness and affection.

Another reason which may help us very much to obtain this compassion for the sins of our neighbour, and hinder us from falling into anger against them, is what Father Avila proposes. The sins of our neighbour, says he, may be looked upon two different ways: either as an offence committed against God, and upon that account we ought to have indignation against them, and to wish they may be punished; or else as an evil against our neighbour, and then we ought to be so far from being angry with them, that we ought to have pity on them. For sin being the greatest of all evils that can happen to men, there is consequently nothing more proper to excite us to compassion than when we consider it in this manner; and even the more a man has sinned, the more he ought to move us to compassion, because his evil is so much the greater, and therefore he is to be pitied. And as the injuries and extravagancies of a madman excite rather compassion than anger, because we look upon his words rather as an effect of his distemper than any offence that he gives us, so our sins do rather excite the compassion than the anger of God, since he is pleased to look upon them rather as an effect of the corruption of our nature than as an offence against himself. Now, what we ought to do in regard of the sins of our neighbour is, to look upon them as a distemper; to look upon them with compassion, and not with indignation; to look upon them, in fine, as we would desire that God should look upon ours; and this will be zeal according to God's own heart, whose bowels are full of mercy.

CHAPTER XIV.

Another means of succeeding in our ministry is, to regard only what belongs to the soul, without letting ourselves be influenced by outward appearances.

ONE of the chief instructions which the saints and masters of a spiritual life give to those who are employed in the salvation of their neighbour, is, to attend only to the soul. There are some, says St. Bernard, who attend to the exterior advantages either of nature or of fortune, and who wish to be concerned only with such as possess these. But the truly clear-sighted look to the interior alone, which is not more beautiful in a handsome than in an ugly person, except when he is more holy, but which is exceedingly beautiful in both when they are not defiled with sin, and which, in fine, is more or less beautiful, the more or less it is exempt and free from sin, or the more or less it is enriched with graces and virtues. The visible beauty of the body is to be esteemed as nothing, if it be not joined with the invisible beauty of the soul. The one is common to us with beasts and inanimate things, but the other belongs peculiarly to the angels and ourselves. Now, as St. Bernard says, it is to the interior alone we are to direct our attention; it is to that soul which God has created after his own image; it is this we are to consider as the living temple of the Holy Ghost, as a member of Jesus Christ, as all bathed in the blood of the Son of God, and as redeemed by his death; and if we perceive that sin has deformed it, and that the infinite price which it has cost our Saviour is lost, we ought to be sensibly afflicted, and conceive a lively sorrow for it. As to what regards the body, we ought, on the contrary, to withdraw our eyes from it as much as we can, and make no more account of it than of a sack of dirt, than of a dunghill covered with snow, or of a painted sepulchre, because in effect it is nothing else. "He who labours for the salvation of souls", as Gerson says, "ought not to attend to the difference of face; no, nor even to the difference of sex". He is to have eyes, not to see the beauty or deformity of his penitents, or even to discover whether they are men or women, but purely to see their soul and their interior necessities. He is to abstract from all things else, to feel no concern about them, for in souls there are no differences of this kind.

This advertisement is of very great importance, first, because when we shall act in this manner, our love for our neighbour will be truly the love of charity, it will be entirely founded in God, and will have no other motive or end but God himself, and so we shall be secure from the dangerous illusions of carnal love; secondly, because those who are employed in the functions of charity may learn hereby to acquit themselves of them as they ought, exercising them as willingly no less towards one than towards another, and as well towards the poor as towards the rich, because the soul of one that is poor and in want of all things, costs God no less than the soul of the richest and the most powerful person in the world. St. Ambrose alleges on our subject the example of our Saviour, who refused to enter into the house of a great prince that came to beg of him to go there to cure his son, for fear, says this father, that in the person of the son of a great prince he might seem to have any respect or deference for riches; but he went to the house of the centurion to heal his servant that was sick, though the centurion came not himself to ask it, but only sent one to him to beg his cure, because he would not have them believe he neglected to go thither by reason the sick person was a man of mean rank, and because he would teach us at the same time that in the offices of charity we ought to look to souls only, and not to the quality or condition of persons. Our eyes and our hearts ought to be so fixed on souls, that we be as willing to take care of the salvation of a peasant as of a prince, because, as the apostle says, "the servant and the master, the slave and he who is free, are all equal in God's sight"—*Gal.*, iii. 28.

But if the love of our neighbour be truly such as it ought to be, we shall rather choose to exercise our functions of charity towards the poor than towards the rich, and towards the people of mean extraction than to persons of rank and quality, and this for divers reasons: first, to follow the example Jesus Christ has given us; and secondly, because the poor do better represent the person of our Saviour, " who, being infinitely rich, would become poor for love of us, that we might become rich by his poverty"—. II. *Cor.*, viii. 9. Thirdly, because we are hereby more assured that it is God alone whom we seek in our functions, and that it is purely for him we labour. For when our functions call us to the great ones of the world, we often act from human respect,— we seek ourselves, and act for our own satisfaction and reputation in the world; in fine, there is no traffic or commerce that is so pure and free from dust and straw, as that which we have with poor and simple people; for many times what appears to us to be zeal, is nothing else than vanity and self-love. Fourthly, because by this means it will be more easy to keep ourselves in humility; and lastly, because experience teaches us that ordinarily more fruit is produced in the souls of the poor than in those of the rich. Do we not see likewise that the poor are those who are more solicitous to follow Jesus Christ, and who make greater profit by his doctrine? And has not he himself told us " that the gospel is announced to the poor"?—*Mat.*, xi. 5. With respect to the rich, he has so few followers among them, that the holy text, speaking of one of the chief amongst the Jews who embraced his doctrine, takes notice that, not daring openly to declare himself, "he came to Jesus by night"—*John*, iii. 2. Moreover, we declare the truth boldly to the poor, we reprehend them boldly, and they receive in good part whatsoever is said to them; and, in fine, it is easy for a confessor to manage them. But it is not so with the rich and great persons of the world—we are often puzzled with them; for a confessor dares not take all the liberty he ought, and is afraid to tell them what he thinks, and afterwards he is troubled with scruples and remorses for neglecting to speak his mind freely, and for showing too much condescension to them. Besides, as we must accommodate ourselves to them, we necessarily lose a great deal of time with them, without producing much, or perhaps any, fruit. Whereas with the poor we advance far in a short time, because with them we may presently come to the matter and to the most essential points. Hence those that are truly disabused of the world, and who wish to make great progress in virtue and to produce abundant fruit in souls, avoid as much as they can meddling with great persons, and look upon them as a burden too heavy for them, according to the words of the wise man: "He shall take upon him a burden who treats with one more honourable than himself"—*Ecclus.*, xiii. 2. Do we not also perceive that those amongst us who apply themselves to hear the confessions of servants and poor people, are very much esteemed for it, and with a great deal of reason? For you may be assured that the rich will never want confessors; and if you should judge that there is some one rich man, to take care of whom would be a very important service to God, believe, if you are humble, that another will do it better than yourself, and with less danger to his own conscience. In the mean time take care of this poor man that has several times presented himself to confess to you, and has been obliged to return without confession.

CHAPTER XV.

Another means to produce fruit in souls is, not to confide in ourselves, but to put our whole confidence in God.

"PUT confidence in God with your whole heart, and rely not upon your own prudence"—*Prov.*, iii. 5. Another means that may exceedingly help and assist us in obtaining what we aim at, is that proposed here to us by the wise man, and which is also proposed to us both by our holy founder and by the bull of our institution, in these few but expressive words: "Diffiding in his own strength, and relying upon the word of God". Would you know how you may produce very much fruit in souls? It is by diffiding in yourself, in your own strength, in your own knowledge, in your own abilities, and in fine, in all sorts of human means, and in placing all your confidence in God. To know that of ourselves we are fit for nothing, and to put all our confidence in God alone, is the best means we can take to advance the work of God in souls, and the best disposition that the workmen of our Saviour can have to execute great things. For it is ordinarily such as are of these sentiments he chooses to be instruments of the wonders he designs to work, and it is this the apostle takes notice of when he tells us: "But we have this confidence in God by means of Jesus Christ, not that we are able of ourselves even to think what is good, but all our sufficiency comes from God, who has rendered us capable of being ministers of the New Testament"—II. *Cor.*, iii. 4.

St. Austin upon these words of our Saviour in favour of Nathaniel, " behold a true Israelite in whom there is no guile"— *John,* i. 47,—it seems, says he, that a man of whom the Son of God had given so advantageous a testimony, ought to have been the first that was called to the apostleship, and yet he was not called at all to it. Would you, says this father, know why? It was because Nathaniel was a very learned man, and deeply versed in the law, and that our Saviour would not choose learned and able men for the preaching of the gospel and for the conversion of the world, but only poor fishermen, simple and ignorant people, who had no knowledge at all.

St. Gregory applies to our subject what the holy Scripture relates of David, when he defeated the Amalecites, who having burnt Siceleg, led all the inhabitants into captivity. One of the Amalecites who retreated with the rest, had left behind him upon the way an Egyptian servant, who was not able to follow because he was sick. David met him when he was already half dead, because he had been there three days and three nights without eating or drinking anything. He made him eat something, recovered him from his weakness, and taking him afterwards for his guide, he pursues the Amalecites and takes them by surprise. For imagining that no one pursued them, they thought of nothing but of making good cheer and recreating themselves. He cut them in pieces, and recovered all the prisoners and booty they had taken. Behold here, says St. Gregory, what the Son of God does, who is the true David. He makes choice of those that the world forsakes, and fortifying them with the food of his word, he afterwards makes them his guides against the Amalecites; that is to say, he makes of them preachers of his gospel against the people of the world, who give themselves up to mirth and pleasures. But how comes it to pass that God selects such weak instruments for a ministry so elevated? Would you, says he, know why? It is to take from man all ground of confiding in himself, and all occasions of attributing any thing whatsoever to himself, and it is to teach him to place all his confidence in God, and to ascribe the glory of all to him alone. And moreover this sentiment is so pleasing to God, that the better to imprint it in our hearts, he would have us see by an infinity of examples, that he pleases himself in choosing weak instruments to execute the greatest projects. It is this proves that it is God, not man, who does all; " it is thus that he makes appear the riches of his glory"—*Rom.,*

ix. 23,—and herein the greatness of his omnipotence is displayed. When God led his people out of Egypt, he wrought many miracles by means of Moses, but there was none of these that made so great an impression upon the Egyptians as when Moses, striking dust with his rod, changed it into sciniphs, with which all their country was filled in an instant. For at the same time the magicians of Pharao having recurred in vain to all sorts of charms and enchantments to do the like, were constrained to acknowledge that Moses acted by the power of God, and to say, " the finger of God is here"—*Exod.*, viii. 19. We read in ecclesiastical history (*Theod.*, in Hist. Eccl., p. ii. 1. iii. c. 6) that Sapores, king of Persia, having declared war against the Romans, and besieging Nisabis, a city of Mesopotamia, with a powerful army, the inhabitants, who had no other hope but in God's assistance, begged of the bishop to curse the enemy's army; and for this end they caused him to go up into a high tower where he might have the whole under his view. But all the malediction that this holy man gave to the infidels, and all the prayer he offered to God agaist them, was to beg that he would be pleased to send so great a number of fleas and gnats amongst them, that they should be constrained to raise the siege, and to acknowledge that this plague came from God. His prayer was scarce ended, when there fell upon the army of the Persians a cloud of fleas and gnats, which so filled the trunks of the elephants, and the ears and nostrils of the horses and other beasts in the camp, that, unable to bear their biting, they ran about in such fury that they cast down those that were upon them, trampled under foot those that endeavoured to stop them, and broke the ranks and files of all their troops. At last the disorder they caused was so great, that Sapores knowing that it was an effect of God's power, and of the care he takes of his servants, was constrained to raise the siege and shamefully to return into his own country. God is able to make war against all the princes of the world with fleas and gnats, and is pleased thus to make use of such weak instruments as these in the execution of the greatest projects, in order to show that it is he only who acts, and to draw greater glory to himself. Now, it is for the same reason that he also very often makes choice of weak instruments to work the greatest conversions. Ecclesiastical history furnishes illustrious proofs of this; for we there find that an infinite number of famous sinners, heretics, and infidels, have been convinced and converted by simple and ignorant persons, after having a long time resisted the eloquence and doctrine of many learned men, and even the authority of general councils, wherein the greatest men of the whole Church were assembled.

Now we ought to receive three instructions from this. The first is, not to be discouraged at the sight of our weakness, and of the slender talents we have for so sublime an end and so elevated an employment as our institution calls us to. So far from this, we ought rather derive new courage, and place greater confidence in God, who is usually pleased to make use of weak instruments to execute his greatest designs. This is conformable to the answer made by St. Francis to his ordinary companion, brother Macius, who, knowing very well how pleased the saint was to receive any humiliation, and being desirous to make trial of his humility, went to him one day and proposed these questions to him. How comes it to pass, says he, that the world runs after you; that they wish to see you, to hear you, and to follow you, though you have not birth, nor engaging countenance, nor learning, nor eloquence? How comes it then to pass that they come from all parts to you? Would you know, dear brother, answers the saint, with his accustomed humility, whence this comes? It is from the infinite bounty of God, who has vouchsafed to cast his eyes upon me, though I be the greatest sinner and the most contemptible creature in the world. "For God has chosen the weakest and most simple to confound the strong and great ones, that no creature may have subject to glory in himself; but he that would glory, let him glory in our Lord, to whom be honour and glory world without end"—I. *Cor.*, i. 20, etc. This is a most holy answer, and ought to give us a deal of comfort and confidence.

The second instruction we ought to derive from this is, that what fruit soever God works in souls by our means, how great conversions soever he works by us, and if he should make use of us even to work miracles, this ought not be to us any subject of pride, but on the contrary ought always to confirm us in the knowledge of our baseness and nothingness, and confirm us in this truth, that we have done nothing at all; because in effect we do nothing of ourselves, and are only instruments that God is pleased to make use of. O how perfect a knowledge had the Royal Prophet of this truth, and how his sentiments and words were conformable to his knowledge! "Lord", says he, "we have heard with our ears, and our fathers have told us, what thou didst in their times, and in those times long before them. Thou didst disperse the nations before them, and didst establish them in their place; thou didst afflict the people, whose land thou wouldst give to them, casting them out of it. For it was not by their weapons that they conquered them, nor was it their own hands that saved them; it was thy hand and arm, O Lord, and the brightness of thy countenance, that preserved them, because thou wert pleased with them"—*Ps.*, xliii. 1, etc. Their merits had no share therein, it was a pure effect of thy bounty and mercy.

When God therefore performs great things by means of us, we have no reason at all to become proud; but on the contrary, the more things he works by us, and the greater they are, the more humble we ought to be, and the more we ought to debase ourselves, seeing that he makes choice of such weak and miserable instruments for the working of so great wonders as he is pleased to work by us. We must do on this occasion as St. Peter did when our Saviour caused him to catch the great quantity of fish which is mentioned in the gospel. The Son of God having ordered him to cast out his nets to fish, St. Peter answered him: "Master, we have laboured all night, and have caught nothing; notwithstanding, in obedience to thy command, I will again cast out my nets"—*Luke*, v. 5. And afterwards he caught so great a quantity of fish that the net broke, and they were obliged to call their companions, who were in another little boat, to come and assist them to draw it out. At last they filled both their boats with only one draught of the net; and then St. Peter, seeing the boat so very full that it was ready to sink, " cast himself at the feet of Jesus, and said to him: Retire from me, O Lord, because I am a sinner. For he was seized with a great astonishment, and not he alone, but all that were with him, to see the quantity of fish they had taken"—*ibid.* St. Peter was surprised to see that after he had laboured all night in vain, he caught so great a quantity of fish as soon as he cast out his net in the name of Jesus Christ; and hence he took occasion to humble and debase himself. Let us enter with him into these sentiments of astonishment and humility, and into the knowledge of our own baseness, whenever it shall please God by our means to execute any great thing. See how far St. Peter was from applauding himself for having taken such a number of fish. Do you also take care not to permit yourself to be carried away with vanity, when God shall have made use of you for the execution of anything; and know that it is a work purely his own, and entirely above your strength; and by this means you will come at length to expect nothing from yourself, but all from God; to attribute nothing to yourself but that weakness and misery which belong to you, and to God that praise and glory which is due to him. Consider what St. Peter did, when in his own name he cast out his nets, and you will see herein what you can do of yourself, and what help you may expect from your own ability, care, and labour; and then consider what he did when he cast them out in the name of Jesus Christ, and you will know what you are able to do by grace and God's assistance. The sight of the one will teach you to have no confidence at all in yourself, and the sight of the other will give you all confidence in God, making you expect all from him. And by this means neither the consideration of those great things which it shall please God to execute by your help, will inspire any vanity into you, nor the consideration of your own weakness will at all diminish your courage.

St. Jerom proposes a question to our purpose, and says, let us see a little which of the two did better—either Moses, who alleged his incapacity, when God desired to send him to lead his people out of Egypt, and who begged of God rather to send a more fit person, or Isaias, who, without being called, offered himself to announce the word of God, and said: "Behold here I am, send me"—*Isai.*, vi. 8. To which the doctor answers, that what he has to say is, that it is a very good thing to have humility, and such knowledge of ourselves as shows us we are good for nothing, and that it is also a very good thing to have a prompt disposition of mind to serve our neighbour. But if we would apply ourselves, adds the doctor, to that which is best for us, we must learn of Moses humility by considering our own weakness, and learn zeal and fervour of Isaias by putting our confidence in God, who, to reward him for his good will, purified his lips, and rendered him capable of the ministry to which he had offered himself. Humility is no enemy to confidence, nor any obstacle to it, but on the contrary it helps and fortifies it, because it causes us to place our whole confidence in God, in whom we are assured we can do all things.

The third lesson we are to learn from hence is, that though it is very true that we ought not to confide in ourselves, nor to rely upon our own strength, we must, however, do everything in our power for the salvation of our neighbour; otherwise, to pretend that God should do all without our doing anything, is to desire and expect miracles, and even to tempt God. He will help us in the conversion of souls, and it is upon this account that St. Paul calls us "assistants and ministers of God"—I. *Cor.*, iii. 9,—and that our Saviour commanded St. Peter to cast his nets, for he would not have bestowed upon him so plentiful a fishing without his having himself contributed something thereunto; and would hereby also teach us that we ought not with folded arms to stand idle. In order, however, that on the other hand we should not attribute the good success of the conversion of souls to our own care and industry, he permitted that St. Peter should work all night unprofitably, and cast his nets without being able to catch anything. So that we ought on the one hand to employ all our care, endeavours, and whatsoever else depends upon us, as if these were sufficient to effect the affairs we have in hand; and on the other, we ought to have no more confidence therein than if we had done nothing, nor expect anything but from God alone. It is this Christ himself teaches us in his own words, "when you have done all that is commanded you, say that you are unprofitable servants, we have done only what we were obliged to do"— *Luke*, xvii. 10. Take notice that he says not "when you have done what you were commanded to do, but when you have done ALL that you were commanded to do", to make us comprehend that whatever we are able to do, we ought never rely on what we do, but ought to put our whole confidence in God, and attribute to him the glory of all; and this, in the opinion of holy men, is the supreme and highest degree of humility.

When St. Peter and St. John cured the lame man who begged alms at the gate of the temple, St. Peter perceiving that all the world were astonished at the miracle, and looked upon them with admiration, he cried out to them, "You men of Israel, why do you look upon us as if by our own virtue and power we had made this man to walk? The God of our fathers has glorified his Son Jesus, whom you indeed betrayed and denied before Pilate's face, he judging it fit to dismiss him; this man whom you see and know, has confirmed the name and faith of Jesus who has fortified him, and it is this faith which he had in him that has thus in the presence of you all entirely cured him"—*Acts*, iii. 12, etc. St. Paul and St. Barnabas perceiving the people of

Lystria ready to adore them upon the like miracle, and that they had already prepared crowns and victims to sacrifice to them as gods, rent their clothes in pieces, crying out, "You men, what is this you are about to do? We are mortals as you are, and men like yourselves"—*Acts*, xiv. 14. It is not we that act in this we do, it is God that acts by us, and it is to him alone that the glory of all is to be given. Thus we see that these great saints, after they had wrought many miracles, remained in as profound humility as if they had done nothing. It is in this manner we must conduct ourselves. When we have done all we can for the salvation of souls, we must keep ourselves in humility and in the knowledge of our own baseness.

CHAPTER XVI.

That confidence in God is another very efficacious means to obtain favours from him.

St. Cyprian, explaining these words of God to the children of Israel, "All places where you have set foot shall be yours"— *Deut.*, xi. 24,—says, "by the foot we ought to understand hope, and the greater our hope is, the more things it will obtain. St. Bernard says the same. You will possess all things, says he, as far as you extend your hope. If you have a great hope and confidence in God, it will do much for you. But if your hope be weak, it will do but very little. We have many examples of this in the gospel. See how the prince of the synagogue who had lost his daughter, speaks to Jesus Christ: "Lord", says he, "my daughter is just now dead, but come lay your hand upon her, and she shall live"—*Matt.*, ix. 18. He had, without doubt, some faith and confidence, because he believed that Jesus Christ could raise his daughter to life; however, he had not much, because he believed it necessary that our Saviour should go to the place where she was, and lay his hand upon her. And hence our Saviour, conforming himself to the faith of her father, goes to his daughter, and having found her dead, he takes her by the hand, and raises her to life. The woman in the gospel, who had been sick of a bloody flux for twelve years, and had spent in vain all she had on physicians, approached the Son of God with a little more faith, "for she said within herself, So that I can but touch the hem of his garment, I shall be healed"—*Matt.*, i. 21. She gets through the press of the people, approaches him, touches the hem of his garment, and behold she is cured at the same instant, God acting towards her conformably to the extent of her faith and confidence. But the centurion had a great deal more; he came to find out our Saviour, and to beseech him to cure his servant who was sick, but he did not beg of him for this purpose either to go to his house, or to vouchsafe to permit his servant to touch his clothes. "Lord", says he, "I am not worthy that thou shouldst enter under my roof; say but the word and my servant shall be healed"—*Matt.*, viii. 8. He also merited that our Saviour should speak in admiration of his faith: "Verily, I say unto you, I have not found so great faith in Israel". And turning himself to the centurion, he said: "Go, and be it done unto thee according to thy faith". He had a firm confidence that Jesus Christ needed only to speak, to cure his servant; and Jesus Christ, conforming himself to his faith, cured him by his bare word. This shows that God is pleased to treat and deal with us according to the confidence we have in him. "Let thy mercy, O Lord", says David, "extend itself towards us, according to the hope that we have in thee"—*Ps.*, xxxii. 22. According to the depth of the vessel of our confidence, says St. Cyprian, such shall be the quantity of Heavenly waters that God shall pour into it.

When Jesus Christ commanded St. Peter to come to him upon the waves, St. Peter walked upon them as if he had land to walk upon, so far was he from being afraid; but no sooner did he begin to lose confidence, perceiving the wind to rise, but he presently began to sink, wherefore our Saviour reprehended him for this fear, saying: "Man of little faith, why didst thou doubt?"— *Matt.*, xiv. 31; as if he would say to him that he sunk only for want of confidence. It is thus that, through our want of confidence, the waves of temptations often seem ready to swallow us up, and that we are not able to resist the storms that arise against us. For if we had firm confidence in God, he would not fail to take us out of all sorts of dangers, and to replenish us with his graces.

The Moabites and Ammonites having joined their forces together to make war against Josaphat, king of Juda, this prince perceiving himself too weak to resist them, was seized with panic fear; but because in this extremity he and all his people had recourse to Heaven, God said to them by the prophet, "Fear nothing; be not at all afraid of the multitude that is assembled against thee, because it is not thine but God's war: it is not thou that shalt fight; have but a firm confidence in God, and thou shalt see the succours that God will give thee"—II. *Paral.*, xx. 15. And in effect they soon received these succours; for without their doing anything, God destroyed their enemies, permitting that they should turn their armies one against the other, and thereby destroy themselves. Now let us consider how little God requires of us to procure his assistance, and to obtain the victory over our enemies. He only requires of us to repose confidence in him, and in the ninetieth Psalm he himself gives no other reason for the succours he promises the afflicted, than their hope in him: "Because he hoped in me I will deliver him: I will protect him because he has known my name"—*Ps.*, xc. 14. "O wonderful liberality of God", cries out St. Bernard upon these words, "who never fails to assist those that hope in him!" "Our fathers", says the Royal Prophet, "have hoped in thee; they hoped in thee, O Lord, and thou hast delivered them. They cried out unto thee, and thou hast saved them: they hoped in thee, and were not confounded"—*Ps.*, xxi. 5, 6. Who has ever had recourse to God, or had an entire confidence in him, without being heard and succoured? "Cast thy eyes upon all the nations of the Earth", says the wise man, "and know that never any one hoped in God and was confounded. For who has ever invoked him and was despised?"—*Ecclus.*, ii. 11, 12. There is still another reason that ought particularly to engage us to put our whole confidence in God; but having spoken of it elsewhere more at large, I shall touch only slightly on it here. It is this, that when diffiding in ourselves, we put our whole confidence in God alone, we transfer all upon him, and trust him with everything, so that this engages him to take care of our interest, as of his own glory. The conversion of souls is your affair, O Lord, and not ours, for what are we able to do if you touch not their hearts? Apply yourself, then, and put your hand to it in a special manner.

The words which Josue said to God, to avert his anger from the people of Israel who had fled from the enemy, are well adapted to this subject: "What will become of the glory of thy name?"—*Jos.*, vii. 9. Humble us, O Lord, if it be your good will and pleasure, and deliver us up to our enemies, as we have deserved! But what will they say of your name? What will the nations say when they shall behold the destruction and captivity of your people? They will say that you could not conduct them into the land that you had promised them. "Give no glory, therefore, to us, O Lord, but to thy name"—*Ps.*, cxiii. 9. "Do justice to thyself, O Lord, but charge us with confusion"—*Baruch*, ii. 6,—as you shall think fit. In fine, let it be taken in what manner it will, it is always a very good means to obtain all sorts of favours from God, to have a great confidence in him, "for our Lord beholds with a pleasing countenance those that fear him and hope in his mercy"—*Ps.*, cxlvi. 11.

But above all, religious have a particular reason to promise themselves God's assistance in their ministry, because, being engaged therein by obedience, they are engaged by the order of God, who consequently will not fail to give them strength and necessary help to acquit themselves as they ought. When God commanded Moses to make for him the tabernacle, the ark of the covenant, the propitiatory which was to be above it, and the altar and table upon which the loaves of propitiation were placed, and, in a word, all the vessels which were for the service of the tabernacle, he did not content himself to mark down the measures and proportions of each one; but, that his orders might well be executed, "he chose Beseleel and Oliab, to whom he gave such ability and understanding as was necessary to know how to work perfectly in gold, silver, precious stones, copper, marble, and all sorts of wood"—*Exod.*, xxxi. 2. Now if God, having chosen workmen to make a material tabernacle, took care to inspire them with all the necessary knowledge they should stand in need of, what will he not do in regard of those workmen and ministers of the gospel whom he has chosen to make the spiritual tabernacle of souls, to raise the living temple of the Holy Ghost, and to extend his kingdom in the hearts of men? Have we not ground to hope that, inasmuch as spiritual things surpass material, even so he will proportionably give us all that is necessary to acquit ourselves well in our ministry. He has so firmly assured us of his help on these occasions, that he would not have us be in pain even about what we shall have to say. "When", says he, "ye shall appear before governors of provinces, and before kings on my account, think not what ye are to say, nor how ye ought to speak, for then God will put words into your mouth. For you do not speak, but it is the Spirit of your Father that speaks in you"—*Matt.*, x. 18. He promises, in fine, such victorious eloquence as nothing shall be able to resist. "I will give you", says he, "a mouth, and wisdom, which all your adversaries shall not be able to resist and gainsay"—*Luke*, xxi. 15. And in effect, do we not read in the Acts of the Apostles that those that disputed with St. Stephen "were not able to resist his wisdom and the spirit that spoke in him"?—*Acts*, vi. 10.

CHAPTER XVII.

The want of confidence is very displeasing to God.

As there is nothing more pleasing to God nor more proper to draw down his graces upon us, than the confidence we have in him, so nothing displeases him more, nor is more capable to provoke his indignation against us, than the want of confidence. He looks upon it as an offence and injury done to his honour, and we see in effect that this was one of the subjects that most of all moved him to anger against the children of Israel, and for which he most severely punished them. When Moses sent persons to view the land of promise, the greater part of them reported at their return that they had seen very strong cities, and such giants that, compared to them, they themselves were but ants; and this caused so great a consternation amongst the people that, despairing of being able to become masters of the land that had been promised them, they already spoke of electing a chief to lead them back to Egypt. Nay, they even went so far as to express a wish of stoning Caleb and Josue, who endeavoured to dissuade them from this design: and then, the glory of God appearing upon the tabernacle, "How long", says the Lord to Moses, "will this people blaspheme against me? How long will they refuse to believe me, after so many prodigies as I have wrought in their presence? I will strike them, then, with the plague, and destroy them"—*Numb.*, xiv. 11, 12. Moses, however, interceded with God for the people, and God pardoned them. "In the meantime", says he, "all those who have seen my glory, and the prodigies I have wrought in Egypt and in the desert, and have frequently risen and rebelled against me, not having obeyed my voice, shall never see the land that I have sworn to their fathers to give them, nor any of those who have blasphemed against me shall ever behold it"—*Numb.*, xiv. 22, 23. In effect, of more than six hundred thousand men that went out of Egypt, there was not one of them who saw the land of promise except Caleb and Josue, who endeavoured to encourage the people. All the rest died in the desert, receiving this punishment for the little confidence they had in God, and as to their children, who they said would become a prey to their enemies, it was of these God made choice to take possession of this land. Even Moses and Aaron, to show how disagreeable to God their want of confidence was, were chastised in the same manner, because when they struck the rock, as God had commanded them, it was with a kind of doubt whether water could spring from it. "Because you have not believed me", says our Lord, "and have not maintained my glory before the children of Israel, you shall not lead this people into the land that I will give them"—*Numb.*, xx. 12. He gave Moses, indeed, a sight of it from a high mountain, but said to him at the same time: "Thou hast seen it with thy eyes, but thou shalt not enter into it"—*Deut.*, xxxiv. 4,—as if he would have said, behold the land of which I promised to give you possession, but to punish you for your little confidence, you shall never enjoy it. This want of confidence is an offence committed against God's honour, as I have already said, and hence it is that he punishes it so severely.

We may draw from this two inferences for our instruction. First, that the discouragement into which we permit ourselves to fall, either in temptations, or in our own advancement in virtue, or finally, in the ministry wherein obedience has placed us, is a very bad thing in itself, and very displeasing to God. If we look to appearances only, it might be said this is a sentiment which springs from humility, when in reality it proceeds only from our thinking that it is from our own strength we are to derive help in our necessities, which indeed is a kind of pride very much to be condemned. The second instruction we may derive, is, that in all our necessities and in all afflictions, the first thing we ought to do is to have recourse to God. We must not begin, by doing all that depends on us, and then recurring to God; for this is one of the great abuses the people in the world are guilty of, who instantly strain every nerve, and adopt all ways and means, to compass their designs, without thinking at all upon God; and have recourse to him only when they have tried all other ways in vain, and when their affairs seem to be desperate. God likewise often permits all human means, in which they placed the greatest confidence, to become unprofitable, and even to turn to their own confusion: "Because thou hast had confidence in the king of Syria", says he to Asa by the mouth of his prophet, "and not in the Lord thy God, therefore the army of the king of Syria has escaped thy hands"—II. *Paral.*, xvi. 7. God is offended that we should seek any other help than his. It is to him, therefore, we must first have recourse; and for this effect, one of the chief things we have to do in prayer, is then to establish in our hearts an entire confidence in God. For since the establishment of virtue in our heart is what we ought chiefly to propose to ourselves in prayer, it is fit that we should employ ourselves therein to gain a virtue so necessary and of so great importance. But, moreover, to do this well, we ought to labour herein without ceasing, till we find a habit thereof well fixed in our heart, and till we come to have recourse to God in all things, and to put our confidence in nothing but in him. We ought continually to have the words of Josaphat, king of Juda, in our thoughts, "Lord, in the ignorance we are, what ought we to do, but only to raise our eyes to thee, O God?"—II. *Paral.*, xx. 12. And then we shall be able not only to do all things with God, but we shall also begin to be happy with him, since the Royal Prophet teaches us, "that blessed is the man whose confidence is in the name of the Lord"—*Ps.*, xxxix. 5.

CHAPTER XVIII.

That we ought not to be discouraged, though we perceive we produce very little or no fruit in souls.

"Wo be to me", says the prophet Micheas, complaining of the little fruit he wrought amongst the people of Israel; "I am become like a man who goes to gather grapes after the vintage is made, and finds not so much as one bunch to eat". The prophet Isaias makes a similar complaint. "The city", says he, "will become a frightful solitude; desolation will cast down her gates; because the same shall happen in the midst of the earth, and in the midst of the people, which happens when they shake down the few olives that are left upon the tree after the others have been gathered; and when they gather together the few bunches of grapes which were left upon the vines after the vintage"—*Isai.*, xxiv. 12. Lastly, one of the things that most discourages those that labour for the salvation of souls, is to see how little fruit they produce by all their sermons, and to see, notwithstanding all their other efforts, how few are converted; how few give themselves to virtue, and how few persevere in it. As then this is a complaint so general, and so productive of evil, I will here apply a remedy to it, and perhaps what I shall say will serve to encourage us in the offices of charity.

St. Austin treats this matter perfectly well. He replies to this complaint by citing the example of our Saviour. Perhaps, says he, the Son of God preached only to his disciples and to those that were to believe in him. But do we not see that he preached also to his enemies, and to those who endeavoured to take him by surprise, and to destroy him? Or perhaps he preached not, but when there was a great crowd of people to hear him. But do we not see that he preached to one single woman of Samaria, and that he discussed with her the famous question, whether they ought to adore only in Jerusalem, or whether they might also adore in other places? But you will say, our Saviour knew she would believe in him, and improve by all he should say to her. It is true, answers the father, he knew it very well; but what will you say of his sermons to the Pharisees, Sadducees, and those others who would not only not believe in him, but would even put him to death? Sometimes he asked them questions that he might convince them by their own answers; and sometimes he answers their questions, which they proposed only to tempt him; "and yet we do not read that any of them was converted by the force of his doctrine". He knew, however, very well what would happen; and though he knew that his sermons, so far from converting them, would, on the contrary, serve to confirm them in their hardness of heart, yet he neglected not to preach to them, in order that we who are ignorant whether any will be converted or not by our means, should learn by his example never to relent in our functions, and never to be discouraged at the little fruit we think we have produced. Perhaps there is one of his elect whose salvation he designed should be wrought by your sermons; perhaps he will touch his heart the very moment you speak; or if this conversion be not then wrought, perhaps he will work it afterwards, and the seed of the word of God, which you cast into his heart, will then produce the fruits of justice and salvation. Hence, let what will happen, we ought never neglect anything for the help of souls that depends upon us.

Gerson, in a treatise he composed on the mode of attracting children to Jesus Christ, speaks very severely against those that refuse to hear the confessions of certain sinners, because they quickly relapse into the same sins, and because all they do to convert them is but to labour in vain, and as it were, to cast water into a sieve. In the same place he exhorts confessors to apply themselves to hear the confessions of children, from whom he says there may be great fruit expected, because they are between two roads, and disposed to follow that to which they shall be directed. They will be for him, says he, who wins their heart. If it is won for the Devil, they will be for the Devil; if it is won for Jesus, they will be for Jesus. So that it is of great consequence to lead them betimes into the way of virtue, and to conduct them to it at first, because ordinarily they remain in that in which they are first placed. Afterwards he answers the objections made by some confessors, who say, it is but lost time to confess children, because they have not as yet a capacity to profit of what is said to them, and therefore after confession they return to the same things from which they came to it, and begin again to play, to quarrel with their companions, and even to fight with them, as if nothing had been said to them. But, says Gerson, if because they return presently to their bad habits you will not confess them, you ought not for the same reason confess those that are advanced in years; for they too return to their vomit as soon as they go from confession, and their sins are far greater than those of children, which ordinarily are only venial. It would, without doubt, be a very strange thing should we send away our penitents, or refuse to confess them, because they quickly relapse into the same sins. Hence, adds he, we ought not refuse to hear the confessions of the one or of the other, so long as they make a true resolution of amendment; and to this subject he applies comparisons that agree very well with it. "Whilst a ship leaks, do they cease to pump, because there enters as much water in as the pump takes out?" And do we forbear washing our hands because they daily grow dirty? We must keep our hand continually to the pump, though we perceive there enters as much water as we take out, because otherwise the vessel would sink, which this prevents. "We must oftentimes wash our hands, though they presently grow dirty again; because the dirt at least sticks not so fast, nor have we so much trouble in making them clean. Let us not neglect, then, to confess such as are penitent, and help them to get up again, though they presently fall, for otherwise they will utterly destroy themselves, and this at least hinders them from entirely abandoning themselves to their disorders; and after all, there is always ground to hope for their salvation.

The example of our holy founder may serve us for a rule on this occasion. We read of him, that amongst other works of charity, which he continually practised, he employed all his power to withdraw bad women from their debaucheries: for this end he obtained the establishment of a house at Rome for such of them as would quit their disorders. For though there was at that time at Rome a monastery of penitents, yet they received none but such as took the veil; and many of these women, how great a desire soever they had to get out of this their unhappy state, either would not embrace a religious life because they found themselves not called thereunto, or could not because of their engagement in marriage. In order, then, that the one and the other might find a place of retreat, he caused a house to be built for them, under the name of the monastery of St. Martha. And because nobody would begin so holy a work, though several offered to contribute to it, he was the first that led the way, giving for this end a hundred ducats, which he got for some jewels that were sold by his order, and which were given him at a time when the society was in distress. His office of general hindered him not from taking this affair so to heart, that when there were any courtezans that quitted their bad life, he himself accompanied them through the streets of Rome, and conducted them to this monastery of St. Martha, or to some other proper house to which they retired. Some people took upon them to tell him that he lost his time in labouring to convert such creatures as these, whose long and vicious habits would easily draw them back into their former disorders. He answered them, that if he could only obtain that any one of them should pass one day without offending God, he thought he had employed his time and care very well, though he should even be assured that presently after she would lead the same life as before. And hence, though we should know that a penitent would not fail to relapse quickly into the same sin, we ought to think our time well employed though he should remain only one hour without offending God, or should commit but one mortal sin less; and this is to have a true zeal for the honour and glory of God. He that digs for a treasure, takes a great deal of pains to dig a long time, and to take out a great deal of earth before he can find anything; and for the little gold he afterwards finds, he thinks all his pains amply recompensed.

But let us go still farther, and put the case that no one be converted, nor even that we be able to obtain that any one for an hour only should abstain from offending God. I say that notwithstanding all this we ought not to cease preaching, or doing whatsoever depends upon us for the help of souls. St. Bernard treats this matter very well in a letter he writes to Pope Eugenius, who had been both his disciple and one of his religious. He exhorts him to reform the people and court of Rome; and having long insisted on it, he starts this objection to himself: but perhaps you are not of my opinion, and you will tell me it is to no purpose to undertake to reform the Romans, who are a proud kind of people, untractable, seditious, incapable of living in peace, or of submitting to their duty but only when they want power to resist, and in fine, from whom nothing is to be expected, and therefore it would be to labour in vain. "Notwithstanding, do not diffide", continues the saint, "you will not perhaps cure them, but you will labour to do so", by applying proper remedies to their indisposition, and this is what God requires of you. "You have been established their governor", says the wise man, "take care of them"—*Ecclus.*, xxxii. 1; and take notice that he says not, "cure them", for he who is put to govern others is not obliged to cure all their defects, because that is not in his power, and God requires no more of us than we are able to do. And hence it has been justly said, that "it is not always in the physician's power to give help to the sick"; and in effect, it is not in this that the duty of his profession consists, but that he does everything in his power to cure them. But setting apart these authorities which I have alleged, I will propose another, that is more formal and more express. Listen to the apostle, who says, "I have laboured more than all the rest"—I. *Cor.*, xv. 10. He says not, "I made more progress, and produced more fruit in souls than all the rest". For being instructed by God himself, "he knew very well that every one should one day receive his recompense according to his labours"—I. *Cor.*, iii. 8,—and not according to the success he had in them, and therefore he ought glory in his labours. Imitate him by labouring on your part, in doing what you are able; plant, water, cultivate the vineyard of our Lord, and hereby you will perform the duty of your charge; the increase and fruit belong not to you. It is God who is to take care of this, which he will do when he thinks fit; but though he should not do it, you will never lose anything thereby, because the holy Scripture assures us, that "he renders to the just the recompense of their labours"—*Wisd.*, x. 17,—and measures them not according to the success. "O secure labours, whose recompense depends not upon the success!" Though no one should be converted, though no one should amend himself, yet your recompense will be as great as if you had produced great fruit, and as if you had been the cause of many conversions. I must, however, tell you, adds the saint, without pretending to give bounds to the bounty and omnipotence of God, that should the people of Rome be more hardened than they are, and though they should have hearts of stone, "God can of these stones raise children to Abraham"—*Mat.*, iii. 9; "and who knows but that our Lord may permit himself to be overcome, and pardon them, and pour also his blessings upon them?"—*Joel*, ii. 14. But we do not here examine what God will do, for it belongs not to us to penetrate his judgments: all that I propose to myself is to show those whose duty it is to labour for the salvation of souls, that the consideration of the little fruit they produce ought not to cause them to relent, because the merit as well as the recompense depends not upon the success, but only upon the manner wherein they acquit themselves of their duty.

There is one thing more, which is, that even though we should know we should be able to produce no fruit at all in souls, yet we ought not neglect to persevere always in our functions, as if we made great progress therein, and this for two reasons: the one is taken from its conducing to the greatness of God's mercy, and the other to that of his justice. Fountains continue to run without ceasing, says St. Chrysostom, though no one goes to draw water; and it is conducive to the beauty and grandeur of a city to have water in it in great abundance, in order to flow and lose itself in divers places thereof. The same thing ought to be in preachers, by whom as channels the water of evangelical doctrine communicates itself to the whole world; they ought never cease pouring forth these wholesome waters of the word of God, whether few or many drink of them. It is in this that the magnificence of God's mercy is more displayed, that he should vouchsafe to let his waters run continually without ceasing for those that were thirsty and had a desire to drink. "Come to these waters, ye that are thirsty; and ye that have no money, make haste, buy and eat; come and buy wine and milk without money and without giving anything in exchange for it"—*Isai.*, lv. 1. Secondly, this conduct is conformable to the justice of God; because in case so many advertisements and sermons are not able to convert men, they will serve at least "that God may be justified in his words, and that he gain his cause when they go to judge him"—*Ps.*, l. 6. God wishes to justify his conduct to sinners, and let them see that it was their own fault if they were not saved; in order that, considering the means which he had given them, they might know that they had no excuse left, and that they had no reason to complain of any but themselves. "What was there that I ought to do for my vineyard which I have not done?"—*Isai.*, v. 4,—says our Saviour, by the prophet Isaias, in order to prove his kind conduct towards his people. "I have planted it, I have hedged it about, I have built a tower, and put a wine-press in the midst of it; and I expected that it should bring forth good grapes, and it has brought forth sour ones fit only for verjuice: wherefore judge now, people of Jerusalem and Judea, between me and my vineyard"—*Isai.*, v. 2, 3,—and see who is to blame, that it produced not what it should have done. Now it is not a small matter, that at least you may be able to defend God's cause at the day of judgment against sinners; for these sermons, these admonitions, of which they make at present so little profit, will convict and reduce them to such a nonplus, that they will not know what to answer. So that on which side soever the matter is taken, we must always employ ourselves with all our power in the help of souls, whether we succeed or not in our endeavours.

St. Austin, explaining the parable of those who, being invited to the marriage feast, would not go, and speaking of the servants whom the master had sent to invite them, do you believe, says he, that these servants ought to be accused of negligence, because those that they invited to the wedding came not to it? By no means. They shall, on the contrary, be looked upon as careful and faithful servants, because they did what was commanded them. They invited those that they were charged to invite; they did what they were able to oblige them to come to the feast. The guests that would not come to it shall be punished; but as to the servants, they shall have the same recompense as if those they invited had come, because it was none of their fault that they did not. The account that God will require of us at the day of judgment is, whether we have done all that we are able, and that we ought to do for the help of souls. For though they should not be converted, and though their conversion be certainly a good, we ought to desire and to rejoice at extremely when it happens, as we read that our Saviour *rejoiced in spirit* for the fruit that his disciples had brought forth in their mission; yet after all we shall not be accountable for it, but they only to whom we have preached the word of God. So that as each one ought to give an account of what regards himself, so we shall only be accountable whether or not we have acquitted ourselves well of our functions, and they, whether they have profited by the instructions they have received from us. Neither our merit, then, nor the goodness and perfection of our actions, depend upon the effect they produce in others; on the contrary, I may here add one thing that cannot but comfort us when we do not succeed in our endeavours. It is, that our recompense and merit are so far from depending upon what we do, that in some measure we merit more when we produce no fruit than when we produce a great deal; as we merit more by persevering in prayer, notwithstanding all distractions and dryness, than when we persevere amidst sweetness and consolations. For, as St. Gregory justly observes, it ought to give a preacher a great deal of satisfaction, courage, and force, to see himself followed by crowds, and to know that he produces great fruit by his sermons; and, on the contrary, it is of itself sorrowful and afflicting not to see himself followed, nor to produce any fruit. So that not to be dejected by this, but still to continue to preach the word of God as if we were numerously followed, and as if we made great progress in souls, this is to have great purity of zeal, and is a true mark that we labour purely for God.

It is with this purity of zeal, and this disengagement from ourselves, we ought to exercise our functions, proposing for our chief end and aim not to produce fruit, but faithfully to acquit ourselves, and to accomplish the will of God, for this is precisely what he requires of us. And thus neither the pains we take will check us, nor our ill success discourage us or deprive us of peace of mind, to which those are strangers who aim at success alone.

THE SECOND TREATISE.

ON THE THREE PRINCIPAL VOWS OF RELIGION—THE ADVANTAGES OF A RELIGIOUS STATE.

CHAPTER I.

That the perfection of a Religious consists in an exact observance of the vows of poverty, chastity, and obedience.

BEFORE I speak of these vows individually, I shall say a little of them collectively; and first, I say, that they are the chief and principal means we have in a religious state to attain perfection. St. Thomas says, that a religious is in the state of perfection; and this doctrine is taken from St. Denis, and is universally received by divines. It is not that as soon as we take the habit we are perfect, but that we then make profession to aspire to perfection. For the state of a religious life is not like the state of episcopacy. We consider perfection in a bishop as a thing already acquired, but we consider it in a religious as a thing he is obliged to acquire. The one ought to be already perfect; and it is sufficient for the other to endeavour to become so. The same St. Thomas founds the difference between these two states on the words of our Saviour, remarking that in the counsel Jesus Christ gives of voluntary poverty, which implies a vocation to a religious life, "he does not suppose that he to whom he gives it is already perfect, but that he will become so if he practises the counsel he gives. For he says not, if thou art perfect, go and sell what thou hast, but only, if thou art willing to be perfect"—*Mat.*, xix. 21. He acted quite otherwise when he appointed St. Peter bishop, for he asked him thrice not only if he loved him, but if he loved him more than all the others; and this he did to show what charity and what perfection the state of episcopacy requires in those that are elevated to it, so that the state of a religious life and the state of episcopacy are two states of perfection, but after a different manner; because the one supposes it already, and does not give it; and the other does not suppose it, but gives it. At the moment you become religious, you are not obliged to be perfect, but you are obliged to aspire to perfection. Hence St. Jerom says, that "it is a prevarication or apostacy in a religious not to desire to be perfect". And St. Eusebius tells us, " that as it is the way to sanctity and perfection to retire into the desert, so it is in like manner the way to damnation not to live piously in it". St. Thomas also tells us, that a religious who aspires not after perfection, and uses not all his endeavours to become perfect, is not truly religious; because he does not perform that for which alone he ought to have embraced a religious life. " Our life ought to be conformable to our name, and our profession ought to be known by our actions".

Now the chief means we have in religion to acquire perfection consist in the three vows we make, of poverty, chastity, and obedience, as is perfectly well explained by St. Thomas. The state of a religious life, says he, may be considered three ways; either as an exercise that leads to perfection; or as a tranquil state which excludes worldly cares; or as a sacrifice which we make of ourselves and property to God. If it is considered as an exercise which leads to perfection, we shall find that it destroys in us all the obstacles that oppose the love of God in our hearts—which obstacles are of three kinds. The first is covetousness of temporal goods, which is destroyed by the vow of poverty ; the second is concupiscence, or the desire of carnal pleasures, which is destroyed by the vow of chastity ; and the third is the disorder of our own will, which is destroyed by the vow of obedience. But if we look upon it as a state that frees us from all kind of care, according to the words of the apostle, "I would have ye be without care or solicitude"—I. *Cor.*, vii. 32,—we shall see that these three vows which we make entirely free us from three sorts of the principal cares with which seculars are molested. For the vow of poverty delivers us from the first, which is the care of riches ; the vow of chastity delivers us from the second, which is the care of governing a family and the bringing up of children ; and the vow of obedience, by which we entirely abandon ourselves to the guidance of our superior, delivers us from the third, which is the care of behaving and conducting ourselves properly in the different occurrences of this life. Finally, if we consider it as a sacrifice which we make of ourselves to God, we shall find that this sacrifice becomes entire and perfect by means of the same vows. For all the goods that men possess are reduced to three; to those of fortune, which regard riches; to those of the body, which regard pleasure; and to those of the soul, which regard the will and desires. We entirely sacrifice the first by the vow of poverty; we entirely sacrifice the second by the vow of chastity; and we entirely sacrifice the third by the vow of obedience, whereby a religious renounces his own will, and puts himself into the hands of his superior, whom he beholds and takes in place of God: so that in what manner soever we look upon this state, we shall always find that the three vows we make in it, are the principal means we have of attaining perfection.

It is related in the chronicles of the order of St. Francis, that Jesus Christ once appearing to this saint, and having commanded him to make three offerings: You know, O Lord, answers the saint, that I have already offered you all I have, and that I am yours, and that I have nothing left but this habit and cord, which in like manner are also yours; what, therefore, can I offer you? I wish I had for this purpose another heart and soul; but since I have nothing which I have not already given you, bestow, O Lord, something new upon me, that I may make an offering of it to you, and that thereby I may obey you. Then our Saviour commanded him to put his hand into his bosom, and to offer him what he should find there. And the saint having obeyed him, drew out a large piece of gold, which he presently offered him; our Saviour gave him the same command twice more, and the saint having drawn out each time the like piece of gold, he in like manner still offered it to him: to whom our Saviour then declared, that the three pieces of gold signified his three vows of obedience, poverty, and chastity, of which this great saint had made so perfect an offering to God, that his conscience, as he said, never reproached him with having broken them in anything. Let us endeavour to imitate him in this kind of offering, that our conscience may never be able to reproach us with anything, and that we may truly say with Job, "My heart has reproached me with nothing throughout my whole life"—*Job,* xxvii. 6.

CHAPTER II.

Why we bind ourselves by vow to these three virtues.

BUT some say, why do you bind yourself by vow to observe poverty, chastity, and obedience, since they may be observed without such ties or engagements as these? All divines answer with St. Thomas, that vows are necessary, because a religious life essentially consists in them, and that without vows it cannot be a state of perfection. The reason of this is, because the state of perfection necessarily supposes a perpetual obligation to perfection: for when we say it is a state, it is the same as to say that it is a stable and permanent thing; so that as religion cannot be a state of perfection without a perpetual obligation to perfection, it consequently cannot subsist without vows, whereby it contracts this obligation. What causes bishops, says St. Thomas, to be in a state of perfection, which parish priests are not, is, because the latter are not always obliged to the care of souls, but may disengage themselves from it whensoever they please; but the pastoral care and solicitude of bishops carries along with it a perpetual obligation, with which the authority of the pope only can dispense. The same difference is likewise found between the perfection of a secular and of a religious; for though it may happen that a secular may be more perfect than a religious is, yet it is true that the secular is not in a state of perfection, and that the religious is in one; because the perfection of a secular not being confirmed by vows, as that of a religious is, it consequently has not that constancy and stability in good, which that of a religious has, inasmuch as regards the state of the one and the other. A secular person leads a very pure and holy life today, and to-morrow he relents; but a religious is always in a state of perfection, although he be not perfect; because he is obliged to perfection by those vows which always engage him, and from which it is not in his power to disengage himself. Accordingly, a holy man being asked whether it were possible to gain Christian perfection in the world, he answered that it was possible, but that he had rather have one degree of grace in religion than two in the world; because in religion, where we are separated from the world, which is a capital enemy of grace, and where we are continually excited to virtue by good example, grace is easily preserved and augmented; whereas, in the world, it is very easily lost, and is very hard to be preserved. Hence he concluded that in religion, a less grace with such secure guards to preserve it, and with so many helps to augment it, was to be preferred to a far greater, with all the dangers wherewith persons are surrounded in the world.

We may hence learn how great is the error of some novices, who imagine that if they were in the world, they should live in so great piety and retirement as to edify their neighbour by their example. This is an illusion of the Devil, who only seeks under this pretence to deprive them of the inestimable good they possess, and to draw them out of religion. For in the world perhaps they might have in the beginning the same fervour; they might go every week to confession, they might make their prayer, and withdraw themselves far from the occasions of sin; but as they are no longer under the government of any one, they are obliged to do nothing under a perpetual obligation : and as every moment they will find new obstacles, so they will this day quit their prayer; the next day, dispense with themselves in going to confession; the day after, expose and distract themselves in company, and at length unhappily come to destroy themselves. It is not the same in religion; for a religious has not the liberty to dispense with himself in his spiritual exercises, nor to disengage himself from the obligation he has contracted by his vows, which is that "triple cord", of which the wise man speaks, "that is very difficult to be broken"—*Eccl.*, iv. 12.

Thus we see then, that it is properly the vows which make the kind of life to which they oblige, to be a religious state and a state of perfection. Many saints also hold that the apostles are the authors of it, and that when they renounced all things to follow Jesus Christ, they laid within themselves the foundation of this state, confirming by vow the offer they made to him, and that from thence the Catholic Church took up the practice of consecrating its members to God by means of these vows.

CHAPTER III.

Other advantages derived from the obligation of vows.

WHAT is still very beneficial in vows, besides what I have already said, is, that what is performed by vow is more laudable and meritorious in the sight of God than what is voluntarily done without being thus obliged to it after this manner by vow. St. Thomas assigns three solid reasons for this, and the first is, that religion being the most excellent of all moral virtues, and a vow being an act of religion, it hence follows that it enhances the value of all the acts of virtue that accompany it, making them become acts of religion, that is to say, holy, and already sacrificed and consecrated to God. It is thus that it makes a fast, which is an act of temperance, become an act of religion, and attaches double merit to it—to itself as an act of temperance, and of the vow as an act of religion. Likewise, generally speaking, in all things we do out of obedience, we gain double merit, that of the thing performed, and of the obedience also through which we perform it; so that we merit more when we act out of obedience than when we do a thing out of our own pure inclination and without being obliged to it by obedience or vow. This will be better comprehended by reasoning from the contrary— as a religious who sins against chastity commits two mortal sins, one against the sixth commandment, which he breaks, and the other against his vow, which is still worse, because it is a sacrilege he commits; so a religious who faithfully keeps the vow of chastity, has two sorts of merit, that of observing God's commandment, and that of fulfilling the vow he has made to God; and this latter being a pure act of religion, is of far greater price and value than the former.

Secondly, what makes a vow attach new merit to our actions is, that in those which we perform by vow, we give much more to God than in those we perform without vow, because we do not only offer what is done, but we offer him also that impossibility in which we have put ourselves, of doing otherwise, and we offer him our liberty, which is the greatest oblation and sacrifice we can make him. It is good to deprive ourselves of all things for Jesus Christ. Now, by the vow of poverty we not only deprive ourselves of what we possess, but, what is far more, we take from ourselves the power of ever possessing anything. In fine, to make use of the comparison of St. Anselm and St. Thomas, we give to God the tree together with the fruit, so that, as the saints say, he who gives the fruit and tree together, gives more than he that gives only the fruit, keeping the tree to himself; so religious offer more to God than those of the world do. For worldlings at most give only the fruit of the tree, that is to say, their good works, but they keep the tree to themselves;

that is to say, they always reserve the liberty of disposing of themselves, and give not themselves entirely to God, whereas religious, putting themselves entirely into his hands, give him both the tree and the fruit; they give him their actions, their words, their thoughts, their will, their liberty; in fine, they give him all things, so that they keep nothing to themselves, and nothing more remains for them to bestow. St. Bonaventure makes use of another comparison upon this subject, and says that as he who gives the property and use of a thing, gives more than he who only gives barely the use, so a religious who by vow gives and consecrates himself to God, gives him more than a secular who does not consecrate himself in this manner to him, because the secular, as I may say, gives only the use of himself to God, whereas a religious, giving his will and liberty as well as all other actions, gives himself entirely in propriety to God.

The third reason why those actions that are accompanied by vow are more meritorious than others, is, that the goodness of all exterior actions comes chiefly from the will, so that the more perfect the will is, the more perfect also are the works it produces. Now it is very certain that the more firm and constant the will, the more perfect it is, because it is farther removed from the defect which the wise man reprehends in timid persons, when he says: "The slothful man wills and wills not"—*Prov.*, xiii. 4,—and because it becomes more "fit to work with this unshaken constancy", which philosophers look upon as one of the chief conditions of virtue, and which is infallibly acquired by the vows. Divines say that as he who is hardened in sin offends more grievously than he who sins out of frailty or sudden passion, because he sins by a will determined to evil, which they say is to sin against the Holy Ghost; even so, those good actions that proceed from a firm and determinate will to what is good, are, without doubt, of greater merit and of far greater perfection than all others can be.

We must add to all this that, on the one hand, if we consider our frailty and weakness, and on the other, the obstinacy of the Devil to tempt us, we shall find that there is not a better remedy both to fortify ourselves, and to shut and secure all the avenues against the Devil, than to bind ourselves to God by the vows we make. For, as a man that courts a young woman in order to marriage, loses his hopes and ceases his pursuit when he sees her married to another; so when the Devil perceives that a soul has taken Jesus Christ for her spouse by means of these vows, he ordinarily loses all hopes of reëngaging her any more to the world, and oftentimes totally ceases to tempt her, lest his temptation should serve only to augment her crown, and that instead of gaining upon her, he should gain only shame and confusion to himself.

CHAPTER IV.

Why the oblation we make of ourselves to God in religion by means of vows, is styled by the saints a second baptism and a martyrdom.

THE oblation of ourselves entirely to God by means of religious vows, is of so great value and merit in his sight, that St. Jerom, St. Cyprian, and St. Bernard, call it a second baptism; and divines hold that an entire remission of all sins is obtained by it; so that if we should happen presently to die, we should not pass through the fire of Purgatory, but go direct to Heaven, as they do who die as soon as they have received baptism. This, however, is not to be understood as if it were said on account of the indulgences that may be annexed to a profession of vows, because there is a plenary indulgence also given to novices upon the day they take their habit; but it is to be understood as simply expressing the merit itself of the vows, which is so great and excellent, that without the help of any indulgence it is capable of satisfying the justice of God for the punishment due to our sins. This truth, which rests on a strong foundation of its own, is confirmed by what St. Athanasius says in the life of St. Anthony. This great saint had once a vision, wherein it seemed as if the angels carried him up to Heaven, and the devils meeting them, endeavoured to hinder them, accusing him of several sins he had committed in the world; but the angels said in reply, if you have anything to accuse him of since he became a religious, you may do it; but as to the sins he committed in the world, they are already pardoned, and it is a debt he has entirely satisfied by consecrating himself to God in religion.

"Redeem your sins by alms"—*Dan.*, iv. 24,—said Daniel to Nebuchodonosor. Now, if by alms, which are only a distribution of some part of the goods we possess, we can satisfy for our sins, in what manner ought we not believe we satisfy for them by an unlimited donation of all we have? "It is good to give alms to the poor, giving charitably these goods to them, as if we were only the distributers of them. But it is also much better to give away all things at once, to follow Jesus Christ, and to free ourselves from the cares and turmoils of riches, to become poor with him". St. Jerom proves this proposition against Vigilantius the heretic, by the testimony of our Saviour himself, who says in the gospel: "If thou wilt be perfect, go, sell what thou hast, and give to the poor, and thou shalt have a treasure in Heaven, and come and follow me"—*Mat.*, xix. 21. St. Gregory, upon Ezechiel, says, that worldlings, in distributing part of their goods to the poor, offer a sacrifice to God of their goods; but religious, by entirely spoiling themselves of their goods for the love of God, offer to him a holocaust which is far more excellent than a sacrifice. But if to renounce riches is so meritorious, how meritorious must it not be to renounce ourselves entirely; to renounce our body by the vow of chastity, and our will and liberty by the vow of obedience! What will it be continually to renounce ourselves, and to mortify ourselves for the love of God without ceasing! For the life of a religious is "continually to carry in his body the marks of the sufferings of Jesus Christ"—II. *Cor.*, iv. 10.

What shows still more clearly the excellency of this entire oblation of ourselves to God, by means of the three vows made in religion, is what all canonists hold for certain, viz., that a man who should have made a vow, for example, to go to Rome or Jerusalem, to give to the poor all the property he could possibly acquire, to serve all his time in an hospital, to discipline himself daily, to fast every day on bread and water, to wear a continual hair-shirt, and in fine what kind of vow soever he should make, he would entirely be freed from it by making himself a religious; all the obligations he should have contracted by any precedent vow being included therein, and changed into that of a religious life, as into a thing more perfect and more pleasing to God.

But there is yet more: this abandoning ourselves entirely into the hands of God by the three vows, as we have said, is a thing so heroical and excellent, that the saints compare the state of a religious life to that of martyrdom; and in effect it is a continual martyrdom, which, as St. Bernard says, has something indeed less terrible than that whereby the body is mangled, but it is also more painful, by reason it lasts longer. "What tyrants inflicted upon the faithful, terminated by a blow of a sword, but the martyrdom of a religious is not ended by one blow, it is a long suffering which is daily revived in us"—*Bern., Serm.* 3, *sup. Cant.*,—sometimes by debasing our pride, sometimes by annihilating our own will and judgment in such a manner, that we may say with the Psalmist: "For thy sake, O Lord, we are daily mortified or put to death, and are looked upon as sheep led to the slaughter"—*Ps.*, xliii. 22. However, our submission ought to be such in this state, that as the martyrs chose not the kind of their sufferings or death, but were always ready to receive that which should be inflicted upon them; so a religious ought always be disposed to undergo all those mortifications that shall be given him.

To conclude, martyrdom is so heroical an act of love, that a more excellent one is not to be imagined. "No one can have a greater love", as our Saviour says, "than to lay down his life for his friends"—*John*, xv. 13. And as, for this reason, the saints hold that martyrdom absolutely cancels sin, so that he who dies for the faith goes direct to Heaven without passing through Purgatory, "and that it would be an injury to him to pray for him"; in like manner they hold that as nothing can excel the entire oblation of ourselves, because we have nothing else to give after we have entirely given ourselves, this oblation which a religious makes to God by means of his vows, obtains for him also both an entire remission of his sins and of the pains due to them; and this is the reason why they compare it to baptism and martyrdom.

CHAPTER V.

That the obligation we contract by the vows of religion, so far from diminishing our liberty, renders it more perfect.

ONE may object and say, that he sees very well all the advantages I have spoken of, which are found in the sacrifice we make of ourselves to God by means of these vows; but the inconvenience of them is this, that they deprive a man of his liberty, "which is of inestimable price". You are mistaken, answers St. Thomas, it rather perfects than destroys liberty: for the effect of these vows is to confirm and strengthen the will in what is good, and to hinder it from letting itself be drawn to what is evil. Now this no more destroys liberty in us, than the perfect liberty which God and the saints enjoy in Heaven is destroyed in them by the impossibility of their committing sin. The apostles could not sin mortally after they were confirmed in grace, yet this grace did not destroy their liberty, but on the contrary perfected it; because it helped to confirm their will in the good for which they were created. Do not, says our holy founder, in his letter on obedience, believe it a small advantage for your free will to be able to restore it entirely into the hands of him who gave it; for by this means you do not destroy it, but render it far more perfect, by conforming it to the sovereign rule of all perfection, which is God, whose interpreter and substitute your superior is. This agrees very well with what St. Anselm says—"that liberty consists not in being able to sin; and that the power of sinning is no power at all, but is rather a mark of weakness and misery than perfection"—*Ansel.*, *c.* 9, *de fortit.* "Would you clearly see this?" says St. Austin. "He that can do all things, cannot sin, cannot lie"—*Epist.* 45 *ad Armen. et Paul.* It is to be under the power of sin, to have the power of sinning; and the power of sin, in regard of man, is more or less great, according as the power of man in regard of sin is less or greater. Hence the more we diminish in us the power of sinning, by determining our will to good, the more we perfect it; and this is precisely the effect produced by the vows by which we oblige ourselves to the practice of perfection. "O happy necessity", say St. Austin, "which continually forces us to do that which is best!" "Wherefore, do not repent your being bound by vows, but on the contrary rejoice; because hereby you are deprived of a liberty which you could not make use of without prejudice to yourself". If any one saw you walk towards a precipice, would they not do you a very great favour by so stopping up the passage, that though you should be inclined to destroy yourself, yet you would not be able to do it? Now if you wish to destroy yourself, it is by the way of your own will; "for if there were no self-will", says St. Bernard, "there would be no Hell"—*Serm.* 3, *de Resur.*,—and consequently the more this way is stopped, by hindering you from making bad use of your liberty, the greater good is done you. So then it is not to lose our liberty, to subject our will to that of our superior by the vow of obedience; but, on the contrary, it is more strengthened and perfected by being thus perfected in the practice of obedience and of the will of God.

A celebrated doctor adds one thing more, which is deserving of attention. The vows, says he, are so far from lessening our liberty, that, on the contrary, he who binds himself to God by them, and submits himself to the yoke of obedience, enjoys a more true and perfect liberty than any one else; for true liberty consists in being master of ourselves, and he who is thus bound and united to God, is without doubt more his own master than he who is not thus bound. But to show this more clearly by some instances. What engages you, for example, to make the vow of chastity is, because you hope that by the grace of God you shall become so much master over yourself as to keep this virtue; and what hinders another from making this vow is, because he does not believe he is so sufficiently master of himself as to be able to keep it. Thus you see that you are the person that have the greatest power over yourself to do what you wish, and to do what you believe you ought to do. But it is properly in this that liberty consists; for the liberty which the other keeps to himself is not a true liberty, but a subjection, nay, a slavery, because in effect, like a slave, he obeys his appetite, which has got the mastery over him and makes him fall into sin. He is a slave to his appetite, "which leads him captive to the law of sin"—*Rom.*, vii. 23. "For he who is overcome is a slave to him who overcame him; and whosoever sins, is a slave to sin"—*John*, viii. 34. It is the same in obedience. What moved you to make the vow of obedience was, because you believed by the assistance of God's grace you should have so much power over yourself as always to follow the will of your superior, and always to mortify your own; and what hinders another from making the same vow is, because he finds he has not so much power over himself as to be able to renounce in this manner his own will, and to submit it to that of another; and consequently you see that we cannot but have more power over ourselves, and more real liberty, by subjecting ourselves to the yoke of obedience, than by not doing so. Nay, there is even a greatness and nobility in carrying this yoke; for it is to carry a yoke of this nature to which the wise man exhorts us when he says: "Thrust your feet into the shackles and your neck into the collar: submit your shoulders to bear his yoke, and be not afraid of his chains"—*Ecclus.*, vi. 25. Happy chains, happy fetters, that rather give liberty than restrain it to those that bear them! These are not the chains of a slave and the marks of captivity, but they are the ornaments which belong only to freemen—they are marks of greatness and dignity. At all events, it is of very great importance, and adds to our comfort and happiness, to view things properly in this manner; "for the yoke of Jesus Christ", as St. Ambrose says very justly, "is sweet and easy to carry when it is viewed as an ornament and not as a burden".

CHAPTER VI.

The great advantages of religion—the obligation we have to God for having called us to it.

"God is faithful", says the apostle, bless him for ever, "because it is by him you have been called to the society of his Son Jesus Christ our Lord"—I. *Cor.*, i. 9. When God led the children of Israel out of the bondage of Egypt, he so expressly recommended to them to remember the day upon which he did them this favour, that, the better to preserve the remembrance of it, he ordered them to celebrate it as a feast for eight days together, and on the seventh day to offer and eat a lamb, with the same ceremonies as they did upon the day of their deliverance. Now, if he would have them keep with so great solemnity the memory of the day upon which he led them out of the captivity of Egypt to bring them into the land of promise, which was only a temporal favour, the effects of which had no influence upon their souls, what ought we not do to celebrate the memory of a day upon which an all-powerful hand has delivered our souls from the bondage of the Devil, to lead them into the way of Heaven? It is related of St. Arsenius, that he was wont every year to celebrate and solemnize the day upon which God did him the grace to bring him out of the world, and his manner of celebrating it was to communicate, to give alms to the poor, to eat a few boiled herbs, and to leave his cell open, that all hermits who pleased might come to visit him.

St. Austin applies to the subject of retiring from the world the answer that Moses made to Pharao, who refused to let the children of Israel go into the desert to offer there a sacrifice, but would oblige them to offer it in Egypt itself. "That cannot be", answered God's holy lawgiver, "because thereby we shall offer the abominations of the Egyptians to our God", that is to say, those very creatures which they adore as gods. "Now, if we kill in their presence what they adore, they will stone us: wherefore we will go three days' journey into the desert, there to sacrifice to the Lord our God, as he has commanded us"—*Exod.*, viii. 26, 27. Those whom God calls to the perfection of evangelical counsels feel themselves in the same situation. They must sacrifice the abominations of the world, that is to say, the things which the world adores—riches, honours, pleasures, love of themselves and of their own will; and because they should be exposed to the obloquies and mockeries of worldly people if they made this sacrifice in the world, therefore they ought to go out of it, and retire to the solitude of religion, there to sacrifice to God in peace. We are in this state, and God, by his infinite mercy, has brought us out of the servitude of the world, and has led us into the solitude of religion, that by means of our three vows we may sacrifice to him the gods of the world, and that we may do it with fewer obstacles; because, in religion, glory and honour consist in sacrificing them, and he who makes a more perfect sacrifice of them is of greatest esteem in religion.

But to show more clearly what thanksgiving we ought to make for this favour, I shall here set down what the saints say of the excellency and advantages of this great benefit. St. Jerom, explaining these words of the Royal Prophet, "going out of Egypt, he heard a language he knew not, and cast off his shoulders the burden he was wont to bear"—*Ps.*, lxxx. 6, 7,— enlarges on the mercy God has done us in bringing us out of the world, and representing to us the miserable servitude we lived in under the tyranny of the Devil, and the liberty to which the children of God are called, God, says he, has delivered us from a great yoke and a burden that was very heavy. We were slaves of Pharao, "and the Lord by his all-powerful hand has brought us out of the land of Egypt, and out of the house of servitude"—*Exod.*, xiii. 14. "When we were in Egypt, we wrought in Pharao's buildings—we carried brick and mortar, and all our care was to seek straw, and gather it together—we had then no corn, we had not the celestial bread which was given us from on high, and manna had not yet fallen down from Heaven upon us. How heavy were the burdens we carried?" In effect how heavy are the burdens of worldly people? What care, what pain, even to subsist, or at most to obtain some honourable employment? What difficulty afterwards in maintaining themselves and in advancing themselves? What intrigues, what hardships, what attentions, what constraints? In fine, how hard and how many subjections are to be undergone, the misery of which is not known until it is experienced? Certainly the yoke which worldly people carry is a yoke of iron, a very heavy and insupportable yoke, "but God has removed our backs from it", and has imposed his own yoke upon us, which is "easy and light", and has called us to a state wherein we have nothing else to do but to love and serve him.

The apostle, speaking of the difference between those that are engaged in the state of marriage and those that are not, says, "He who has no wife is employed in the affairs of our Lord, and is solicitous to please God; but he who has a wife is taken up with the things of the world and with the care how to please his wife, and is divided between God and the world. A woman who is not married and a virgin, thinks always of what belongs to our Lord, and of the means how to become holy, both in body and mind; but she who is married thinks of the things of the world, and of the means how to please her husband"—I. *Cor.*, vii. 32, etc. Now if, as the apostle says, all the care of those that live in the world in the state of chastity ought to be to please God and to sanctify themselves in body and mind, what ought to be the obligation of religious persons, whom God has freed from all the cares of the world, and even from that of getting themselves a livelihood, that they might have no other care but daily to render themselves more pleasing in his sight, and daily to increase in sanctity? St. Austin says, that the difference of these two states is figured by what Abraham did when sacrificing the victims that God had commanded him, which were a cow, a goat, a ram, a turtle, and a pigeon. For the Scripture takes notice that having cut the three first victims in two, "he divided not the birds", but offered them whole and entire. By the terrestrial beasts, says this father, are to be understood carnal men and the people of the world, whose mind and heart are continually divided by divers cares; and by the birds are to be understood spiritual men, who, whether they remain in retirement, as the turtle, or live in commerce and conversation with men, as the pigeon, are never divided, but offer themselves entirely to God, and employ themselves in his service only. Now this is one of the advantages of religious, to be able to sacrifice themselves entirely to God, without any division, and to have nothing to do but to please him. It is for this reason we make the vow of chastity, that being disengaged from the care of pleasing a wife, and of governing a family, we may apply ourselves to nothing else than to render ourselves more holy and more perfect. It is for this end that we make the vow of poverty and renounce riches, that being also freed from the disquiets they occasion, which are thorns that choke the good seed, we may endeavour to cause it to bring forth an abundant increase in our hearts, and there gather together the treasures of grace. And lastly, it is for this purpose we make the vow of obedience, and renounce ourselves and our own will, in order that, having nothing more to put ourselves in pain concerning our own conduct, and having entirely put the care thereof into the hands of our superior, who is charged with it, we may think of nothing else than what regards our spiritual advancement. St. Jerom, writing upon these words of the Psalmist, "Bless ye the Lord, ye his servants, who dwell in his house, in the courts of our God"—*Ps.*, cxxxiii. 1, 2,—says, that as a great lord has many servants, of whom some are near his person, and others look after his lands in the country, "so God has many servants, of whom some", as I may say, "are bound to wait upon his person, and others are employed abroad". Religious are like household and menial servants, who never leave their master, but are always speaking and conversing with him; and worldly persons are like the servants who are sent abroad to take care of their master's lands and to cultivate them. Now, just as, continues the holy doctor, when those who serve abroad wish to obtain some favour of their master, employ the others that are commonly with him to obtain it, so when there happens any particular affair to worldly persons, and when they would wish to obtain any favour of God, they ordinarily address themselves to religious, who have more easy access to God than themselves, and are more favoured by him. Nay more, as the servants who are employed in taking care of cultivating his lands, have all the trouble and pain, whilst the others enjoy a quiet and easy life at home with their master; so people of the world are those who have the pain and care of all, whilst religious have nothing else to do but to live in quiet and repose, and to entertain themselves with God. St. Gregory says, that the difference of these two states is also figured to us by the different kinds of life which Jacob and Esau embraced. "Esau was a hunter, who loved the country; Jacob was a plain, honest man, who loved to remain at home"—*Gen.*, xxv. 27. By Esau, who was given to hunting, are to be understood, says this father, the people of the world, who continually employ themselves in the cares of earthly things; and by Jacob, a plain, honest, countryman who lived at home, are to be understood, religious, who live in a continual recollection of mind and a constant application to what regards the advancement of their souls, and who are for this reason the favourites and beloved children of God, as Jacob was the beloved child and favourite of his mother. Now, let us here consider a little how great a favour our Sovereign Master has done us in raising us so far above the people of the world, who are like servants employed in mean and painful offices in the country, whilst we are like the servants who never quit his person. Certainly, we can justly say to him what the queen of Saba said to Solomon, after she had seen the magnificence and excellent order which was kept in his palace: "Happy are thy people, and happy are thy servants, who are always in thy presence, and who hear thy wisdom"—III. *Kings*, x. 8. Happy are the religious whom God has made choice of to remain in his house, there always to enjoy his presence and the treasures of his infinite wisdom.

By all that I have said it is easy to judge how great the blindness is of those who think they have done much for God by quitting the world, and who imagine that God is very much indebted to them for it. You deceive yourselves; it is God, on the contrary, that has bestowed upon you a very great favour in bringing you out of the world, to place you in religion, and to elevate you to so high a state—it is you that are beholden to him, and are obliged anew to render him great service and a more thankful acknowledgment for so great a benefit. If a king should cause a gentleman to come to him to give him one of the chief employments at court, this gentleman would be far from believing that he had done a great deal in quitting his house, and that the king was indebted to him for it; on the contrary, he would believe that the king, in calling him to be near his person in this employment, had added a new favour to those he had already bestowed upon him, and would endeavour to merit and thankfully acknowledge it by new services. Behold here what we ought to do. For we have not chosen God, but it is God who has made choice of us, and has done us the favour to call us, not only without having merited it, but even after having rendered ourselves unworthy of it.

Alas! O Lord, what could you perceive in me, to choose me, rather than my brethren, whom you have left in the world; and what was there in me that could be pleasing to you, that you have chosen me in preference to them? But take heed, some may say, you go not too far, because all divines hold that there is nothing in us which can contribute to the cause of our predestination. St. Austin explains this very well by a fit comparison. A carver, he says, passes through a wood, he beholds the trunk of a tree, he stops, he considers it, he likes it, and resolves to make something of it. But what was in it could please him? "He saw in it what he could work on by means of his art, and he liked it, not for what it was then, but for what he proposed to make of it afterwards; he liked in it that piece he designed to make out of it. Behold here the manner wherein God has loved us, even when we were sinners. He did not love the state in which we were, he did not love us in order that he might leave us in it, and that we might remain like the trunk of the tree, but he looked upon us as an excellent workman looks upon a piece of wood cut down in a forest, and thought only of the piece of work he would make it"—*Aug., tract.* viii. *sup.* 1, *Ep. Joan.* Behold here what has pleased God in us, not what we were then, for then we were shapeless and unprofitable pieces of wood, but what he had a design to make of us. It was the wish of this admirable workman, who made Heaven and Earth, and who "predestinated to be conformable to the image of his Son those whom he foreknew"—*Rom.*, viii. 29,—it was his wish to make of you an image, which should be perfect, and should resemble himself; and this is what moved him to make choice of you. "For it is not you", says our Saviour, "who have chosen me; but it is I that have chosen you, and established you, that you might go and bring forth fruit, and that your fruit might last for ever"—*John*, xv. 16. Consider what image God would make of you, and how like he would make you to his only Son, whereas he has chosen you for the same employment for which he sent his Son into the world—viz., the salvation of souls.

The same saint, explaining this verse of the hundred and thirty-sixth Psalm, "On the banks of the rivers of Babylon, there we sat and wept at the remembrance of thee, O Sion"—*Ps.*, cxxxvi. 1,—gives it a sense which is suitable to our purpose. The rivers of Babylon are, says he, the transitory things of this world, and there is this difference, says he, between the children of Babylon and the children of Jerusalem, that those remain in the midst of the rivers of Babylon, where they are continually exposed to tempests, that is, they plunge themselves in pleasures, where they are continually afraid of being surprised by death; whereas these, "who perceive the misfortune of the others, keep themselves upon the banks of the rivers, and bathe themselves in tears". But why do they weep, and why do they sit upon the banks of the rivers? First, says this father, they lament their banishment. The sight of these storms that continually rise upon the rivers of Babylon, and the remembrance of their Heavenly country, which is at so great a distance, draws these tears from them, and makes them cry out with sighs: "O holy Sion, where all things are permanent, and where nothing passes, who has cast us headlong into this misery? Why are we separated from him who has built thee, and from the company of the inhabitants?" When shall we be delivered from these dangers that encompass us? When shall we be recalled from our banishment? When shall we have nothing to fear, and when shall we behold you within your walls? In the second place, they lament those who let themselves be carried away with the torrent of the rivers of Babylon; they bemoan their brethren whom glory, ambition, love, hatred, and envy have dragged to the precipice, into which they daily fall by thousands. A great saint one day in a vision saw souls fall as thick into Hell as flakes of snow fall in winter on the earth. Who would not lament this loss? And who can behold these miserable souls without feeling his bowels torn in pieces with tender compassion? Finally, they sat upon the banks of the rivers of Babylon to help their brethren, who were in danger of being lost—to stretch out their hands to them, and to see if they could save some of them. Behold here what ought to be the employment of all religious, who are here described as children of Jerusalem, and what ought chiefly to be ours: "For God has particularly called us to make us become fishers of men"—*Mat.*, iv. 19. And he has placed us as it were upon the rivers of Babylon, that we may do our duty to save those who are daily shipwrecked, and that we may stretch out our hands to the souls which are on the point of being lost. Let us now consider, on the one hand, how great a favour God has bestowed upon us above those who are in the world, in having placed us upon the bank, whilst he leaves them in the middle of the water, where they are every moment in danger of being lost; and, on the other, how great strength, skill, and ability is required to help those that are drowning, without exposing ourselves to the danger of being drowned with them—it being very common that he who is drowning takes hold and drags in with himself the person who wishes to save him. We must, therefore, be very skilful in the art of gaining souls to God. Great virtue and sanctity is required to bring others out of danger, without being exposed to it ourselves

It is related of St. Anselm, that being one day in an ecstasy, he saw a great river, into which were cast all the dirt and filth of the world. The waters became in consequence so muddy and stinking, that nothing could be imagined like it, and the torrent was also so rapid and violent, that it carried away whatsoever it met, men and women, rich and poor, now plunging them to the bottom, then casting them up, and then casting them down again, without letting them rest one moment. The saint, astonished at this vision, and surprised to see that those who were in the river were still alive, asked how it was possible they could live there, and how they were nourished. He received for answer, that they were nourished by the filth of those muddy waters, into which they were plunged, and after all, that they were contented to live in them. Afterwards this vision, was explained to him, and he was informed that this rapid river was the world, where men, plunged in vice and hurried along by their passions, live in so strange a blindness, that though the continual agitation they are in permits them not to feel the least repose, yet still they believe themselves happy. After this he was again wrapt in spirit into a very spacious park, encompassed by walls covered with plates of silver which reflected a shining light. In the midst of this there was a great meadow, the grass whereof was all gold, but so soft and fresh that it easily yielded when persons wished to sit on it, and that without the least appearance of withering, it returned to its first state as soon as they stood up. The air of that place was sweet and pure, and in a word, all things in it were so pleasant and delightful, that it seemed a terrestrial paradise, and that it possessed everything which constitutes sovereign felicity. The saint was told that this was a lively representation of the state of a religious life.

CHAPTER VII.

A continuation of the same subject.

ST. BERNARD wishing to comprise in a few words the advantages of a religious life, says that "the sanctity and purity of religion causes him who is engaged in it to live more purely, to fall less frequently, to rise sooner, to walk with greater precaution, to be refreshed more frequently with Heavenly comforts, to repose with greater security, to die with greater confidence, to be sooner purified from his defects, and to be more gloriously recompensed. Your profession", says he, speaking in another place to religious, "is most sublime; it is higher than the heavens, it is equal to the angels, it resembles angelical purity, because you have vowed not only all kind of sanctity, but also the perfection of all kind of sanctity, even the highest perfection. It is for others to serve God, but for you to be united to him; what name, therefore, shall I give you that is worthy of you? Shall I call you Heavenly men or Earthly angels? For though you live upon Earth, your conversations and your thoughts are in Heaven"— *Ep. ad Frat. de Monte Dei.* "For you are no longer strangers and pilgrims upon Earth, but fellow-citizens of the saints, and domestics of God"—*Eph.*, ii. 19. You are like the blessed spirits whom God gives us to be our guard, and who so exercise themselves in their employments that they never lose the sight of God. Behold here the life of a true religious: his heart is in Heaven while his body is upon Earth: all his entertainment, all his conversation is either of God or of things belonging to God; and he may truly say with the apostle, "Christ is my life"— *Phil.*, i. 21. And as in the world it is said of him who loves hunting extremely, that hunting is his whole life; and of him that very much loves his study, that study is his life; so the apostle says here of himself, "that Jesus Christ is his whole life", because he gave himself to nothing else but to Jesus Christ, and was entirely consecrated to him. A religious, also, is consecrated to him in the same manner, and consequently may say the same thing.

The same St. Bernard applies to a religious life these words of the Canticles: "My bed is all covered with flowers"—*Cant.*, i. 16. He says that amongst the things of the world there is nothing conduces more to repose than a bed, so in the Church of God there is nothing more conducive to tranquillity of mind than religion, and that it is a kind of bed, where the soul, disengaged from all the cares and disquiets of the world, reposes continually in God. ' We daily experience in the society the advantage it has pleased God to give us herein, superiors taking such particular care to provide us with all things that are necessary for life, for clothing, for studies, for journeys, for sickness, and for health, that we want not at all the help of our parents, nor need we think of them any more than to recommend them to God. For whether they are dead or alive, whether they are rich or poor, the society, and these superiors it gives us, are to us in place of father and mother, and with a tenderness which even exceeds that of a father and mother, provide for all our necessities, in order that, having no trouble about temporal things, we think of nothing else than of the end for which we embraced religion, which is to labour for our own spiritual advancement and for that of our neighbour. Clement of Alexandria says that God having put man in the terrestrial paradise, delivered up the possession of all things into his hands, that there being nothing more he could desire upon Earth, he might raise his thoughts and desires to Heaven. The society uses the like method with us. It charges itself with the care of all things we stand in need of, that being freed from the care of Earthly things, we may continually raise our thoughts towards Heaven.

CHAPTER VIII.

The renewing of vows, which is a custom practised amongst us.— The fruit which may be reaped from it.

IN the year one thousand five hundred thirty-four, upon the feast of the assumption of our blessed Virgin, the first fathers of the society being assembled at Paris with St. Ignatius, went from thence to Mont-Martyr, into the church there dedicated to the blessed Virgin, where having confessed and communicated, they solemnly promised to God that upon the day then specified, they would quit all they had, without reserving anything to themselves but what was absolutely necessary for their journey to Venice. They also vowed to employ themselves in the spiritual advancement of their neighbour, and to go on a pilgrimage to Jerusalem, on this condition, that they would wait a whole year at Venice for an occasion to pass into the Holy Land, and if within the year they found one, they would go to Jerusalem, and use all their enendeavours to remain there all their lives in those holy places; but if within a year they found no convenient passage, or if, after having visited those holy places, they found it impossible to establish themselves there, then they would go to Rome to prostrate themselves at the Pope's feet, and make an offer of themselves to him to dispose of them as he pleased for the good and salvation of souls. They renewed these vows two years together upon the same day, in the same church, and with the same solemnity, and from this the renovation of vows, which is practised in the society before profession, had its beginning.

Our holy founder, speaking of this renovation of vows, says, that "to renew those vows is not to engage ourselves anew to God, but to call to mind the engagement we have made to him, and to confirm the same"—IV. *part. Const. c.* 4, § 5. It is to renew what we made before, and to confirm it with joy, in order to show that we have no regret for having made it, but on the contrary, that we give thanks to God for having accepted the offering which we have made; that we would offer it anew if it were still to make; that, had we a thousand worlds to forsake, we would leave them all for love of him; and if we had a thousand wills and a thousand hearts to sacrifice to him, that we would sacrifice them all with joy. It is in this manner that renovation of vows ought to be made, and when we make them thus we may assure ourselves they are of very great merit. For as the joy and satisfaction which we take in sin is a new sin and a new subject of punishment, so the joy and satisfaction we take in a good action is a thing very pleasing to God, and a new matter of recompense. The joy of a good action is meritorious, proportionably to the goodness of the action.

The renovation of vows, says he afterwards, to descend more to particulars, is made for three reasons. The first is "to increase devotion in our hearts"; for, in effect, it does not a little increase it in the heart of those who prepare themselves as they ought to do it well. The second, "to awaken in us a memory of the obligation we have contracted with God", and thereby to excite us faithfully to acquit ourselves of our promise, by daily endeavouring to render ourselves more perfect. And the third, "to confirm us more strongly in our vocation". For as it is a great remedy against temptations to produce acts of virtue contrary to the vice to which one is tempted, because contraries are cured by contraries; so to renew the vows we have already made is a great remedy against the interior troubles and disgust which the Devil endeavours to give us upon occasions. He becomes weaker, perceiving us thus to fortify ourselves in our holy resolutions, and loses courage to attack us with the like temptations, and if we have been guilty of any negligence, it is then repaired with interest by the new strength we acquire.

Virtue and perfection is a thing very difficult to our corrupt nature. For the misery and weakness we have contracted by sin is so great, and the inclination we have to evil so violent, that though we should sometimes begin our spiritual exercises with fervour, yet we permit ourselves by little and little to relent, and soon return to our weakness and tepidity. We are like weights of a clock, which continually draw downwards. Our flesh, which is earth, still draws us towards the earth, and therefore we need so much help that if we come to fall, we may presently be able to get up again. It is for this reason that, as the Church has established Advent and Lent, that there may be two periods in a year in which its children might gather new strength to begin again to serve God with new fervour; so our holy founder would have us twice a year call to mind the vows we have made to God, that this remembrance of them might rekindle in us our first fervour, and give us new strength to acquit ourselves well of the duties of our vocation. Behold here what chiefly moved him to institute in the society this solemn renovation of vows, and the fruit which we ought endeavour to reap from it.

St. Francis Xaverius said that we ought to renew them, not only at the times appointed for doing so, but, in imitation of the holy abbot Paphnucius, we ought to renew them every day; and as he knew not better arms than these for a religious man to use against all sorts of temptations, so he counselled us to arm ourselves with them every night, and every morning after prayer, against the enemies of our salvation. But if we have not sufficient fervour to embrace this practice, yet it is good at least to follow the example of those who renew their vows as often as they communicate, and who exact of themselves an account of the manner how they observe them, and carefully examine themselves whether their conscience reproaches them with anything contrary to the fidelity of their promise.

The better to attain the end which we ought to propose to ourselves in this solemn renovation of vows, it is the custom of the society, that, besides the austerities and corporal mortifications practised in the times appointed for this renovation, we practise three things to prepare ourselves for it. The first is, to make a retreat of some days, during which time we ought to abstain from all sorts of employments, in order to give ourselves more tranquilly to prayer and spiritual exercises. The second is, to give an account of conscience to our superior, which ought to be given from the last six months, and ought to be made more exactly than at other times of the year; but as this is one of the most essential obligations, it shall hereafter be the subject of a particular treatise. The third is, to confess all the sins we have committed for the last six months, addressing ourselves to one of those confessors who shall be appointed for this end, according to the ancient custom of the society, and according to the rule that obliges us to it. Now, all these means are most proper for the end we here propose: because, in taking a review of all our faults, and comparing the six last months with the preceding, we may easily know whether we have made more progress in the one than in the other, and whether we have advanced or gone back in the way of God; and when we find we have gone back instead of advancing, we may come hereby to have a great confusion to see ourselves so far from that perfection to which we are called, and we may feel ourselves excited to use new endeavours to obtain it.* Moreover, when a man coolly and deliberately reviews all his faults together, he judges by seeing those into which he has oftenest fallen, what passion most reigns in him, and what makes the rudest war against him, and then with additional fervour he applies convenient remedies, making this passion the subject of his particular examen. There is still another advantage, which is, that as we make the review of our faults in the time of renovation of vows, when we also take a review of all those favours we have received from God, and particularly of that of his having called us to religion, it is impossible that, considering on the one hand so many graces received, and on the other so many faults committed, we should not come to humble ourselves before God, and make a firm resolution of amendment, and of serving him better than we have hitherto done. "The things which are opposite to one another appear greater by approaching the one to the other, so that black throws out the white when placed near it". Now, compare what God has done for you with what you have done against him; consider what obligations you have to him, and after what manner you have fulfilled them, and you will see how great a subject you have to be confounded and to debase yourself before him. What have you gained by frequenting the sacraments? What have you got by so many mortifications, austerities, and prayers, by so many examens, exhortations, and spiritual readings? Into what an abyss are all these fallen? What fruit and profit have you received from them? It is after this manner we ought to examine ourselves, when we are to give an account of conscience to our superior, or to make a general confession; but, above all, we ought endeavour to discover what way the waters of so many graces have run out and been lost, in order that, having discovered it, we may hereafter apply a proper remedy.

CHAPTER IX.

A continuation of the same subject.

THE renovation of vows is, moreover, instituted amongst us as an acknowledgment of the grace that God has done us in bringing us out of the world and calling us to religion; and it is properly a feast which we celebrate in memory of this great benefit, which is the source of all our happiness, and a great mark of our predestination. As the Church yearly celebrates the feast of the dedication of material temples, so it is very just that we should celebrate the feast of the dedication of our souls, which are the living temples of the Lord. But the better to celebrate it, and to render our thanks more pleasing to God, we must testify our thanksgiving by effects, which is the best mark of it: we must renew ourselves in renewing our vows. We must so fortify ourselves in the observance of all our duties, that for the future we may come to acquit ourselves of them with greater exactness and fidelity than ever we have done before. It is to this renovation of ourselves, says St. Gregory, to which the apostle exhorts us by these words: "Be you renewed in spirit"—*Eph.*, iv. 23. For, as to this exterior renovation we make by our mouths, to what can it serve if it be not accompanied with the interior renovation of our souls? When the colours of a picture are so worn out and effaced by time that one can scarce distinguish the strokes and figures, we refresh it with new colours, and it becomes again as beautiful as if it had been newly painted. The colours of virtue are soon worn out and effaced in us by time, because we are dragged by our depraved nature, which carries us to corruption and disorder, "and this corruption of the body renders the soul heavy and uneasy"—*Wisd.*, ix. 15. Hence there is need from time to time to apply new colours, and to touch or move ourselves again, by renewing those holy resolutions we have already made, and strengthening ourselves more and more in them. "If we desire not to relent in virtue", says St. Gregory, "it is very necessary to imagine every day that we only now begin, as when first we came to religion". Now, therefore, begin anew with the same courage and fervour you did then, and by this means you will renew yourself. This will be to give God a pleasing mark of that lively gratitude which you have for all his benefits.

Cassian relates a short and solid exhortation, which the Abbot Paphnucius made, in the presence of all his religious, to a novice he received, and each one may apply it to himself as a means that may very much help to dispose him to the renovation of vows. You come to give yourself to God, says the saint, and to renounce all the things of the world; "take care you take nothing back again that you have quitted by this renunciation". You have renounced riches by the vow of poverty; take care not to attach yourself to the possession of the least thing in religion; for it will signify nothing to you to deprive yourself of what you possess in the world, if in religion you adhere to the possession of anything. You have renounced your own will and judgment by the vow of obedience; beware of taking them back again, but say with the spouse, "I have taken off my coat, how shall I put it on again?"

—*Cant.*, v. 3. I have divested myself of my own sentiments; may I never resume them. You have renounced all the pleasures and vain entertainments of the world; take great care never to admit them again into your heart. You have trampled under foot pride, vanity, and the opinion of the world; beware of suffering them to take root anew in you, when you shall teach, or when you shall enter on some honourable employment. Do not, then, build up again what you have now destroyed, for that will be to become in a manner an apostate, "and to look back after you have put your hand to the plough"—*Luke*, ix. 62. But persevere to the end in poverty, and in stripping yourself of all things, and in the place you have promised God to live, persevere in that humility and patience which you had, when with tears you begged to be received into religion.

St. Basil, St. Bernard, and St. Bonaventure add another consideration. Consider, say they, that you no longer belong to yourself, but that all you are, and all you possess, belongs to God, to whom you have given it by means of your vows. Beware, then, of taking back what you have already given, because this would be to commit a theft, "since it is a robbery to dispose of anything against the will of him to whom it belongs". Did I not say in the beginning of this treatise, that he who enters into religion gives to God the fruit and the tree? But if any one had given a tree to another to plant in his garden, and should afterwards reap the fruit of it, would not this be a theft? This is what a religious does who follows his own will, instead of doing what obedience prescribes. Nay, he does what is worse, for he commits a sacrilege; for there is question of a thing that is consecrated to God, and even a sort of sacrilege which God very much abhors, as he himself declares in these words: "I am the Lord, who love justice, and hate rapine in a holocaust"—*Isai.*, lxi. 2. What greater crime can there be than to steal any part of a "holocaust", which entirely belongs to God, and is wholly consecrated to him? Hence St. Bernard says very justly, "that there is not a greater nor more enormous crime than to resume power over a will which has been once offered to God in sacrifice"—*Bern.*, *Ep.* cccliii.

St. Austin, explaining this passage of Genesis, "God took man, and put him in a paradise of pleasure, that he might work and take care of it"—*Gen.*, ii. 15,—interprets it after a manner that suits very well with our subject. Let us examine a little, says this father, what the Holy Ghost would have us understand by these words. Is it that God placed Adam in the terrestrial paradise to cultivate the ground? There is no probability at all that before sin God would oblige him to work, yet certainly there was no inconvenience that he should then exercise him in something by way of amusement or recreation, as those do who take pleasure in working in their own gardens: but was he obliged to it by constraint? This was neither convenient to his state, which was the state of innocence, nor necessary to the nature of the earth, which brought forth all things of itself, without being cultivated. Therefore what is there more to be understood, adds this great saint, by these words, "God put man in paradise to take care of it"? From whom ought he guard it, as there was no other man but himself in the world? Ought he not preserve it from the beasts? Before sin, the beasts did no hurt at all to man, nor to anything belonging to him; and how was it possible that one man alone should be able to guard a place of so great extent from so many sorts of beasts? Should not he at first have made an enclosure so securely fenced as to be sufficient to have hindered the serpent from entering into it? And before he had finished it, ought he not to have hunted out all the beasts that were in it? But how was it possible that a single man should be able to compass so many things? Hence it is not to be understood from this passage of Scripture, that God put man in Paradise to guard it after this manner, and to cultivate the earth. But what then is the meaning of these words, "to work therein, and to guard it"? Their meaning is, answers this father, that he should take care to put in practice those commands that God had given him, in performing which he would have kept Paradise, which afterwards he lost by his neglect to practise them. Let us now apply this to our subject: why, think you, has God placed you in this paradise of religion? for this is a name which the saints give it, and which agrees very well with it: would you know why? it is that you may practise the commandments he has given you, and the evangelical counsels which are contained in your rules, that by practising them you may preserve this terrestrial paradise for yourself, which others have lost in consequence of their not practising them.

The same saint attaches another meaning to this passage. He observes, that the words of Scripture are, "ut operaretur, et custodiret illum". Now the word "illum" may refer to "man", as well and better than to Paradise. God therefore, adds the father, placed man in Paradise, not that man should cultivate and guard Paradise, but that God himself might there cultivate and guard man. For. as we say that man cultivates the ground, when he labours to render it fruitful ; so we may say also that God cultivates man, when he labours to render him more just, more holy, and more perfect. But it was precisely for this that God placed him in the terrestrial paradise, to cultivate his soul by sanctity, to guard him by this means till such time as he should be pleased to transfer him from this Earthly paradise to that of Heaven, and render him for ever happy in glory. Be you persuaded, in like manner, that God has not placed you in this terrestrial paradise of religion, that you may cultivate and keep it, because it is guarded and cultivated by better hands than yours, but he has placed you in it, that he may cultivate you, that he may make you a man filled with the spirit of mortification, an interior man, a holy man, a perfect man, and that he keep you by this means till he shall vouchsafe to transfer you from this house of peace into the eternal mansions of his glory.

We ought to help ourselves with these and similar considerations, and excite ourselves with all our strength to fulfil our obligations to God, and to reap from the renovation of our vows the fruit we ought to propose to ourselves therein. But if you regard pains and difficulties in the practice of the things which you have promised, think at the same time of the price annexed to them, " and how great the recompense is"—*Heb.*, x. 35. "We have promised great things", says St. Francis to his religious, "but greater things are promised us". Let us be faithful to our promises, and God will not fail to be faithful to his. Hence, when a religious makes his profession in the order of St. Francis, as soon as he has ended his vows, and made them to his superior, the superior answers him saying, "And I promise you in God's name life everlasting". I now make the same declaration. If you keep your promise to God, I promise you, on his part, eternal life; and I make you this promise by virtue of the words of Jesus Christ, who assures us in the gospel, that those who leave all to follow him, "shall have a treasure in Heaven"—*Mat.*, xix. 21.

THE THIRD TREATISE.

THE VOW OF POVERTY.

CHAPTER I.

That the vow of poverty is the foundation of evangelical perfection.

"BLESSED are the poor in spirit, for theirs is the kingdom of Heaven"—*Mat.*, v. 3. With these words the Saviour of the world began his admirable sermon on the mount. Some doctors and saints say, that by "poverty of spirit" Christ meant humility; but others with a great deal of reason say, that he meant voluntary poverty, and chiefly that poverty which religious profess. We adhere to the latter, which is the opinion of St. Basil, and of many other saints. Certainly it is no small praise to this virtue, that our Saviour began with it his sermon on the mount, and that it was by him ranked the first of the eight beatitudes. But what makes far more for its commendation, is, that during his whole life he taught it to us by his example, and that it was the very first lesson he taught us on coming into the world. The stable, and the manger where he was born, the rags, his swathing bands, the hay on which he lay, the breath of poor beasts to defend him from the cold, declared his poverty at his birth: and as this was the first, so it was also the last lesson he taught us. As soon as he was born he preached it to us from the crib; and dying he recommended it to us from the pulpit of the cross. He died naked, and so poor, that Joseph of Arimathea was forced to buy him a winding-sheet. What greater poverty can be imagined? His whole life was the same; for he had not a farthing to pay the tribute which was asked of him; nor had he a house to eat the paschal lamb in with his disciples; and what was yet more, he had not as much as any place to dwell or rest himself in. "Foxes have their dens", says he, "and birds their nests, but the Son of man has not where to lay his head"—*Mat.*, viii. 20. The Saviour of the world wished to establish voluntary poverty as the foundation of evangelical perfection : " If you would be perfect, go and sell what you have, and give to the poor"—*Mat.*, xix. 21. And therefore it was necessary that his own example should give it authority. Hence it was that poverty was so much practised in the beginning of the primitive Church, and that all the goods of the Christians were in common, so that they who had houses and lands sold them, and laid the money at the apostles' feet, to distribute it according to each one's necessity. St. Jerom says, this was done "to show that riches ought to be contemned and trodden under foot". The same holy doctor, together with St. Cyprian and St. Basil, tells us, that the Christians in those days made a vow of poverty; the proof of which they derive from Ananias and Saphira, who were punished with sudden death for retaining some of the money they had received for their goods. For they would not have deserved so severe a punishment, say these three saints, had they not acted contrary to the vow or promise they had made to Almighty God, by retaining something to themselves of what they had offered to him.

In conformity to the sanctity of this doctrine, and the antiquity of this practice, all holy men and founders of religious orders, have placed the vow of poverty as the foundation of a religious life. And our holy founder, following their example, says in his rule, " that poverty is to be looked upon as the wall or fortress of religion; and that it ought to be preserved by us in its purity, so far forth as God's grace shall enable us"—6 *p. Const. c.* 2. § 1. *et. Reg.*, 3. *summ.* As in the world, estates and great families are founded upon riches; so on the contrary, religion and Christian perfection is built upon poverty. For as the building which we raise in religion is quite different from that of the world, so it is very reasonable that their foundations also should not be the same. This truth was laid down by our Saviour in the Gospel, in these words: "Who is there amongst you, who, being to build a tower, does not first compute the charges that are necessary to finish it, lest having laid the foundations, and not being able to carry on the work, those that see it should laugh at him, and say, Behold a man that began to build, and could not finish it? Or what king going to make war against another, does not first consider whether he be able with ten thousand, to meet him that is coming against him with twenty thousand men? Otherwise while he is afar off, he sends his ambassadors with propositions of peace. In the same manner, if any of you do not renounce all he possesses, he cannot be my disciple"—*Luke,* xiv. 28, etc. By these two comparisons, our Saviour gives us to understand, that as men and money are necesssary to maintain a war and carry on a building; so to be poor and stripped of all we have, is necessary to carry on a war against the enemies of our salvation, and to raise the spiritual building of perfection which we have undertaken. St. Austin, explaining this very passage, says, that the tower signifies the perfection of a Christian life, and the stock required for building imports a total renunciation of our goods, which makes us be in a better state of serving God, and have less reason to fear the Devil; for hereby he has scarce anything left to lay hold on, and his points of attack are reduced in number.

St. Jerom and St. Gregory are of the same opinion. We are come into the world, say they, to combat and fight with the Devil, who is poor and possesses nothing; and consequently, we ought to deprive ourselves of all things, to fight against him. "For he that wrestles with his clothes on, against one that is naked, is easily thrown; because he has so many things to be laid hold on. Do you desire to fight valiantly against the Devil? Throw off your clothes, lest he throw you. For all Earthly things are no more than clothes which do you harm, and he that has most of them is soonest overcome, by reason of the advantage they give his enemy"—*Hier. et Greg. Hom.* xxxii. St. Chrysostom, inquiring into the causes of the zeal and fervour of the primitive Church, and the tepidity and remissness of Christians in his days, gives this reason for it, that the former deprived themselves of their goods to fight naked against the Devil, but the latter fight in their clothes; that is, they are charged with plenty and riches, which are very prejudicial to them in the combat. Now we have disengaged ourselves from all these trammels, to be in a better state to fight against the Devil, and to follow Jesus Christ; and this makes the same saint say, "that a man strips in order to wrestle the better; that he who wishes to swim over a river, takes off his clothes; and that a traveller on foot walks much easier when he has nothing to carry".

Besides, as "covetousness is the root of all evil"—I. *Tim.*, vi. 10,—so poverty is the source and origin of all good, and it is for this reason that poverty is the first of the three vows made in religion. St. Ambrose, upon these words of the apostle last cited, says "that as riches are the instruments of all vices, because they render us capable of putting even our worst desires into execution, so a renunciation of riches is the origin and preserver of all virtues". First, with respect to humility, St. Gregory says, "that poverty is its guardian". As for chastity, it is easy to show that a poor habit and poor diet procure and preserve it. It is also no hard matter to prove how far it conduces to abstinence and temperance; nor, lastly, is there any difficulty in proving the same, in respect of all other virtues, should we take a survey of them all. Hence it is that holy men, speaking of poverty, call it sometimes the guardian and mistress, at other times the mother of virtues. St. Ignatius in his constitutions commands us to "love poverty as a mother"; because it produces and nourishes all other virtues in our souls, and keeps up regular discipline. And hence, the orders which have not observed holy poverty, whose children they ought to be, have scarce the appearance of religion, since they have ceased to resemble their mother. Let us then love her, in order to preserve the spirit of religion among us, and let us caress her with all the respect and tenderness due to a mother. St. Francis used to call poverty his mistress; and hence it is, that in the rule of St. Clare, it is expressly said, we bind ourselves for ever to our mistress, holy poverty.

CHAPTER II.

Of the greatness of the reward God bestows upon the poor in spirit.

THE young man in the gospel, who aspired to perfection, and was not content with a bare observance of the commandments, went away very much afflicted, when Christ said to him, that if he would be perfect, he should sell all he had and give it to the poor. He had so great an attachment to his riches, which were very considerable, that he had not the courage to quit them, and hence he had no foundation on which to build the tower of evangelical perfection. Now, that the like may not happen to us, and that we may be able to detach ourselves absolutely from all things of this world, Jesus Christ proposes to us the greatness of the reward which is annexed to this absolute disengagement. "Blessed", says he, "are the poor in spirit, for theirs is the kingdom of Heaven"—*Mat.*, v. 3. Consider here, whether you would not do well to exchange all your substance upon Earth for the kingdom of Heaven? Can you make a bargain more advantageous, than in giving the little you possess in this world for an infinite treasure in the next? St. Bernard makes an excellent remark on this passage, and says that our Saviour does not speak here, as in the other beatitudes, of the time to come. He does not say that the kingdom of Heaven shall be yours, but that it is so already; and in reality, though you do not enjoy it at present, yet it does not still cease to be yours; because you have really purchased it by abandoning all you had in this world. For example, if you have given an hundred guineas for a jewel, but left it in the hands of the seller, the jewel is certainly yours, though it is not yet delivered to you, because you have bought and paid for it. In like manner, the kingdom of Heaven belongs to a person poor in spirit, because he has given all he was worth to purchase it. "The kingdom of Heaven", says our Saviour, "is like a merchant that seeks for fine pearls, who having found a rich one, goes and sells all he has to buy it"—*Mat.*, xiii. 45. Now as this pearl belongs to this merchant, because he bought it with his money, so the kingdom of Heaven belongs to you, because you have bought it by a sale of all your goods.

But the recompense which the Son of God proposes to the poor of spirit does not end here. He promises still more. Can there be anything more, you will say, than the kingdom of Heaven? Yes, for as in the world there are degrees of honour and command, so are there of glory and excellence in Heaven; and our Saviour has promised the most eminent degrees of glory to the poor in spirit. Christ, upon the young man's unwillingness to sell all he had to follow him, took occasion to show the difficulty of rich men entering into Heaven. And St. Peter having then said, "we have left all and followed thee; what reward shall we have?" our Saviour answers, "Amen, I say to you, that you who have followed me in the regeneration, when the Son of man shall sit in the seat of his majesty, you shall sit also upon twelve seats, judging the twelve tribes of Israel"—*Mat.*, xix. 27, 28. It is the common opinion of holy men, that these words ought also to be extended to all those who have imitated the apostles in voluntary poverty, and chiefly to those who have engaged themselves to it by vow, as all religious do; for suppose they die in that condition, and in the grace of God, St. Austin, with St. Gregory and Venerable Bede, hold, that they shall all appear sitting on the great tribunal of God at the day of judgment, rather to exercise the office of judges, than as criminals; and they apply these words of Isaias to them, "the Lord shall come to judge with the elders and princes of his people"—*Isai.*, iii. 13; as also these of Solomon, which they interpret of the spouse of the Church, "her bridegroom shall be illustrious in the assembly, when he shall sit with the senators of the Earth"—*Prov.*, xxxi. 23. All which titles of senators, elders, and princes, of whom the Holy Ghost speaks, the same holy doctors give to the poor of spirit. It is true some would have this privilege granted to all those whom the Church acknowledges for saints; but St. Thomas of Aquin, whom most follow in this point, limits it to those who have made profession of holy poverty, whether they be canonized or not, and he brings a great many plausible reasons to prove why this privilege ought to belong to them, rather than to other saints. St. Gregory, upon the consideration of this great prerogative, cries out with the Psalmist, " Thy friends, O Lord, are even too much honoured; and their dominion confirmed to admiration!" —*Ps.*, cxxxviii. 16, 17. Be thou for ever blessed, O my God, who hast thus honoured thy friends, particularly those who have made themselves poor for love of thee. Thou art not content to give them part in thy kingdom, but thou advancest them to the glory even of sitting as judges with thee to judge the whole world.

CHAPTER III.

That God rewards the poor in spirit, not only in the other life, but in this also.

THAT you may not think all your reward reserved for the other life, or imagine you trust Almighty God too long by giving him so much time to repay you, since you have paid him in ready money, I must assure you that the poor in spirit are not only recompensed in the other world, but in this also, and that with considerable interest. All men are so self-interested, and so sensibly touched with what is present, that they seem to lose courage if they have not a prospect of some present advantage. It is for this reason the Son of God, who knows our weakness, was unwilling that those who renounced all for his sake, should be without reward in this world; and hence, immediately after the promise we spoke of in the foregoing chapter, he adds, that "he who shall leave his house, or brothers, or sisters, or father, or mother, or wife, or children, or estate, for my sake, shall receive a hundred fold, and enjoy everlasting life"—*Mat.*, xix. 29. This hundred fold is to be understood of this present life, according to our Saviour's own explanation of it in St. Mark: "He shall at present receive a hundred fold here in this life, and eternal life hereafter in the world to come"—*Mark*, x. 30.

St. Jerom, speaking of this hundred fold, interprets it of spiritual goods, and says, "that he who shall forsake temporal goods for the love of our Saviour, shall receive spiritual for them, which being compared with the others, are as a hundred in respect of a small inconsiderable number"—*Lib.* iii. *in Matt.* But Cassian interprets it of exterior and visible goods, and says, in conformity to the words of St. Mark, that religious receive this hundred fold even in this life, as you shall see made clear by what follows. You have left one house for the love of Christ, and in place of that God has given you a great many; you have forsaken one father and mother, and God has given you a great many other fathers, who love you much more tenderly than the former, take more care of you, and are much more solicitous for your good. You have quitted your brothers, and God has given others, whose love of you is more sincere, because, having but God in view, it is free from self-interest; whereas your brothers in the world scarce loved you any longer than they had occasion to make use of you in order to serve their own ends. You have left those who waited upon you in the world (if indeed you had any such to leave), and now you find a great number always employed in your service; one serves you as your steward, another as your porter, a third as your cook, and a fourth attends you when sick. And what is more, should you travel into Spain, France, Italy, Germany, nay even to the Indies, or any other place in the world, you would always find a house ready to receive you, and the same attendance to wait upon you, which is an honour and advantage that no prince in the world can boast of. Is not this to receive a hundred fold, and more than a hundred fold, even in this life? What shall I say now of what you have left,—I mean your riches? Have you not much more in religion than in the world? Has not God, therefore, rendered you the hundred fold? For you are more a master of all the riches of the world than those are who possess them, since they are rather slaves than masters; which makes the Royal Prophet call them "men of riches"—*Ps.*, lxxv. 4,—as if he would say, their riches do not belong to them, but they to their riches, since their riches command and domineer over them. They continually take pains to get, to increase, and keep their riches; and the more they have, the more uneasy and the greater slaves they are: "their wealth", says Solomon, "even robs them of their sleep"—*Eccl.*, v. 11. On the contrary, religious have everything they want, without the trouble of knowing whether it be dear or cheap, or whether the year be scarce or plentiful; and they live, to make use of St. Paul's own terms, "as having nothing, yet possessing all things"—II. *Cor.*, vi. 10. As for ease of mind, you have a hundred times more in religion than you would have had in the world. Ask worldly persons, and those whom you think most satisfied with their condition, and you will find them hourly exposed to a thousand misfortunes and disquiets, from which religious are exempt. As to honour, you have it much more in your religious habit than if you were living in the world. Princes, lords, bishops, and magistrates, who perhaps would not have taken notice of you before, now pay you deference and respect on account of the habit you wear. And God gives you much more peace and quiet in religion than the world can give; in fine, he returns with usury whatever you renounced in the world for his sake.

But upon what account does God treat religious thus? It is because they are disengaged from all things of this world, and think of nothing but Heaven. The time they would have spent in providing necessaries for their bodies in the world, is now employed in rendering themselves more pleasing to God, and in hourly increasing in virtue and perfection. This is what the Psalmist testifies when he says, "God gave the nations of the Gentiles to the children of Israel; they possessed the labours of other people, that they might keep his commandments and observe his law"—*Ps.*, civ. 43, etc. It is for this reason that

God himself speaks thus by the mouth of the prophet Ezechiel concerning priests, "There shall be no inheritance assigned them —I myself am their portion; you shall not give them any possession in Israel; I am their possession and inheritance"—*Ezech.*, xliv. 28. Thrice happy portion of religious, to whom God himself is portion and inheritance! So that we can truly say with the Royal Prophet, "My part is fallen very well to me, and the inheritance which has happened to me is admirable"—*Ps.*, xv. 6. Our condition is much to be preferred before that of our brethren in the world; for they have Earth, and we Heaven for our portion; God himself is our lot and possession. "Thou art the part of my inheritance, O my God"—*Ps.*, xv. 5. "Thou art the God of my heart, and my portion for eternity"—*Ps.*, lxxii. 26. St. Francis called poverty a divine and Heavenly virtue, because it makes us despise all Earthly things, and disengaging the soul from embarrassments, it enables her to direct all her thoughts to Heaven—to soar more easily to God, and to unite herself more closely to him.

CHAPTER IV.

In what true poverty consists.

THE Son of God gives us a sufficient notion of true poverty in these words: "Blessed are the poor in spirit", and, at the same time, shows us wherein it consists; for by these words he declares that it ought to be in the heart and mind, and that it is not enough to forsake riches to become truly poor, unless we also bid farewell to all attachment to them. It is the part of true poverty, not only to despoil us of all Earthly things, but even of all desire of them, that by this means we may be more capable of following Christ and devoting ourselves entirely to evangelical perfection, which is the end of a religious life. St. Jerom makes an observation to this purpose upon the answer our Saviour made to these words of St. Peter: "We have forsaken everything and followed thee: what shall we have for our reward?" Our Saviour answered: "Verily I say unto you, that you who have followed me", etc. Observe here, says St. Jerom, the Son of God does not answer: "Verily I say unto you, that you who have left all", but "you who have followed me"—*Mat.*, xix. 28; for to leave all is not here the essential part, since several heathen philosophers, as Diogenes, Antisthenes, and others, have done this. It is related even of Crates, the Theban, that, being a man of great wealth, and desirous to go to Athens to study philosophy, he sold all he had, lest his riches should divert him and call him home; and, having got all his money together, he threw it into the sea, saying: "Get you gone, you covetous desires, to the bottom of the sea; I will drown you now, lest you should one day do the same by me". There is also a story of Phocion, the Athenian captain, which expresses an equal contempt of riches and no less love of poverty; for Alexander the Great having sent him a hundred talents, which make about sixty thousand French crowns, Phocion asked the messengers why Alexander sent it him. They answered, that Alexander sent it because he looked upon him to be the most virtuous man in Athens. Let him permit me then to remain so, says Phocion, and so dismissed them without receiving a farthing. This refusal, with the answer, was very much admired and spoken of by the Grecian philosophers, who disputed very much which was the greater act— Alexander's liberality or Phocion's generous contempt of his present. Antiquity furnishes us with many instances of this nature, all which prove that the heathen philosophers looked upon riches as an impediment to virtue, although, as St. Jerom and St. Austin justly observe, riches of themselves do not properly any harm; and for proof of this, they allege several examples out of the Old Testament, as that of Abraham, Isaac, and Jacob, who were all very rich men; of Joseph, who was next to Pharao in power and wealth; of Job, who had great possessions; of David, who was a powerful monarch; of Daniel and his companions, men of great authority in Babylon; of Esther and Mardochai, who were also very considerable in the reign of king Assuerus; and of several others who lived in all the splendour and greatness this world could afford, and yet with an absolute disengagement from all Earthly things, which is the greatest sign of true poverty of spirit, and recommended to us by the Holy Ghost in these words, "If riches abound, set not thy heart upon them"—*Ps.*, lxi. 11.

But, to return to our subject, you must know that there are two things necessarily required for that poverty of spirit which religious make profession of. The first is, to leave ourselves nothing in this world, and this is done by the vow of poverty.

The second is, to retain no attachment to Earthly things. Now, this second is the principal, because really disengaging our heart from the love of riches, it enables us to give ourselves totally to God. This makes St. Thomas say, that the first is only a disposition to the second, and a help to shake off more freely, and bid farewell to, all that we have in the world: insomuch that St. Austin says, "We love those things that we really possess, far better than those we do not possess"; and, consequently, we can far more easily wean our affections from what we do not possess, than from what we are real masters of. It is much easier not to trouble ourselves about what does not belong to us, than to abandon that which does; for that which we have not, we look upon as a thing quite foreign to us—but that which we actually enjoy, we esteem as a part of ourselves and as incorporated with us. Hence, when we are to part with it, we feel the loss of it as much as of a leg or an arm.

St. Jerom, St. Austin, and St. Gregory, discoursing upon these words of St. Peter, "Behold, we have left all", treat this subject admirably well. "What great confidence", says St. Jerom, "does this manifest in St. Peter! Though he had been but a fisherman, always poor, living upon his trade, and getting his bread by the sweat of his brow, yet with great confidence he says, we have left all". "Which he might very well do", says St. Gregory, "for we are not to consider the things he left, but the will with which he left them; he left a great deal who reserved nothing to himself. It is a great matter to quit all, though the things be very inconsiderable that we leave. Do not we see with what passion we love what we already have, and how earnestly we search after what we have not? It is for this reason that St. Peter and St. Andrew left much, because they denied themselves even the desire and inclination of having anything at all"—*Hom. 5, in Matth.* St. Austin is of the same opinion, and says, "that the apostles even gloried that they had left all to follow Christ; because, upon his call, they had forsaken their nets and fishing-boat. And in effect he really despises and leaves everything, who quits and despises not only those things which he possessed, but all other things likewise to which his desires might have carried him"—*Epist.* 34, *ad Paulin.* This is no small comfort for those who have forsaken only a little because they had no more to forsake. This is what the same father observes, when he speaks of the reward he hoped for, for having sold and left all for Jesus Christ. "Though I have not been rich", says the same holy father, "yet I shall not have the less reward for that. For the apostles, who have done the same thing with me, were no richer than I; he therefore leaves all the world, who leaves all he has, and all desires of ever having more"—*Epist.* 89, *ad Hilar.* If, for the love of God, you forbear to desire a thing, you are justly said to renounce it for his sake; and, therefore, you renounce all Earthly things, if you forsake the desire not only of what you have or might have had, but even of those things to which your affection might have led you; and by consequence you may rejoice, and say with the apostles, "Behold, we have left all"—*Mat.*, xix. 27. On the contrary, he that was a rich man in the world ought not to glory the more upon this account, nor imagine that he has left more than another has done; for he has forsaken very little, if he has not also forsaken the thoughts and desires of all Earthly things. Whereas, he that had but a little in the world, has left a great deal, if in leaving the little he had, he has left the desires of having what he had not.

This is the nature of that poverty of spirit we now treat of. It consists in an absolute disengagement from all things of this world; in treading them under foot by a generous contempt of them; and in believing with the apostle, "that if we can but gain Jesus Christ, all the rest is but filth and ordure"—*Philip.*, iii. 8. Those who are thus truly poor in spirit, are the persons whom the Son of God calls happy, and they are really so; for the kingdom of Heaven does not only belong to them, as we have already shown, but they are at present in a state wherein they desire nothing, which is they highest idea that can be formed of temporal happiness. For happiness, according to Boetius, does not consist in the fruition of a great many things, but in the accomplishment of our desires; or, as St. Austin says, "he is happy who has all he desires, and desires nothing but what he ought". The poor in spirit have a greater advantage than rich men of the world; for they have all they desire, because they desire nothing but what they have, and look upon the rest as superfluous; whereas the rich are never satisfied, and their desires are boundless. "The covetous man shall never have his fill of money"— *Eccl.*, v. 9,—says the wise man, and avarice will never say, it is enough. The reason is, because nothing here below can satisfy the heart of man, but renders it rather uneasy than quiet. A covetous man is like one in a dropsy: the more he drinks, the more he thirsts; just as the miser's "desire of having more, grows and increases with his riches". Let his wealth be ever so great, his wishes are still greater; he daily languishes after what he has not; and looking upon what he already has as nothing, he is always solicitous how to get more. His trouble also for what he has not, exceeds the pleasure acquired by what he has; and by giving way to his insatiable desires, he spends his days in care and anxiety, and in vain searches after what he can never obtain.

Alexander is said to have wept when he heard Anaxarchus's opinion of many worlds; and that he made this answer to one who asked him the cause of his tears: Have I not sufficient reason to weep, says he, since there are so many worlds, and I have not as yet conquered one? This very idea alone, of something being wanting to his greatness, damped the joy he felt at all his success in war and at the vast extent of his empire. Crates, on the contrary, though only master of a poor wallet and a cloak, was always merry and pleasant, and always looked as if every day had been a festival with him, and was richer and more content with his poor condition, than Alexander with the empire of the world. This same emperor, happening one day to meet Diogenes, and seeing him very poor, said he thought he was in great necessity, and therefore bid him ask what he pleased, and it should be granted him. The philosopher immediately replied, who do you think, Alexander, is more in want—you or I? I have nothing but my cloak and wallet, nor do I desire anything else. But you, though you are so great a prince, yet expose yourself to a thousand dangers to enlarge your dominions, and the whole world is not able to satisfy your ambition; be therefore assured that I am richer and happier than you. St. Basil says, that Diogenes spoke very rationally. For after all, pray, who is richer—he that wants nothing, or he that wants many things? Certainly the former. Diogenes wanted nothing, because he was content with what he had; but Alexander wanted, because he desired many things, and consequently poor Diogenes was richer than Alexander the Great.

Therefore, as the most substantial riches and the truest happiness of this world, do not consist in the possession of many things, but in the accomplishment of our desires and in the satisfaction of our will, so poverty does not consist in being deprived of all things, but in the desire of not possessing any of them at all, and of being free from that insatiable desire of still getting more, "which", says Plato, "is no sooner quenched but a good man becomes rich upon it". St. Chrysostom has a comparison well adapted to our purpose. If a man, says he, is so very thirsty that he is obliged to drink continually without being able to quench his thirst, shall we think this man happy because he has at the same time plenty of water? By no means; for if at the same time we should see another, who in all appearance had no thirst upon him, certainly we should look upon the one as troubled with a dropsy, or else in a burning fever, and upon the other as a person in perfect health. The same difference is found between those whose thoughts are always employed in the pursuit of riches, and who are never content with what they have, and the truly poor in spirit, who are satisfied with the little they enjoy, and never seek after more. These are in perfect health, and the others are indisposed; these are fully satisfied, and the others suffer extreme hunger; these are truly rich in their poverty, and the others really poor, notwithstanding all their riches. This is what the Holy Ghost would have us understand by these words of Solomon: "There are some who seem rich, yet have nothing, and others who seem poor, and yet abound in riches"—*Prov.*, xiii. 7. But you will ask me whence this difference comes? I answer, from the very nature of riches themselves, for nothing here below can fully satisfy the heart of man, and from the nature of poverty of spirit, which is capable of abundantly satisfying those who are masters of it. Socrates used to say, "that he who wanted very few things, did in a particular manner resemble God, who wants nothing". And passing once through the market-place of Athens, where he saw a great deal of merchandize exposed to sale, he cried out, "How many things are there here which I have no need of!" On the contrary, ordinary people who judge only according to outward appearance, and the covetous, who set no limits to their greedy desires, are troubled at the sight of such things as they have not, and, sighing, cry out: Alas! how many things do I still stand in need of!

CHAPTER V.

Of the fault of some religious, who in religion place their affection upon trifles, having left considerable estates in the world.

It follows from what I have already said, that if a religious, when he forsakes the world and all its riches, does not at the same time disengage his affections from all things, he is not truly poor in spirit: for poverty of spirit essentially consists, not only in the bare depriving ourselves of all Earthly goods, but chiefly in cutting off and for ever destroying all inclination or affection towards them. If any inclination to them still remains in you, you cannot be truly said to have left them; no, you have only transplanted them out of the world into religion; for you retain them in your heart, and therefore you are not truly poor, but are only so in appearance, and by consequence only religious in the exterior; and therefore you are unjustly called religious, since it is only your body that is in religion, but your better part is still in the world.

From hence we may conclude, that, should a religious man, after he has generously renounced his worldly possessions, set his affections upon such trifles as a pretty cell, a good habit, choice books, or the like, he is no longer truly poor in spirit. The reason of this is the same as that already given, and is taken from the nature of true poverty of spirit, which consists in an entire disengagement of our affections from all things of this world, and such a person as we have now spoken of is by no means in this happy condition. He has only changed the affection he had for temporals in the world, to the affection for temporals in religion, and has forsaken great things to cleave to little ones, and in the main he is as much engaged and attached to these little things in religion, as he could have been to greater in the world. Cassian treats this subject incomparably well. I am at a loss, says he, when I would speak of that childish weakness of some religious, who, after they have bid adieu to what they had in the world, fall in love with trifles in religion, and seek their little conveniencies with the greatest zeal and solicitude; "so that their inclinations are sometimes more violently bent upon these trifles, than they were before upon the riches they had in the world. What does it signify to these men to have left great possessions, if they have not also left all irregular desires towards them? By retaining a desire and an inclination to little things, since they cannot aim higher at present, they discover too clearly that they have not quite destroyed their former passions, but only changed their objects. Their care and anxiety is still the same, yet they make little or no account thereof, as if different objects, and not disorderly passions, made avarice a crime. They are of opinion that we may leave great things to fix our affections upon less, and that it may be done for this reason; but they are in an error, for we renounce greater in order to despise smaller things with greater ease"—*Cass. Coll.* 4. *Ab. Dan.*, c. 2. For if our affections continue irregular, and avarice domineers in our hearts, it imports very little what is the cause, since our hearts are as much troubled and disquieted for trifles in religion, as they could have been for an estate in the world. The one and the other produce the same effect. If a man were to be deprived of the sun, were it not all one whether a plate of gold or of brass be put before his eyes, for he would be equally hindered from seeing the light. This is the sentiment of St. Mark the Abbot, who had the following conference with his own soul upon this matter. "You will tell me, my soul, that we do not heap up riches, that we neglect getting an estate; but I answer thee, that the abuse of riches, not the true use of them, does a man prejudice, as we see in Abraham, Job, David, and several others, who were masters of great estates, and at the same time great favourites of Heaven, because they did not set their hearts upon their riches. We, though poor, yet nourish avarice in our hearts; and though we heap up neither gold nor silver, yet we pick up a great many trifles, to which we tie our affection, and suffer as much uneasiness from them as from all the riches in the world. We renounce all dignities, nor do we aspire to the greatness of the world; yet we court the praises of men, and desire to be honoured and looked upon as somewhat considerable"—*In Biblioth. S.S. Patr.* These disorders of our mind make us more unhappy and less excusable than worldlings, and we show a meaner spirit than they do. For they set their hearts upon what has at least some appearance of greatness in it, whereas we, after having forsaken all, debase ourselves by a degenerate pursuit of what we ought generously despise. We ought to increase in perfection, and grow into a perfect man, as St. Paul says; but we act quite contrary, and instead of becoming men by entering into religion, and by generously forsaking the world, and disengaging ourselves from it, we are, by an over-foolish affection to toys and childish baubles, become children. A child cries when you take his rattle from him, or deny him anything he calls for: just so, the parties we speak of, fret themselves, and are troubled, when they are deprived of anything they fancy, or when all their demands are not granted. And certainly it is a thing very ridiculous, and much to be pitied, to see a grave religious person, who had the courage once to contemn the world, become so strangely fond of trifles, as to be as uneasy and troubled at the parting with them, as a child is, when you deny it an apple or take away its baby.

"We religious", says St. Bernard, "are the most miserable of all men, if we permit things of so little consequence to do us so much harm. For what blindness, or rather what folly and madness, is it to set our hearts thus shamefully upon trifles, after we have renounced things far more considerable! For if we have renounced all Earthly possessions and all carnal love to our parents, and confined ourselves within the walls of a monastery, and lastly, if we are come to religion to deny our own wills and freely submit to another's in everything, what is it that we ought not to do in order to preserve the merit of all these good actions, and never to forfeit it by any folly or negligence!"—*Ad Mon. S. Bertin.*

CHAPTER VI.
Of the three different degrees of poverty.

THE saints and masters of a spiritual life assign three degrees of poverty. The first degree is to be found in those who exteriorly quit all the things of the world, but who love them interiorly, and detach not the heart from them. It is proved already that these persons are not really, but only hypocritically poor, and that they do an injury to the name they bear. The second comprehends all those who have left the world, both in will and deed, and whilst they are in religion do not seek after superfluities, but are extremely careful to have all things necessary,—as good victuals, good clothes, convenient lodgings, and such like,—and are much troubled and complain when they are denied what they desire. This is no true poverty; and, as St. Bernard says, it is strange that so many at present should glory in the name of poor men, and at the same time be unwilling to want the least conveniency. This is the way to be rich rather than to be poor; and such as these outdo even secular persons, who are not always provided with conveniencies, some, because they have not wherewith to procure them, and others who had rather bear them than be at any expense, so that a thrifty disposition does in them what virtue should do in us; others, in fine, though they have much, and put themselves to vast expenses, yet they are never served according to their will. Yet you, who are religious, and have made a vow of poverty, would have everything you want, and suffer no manner of inconvenience. This shows no desire of poverty, but rather a desire to live in ease and plenty. Had you been in the world still, perhaps you would have suffered a great deal more in this point; is it therefore just, that we, who entered into religion to mortify our passions and to lead a penitential life, should be solicitous for those very conveniencies which we would not have met with in the world?

If, then, we wish to attain this perfection of poverty of spirit, and to correspond to the name and duty of a religious person, and to render our life conformable to our profession, we must advance one step higher, and be content to want even what is necessary, which is the third degree of poverty; for he who is truly poor despises even necessary things. It is not enough to be detached from unprofitable and superfluous things, but we must also break off all affection even to those that are necessary, and show our love of poverty by a want as well of these as of other things. Unable to do without the things which are necessary for life, we must take of them no more than is absolutely necessary; and by keeping this necessity within very narrow bounds, rather than by extending it, we must show that we are glad of any occasion to give testimony of our love of poverty.

It is nothing to be poor, says St. Vincent, unless we love to be so, and even rejoice to suffer for Jesus Christ all the inconveniencies of poverty. He that would bring his love of poverty to the test, must consider if he loves the effects of it, as hunger, thirst, cold, weariness, and a real want of all things. See if you are glad when you have an old threadbare habit given you,́ when you want part of your dinner, when the server forgets you, or gives you what is displeasing to your palate, or, lastly, when you have a very poor cell assigned you. For if you do not take a satisfaction when these things happen, but rather endeavour to avoid them, be assured that you are not yet arrived to the perfection of poverty of spirit.

CHAPTER VII.

Means to acquire and preserve poverty of spirit.

ST. IGNATIUS, in his constitutions, provides us with the first means or help towards it, in these words, "Let no one make use of anything as if it were his own property"—*Reg.* 4, *Sum.* A religious, says this saint, ought to be in all things he has for his use, like a statue, which is dressed and stripped again without being troubled or without making any resistance. It is thus you ought to look on your books, habit, chamber, or anything else you make use of; if you are ordered to give them up, or to make an exchange with others, you must be no more concerned than a statue is when it is undressed; and by this means all propriety will be avoided. Whereas, if when you are bid to change your chamber, or to part with this or that, or to exchange it for another, you find any repugnance, and are not like a statue herein, it is a sign you look upon those things as properly belonging to yourself, otherwise you would not be vexed to part with them. For this reason our holy founder appoints superiors to try their religious, as God did Abraham, and particularly in poverty and obedience, in order hereby to make a trial of this virtue, and to give them an occasion of making every day new progress in perfection; and without question, it is an excellent trial of their virtue, to take away now and then from every religious the things which he has the use of. It usually happens, says St. Austin, that we believe we do not love a thing whilst it is in our possession; but when we come to be deprived of it, it is then we certainly know how we stand affected to it. If you find yourself troubled and uneasy when anything is taken from you, there is no doubt but you loved it; for all that trouble and uneasiness arise from your too great attachment to it. On the contrary, if you felt no grief at all in parting with it, it is clear you had no tie to it. For, as the same holy father says, "we forsake without pain what we possess without love, but we cannot without grief give up that which we enjoy with pleasure". Hence we may infer how profitable it is that superiors sometimes exercise their subjects in making them change their chambers when they find some convenience in them and begin to love them but too well: in taking such books away as they wish most to retain; in obliging them to exchange a good habit for another that is worse. For otherwise there would be a kind of propriety pretended over everything, and by degrees the wall of poverty, which environs us, and is the bulwark of religion, would at last be quite demolished. The old fathers of the desert exercised their religious in this practice, in order to disengage them from everything, and to make them count nothing as their own. Thus St. Dorotheus treated his scholar, St. Dositheus. He used to give him a habit to make up for himself, and take it again from him and bestow it upon another, after he had taken a great deal of pains about it. This is conformable to what we practise at present; and the book of instructions which St. Dorotheus left, whence this example is taken, affords a great many more of this nature, which are very profitable to maintain religious discipline. In this book it is related that the same St. Dositheus, being infirmarian, wished very much to have a knife, and asked it of St. Dorotheus, not for himself, but for the use of the infirmary which he had care of. Whereupon the saint replied: "Well, Dositheus, does the knife please you? Had you rather be a slave to a knife than to Jesus Christ? Do you not blush to think that a knife is your master? Henceforward I charge you not so much as to touch it". And St. Dositheus never touched it after, so much effect had this grave rebuke and prohibition upon him. I wish we would in like manner often reproach ourselves, and say: Are you not ashamed that the love of a trifle should prevail so much upon you and cause you so much uneasiness? And do not believe withal that these things are so frivolous or of such little consequence as is, through want of due examination, generally imagined. For, as St. Jerom says, perhaps they may seem trifles and very inconsiderable to those who are strangers as yet to virtue and perfection, but at the bottom they contain things of profound wisdom and exquisite perfection, which God has hid from the wise and prudent, but discovered to the simple and humble of heart.

The second help to maintain poverty of spirit is, to have nothing superfluous; and the mercy of God has admirably provided for this by the conduct which is observed in the society of Jesus. Our chambers are like to that which the Sunamite fitted up for the prophet Eliseus, who, having occasion to pass frequently that way, used to call in to refresh himself. "I observe", says this woman to her husband, "that he who comes often hither is a man of God, and therefore let us provide him a little chamber with a bed, a table, a chair, and a candlestick in it, that he may lodge with us when he comes"—IV. *Kings*, iv. 9, 10. Such ought to be the furniture of our chambers, such ought to be our moveables; these are all really necessary, the rest superfluous. For this reason we are not permitted to adorn our chambers with pictures or such like ornaments. We have no great armed chairs or couches, tapestry, desks, or wrought carpets. We cannot keep anything in our chambers, either for ourselves to eat, or to entertain strangers with; nay, we are obliged to ask leave to go to the refectory, though it be but to drink a glass of water; nor can we have any book in our chambers in which we may write so much as one line or carry away with us. And as it is not to be doubted but this is true poverty, so it is at the same time to be granted that it is a great happiness, and no less perfection; for were we permitted to have superfluities, the care and trouble of getting them, of preserving them, and of increasing their number, would take up a great deal of time and be too great a distraction to a religious; whereas this wise prohibition removes all these inconveniencies. And one of the chief reasons why the society does not permit secular persons to come into our chambers, is to preserve us in this holy poverty. For we are men, and should we receive visits in our chambers, we would perhaps be tempted to exceed the limits prescribed us concerning poverty, and at last procure a handsome library, in order to make people believe we are learned. Hence this exact observance in the society is a mighty help to make us live up to the rules of poverty, and to cut off all desires of what is superfluous; and certainly this conduct is so prudent, that we can never esteem it enough, nor observe it too strictly.

Another proper help, which also conduces much to this virtue, is, that a religious, as soon as he perceives himself to have a particular inclination for anything he makes use of, should carry it immediately to the superior, and leave it to him to dispose of, even though this religious should have leave to keep it. This practice was very religiously observed heretofore by the monks of St. Jerom, who were also very vigilant to see that none should have anything superfluous; and if at any time they found a monk to have any vain or curious thing about him, they presently assembled, and burnt it before his face, saying that such things as these were the idols of religious. In imitation of them, we ought to deprive ourselves of every thing which we have not a real need of, and put it in the hands of our superior, without hopes of recovery. Moreover, to make this kind of sacrifice, it is not necessary to wait till we have an affection to the thing itself, for if it be not really necessary, this is a sufficient motive for us to make this sacrifice itself.

St. Bonaventure goes farther, and says he does not approve that any should heap up superfluous things in order to make presents, even under pretence of devotion, or upon any other account whatsoever. For, says he, besides that this makes the person singular, and be looked upon as one that traffics in such ware, and as one to whom application is to be made for them, it is certain that this takes up his thoughts too much, and by consequence diverts him from his duty. The same saint finds this other inconvenience in it, that a religious may sometimes dispose of such things without leave, either out of haste or inadvertency, or through shame of troubling the superior with his frequent petitions about such frivolous things. Hence it also happens that the party he gives it to receives the present without leave, either because he has not courage to refuse it, or because he is unwilling to put the other to the blush, and thus he gives at once both bad example and matter of scruple to his brethren. Besides, these little presents serve ordinarily either to create or continue particular friendships amongst religious, which holy men have always condemned as highly prejudicial to union and fraternal charity. And it was for this reason, says St. Bonaventure, that our ancient fathers would never allow of it. It is the same amongst us; for although we permit some religious to have such things upon account of their employments, yet certainly this can be no reason why others pretend the same privilege; and if any one should, he would both displease his superior and disedify his brethren. A religious ought to be so poor as to have nothing to dispose of, and it is this that truly edifies. With respect to those that wish to have some little things to make presents of, they are never looked upon as the most regular persons; and therefore it is best to follow St. Bonaventure's counsel in this matter in order to live up to the rule of true poverty.

There is another thing observed in our society, which helps very much to keep true poverty in its purity, and wherein the Lord bestows on us a particular favour. Our chamber doors are never locked, nor can we have a box, desk, or cupboard locked without leave from the superior. All things are to be exposed to the superiors' eyes, so that we can say we have nothing which they may not take. This agrees with these words in St. Jerom's rule: "Let all use of locks and keys be prohibited amongst you, that all the world may see by your exterior you possess nothing but Jesus Christ". But although our chambers lie open, yet all things in them are secured from the rest of the religious, by a prudent foresight of our holy founder, who, in another rule, forbids any religious to enter another's chamber without leave of the superior, and in another place prohibits all his subjects to carry anything out of the house, or even out of another's chamber, unless the rector consents thereunto. These are the securest locks and keys, which being defended with the vow of poverty, are rendered almost incapable of being broken open. And, without doubt, our chambers, though so exposed, are safer by this means in respect to our own religious, than if they were shut up with bolts and padlocks. Let us then endeavour to maintain this holy practice; and certainly should any religious give the least blemish thereunto by endeavouring to violate it, he would deserve a most severe punishment, and run the hazard of making a change in the purity and simplicity of what we practise, wherein true poverty appears and shines so bright. St. Basil and St. Bonaventure exclaim very much against such persons as these.

CHAPTER VIII.

Another efficacious help to obtain and preserve this poverty of spirit.

CERTAINLY it is of very great advantage to us, in order to increase this virtue of poverty, and gain it in perfection, not only to deprive ourselves of things superfluous, but also to retrench those which are absolutely necessary for us, thereby to show our love of poverty, and to appear what we really are, I mean poor men. This is what St. Ignatius enjoins in his constitutions, when he says: Let their diet, clothes, and lodging be like those of poor men; and let every one, for his greater spiritual progress and greater abnegation of himself, always think that the worst things in the house ought to be given to him. And he recommends the same over and over in several other parts of his rule, in these words: Let every one love poverty as a mother, and according to their zeal, endeavour now and then, so far as prudence and discretion shall admit, to feel some effects of it. Our holy founder desires that we should always incline to have the meanest and most ordinary things; but he does not pretend that our love of poverty should rest in these bare desires, and go no farther—no, he would have us feel the effects of it so far as to put it really in practice, though he would not have us want anything that is necessary for life. Nor is he content to speak in several other places of poverty in general, but in the sixth part of his constitutions he descends to particulars, and assigns habits to us, according to the offices we are employed in, but always conformable to the poverty we profess. And in order to this effect, he appoints that our clothes should be decent, as becoming religious; that they should suit the place we live in, since our way of living is common as to the exterior; and, lastly, they should be poor, which they would not be, says he, if they should be made of fine stuff or cloth that is dear. And, therefore, when the parents or friends of any religious would give him clothes of this kind, he must not accept of them, as being contrary to our constitutions, and not being suitable to the poverty we profess. Some may hereupon object that it is good economy to buy the best cloth, because it lasts longer, and consequently is less expensive. These reasons are the dictates of flesh and blood, and may hold in the world, but not in religion; for this economy is not of so much importance to true religious men, as is the obligation they have to manifest to the world their poverty by the clothes they wear, and to appear such as they really are. Nor ought this poverty appear only in the cloth, but also in the fashion and cut of it; for should any of us have a cassock too wide in compass, or with too many plaits in it, or trailing upon the ground, it is certain we would transgress against the poverty we made profession of.

11 B

St. Ignatius requires that our clothes be religiously decent and warm, which are the two chief ends for which clothes were first invented. This is St. Basil's doctrine, in his explanation of these words of St. Paul, "having food and raiment, let us be content" —I. *Tim.*, vi. 8. Another saint observes, and very much to our purpose, that St. Paul says, "food, and not delicacies, and raiment to cover us, not to make us gay and fine". We ought to content ourselves with what is barely necessary, and absolutely banish everything that looks rich, or has any appearance of ostentation, as savouring too much of vanity and profaneness. Let us never suffer such things, nor ever permit the pride and vanity of the world to find way into our order. St. Francis used all possible precaution in this point. We read in the chronicles of his order, that Friar Elias, one of the chief men of the order, and afterwards general of it, got himself a habit made that was very large and full, with sleeves that hung down to the ground, and of very fine cloth. As soon as St. Francis knew of this, he sent for him, and in the presence of several religious desired to see his habit. When he had brought it, St. Francis put it on above his own, and began to set the plaits in order, and to let fall the sleeves with an air that was vain and fantastical; after this he put on a haughty mien, and strutting along, paid his honours to the religious with affected voice and affected gesture. The religious, surprised at this, looked at one another with amazement, when the saint, transported with zeal, hastily pulled off the habit, and, casting it with violence upon the ground, told Friar Elias, before all the company, that the bastard sons of the order were clothed in that manner. After this he re-assumed his sweet and mild countenance, and, conversing with the religious according to his custom, recommended mildness, humility, and poverty to them. Let us take care, then, that we do not declare ourselves illegitimate by a similar vanity; let us, like the lawful issue and true children of holy poverty, endeavour to resemble our mother, and in this quality wear no habit that may distinguish us from poor men. For this effect, we ought to retrench something even of what we might wear with decency, as also something which the world might judge really necessary for us. For he cannot be called poor in his clothes, who is well clothed from head to foot; and he alone who wants something of what in this part is really necessary, deserves that name. And for this reason we have declared all along in this treatise, that true poverty consists in being satisfied to want things really necessary; and he that finds not an ease and content of mind in this point, is by no means as yet arrived to the perfection of poverty of spirit.

What I have said of clothes, may be applied to other things; for in all things we ought to appear like poor men, and endeavour to make known our poverty. And therefore, our chambers ought to be provided with nothing but what is precisely necessary, and that too ought to be the worst in its kind; as for example, the worst table, the worst chair, the worst bed. Nay, we ought to desire the worst of everything in the house, and return those books to the library which we do not actually stand in need of, and never to affect the honour of having a great number of them upon our shelves. St. Bonaventure, treating this matter, descends to particulars. He recommends to his religious that they should have nothing but bare necessaries, bids them take particular care that even those should not be curious or finely wrought, but rather coarse, ordinary, and plain; that they should not seek after books neatly bound; that their breviaries and diurnals should be plain and like those of others; that they should not have any pictures or beads of any considerable value; and that if they had any *Agnus Deis*, crosses, or relic-cases, they should be conformable to the poverty they had vowed; and be assured, says the same saint, that the more your poverty appears, the more agreeable you are in the sight of God and his saints. The humble St. Francis said, that an affection in a religious person to curious and unnecessary things, is a sign of his soul's being dead to grace; for it cannot proceed but from the want of the life and warmth of divine grace, and thus, not finding any satisfaction in spiritual things, the soul seeks its comfort and ease elsewhere. Daily experience confirms this truth, and makes our superiors most vigilant in this point; because not only poverty, but fervour of spirit is destroyed by these trifles. If we desire to be truly poor, it is not enough to disengage our affection from these, but also even from necessary things; and we must be glad of the occasion of suffering this want of necessaries, the better to resemble Jesus Christ, " who, when he was rich, became poor for our sakes"—II. *Cor.*, viii. 9, —who suffered hunger and thirst, cold and heat, weariness and nakedness, and several times wanted the necessaries of life.

St. Bernard says, that there was in Heaven a great abundance of riches, but that poverty was a species of merchandise not found there; and though it was common in the world, yet men did not esteem it nor know the value of it. What, therefore, did the Son of God do? Knowing the true value of poverty, he came to Earth, and like a prudent merchant, he purchased it, in order that men might, from his example, be convinced of its worth, and bring it with them to Heaven, where it is in so high estimation.

CHAPTER IX.

What has been said in the preceding chapter, is confirmed by several examples.

IN the book of the illustrious characters of the Cistercian order, —*Lib. Viror. Illust. Ord. Cisterc.*—we read that one of their abbots in Saxony, not being content to wear the cloth of that country, sent every year into Flanders to buy finer for his own habit. After his death, his clothes were distributed amongst the religious, and the prior kept an under garment for himself, which he put on upon the eve of a great festival, and had no sooner done so, but he cried aloud, as if hot plates of iron had been applied to his flesh, so great was the pain he felt. The religious hearing this noise presently ran to him, in whose presence he immediately pulled off the garment, and threw it upon the ground. They were much surprised to see it look like red-hot iron, and all those who had got any of the deceased abbot's clothes, being terrified at this sight, immediately brought them to the same place, and threw them all in a heap together, when they forthwith took fire, and by their sparks and flame seemed a burning furnace. The fire miraculously lasted so long, that they had time to advertise the abbots of the neighbouring monasteries, who saw it, and bore testimony of it afterwards.

Cæsarius tells us, that the Benedictine monks of a monastery in France, being much oppressed by a gentleman that lived near them, resolved to make their complaints to Philip I. They made choice of a young religious of noble extraction to present their petition, in hopes that the consideration of his family might procure him a more speedy and favourable audience of his majesty. The young monk being presented to the king, prefers his complaints, demands justice, and begs that the gentleman might be obliged to restore what he had taken from their monastery. The king for some time looking upon him, and observing his habit and comportment, asked him who he was? Having answered that he was the son of a person of quality well known to the king, he began to talk of another matter, till the monk interrupted him, saying: Sire, it is certain that this gentleman has deprived us of almost all we had, and scarce left anything in the monastery. I easily believe it, replied the king, for it appears so by your shoes, which would not have been so tight, had he left one bit of leather more in your convent. This remark, however, his majesty graciously sweetened, by adding: Make it your business for the future, to surpass the rest of your religious as much in humility as you exceed them in quality, and be not troubled at what I have said, since it is for your good; return home to your monastery, and I will give orders that you be no longer annoyed by this gentleman.

The same Cæsarius sets down a similar answer made by another Philip, king of the Romans, to a Bernardine abbot, who was representing the great poverty of his convent. His majesty noticing the tightness of his shoes, told him that he perceived by them that his convent was very poor, seeing they were so sparing of leather.

We read in the chronicles of the Franciscans, that a guardian of that order, and an intimate friend of St. Francis, having built a chapel for his religious, ordered that a cell should be built very near it, to which the saint might retire to perform his devotions when he came there, and be in consequence induced to stay the longer with them. The first time he came there, the guardian conducted him to his cell, which was made only of ordinary timber: the saint, however, no sooner saw it, but he said, that if the guardian wished him to stop there, he should cover it at the top, on the inside, with boughs of trees tied together with osiers, that he might have a true picture of poverty, and this being done accordingly, the saint staid there for some days.

St. Francis Borgia, as may be seen in his life, gave most signal proofs of his real love of poverty. His habit, his diet, his chamber and bed were truly poor. Poverty appeared in the very paper he used to write his sermons on, in the fire they made sometimes for him in his greatest necessity, and in a thousand other things like to these. He came to such perfection of poverty that they could not prevail on him to change his shoes and stockings; and once, his old stockings being taken away, and a pair of new ones put in their place without his knowledge, he obliged them to bring the old ones back again. When he went begging, he chose rather to eat of the scraps of bread he brought home with him, than of the loaves that were laid upon the table. In his longest journeys and worst health, he would never take a pair of sheets along with him, for he thought this against holy poverty. He passed many nights upon a little straw, exposed to the open air; and he took such satisfaction herein as caused astonishment in his fellow-travellers. He had only one cloak, winter and summer, and to preserve it the longer, he caused it to be lined. It was not without the greatest difficulty he was persuaded to ride in boots; and he would never have more than one hat, which he thought a sufficient defence against sun and rain. In travelling, he often came to his inn all wet and shivering with cold, and it was an extraordinary joy to him when he met with no manner of convenience or comfort in this condition. Though he was ever so sick, and the weather extremely cold, yet he would never admit of anything about his bed, or in his chamber, which might keep the wind from him. Nay, he deemed a little mat, which was fastened to the head of his bed, to have too much delicacy in it, and the high state he had forsaken made all these things much more admirable in him.

CHAPTER X.
The obligation of the vow of poverty.

I SHALL now proceed to show what, in religion, we are bound to by the vow of poverty, and to point out when one offends venially or mortally against it; for it is fit that religious should understand precisely the obligation of their profession and of their vows. Hitherto I have spoken of perfection; now I shall treat of what regards the obligation, which should always precede, as being the foundation on which the remainder of the edifice rests. For this purpose, I shall lay before you as briefly as I can what is said on this subject by divines and canonists, whose opinions are maintained by saints, and confirmed even by the decision of the canon law. They tell us that a religious is bound by the vow of poverty to have no dominion, no property, no use of any temporal thing, without license from his superior. Hence, two things necessarily follow: first, that the vow of poverty obliges a religious not to possess, or take, or receive any temporal thing, in order to keep, make use of, or to dispose of it in any manner whatsoever, without leave of his superior; for this cannot be done, but by such as have, or can have, a property and dominion in temporals. The second is, that a religious acts contrary to his vow of poverty, not only when, without permission, he takes, retains, or in any manner disposes of anything that belongs to the house, but likewise when he accepts of anything from persons abroad, though they be his parents, friends, or penitents, and keeps or disposes of it without license from his superior. These two consequences drawn from the premisses above, are admitted by all divines, and looked upon as certain and infallible, and the canon law sets them down as such. These being fixed and undeniable principles, whatever I shall say upon this subject shall be grounded upon them, and whatever decisions I shall give on particular cases, shall be conformable to them.

St. Ignatius, treating of this subject in his constitutions, speaks of it in the same manner; and that his doctrine might be always before our eyes, he has inserted it in one of his rules. Be it known to all, says he in the sixth rule, that no religious can take or lend, or in any sort dispose of anything that belongs to the house, without the knowledge and consent of the superior. Had he said no more than this, some might have believed that they offended not against poverty but by disposing of things of the house, and so might receive presents from strangers without acquainting the superior; but he explains himself still farther upon this point in another rule, and says, that no person shall take the least thing belonging to the house, or out of another's chamber, or receive anything, let it be what it will, upon any account, from strangers, either for himself or another, without permission of his superior. Here you have, in a few words, that to which the vow of poverty binds in rigour: our holy founder has comprised it all in these two rules.

It must be observed, however, that you must be on your guard, lest you deceive yourself by imagining that, as our constitutions and rules do not bind under pain of sin, you therefore commit no sin, at least no mortal sin, by violating these two rules. For it may easily happen that some one may be so far mistaken as to argue thus: To give or receive anything without leave is a breach of a rule; but since our rules do not oblige us under pain of sin, therefore I only transgress the rule, but commit no sin. It is true that St. Ignatius has declared in his constitutions that his rule does not oblige under pain of sin, yet, doubtless, the vows we make in profession bind under pain of mortal sin, as the same saint positively asserts in the same place, lest, though this truth is clear in itself, any one failing in his duty should set up the plea of ignorance. For as it is certain that, by offending against chastity, a religious sins mortally against his vow of chastity and commits a sacrilege, so it is equally certain that, by offending against poverty, he is guilty of a mortal sin against the vow of poverty. This is what no one can deny. Had you not entered religion, and there made the vow of poverty, but continued in the world master of your property, then you might have disposed of it at your pleasure, and you would not have incurred any obligation to the contrary; but, having entered into religion and vowed poverty, it is not in your power to receive or keep anything without leave, this being an obligation arising from the vow you have made. St. Peter's answer to Ananias was something like this, when, after having sold a field, the latter brought in only part of the purchase-money, pretending it to be the whole, and retaining the rest for his wife and himself, notwithstanding the vow of poverty which holy doctors say they had made. "Why has Satan", says the apostle, "tempted thy heart to lie to the Holy Ghost, and by fraud keep part of the price of thy field? Possessing it, did it not remain to thee, and being sold, was it not in thy power? Why hast thou conceived this thing in thy heart? Thou hast not lied to men, but to God himself"—*Acts*, v. 3, 4. Now, what was the event of this? Ananias immediately fell down dead in punishment of his crime, and a little after the same happened to his wife Saphira, who was his accomplice. "Upon this", says the Scripture, "there fell great fear upon the Church, and upon all those that heard these things"—*Acts*, v. 11. Certainly we cannot be too cautious in the vow of poverty, since we see how severely those that break it are chastised by Heaven.

To return to our subject, I say that, were poverty enjoined

only by our rule, a breach of it would not be a mortal sin; but when a rule contains the matter of a vow, there is no doubt but that we are obliged to keep it under pain of mortal sin; not that the rule itself has power to bind us, but because the vow expressed in it binds us. Hence it is that these rules which concern chastity or the law of nature, oblige under mortal sin, not barely of themselves, but on account of the obligation which the vow of chastity and the law of nature impose on us. Now, as the rules here mentioned contain in substance the vow of poverty and all its obligations, it follows that he who violates them sins mortally, not because he violates the rules, but because he breaks the vow of poverty contained in the rules. Whenever, then, we read these rules, we are not to look upon them barely as rules, but to consider that they explain the vow of poverty, its essence, and indispensable obligations, according to the decisions of the canon law and the opinion of all divines. St. Austin, speaking of those religious that live in communities, says: "It is certain that they ought not to have, possess, give, or take anything without permission of their superior"—*de Com. Vit. Cler.* Our rules say the same in express terms, and indeed exterior poverty consists in this. For the power of giving, taking, possessing, or disposing of temporals at pleasure, or without leave from another person, most certainly argues a propriety which is directly opposite to the vow of poverty.

In order that this, which is received as a sort of first principle, may be more clearly understood, I shall here note the distinction which divines and canonists make, between having the dominion, and having but the use of a thing. He that has the dominion of it, can give, lend, sell, or dispose of it as he pleases: whereas he who is not master of it, but has only the use of it, cannot do so; for he can neither give it away, nor buy nor sell it, nor make any other use of it, than that for which it was placed in his hands. This is wont to be made more clear and evident by the following example. You invite a person to dine with you: the invitation does not make him master of what is set upon the table. He cannot carry anything away with him, send it to his friends, or sell or dispose of it at his pleasure, for you only grant him the liberty of eating what is set before him; and hence a distinction between the use and the dominion is made in things which are consumed by using them, nay, in such things as are consumed the very first time they are used. Now the same holds amongst religious, as divines teach, in respect of the things they possess by permission of their superiors. They have only the bare use of them; for they are given to them for this end only, and they cannot dispose of them at their pleasure, seeing they are not masters of them. For example, you cannot, without leave of your superior, give to another the habit you wear; and if you should give it away of your own accord, you would sin mortally against the vow of poverty, because the act of giving it away would show you had been master of it. What I here say of a habit, is applicable to everything else we have the use of; and hence you cannot give away your hat, breviary, or anything, in fine, because you have not the dominion of them. You have only the use of them, just as guests have the use of what is served at table; and I wish this comparison may never be forgotten, for it is a very just one, and very explanatory of our subject. If then it be true, that we cannot dispose at our pleasure of what the superior permits us to make use of, it is most evident that we cannot dispose of what belongs to the house without license from the superior, and consequently that we cannot take a book out of the library, or anything out of the wardrobe, refectory, or any other place, without acting in a still more direct opposition to the vow of poverty.

CHAPTER XI.

How far it is against the vow of poverty to give or receive without permission, anything, though even it should not belong to the house.

WE have said, that in general, all divines maintain, that a religious breaks his vow of poverty, not only when he takes any thing belonging to the house for his own use, or when he gives it to another, but also when he receives anything from abroad, without his superior's leave. For example, should your parents, friends, or any other person give you money to buy a habit, a book, or any other thing whatsoever, and you take it and make use thereof without permission, you sin against your vow of poverty; and this is the case whether you asked the thing or not, though it was given you purely out of friendship, or by way of alms, or through any other motive whatsoever. But some will object, that it is easy to comprehend how the vow of poverty is broken by appropriating to one's self a thing which belongs to the community; but how can it be broken when the thing is given me from abroad; when no injustice is done; nay, when even the house gains so much as it should have expended in purchasing for me what my friends make me a present of? Sure this is no sin, nor is it against any commandment. I answer that this is a sin of theft, and that you offend against the seventh commandment. This St. Austin says expressly in his rule: "If anything", says he, "be given to any particular person, for example, a religious habit, let it be kept for the common use, and be given to him who shall be judged to stand most in need of it" —*Reg.* 3, c. 28. If therefore any one should offer a thing to a religious, he cannot receive it without leave; since it belongs to the superior to receive it, and it is not for him to whom it is given, but for all in common; and he receives it, in order to give it afterwards to the person who, in his opinion, will want it most. If a habit is sent you from a friend, and the superior is pleased to bestow it upon another, he does no injury to you; for it is as much mine as yours, and every one in the community may pretend equal right with you unto it. But to decide this question, St. Austin subjoins these words:—"If any one should have anything given him, and he conceal it, he is guilty of theft"—*Reg.* 3, c. 28. St. Basil is of the same opinion, when he says, "To possess anything as an individual, without the superior's consent, is theft"—*In Const. Mon.*, c. 35. You will ask, from whom it is that the religious person steals. In answer to this, St. Basil tells you, "that you steal from the community, by applying to your own use the least thing imaginable, let it come from whom it would". These are no exaggerations of these holy doctors, nor do they speak on this occasion, as they sometimes do, when they wish to create a horror of a thing. They only assert an evident truth, admitted by all divines, and founded upon this principle, universally approved of, viz., that the vow of poverty renders a religious incapable of possessing or disposing of anything. As he belongs not to himself, but to his order, so whatever he acquires, whatever is given him, whatever he obtains in any manner whatsoever, belongs to his order the very moment it belongs to him. Hence, in all communities, if in consequence of any place he had filled while in the world, a religious has a pension, this pension does not belong to himself, but to the monastery, in whose name the superior orders it to be received, like every other revenue, and with part of it supplies the necessities of this religious, as would be done if had had no pension.

Hence we see clearly that a religious who receives or keeps anything in private, without leave of his superior, is guilty of theft. For theft consists in taking away, or retaining against his will, what belongs to another; now, what a religious has received belongs to his order, and consequently, by retaining it without leave, he usurps it, and steals it from his order. Hence it follows also, that the person to whom a religious gives anything without leave, though by way of alms, acquires no right to it, nor is he the true owner, but is really bound to restore it. This clearly shows that those err, who think that they can, as they please, dispose of a book, a picture, or a relic given them from abroad, or in short, of anything else, provided it does not come from the house. For, as it is a theft and a breach of the vow of poverty, to dispose of anything belonging to the house without leave, so it is an equal crime to receive anything from abroad, and dispose of it without the superior's consent.

But admit that there should be no theft committed, nor any prejudice done to the community, as it may happen, yet to receive anything, and make use of it, or dispose of it according to our own will, without license from the superior, is of its own nature a mortal sin; for this is absolutely prohibited all religious, and by their vow of poverty they are rendered incapable of it. Besides, should any one receive a present from a religious, the receiver would not be the true master of the present, for it belongs to the community, and he would be obliged to restitution, because he received it from a person who had no more power to give it than a minor has.

The truth of this doctrine is confirmed by what St. Gregory the Great did to a monk in the monastery which he built in Rome after he was made pope. I take the following relation from his own dialogues, and from Surius in the life of this holy doctor. One Justus, a religious of this monastery, desired a brother he had in the world to buy him an under garment, and his brother, to free himself from any further trouble, gave him money sufficient to buy what he demanded. Surius says, that they were three Spanish reals, and this author declares he took his history from the original copies. St. Gregory says they were three ducats, but it avails nothing whether they were reals or ducats, as at that time either would be sufficient to buy an under garment. Now, to come to the fact, the religious took the money without permission, and happened to fall sick whilst it was in his custody. Another monk, who by accident knew of it, acquainted the abbot; for, as it is at present practised by us, so it was practised then, that if any one should discover anything of moment done by another religious, he should immediately give notice of it to the superior. The abbot judging this a matter of consequence, thought proper to go and inform the pope of it, that he may learn his will on the occasion. Upon hearing it, St. Gregory, then pope, gave orders, that the sick person should be looked upon as excommunicated, and that none of the monks should visit or have any conversation with him in his sickness, because he had broken his vow of poverty. Moreover, he commanded that he should not be buried in consecrated ground with the rest of the monks, but in a dunghill outside the monastery, and that the money should be thrown upon the body whilst the monks all said, "May thy money perish with thee"—*Acts*, viii. 20. The monk died of this sickness, and all things were put in execution according to St. Gregory's orders, who tells us farther, that this fact created such general fear and consternation amongst the religious, that having most diligently examined everything they had, even the smallest things which they could keep with permission, they brought them immediately to the superior, for a farther assurance that they might retain nothing that was contrary to holy poverty. The sacred canons, in conformity to this example and to the practice of the ancient fathers, have ordained the same punishment for all religious who die proprietors of anything.

CHAPTER XII.

A solution of some difficulties which relate to the vow of poverty.

FROM the principles which have been already laid down, and which are founded on the universal consent of doctors, we can infer the decision of all the particular cases which may occur; and as it will be very useful on this occasion to enter into a detail, we shall, by way of examples, quote some cases which will serve very much to elucidate all others.

The first consequence I draw from these principles is, that a religious, when he receives money from his superior to make a journey, is not permitted to buy beads, pictures, or anything else, either for his own use or to make presents, nor can he so much as get his reliquary mended with it, though he should for this very design save some expenses which he might reasonably make. The reason of this is, because the money is given him barely to defray the expenses of his journey, and he is obliged to give up all that remains, either to the superior from whom he had it, or to him that is superior of the place he goes to; so that if he retains it or devotes it to any other use, he robs his order and sins against his vow of poverty. This is to be understood when the superior gives the religious what is really requisite for his journey, according to the practice amongst us. For, should he only be allowed so much a day and no more, though he should stand in need of it, the case is otherwise; for this would be a tacit consent for him to devote what he saved of his expenses to any other honest and lawful use.

The second is, that though he should be provided by his parents or friends, and not by his superior, with this money, yet he cannot so much as buy a breviary, a pair of tweezers, spectacles, or any other thing, either to keep or give away. The circumstance of its being his friends and not his order that give the money, must not cause any mistake here; seeing the party it comes from signifies nothing, for it being once in his hands, it belongs to his order; and it is the same thing, as we have already observed, as if he received it from the rector or procurator of the house. It is therefore to be devoted only to the expenses of his journey, as the superior permitted him to receive it only for this end, and he is bound to restore what remains; so that if he keep it or spend it any other way, he breaks his vow and robs his order. I say this even on the supposition that the religious received this money from his friends with the superior's leave; and if this is not obtained, it is another breach of his vow, as has been already said.

The third is, that when a religious comes from the mission or from visiting his relations, where he was made a present of a pair of boots, a cloak, or some other conveniencies for his journey, these things belong to the community he is of, and upon his coming home, he ought to deliver them up to the superior or to him who has charge of such things; for, should he keep them without leave, he would become proprietor, and so commit a theft, and offend against his vow of poverty.

The fourth is, that though a religious should have his foot in the stirrup and be on the point of setting out for another house, he can neither ask nor accept of anything from seculars, though it should be only to bear his expenses upon the road, without license from the superior of the house he leaves, even though he should be persuaded that the superior of the house he goes to would be glad he should do so in order to save expense. The reason of this is, because he is still under the authority of the superior he leaves, and not under his to whom he goes; and therefore not to ask his consent, which might still be done, is to receive things without his permission. If he were upon his journey indeed, then he might accept of as much as he should think the superior he goes to would permit, but still with an intention at his arrival to give him an account of it. What makes the difference is, that in this case he may presume of the superior's consent; but never can this be presumed when we can have recourse to him, or when the thing in question may be deferred.

The fifth is, that if a superior permits his subject to receive money, and to put it into the procurator's hands for some particular purpose—for example, to pay for copying out some of his writings—he cannot apply this money to any other use without leave, nor give any part of it to another religious who wants it, either for himself or his relations; nor can he employ it in charity, devotion, or any other way, any more than the other religious can receive it from him, without permission. And should they do it, they would both offend against their vow of poverty; for, as I have already said, this vow is broken either by giving or accepting any temporal thing without the superior's leave.

The sixth is, that as a religious can neither give nor take, so cannot he either borrow or lend, or make any contract without leave; for every species of contract is prohibited by the vow of poverty. Yet, notwithstanding this, there may be presumed a tacit or general consent of the superior, in respect of things of very small consequence; and religious may frequently have occasion to borrow of one another, provided it be but for a short time, and according to the practice of the house they live in.

The seventh is, that it is a breach of the vow of poverty to receive a deposit, either from a domestic or an extern, without leave. For in all deposits there is a kind of contract, which obliges you in law to be responsible for the things put into your hands, and to return the worth of them if they be lost by your negligence. Moreover, the keeping of money, or any other thing of value, brings a great deal of care and trouble along with it, and it would be highly scandalous to find such things in a religious man's custody, when he has no authority to receive them, and when nobody knows whence they came. As to the ordinary things which we are permitted to keep in our chambers, those we may commit to the care and custody of another religious in the same house.

The eighth is, a religious man, without leave, cannot have money, nor anything equivalent, in his own keeping, nor in the hands of a third person; for there is no difference between having it in one's own hands and in the hands of another; so that, should he give some goods or clothes to his relations to keep for him till he should be making a journey, he would offend against the vow of poverty as much as if he had kept them himself without the knowledge of his superior.

The ninth is, it does not look like holy poverty, but rather has an appearance of propriety in it, to carry books, pictures, or anything of that nature along with you when you remove from one house to another. And, therefore, this is not allowed in the Society of Jesus, which takes care that all things which the religious have be accounted community-property, and that they shall not carry anything away with them when they are going elsewhere. And should any religious do it without permission, he would steal the goods of the house, and break the vow of poverty, even though what he took away came not from the house, but from some other place; for it is all the same, according to the reason already given.

The tenth is, he that should spend his money in vain and superfluous things, though with leave of the superiors, would also sin against the vow of poverty: for the holy canons declare such expenses contrary to poverty: nor can the superior himself either buy, or give leave to buy, anything but what is necessary, profitable, and decent. Hence it is, that, should any one receive such vain curiosities from any religious which he has foolishly bought, he would be obliged to restore them to the order, as I have proved in the preceding chapter.

The eleventh is, when a religious hides anything for fear his superior should find it and take it from him, he sins against the vow of poverty; for, as divines observe, this secrecy is a desire of property, and manifests an inclination to keep it against the will of his superior.

The twelfth is, a religious who has the disposal and distribution of things committed to his care for the use of the community, is obliged to follow the orders of the superior, and not his own private judgment. And if he gives either more or less, better or worse, than the superior ordains, he offends against poverty; for by so doing he disposes of the things as if he were the master and proprietor of them, and not as if he depended upon another.

The thirteenth is, that as a religious would sin against the vow of poverty by deliberately wasting or spoiling what is committed to his care, or what is given him to make use of: in like manner, according to the maxim of canon law, viz., "gross negligence is considered a fraud", he would also sin, who, by his notorious carelessness, should lose or spoil anything committed to his charge. For, first it belongs only to the master of the goods, to waste and consume them at his pleasure. Secondly, things are given totally for the service of the religious; and those persons that are entrusted by their employments with things of the house, cannot dispose of them, unless it be for the advantage of the community; so that, if they should dissipate or waste them, they would certainly violate the vow of poverty. It is, moreover, to be observed that though perhaps once or twice doing so would not prejudice the house much, yet the loss would be very considerable in the end. Cassian has an example upon this subject, which shows how exact and strict the ancient fathers were in this point. The dispenser, or he who keeps and gives out all the provisions of a monastery, coming into the kitchen, perceiving that the cook, who had been washing his peas to boil for dinner, had let three fall upon the ground, immediately acquainted the abbot with it, who gave the cook a public penance for the little care he took of what belonged to the community. And Cassian adds, that those ancient religious did look not only upon themselves as consecrated to God, but also upon all the goods of the monastery to be so too; and this made them to be so very careful even of the least thing that belonged to the community.

CHAPTER XIII.

An objection is answered, and thereby this subject is more clearly elucidated.

SOME may object, that this exact observance of every little point relating to poverty is too severe, and that, after all, several other religious, who make the same vow of poverty as we do, receive money from their parents and friends without any difficulty, to buy them a breviary, books, or clothes, and yet are looked upon to be well-informed persons and true servants of Almighty God. Nor do they scruple to give a book to one of their fellow-monks, or to any one of their friends or relations, and perhaps even something of greater consequence, without the superior's leave, nor do they think that they act at all against their vow of poverty in this. Now, if they do not sin, it follows that we do not sin against our vow by disposing of things in like manner. All the fault that can be committed, is, that we do not act herein according to the perfection of poverty, nor show that submission we ought to our superiors, and to the rules and constitutions of our order. This objection is a strong one, and it is selected, in order that the answer to it may elucidate what I have already said, and what I shall hereafter say on this subject. I agree with you, that in some orders, the religious do, and may dispose of some things, as the objection says, without scruple or breach of poverty; but it does not follow from thence, that we can imitate them without committing sin; on the contrary I maintain, that we should hereby not only offend against the obedience we owe our rule, but also violate the vow of poverty. The reason of this difference, is, that these things are now permitted in some orders, either by the express or tacit consent of superiors, which tacit consent exists, divines say, when superiors know of a custom that has been introduced, and though able to prevent it, yet tolerate and connive at it; "for then silence gives consent". Now, a religious when he has either a tacit or express leave from his superior, does not offend against his vow of poverty by receiving or disposing of anything, and consequently the practice of those religious mentioned in the objection is lawful. But this does not hold in the society, where we endeavour to live up to the perfection and purity of poverty, and where there is no leave either tacit or express given for this practice. On the contrary, our custom is directly opposite to this; and hence one of our society would sin against his vow of poverty, should he so receive or dispose of anything, and the other religious above mentioned would equally offend, were he not protected by the permission. Religious women vow poverty, yet some of them have pensions to buy themselves habits, books, and other conveniencies; nor does any body look upon this as a fault in them, since their superiors permit this practice. Yet if any of the society should do this without leave, he would sin against his vow of poverty; nor can the practice of several learned and pious men in other orders, warrant the same amongst us. Other orders have either a tacit or express leave for it, the society has none; nay, its practice is quite contrary; and therefore the obligations set down in the other chapter are not bare scruples, but solid truths, grounded upon the very nature of poverty and the general consent of divines.

St. Bonaventure and Gerson, both of them very spiritual men and great divines, have left in their books several of these very cases we have set down; and in order to decide whether a religious can give or receive anything, they reduce the whole matter to this one point, viz., his having either an express or tacit leave from his superior. If he has not, they declare that a religious can neither give nor take, nor dispose of anything, without a breach of his vow of poverty; for he ceases to be poor and becomes proprietor, who accepts or disposes of things at pleasure. Gerson puts the case in the person of a procurator of a monastery, who has the money of the community in his hands, and he asks the question, whether this procurator would sin against his vow of poverty by buying a knife, a comb-case, or pair of spectacles either for himself or for another—nay, he descends to things yet more inconsiderable, as a needle or a little thread; and answers, that should he do these things by an express or tacit leave from his superior, there would be no sin, but without this leave he would break his vow of poverty; and the great chancellor of Paris, says the same of a religious, who gives to, or receives from a secular person, without his superior's permission. Thus you see how all divines agree, that the giving, taking, or disposing of anything without leave, is certainly forbidden all religious by the vow of poverty. But if any order permits a religious to have something in particular, or to receive presents from his friends and dispose of them, it is because in such order there is a tacit or express leave, otherwise the vow of poverty would be broken. Hence it follows (and pray, observe the consequence well), that in order to decide whether or not a religious has in this or that case violated his vow of poverty, we must first know the practice of his order, that we may thereby judge if it gives express or tacit consent on such occasions. For, unless you know this, you shall never be able to judge aright, there being in some orders many things permitted, by connivance and tacit consent, which are not so in others.

Hence it also follows, that though some authors hold that a religious who receives money from a secular person to buy books or anything else of that nature, does not sin, provided he exposes what he buys to the view of the community, and is ready also to give them up when the superior shall think fit, yet one of our society, by doing so, would break his vow of poverty. For those authors suppose that there is a tacit leave, and that the superiors are content with this act of resignation in the religious when called upon. But amongst us there is no such connivance or tacit leave, but a determination and express practice to the contrary. As to our cassock, cloaks, breviaries, or anything else which we are permitted to use, we must have such submission to, and dependance on our superior's will for them, that we must be ready to part with them when he pleases, otherwise we would act against our vow of poverty, and become proprietors. Nor can we receive money to buy a habit or books, or anything else, though we should expose them to the view of the whole world, and be disposed to give them up at the superior's command; for the practice in the society being quite contrary, involves a breach of the vow of poverty on the part of any that should do so. And should we take this liberty, and relax ever so little in this point, I do not doubt but that it would be reclaimed against in the congregations, and an immediate stop put to all further abuses in this kind, which would destroy the very foundations of that poverty we profess.

Divines make another observation upon this tacit consent or supposed leave, and tell us that it is not sufficient for a religious, in order to ask, receive, take, or keep anything, to know certainly that his superior, on being applied to, would instantly give him leave to do so, no more than it would be sufficient for him to go abroad or to write a letter upon the same presumption. Together with this, they say, that you must be very well assured that your superior would also be very willing you should accept or dispose of the thing without his leave, and that he would not take it ill though his leave were not asked. This is a true description of this tacit permission or leave, which is now introduced into several orders, and by virtue of which they may freely give or take without any farther permission. But this custom is not yet introduced into the society, where superiors are so far from being glad that their subjects do not apply to them on the like occasions, that they hold nothing more dear than to see the contrary strictly observed, and are never more displeased than at the least liberty or presumption in point of obedience. And for this reason we ought to act quite differently from some other orders in the point of poverty, and in some other particulars; for in this respect they are not at present so strictly bound as we are, though without doubt they were so at first, if we may credit their own histories; and we see some orders at present who live up to the primitive strictness and severity of their rule.

CHAPTER XIV.

That the vow of poverty obliges under pain of mortal sin.

It may now be asked if what we have said to be a breach of the vow of poverty is a mortal sin, or in what case is it mortal? All divines agree, as we have said before, that a breach of the vow of poverty is, at the same time, a sin against the seventh commandment, which prohibits theft. This presupposed, I answer, that as this commandment obliges under pain of mortal sin of its own nature, yet, if the thing stolen be very inconsiderable, for example, an apple, or a farthing, it is then only a venial sin; in like manner, the vow of poverty obliges under mortal sin, unless the transgression be so small, that it prove only venial. If you desire to know what kind of transgression against this vow is a mortal sin, you must first inform yourself what kind of theft is a mortal sin; for one is the measure of the other, and the theft which amounts to a mortal sin is a mortal breach of the vow of poverty, as all doctors hold who have written upon this subject.

For the further elucidation of this matter, some divines say, that there are two causes, whence arises the grievousness of this sin. The first is, an unjust usurpation of another man's goods against his will: the second is, a breach of a vow made to God. As to the first cause, they require the thing should be more considerable to make a sin mortal against poverty, than against the seventh commandment; because the goods a religious man disposes of, are not so properly another person's, as when an ordinary theft is committed; nor is the disposition with which it is done so contrary to the owner's intention as in theft. But if we consider the second cause, that which is sufficient to make theft a mortal sin, is also a mortal breach of the vow of poverty; the obligation we have contracted by the vow of poverty, of not taking or disposing of anything without our superior's consent, being far greater than that which the seventh commandment imposes upon us—namely, not to take another man's goods against his will.

In the affair of St. Gregory, which we lately quoted, we see that the money given the religious by his brother to buy him an under garment, was no more than three crowns, both according to the relation of Gregory and Surius, and it was to purchase that, which the monastery must have furnished him with, had not his brother's kindness prevented them; and yet St. Gregory judged it a mortal sin, as appears by the severe punishment and the excommunication he inflicted. Amongst modern authors who treat of this subject, some require three reals to make a mortal sin, others four, others five. And amongst the Carthusians a far less thing would be a mortal sin, and be sufficient to incur an excommunication, and to deprive one of their monks of Christian burial.

But let us put the case, that the thing be of greater value than divines require, and that three reals be too little to make a mortal sin against the vow of poverty: shall a religious who ought daily promote his advancement in perfection, expose himself to the danger and trouble of examining if the thing he has received, given, or kept, amounts precisely to six, or only to four reals, and thereby be at least in danger of plunging himself into mortal sin? It is ordinary for servants that go to market, to defraud their masters of a penny or a halfpenny in their bargains, and yet nobody says they sin mortally, by reason of the smallness of the sum; but does it become a religious to do the like, though it be only a venial sin? If therefore you are ashamed to do this, and you look upon it as an infamous thing, take care not to receive or give the least thing, under pretence that it is only a venial sin, for this is as infamous in you, as it is in a servant secretly to play the thief. We ought to be very cautious in a thing so essential as that which relates to one of the three vows. For he that would deliberately commit a sin against poverty under pretence that it is only venial, is in very great danger of sinning mortally against his vow. The desire of having and of giving and receiving, is a passion natural to man, and so violent that we may be easily deceived by it, and carried farther than we imagine. Besides, it will often happen that we are left in doubt and perplexity, whether the sin be mortal or not; now a religious ought never expose himself to doubts and incertitudes of this nature.

CHAPTER XV.

Whether a religious can, without leave of his superior, receive money in order to do works of charity with it; and what those cases are, wherein he would sin against his vow of poverty by doing so.

THE society requires of us so much purity and perfection in all things which concern holy poverty, and is so careful to take from us all pretences to have money at our own disposal, that we are forbidden by our institute to ask or receive money from any person, even our very penitents, in order to give alms or make restitution. So that if a penitent, who is obliged to restitution, should desire to leave money to be restored, in the hands of his ghostly father, he cannot take this charge upon him without leave of his superior. This rule is grounded upon reason, experience, and the doctrine and examples of holy men. It is conformable to the opinion of St. Basil; St. Francis Xaverius also very earnestly recommended the practice of it; and what St. Jerom relatès concerning St. Hilarion upon this subject is very remarkable. A rich man, out of whom St. Hilarion had cast a legion of devils, finding the saint to refuse a considerable sum of money, which he would have presented him as an acknowledgment of the favour done him, pressed him at last to accept of it and distribute it amongst the poor. The saint persisting in his refusal, said to him : You can distribute it yourself much better than I can; you who know many great cities, and can inform yourself of their poor inhabitants; as for me, I did not relinquish my own property in order to charge myself with that of another. It is our duty to assist our neighbours by good advice and all other charitable works of that nature, but not to become their almoners; for such a concourse of indigent persons as would come to us, would create so great confusion, that two porters at the gate would not be sufficient to give answers to them all, and the confessors would be also disturbed in their confession-seats, and hindered from preaching and other spiritual duties. The apostles themselves knew by experience that they could not be employed in such affairs without failing at the same time in their duty of preaching the word of God. "It is not fit", said they, "we should leave the word of God to serve at table"— *Acts*, vi. 2,—and therefore they committed that charge to others, that hereby being disengaged from the care of temporals, they might attend only to the conversion of souls. There are some who imagine this distribution of alms to be a very good way to gain the people's hearts and induce them to a frequent use of the sacraments, but they live under a very great mistake; for a man rather loses than gains by it on account of the persons displeased, who are always the greater number. For some are dissatisfied because they had nothing given them, others because they had not as much as they desired, and in the end most will complain and cry out that the charity was distributed rather according to favour than justice, and that we converted part of it to our own use. Besides, it can never be a good motive to bring people to confession, but, on the contrary, becomes prejudicial thereunto, giving occasion to penitents of inventing many lies and forgeries, thereby to move their confessor to have compassion, and bestow on them part of the charity he has to distribute. Notwithstanding this, a religious may, with leave of his superior, receive money to make restitution: for example, when the thing requires secrecy, and the penitent cannot restore it himself without loss of his reputation. Yet, in this very case, divines counsel the confessor to take an acquittance from the person to whom he makes restitution, and to give it afterwards to the penitent, who, though he may endeavour to hinder his confessor from doing it, and give signs of his great confidence in him, yet will be always glad when he sees the acquittance; he will be more edified at his confessor, and more easy within himself: nor will he give way to any of those suspicions which sometimes occur when the confessor neglects this precaution.

But since we are speaking of what the vow of poverty obliges to in rigour, it will not be amiss to propose those cases wherein, by receiving money for charitable uses without leave, we either sin against the vow of poverty, or barely trespass against the obedience due to our rule. Divines discuss this very question, whether or not a religious would sin against the vow of poverty, if he should, without permission of his superior, receive money of a secular person, not for himself, but to apply to charitable uses, in the name of him who gave it? One would think that in this he would not sin against his vow of poverty, since the money is not for his own use, nor to be distributed in his own name, but in the name of the party from whom he received it. Yet the decision of this question is, that there are two ways of receiving money or anything else that is to be given to another. If the giver says expressly that it is to be disposed of in his own name, and mentions the charities he would have it employed in, as, for example, when money is put into the hands of a confessor, either to make restitution or to distribute to the poor, then the religious that so receives it without leave of his superior, would only offend against the obedience he owes his rules, but not against his vow of poverty; for the giver would still remain master of it, and it would be disposed of at his pleasure, and the confessor would only be the instrument to convey it according to the other's will. But should the giver leave the free disposal of it to the confessor, and should the latter employ it all in charity, or in any other way, he would sin against his vow of poverty by receiving and disposing of it without permission from his superior. For, first, the giver, by doing so, deprives himself of all propriety in the thing, and transfers it as much as he can to the religious, in order to dispose of it as he pleases, and certainly no religious is capable of propriety. Secondly, it is not propriety only which is inconsistent with the vow of poverty, but also the use and free disposal of anything without leave, these two latter being a breach of the former, and equally prohibited all religious by their vow of poverty. Again, this use and free disposal of things is still more opposite to the vow of poverty than dominion or propriety, by reason it diverts a religious more from his duties, and proves a greater prejudice to him than propriety alone. Hence, the reason why the Church and holy fathers wish that no religious should have anything he might call his own, is, that being delivered from the care and trouble which the administration of temporals draws along with it, he might be the better qualified for the service of Almighty God: and by consequence, though a religious has neither the dominion nor propriety of another man's goods, but only the bare administration and use of them, without leave of his superior, yet hereby he sins against his vow of poverty. Would it not be very ridiculous, says St. Denis the Carthusian, speaking on this subject, if a father that had a son mad should content himself to take the propriety of a sword from him, but leave him the use of it? This, says he, is the practice of some religious, who are content not to hold anything in propriety, yet take upon them the use and administration of other people's goods, which is the most dangerous thing that attends riches, and which most diverts them from the duties of religion. There are some who assert the first cause I laid down concerning this matter to be equally with the rest contrary to the vow of poverty, it being an acceptance and disposal of money or something equivalent, without leave of superiors; yet they say the sin is only venial and not mortal, because they apply the money to the person's use for whom it was designed.

Here we find an answer to the difficulty which frequently occurs, which is, whether a religious would sin against his vow of poverty, in case he should, without leave of his superior, ask money of any one to assist his parents or friends, and having got the money, should either effectually give it himself, or desire the party who does the charity to give it, or send it, to the person for whom he begged it? To this I answer, that this religious, if he asks and receives this money with an intention to be master of it, and to dispose of it as he pleases, sins against his vow of poverty, although at the same time he should design to give it, and should accordingly give it afterwards, or send it in the name of the party from whom he had it. But if he does not take it to dispose of at his pleasure, and should speak thus to the giver: For my part, I have no need of it, nor can I receive it for my own use, but if you please to give it to such a person in necessity, or to leave it with me to give or send it to him as from you, I should be very much obliged to you, and thereby you would do a real act of charity. In this case, though the person should do this charity for the sake of the religious, and the religious should afterwards return him thanks for it, yet he would not sin against his vow of poverty, because he does not receive this money for his own use, nor pretend to be master of it, but is only an executor of the giver's will, and an intercessor for the poor. Much less would he offend against his vow, should the giver, at his request, send or give the money himself to the party for whom he petitioned; for though the charity really proceeds from the prayers and intercession of the said religious, yet this does not alter the case, nor attach either propriety or use of the thing to the religious. But, after all, though this practice be not contrary to the vow of poverty, yet it brings several inconveniencies along with it, when it is done without permission. And it is to be feared that these limits here prescribed would not stop persons thus disposed, but that they would go on even to a breach of their vow of poverty. For I cannot always examine whether the present be made to myself, or in what manner I received it, nor whether I am to give it in my own or another's name, or whether it comes from another or from myself. Besides it often happens that the desire of having money at our own disposal blinds us, and at last, under some plausible pretence, we come to act directly contrary to the vow of poverty, and therefore we ought to be very careful to avoid all danger of this kind. Wherefore, let us give no occasion of having that applied to us which St. Basil, as St. Cassian relates, said to a senator, who, having forsaken his dignity to become religious, reserved a small part of his estate to live upon, without being obliged to work and labour as the other religious were: "You have ordered the matter so", says St. Basil to him, "that now you are neither a senator nor a religious".

CHAPTER XVI.

Some examples in confirmation of what has been said.

It is related by St. Jerom, that one of the hermits that lived in the desert of Nitria, and who maintained themselves by labour, had a great desire to lay up a little money. This man, by eating little and working hard, got at last a hundred crowns together, and so died. When they came to bury him they found this money in his cell. Whereupon all the other hermits, who were about five thousand, dwelling in little cells at a distance from one another, assembled to consult what was to be done in this matter, and how they should dispose of the money. Some were for giving it to the poor, others to the Church, and others to the relations of the deceased party, who perhaps might stand in need of it. St. Macarius, and the Abbots Pambo and Isidore, with some more of the most ancient amongst them, inspired by the Holy Ghost, counselled them to bury the money with the corpse, and to pronounce over it these words of St. Peter, "Thy money be with thee to perdition"—*Acts*, viii. 20. This advice was followed. And St. Jerom would not have us think this sentence too severe or rigorous, but rather prudent and charitable; for it struck such a fear into all the fathers of the wilderness in Egypt, that they looked upon it as a very great crime to have any money found about them at the hour of death.

St. Austin relates an example very like the former, of one Januarius, a religious, who was looked upon as a saint; and I shall repeat his own words, which are very expressive and pathetic. We cannot, says he, sufficiently lament the loss of our brother Januarius, who, though he seemed the very model of obedience and poverty, yet has made an unhappy end. He begged his admittance amongst us with tears in his eyes, he promised to be a faithful observer of poverty all his life; and yet, at the same time, he reserved to himself without our knowledge the enjoyment of an estate in the world. O unfortunate profession, and faithless promise! His words promised what his heart detested, and we thought him holy and virtuous, who now proves a deceitful and impious impostor. He lived thus above twelve years, and his death was answerable to his life by secretly possessing what did not, or could not, belong to him. He died most miserably in sin, without acknowledging his fault, making a will in favour of a son he had in the world, without ever acquainting us with it. I wish he had but owned his crime at the hour of his death, for then we might have endeavoured to procure his pardon by our prayers; but, alas! he neither confessed it, nor repented of it; and, therefore, we ought not to look upon him at present as one of ours, but like one that had never been amongst us. Bind, then, his hands together; tie up in a cloth the hundred and eleven shekels which he had hid in the wall of his cell; put them into his hands, and bury them both together; and, with very deep sighs, pronounce these words, "Thy money be with thee to perdition"; for it is not lawful for us to employ that upon the necessities of our monastery which has been the price of his eternal damnation.

Cæsarius has a story of a Cistercian monk, who, lying upon his death-bed, confessed to his abbot, and forthwith had the blessed sacrament brought him, which he received into his mouth, but was not able to get it down his throat; hereupon the priest, taking it out, gave it to another religious that was sick, who received it with a great deal of devotion, and swallowed it with no less ease. A little after, this first religious died, and then they discovered the reason of this impediment, as well as of his ruin. For, when they washed his body before his burial, they found five pieces of money about him, which, though only brass, yet rendered him no less in fault than if they had been silver. The religious, seeing this, admired the judgments of God, and, by the abbot's orders, whom they had advertised of the matter, they buried the corpse in an open field, throwing the money upon it, and saying, "May this money, which thou hast kept in private, contrary to thy profession, perish with thee eternally". The abbot gave an account of this passage in the next general congregation of his order. The historian adds, that none ought to impute his not swallowing the sacred host to his sickness, for the very same day he had eaten a whole chicken that was boiled for him.

We read in the chronicles of St. Francis (p. ii. l. 1. c. 28), that there was a brother in one of the convents of his order who knew how to read a little, and, desirous to learn more, found means of procuring himself a Psalter. But, as St. Francis's rule prohibited all lay brothers to learn to read, the father-guardian, understanding he had got this book, asked him for it. He answered that he had it not. The guardian pressed him to tell where he had put it, and showed him that to live proprietor of anything, was to live in a continual breach of his vows; yet the brother would not hearken to what he said nor obey him. Not long after this, he fell dangerously sick, and the guardian, for fear that he should die in that state, commanded him, in virtue of holy obedience, to restore the book or tell him where he had hid it; but this unhappy man, being hardened in his sin, died without declaring anything. The night after he was buried, when the sacristan rung to matins, he saw a frightful ghost coming suddenly towards him, and hearing a melancholy mournful voice, without being able to understand anything distinctly, he was seized with such fear, that he fell down as if dead. The religious, having heard the first peal to matins, wondered why the bell did not ring again, and, after having waited a little, they went to the church and found the sacristan lying along as a dead man, who, coming to himself, told them what had happened. After they had begun to sing matins, the same ghost appeared again, crying and howling most lamentably, but did not utter any word so clearly as to be understood. The guardian, to encourage his religious, who seemed very much affrighted, commanded the spirit in the name of God to tell who he was and what he wanted there. To whom it replied: I am the lay brother whom you buried yesterday. Then the guardian asked him if he stood in need of the prayers of the religious; to whom he answered, no; for they could do him no good at present, as he was eternally damned on account of the book which he had kept in propriety at the hour of his death. Since, therefore, replied the guardian, we cannot do you any service, I command you in the name of our Lord Jesus Christ to depart hence immediately, and to return no more to disturb us. These words were scarce uttered, when the ghost disappeared, and was never seen after.

Denis the Carthusian relates the following passage (*in Scala Relig.*) A religious finding his habit torn, went into the tailor's shop and took a piece of cloth to mend it without having leave. He fell sick soon after, and thought himself a great servant of God: for he felt no remorse of conscience; nor could the devils find anything wherewith to disturb him, which made him wait for death with a great deal of resignation and comfort. Being thus disposed, he chanced to look towards the corner of his cell, where his habit hung, and saw the Devil in the shape of a monkey sitting upon it, and licking with satisfaction the piece of cloth wherewith he had mended it. He presently perceived the fault he had committed in taking the piece of cloth without leave; and sending for his superior, he confessed it to him; and he begged his pardon, and the Devil immediately vanished out of his sight.

It is related in the history of St. Dominic's order, that whilst the holy man Regnadus was prior of the convent at Boulogne, a lay brother of the same house received a piece of cloth to mend his habit from a person in the world without leave of his superior. The good prior having notice of this, called the brother to the chapter-house, where he gave him as severe a check as if he had been a thief and traitor, and enjoined him a public discipline, and burned the piece of cloth in full chapter before him and all the rest of the religious.

We read in the same history, that Albertus the Great, when provincial of the Dominicans, prohibited all his religious, under great penalties, to have even the least sum of money either in their own or another's keeping, either for their own or another's use. When, some time after, they held their provincial congregation, in which it was proved that a certain religious who died a few days before, had not observed this prohibition, Albertus punished this transgression so severely, that he caused the body to be taken and buried in a dunghill, in imitation of the ancient fathers of the desert, who treated thus their monks that died proprietors of anything, however trifling.

THE FOURTH TREATISE.

ON CHASTITY.

CHAPTER I.

Of the excellency of chastity, and the degrees by which we ought to raise ourselves to perfection in this virtue.

"THIS is the will of God, that you become holy, that you abstain from all uncleanness, and that every one of you keep your body entire and undefiled; for God has not called us to impurity, but to sanctity"—I. *Thess.*, iv. 3, 4, etc. St. Bernard says, that chastity is meant here by the word sanctity: and our blessed Saviour himself observes, that chastity renders us like unto angels: " In the resurrection", says he, " they shall neither marry nor be given in marriage, but be like the angels of Heaven"—*Matt.*, xxii. 30. St. Cyprian speaks thus to virgins: you already enjoy part of the blessing which one day you shall fully possess in glory; for you are not inferior to angels, as long as you remain chaste and poor. In like manner Cassian assures us that no virtue renders us so like to angels as chastity, by the help of which we live in bodies, yet so as if we carried no flesh about us, being now transformed by it into pure spirits, according to these words of St. Paul, " You live no longer in flesh, but in spirit"—*Rom.*, viii. 9. And in this we are superior to the angels themselves, who being incorporeal, it is no wonder they live pure and spotless; but it certainly deserves far greater admiration, that man in this frail and mortal body, which continually wars against the spirit, should live as if he had no flesh about him.

Morever our blessed Saviour, to show how pleasing this virtue is to him, when the mystery of his incarnation was to be accomplished, chose a virgin for his mother, who by vow had consecrated her virginity to God, as the holy fathers observe. St. John also saw virgins follow the Lamb Jesus upon Mount Sion, that is in Heaven, wheresoever he went, and heard them sing a new song to him which none else could sing. " I saw", says he, " the Lamb upon Mount Sion, and one hundred and forty-four thousand with him, singing, as it were, a new song, and which none else can sing, but only these hundred and forty-four thousand which he had redeemed from the Earth. These are such as were never defiled by women, they are virgins, who follow the Lamb wheresoever he goes"—*Apoc.*, xiv. 1, 3. St. Gregory on this passage says, that virgins are described on the mountain with Christ, because the highest degree of glory is due to the merit of chastity.

St. John the Evangelist is styled in Scripture, "the disciple whom Jesus loved"—*John*, xxi. 7,—and St. Jerom and St. Austin assign his virginity as the reason of this his title. And the holy Church in the office of St. John says, "that Jesus loved him more tenderly than the other apostles; the prerogative of his chastity claiming this privilege as its due; for he was not only a virgin when he called him to be an apostle, but remained so all his life". And hence the words of the Proverbs are by some not unfitly applied to him, "he that loves purity of heart shall, by the grace of his discourse, be in the king's favour"—*Prov.*, xxii. 11. It was on account of his virginity that our Saviour loved him so well as to permit him to sleep upon his own breast, and that he bestowed several favours upon him which he did not confer upon the rest of the apostles. Hence it was, that St. Peter, who had been married, durst not ask Jesus when he would eat his last supper, but desired St. John to propose the question for him. On Easter-day, blessed Magdalen bringing the news of Christ's resurrection, St. Peter and St. John ran immediately to the monument, but St. John got thither first. At another time, when some of the apostles were fishing in a little boat upon the sea of Tiberias, Jesus stood on the shore, and there was none of them knew him but St. John, who said to St. Peter, "Look yonder, behold, it is our Lord"—*John*, xxi. 7. "There was none in the company", says St. Jerom, "that was a virgin except John, and therefore one virgin knew another". And what other reason was there but this, that induced our Saviour, by his dying words upon the cross, to recommend his mother to him, "who", as St. Jerom says, "recommended his virgin mother to his virgin disciple"?

Intending to be brief in this treatise, in imitation of our holy founder, I will not enlarge, or write a panegyric upon chastity, but will lay down the seven degrees of it which Cassian has established, and by which, as by so many steps, we can mount to the most sovereign perfection of this angelical virtue. The first degree, is not to suffer ourselves to be overcome by any impure thought or motion whatsoever. The second is, not to entertain such thoughts for a moment, but immediately to fly from them and remove the occasion of them. The third is, not to be moved at the sight of a woman. This degree is more perfect than the two former, by reason of our frail and vicious nature, which is too apt to rebel on such occasions. The fourth is, not to encourage, upon any account, the least unchaste motion of our body when we are awake. The fifth is, that when we treat of or study this matter, we do it with all tranquillity and purity of mind, and keep our imagination as steady and quiet as if we were studying architecture, the art of gardening, or any other subject of that nature. St. Ignatius attained this degree of perfection at the very first beginning of his conversion. The sixth is, not to have, even in our sleep, any impure fancies or unchaste dreams, which certainly is an argument of a pure heart, as well as of a memory freed from all those filthy representations. Whereas on the contrary, impure illusions of the night, though they happen without sin, yet prove that the sensual appetite is not yet subject to reason, and that the imagination still retains some of those bad ideas. The seventh and last degree is a particular grace, says Cassian, which God has bestowed upon some few, as upon the Abbot Serenus and some other saints, and consists in being freed, both asleep and awake, from all those motions of the flesh which nature alone excites in us. This shows that by virtue of this grace, our concupiscence is rendered so peaceable and obedient, that we, in some sort, enjoy the happiness and privilege, which man enjoyed in the state of innocence, and that "the body of sin is destroyed in us"—*Rom.*, vi. 6,—as St. Paul says. Grace works so powerfully in those that have arrived at this last degree, that it takes from sin all the force and power it usually has. They feel no disordered motions in their flesh, nor anything that tends that way—nay, they live in a body of flesh as if they had no flesh about them. I do not, however, mean to say, that these kinds of motions in the flesh, either in sleep or otherwise, are contrary to chastity, even when it is in the greatest perfection, since they are no more than a natural effect, and consequently may happen to the greatest saints. God by a special grace has exempted from these, some of his servants, whom he has been pleased to raise to the most sublime perfection. There are others whom he scarce permits to be molested by them; and he has been mercifully pleased to grant to others the grace of appeasing and suppressing the rebellion of their flesh so quickly and easily that they enjoyed a perpetual peace. These are the persons that live like angels, whom we ought to propose to ourselves for imitation, as St. Ignatius advises us in his constitutions, by forcing ourselves "to imitate their angelical purity". And here it is to be observed, that the word "force" implies more than a bare essay, endeavour, or labour. The saint would have us offer violence to ourselves in this case, and even to use our utmost endeavours, as we ordinarily do in the most difficult enterprises. His meaning is, that we should employ all our force in order to make ourselves masters of this evangelical virtue—we must offer early violence to ourselves by a constant application to the practice of all the virtues, and particularly of mortification. For though chastity be the free gift of God, and placed beyond the reach of our endeavours, yet God requires that we should do as much as lies in us in order to obtain it; our endeavours being as it were the price by which it is to be purchased.

CHAPTER II.

That to live chaste, we must necessarily mortify ourselves, and keep a strict watch over our senses, particularly our eyes.

"THE ancient fathers, taught by long experience", says Cassian, "thought it impossible for religious, especially the younger sort, to subdue concupiscence, unless they had first been accustomed to mortify their will by obedience". St. Basil and other holy fathers prove that the practice of all the other virtues is necessary in order to obtain and preserve chastity in its perfection, because in effect they all contribute to it and are its guardians. But as this is sufficiently treated of throughout this work, and chiefly in the second volume, I shall only speak at present of such means as are in a particular manner conducive to this end. The first is, that if we desire to acquire chastity in perfection, and to keep it in the same degree, we must guard very diligently all the avenues of our soul, and chiefly our eyes, the ordinary and most common passage of evil to our heart.

St. Gregory, writing on that passage of Isaias, "who are these that fly like clouds, and sit at their windows like doves?"—*Isai.*, lx. 8,—says, that the just are compared to clouds, because they are above all Earthly things; and to pigeons, which retire to the dove-cot, because being recollected within themselves, and not carried away by the consideration of exterior things, they are thus prevented from even desiring them. But it is not so with those who give a liberty to their eyes; for they frequently desire what they see, as David did, who, though he had frequently raised himself as a cloud to Heaven, and employed much time in divine contemplation, yet by one glance of his eye consented to very unlawful desires. "Death", says Jeremiah, "has entered by my windows"—*Jer.*, ix. 21; "and my soul is become a prey to mine eyes"—*Lament.*, iii. 51. And St. Gregory gives us this wholesome counsel, "never to cast our eyes upon what is forbidden us to desire"; for it is much to be feared that the object will captivate our hearts by means of our curiosity, and that when we least think on it we will be unfortunately surprised.

This was the reason why Job took so great precaution that he said, "I have made a league with my eyes not even to think on a virgin"—*Job*, xxxi. 1; and on these words St. Gregory the Great starts this objection: What kind of treaty would he make with his eyes in order to thinking? Methinks he should rather have made it with his understanding and imagination; for only shut your eyes, and there needs no further treaty with them. In reply, however, to himself, this holy doctor commends this league of Job as a very wise and rational one. Job knew, says he, that the eyes were the inlets to all the malice of the heart, and that if he kept a strict guard upon them and the avenues of his senses, his interior would be secure and out of danger. If you therefore wish to prevent all evil thoughts, let your eyes be modestly reserved, and make a league with them never to look upon anything which is not permitted you to desire. Who would not be astonished, says St. Chrysostom, writing upon the same passage, that so great a man as Job, who had made head against the Devil, fought hand to hand with him, and triumphed as well over all his stratagems as his power, should not dare to look a woman in the face? He did this, adds the same holy father, to teach the greatest proficients in virtue to keep a restraint and guard over themselves.

St. Ephrem prescribes temperance, silence, and a modest custody of the eyes, as extremely conducive to the preservation of chastity in its purity. For though you practise the two first, yet a neglect of the last will endanger your chastity. And as water is lost when the conduit pipe is broken, which, instead of keeping it, lets it out, so when the soul sallies forth through the eyes, and wanders abroad, chastity will quickly be lost. Another saint compares the sight of a woman to a poisoned arrow, whose every wound reaches the heart; and also to a spark of fire, which lighting upon a straw, unless immediately put out, sets it all on fire. In like manner the evil thoughts caused by the sight of a woman, bring along with them nothing but fire and confusion into the soul, unless timely stifled and prevented.

Surius says, that Hugh, bishop of Grenoble, heard women's confessions every day for above fifty years together, and conversed with all sorts of persons, who addressed themselves to him concerning their affairs by reason of his great sanctity, and yet that he never looked any woman so much in the face as to know her by sight, except one, and this so slightly that he did not know whether she was old or young, handsome or ugly. This saint used to say, that we ought to be extremely cautious in this point; for if we once give scope to our eyes, we shall never be able to deny admittance to bad thoughts into our hearts.

St. Bernard one day stood still to look upon a woman, without reflecting upon the action; but, taking himself in the fact, he conceived such indignation against himself, that he immediately went and stood up to the neck in a frozen lake, where he remained till he was taken out half dead.

CHAPTER III.

That we ought to be very nice and careful, even in the least thing which relates to chastity.

THE more excellent chastity is in itself, the more it ought to be our care to preserve it. For, generally speaking, in all virtues we ought to be very cautious, even of the most minute things that relate to them, since he "that contemns small ones falls by little and little"—*Ecclus.*, xix. i.,—even into the greatest inconveniencies. But this rule holds chiefly in chastity, wherein the least thing may be of very great prejudice. The better a thing is in the esteem of the world, the more the least defect is taken notice of. This observation is in a particular manner applicable to chastity; for, being the most delicate of virtues, it is, of course, the most easily wounded. A holy man very justly compared chastity to a looking-glass, which is tarnished by the least breath. It is thus the least thing tarnishes chastity and makes it lose all its lustre. Hence it is that we ought to be very careful in preserving its beauty by mortifying our senses, rejecting every evil thought as soon as it offers itself, and by carefully avoiding everything from which we may apprehend any danger. A flame leaves always more or less some mark behind it where it has been, and though it does not burn yet it blackens. In the same manner some things, though they do not burn us, yet blacken us, inasmuch as they create in our souls black and cloudy thoughts, repugnant to chastity, and inciting the body to impurity.

It is an admirable saying of St. Ignatius, that whatever regards chastity admits of no interpretation. No one must trust himself in this case, nor presume that he can go so far and no farther, without danger; for how can any man be secure of this? Yet, suppose he were, I would fain know whether he can promise himself not to transgress those bounds he has prescribed, since the least thought may carry him farther than he is aware of. When we walk upon slippery ground, we go step by step, and propose to ourselves to go only so far; however, the weight of our body and the nature of the ground often carries us farther than we designed. So fares it with us in the business of chastity: every step we make is upon slippery ground, and the corruption of nature hangs so heavy upon us, that it easily carries us beyond our mark. In fine, chastity is so delicate that the least thing wounds it, and therefore we ought to be extremely cautious of exposing it to the least danger. "This is the rich treasure which we carry in earthen vessels"—II. *Cor.*, iv. 7,—which, if once broken, all is lost; therefore we ought to be more attentive and vigilant in blocking up every passage by which impurity may find a way to our hearts.

We read of a certain religious, who, though favoured by God with the gift of chastity, yet never omitted his former care and moderation both in his looks and words, and was extremely vigilant in avoiding the least occasion of unclean thoughts. The religious of the same monastery asked him once, why he was so much upon his guard, since God had favoured him with the gift of chastity. To whom he answered thus: If in the smallest matters I endeavour to do what I ought, and as well as I can, God will give his grace to carry me through greater: whereas, should I neglect the former, it is more than I know whether God's grace will assist me in the latter; or I should at least hereby deserve to be forsaken by him, and so fall into sin. This is the reason why I keep continual watch over myself; for though the things seem small and inconsiderable in themselves, yet I am resolved to do what lies in me, thereby the better to discharge my duty. Surius says, that St. Thomas of Aquin, though he had received the gift of chastity, and been assured by an angel that he would never lose it, and that he need not be uneasy at any unchaste temptation, yet made it his business to avoid even the sight of a woman, and banished far from him every object whence the least impression of impurity might arise.

If we desire to preserve chastity unspotted and in its vigour, we must adopt these holy practices, or else we may justly fear that sad disaster which Job, after he had said, "I have made a league with mine eyes never to think of a woman", subjoins: "For without this, what part will God have in me?"—*Job*, xxxi. 1, 2; which is as much as if he had said: If I do not take care to guard my senses, to avoid all occasions of evil, to reject impure thoughts, and to make account of the smallest things in this matter, I shall presently give way to unlawful desires, and so forfeit the grace of God. The Devil acts in this business as a thief that is going to break into a house, who, finding the windows too narrow for himself to enter in, thrusts in a boy to open the door on the inside. Bad suggestions, want of recollection, too much liberty of our senses, and a thousand such like occasions, are the engines the Devil makes use of to force a passage into our soul. We must endeavour, therefore, to see beforehand all occasions, and to avoid them with all possible care; for we cannot take too many precautions in this matter.

Cassian applies these words of St. Paul to our purpose:

"And every one that striveth for the mastery refraineth from all things"—I. *Cor.*, ix. 25,—and says, if those who are to run or wrestle at the Olympic games, abstain from anything which might in the least weaken their bodies; if they deny themselves all sorts of victuals which might do them the least harm, and continually give themselves to such exercises as improve their strength; if they even wear plates of lead upon their reins, as well to increase their agility as to prevent the illusions of the night, which might affect their strength, and all this "to gain a corruptible crown"—I. *Cor.*, ix. 25,—what ought we then to do in defence of our chastity, which will procure us a crown that is everlasting?

CHAPTER IV.

That the least offence against chastity is to be told in confession.

ST. BONAVENTURE, speaking of confession, lays down this rule, which is very profitable and useful for all sorts of persons. He says that, however trifling the things which occur against chastity may be, yet they are never to be concealed in confession under pretence that they are no sin, or at least but a venial one, which is not necessary to be confessed; for this has been the occasion of infinite disorders. The ruin of many a soul has begun with this. God preserve you, therefore, from ever giving the Devil this entrance into your heart, or opening this gate to him; he will require nothing more to destroy you. For, in a short time, shame, joined to the little account you make of these things, will impose a belief upon you, that those which really are sinful, or which, at least, are much to be doubted of, are not so in effect; and thus at last you will dispense with yourself from declaring anything of it in confession. Persons who are naturally inclined to virtue, and who very rarely commit mortal sin, are very subject to this vicious bashfulness when they fall into any sins of the flesh. It is then that pride and a desire of being esteemed (two vices rooted in our nature) awake, and make us believe that we shall hereby lose our credit, at least with our confessor, and so put us upon finding out reasons why the thing we blush to own should be no mortal sin, and consequently that it is not to be confessed under a strict obligation. But, supposing we proceed to accuse ourselves of it, yet we oftentimes so mince the matter, that our confessor is at a loss to know what we would be at, and hence we might as well have concealed it entirely. For an accusation in confession ought to be so clear, that the confessor, on hearing it, should understand the grievousness of the sin; and hence, when the penitent speaks in such obscure terms, that he does not make known either the sin itself or the grievousness and necessary circumstances of it, he, in this respect, might as well have not confessed at all. Now, it is bashfulness, or rather pride, that blinds the penitent and leads him into this error of not confessing in clear terms. This is, moreover, a sign that he has no true sorrow for his faults, since he has not the courage to declare them as he should do in confession; for had he a real regret for his sins, he would offer this shame to God in order to satisfy for them. And I must needs say that the bare repugnance we find to accuse ourselves of a fault ought to make us suspect all the reasons or plausible pretences which dissuade us from revealing it; and it is worth our while thus to discover it, though it were only to overcome the difficulty we feel to mortify ourselves, and to prevent the flesh and the Devil from domineering over the spirit.

But what renders this still more necessary is, that in the matter of chastity there are many things which ignorant people do not think to be mortal, when they really are so. There are other things so doubtful, that it is not easy positively to determine whether they be mortal sins or not, and yet we are obliged under pain of mortal sin to confess these as well as those which are so in reality. So that the bare doubt whether sin be mortal or not, is sufficient to oblige the penitent, under pain of mortal sin, to confess it, and his omitting to do so will render his confession and communion sacrilegious. It happens sometimes that even the confessor himself, though an able divine, cannot decide whether the sin be mortal or venial; how then shall the penitent dare to take upon him to be a judge in his own cause, and deciding the fact he has committed to be no mortal sin, exempt himself from the obligation of confessing it? This is too great a risk, especially when we find ourselves inclined to conceal the fault, or at least to diminish it and make it appear less, in order at the same time to diminish our shame. For my part, I would not answer for a penitent thus disposed. But every man's conscience is the best judge in this case: for he that accuses himself of several small things in confession, cannot but feel remorse at his attempt to conceal other things which he knows to be of far greater consequence. Would you venture then at the hour of your death to pass such things over in silence? No certainly; wherefore take care not to do it at present. For not only our confessions, but all our other actions, ought to be done as if we were going to die. St. Gregory says, " that it is a sign of a good soul to find a fault where there is none"; on the contrary, it is a sign of being ill-disposed, not to fear sin where there are grounds for such fear.

Some will say, that they may lawfully do this to prevent scruples; and this is another wile which the Devil practises in order to deceive them. To accuse one's self of the things I speak of, is not to be scrupulous; for persons who make profession of piety accuse themselves of things far more inconsiderable, and that not from necessity or scruple, but from respect and veneration for the most blessed sacrament, which they are to receive after confession. So great purity is necessary to approach this sacrament, that the masters of a spiritual life advise us to accuse ourselves of all things relating to chastity, though in themselves they are no sins at all. I accuse myself, Reverend Father, you ought to say, of having had some temptations of impurity; and if you think that there was on your part a little negligence either in your admitting them, or in your not instantly banishing them (as happens but too frequently on account of our corrupt nature), then are you to declare this negligence, however trifling it may be. But if you believe that all this passed without any fault of yours, you can still accuse yourself to have had evil thoughts, and humbly add, but by the grace of God I hope they happened through no fault of mine, for I resisted them as much as in my power. We are to do the same whenever we have any thoughts against faith. Nay, in the matter of chastity, it is recommended to us to accuse ourselves of things which are less than even these I have mentioned: for example, of what happens to us in our sleep, which really is no sin, by reason it is not voluntary in us. Not that it is necessary to accuse ourselves of these night illusions, when we know that we have noways given occasion to them beforehand, nor consented to them when they happened; yet notwithstanding it is laudable to confess them for our greater humiliation; and the best and devoutest persons being in the like circumstances, always confess them before they go to communion, out of respect to the holy sacrament of the altar. Divines are wont to inquire whether or not such an illusion ought to hinder us from communion. And they answer, that it would show far greater respect to defer it to another day; unless there be some obstacle, as would be that of the scandal which an individual would give by abstaining from communion on a day that all the religious communicated. But when on such occasions a person avails himself of the permission he has to communicate, it is good at least to follow the advice which we have given.

CHAPTER V.

Of the nature of love; how violent and dangerous a passion it is— how much we ought to dread it.

LOVE is the most dangerous of all passions: for, as it is the most strong and violent of all, so we find that it is the most difficult to be conquered, and the most capable of bringing on our utter ruin. St. Austin, to show the power of love, and how much we ought to fear it, selects two examples from holy writ: the first is taken from the disobedience of Adam. What made Adam, says this saint, break God's command and eat the forbidden fruit? Was he so credulous as to fancy that eating it would make him like God, as the serpent told Eve? No; it is not at all probable that he, who was endowed with so much wisdom, should be so blinded as to believe such an improbability. This is what the apostle says, "Adam was not seduced, but it was the woman who being seduced was the cause of his fall"—I. *Tim.*, ii. 14. It was Eve, therefore, and not Adam, that was deceived; he gave no credit to the serpent. Hence Almighty God asked Eve, "Why hast thou done this?" And she replied, "The serpent deceived me, and I did eat"—*Gen.*, iii. 13. But when he put the same question to Adam, he did not answer: The woman whom thou gavest me deceived me, and I did eat; he only said, "The woman whom thou didst assign me for my companion, gave me some of the fruit of the tree, and I did eat"— *Gen.*, iii. 12. His affection and love for her were so great, that rather than afflict her, he complied with what she desired, so that it was love deceived him. Nor was it a sensual love which subdued him; no, but he was subdued by a love of benevolence, as those sometimes are who offend God rather than displease a friend. This was the gate by which sin, death, and all other miseries and misfortunes entered into the world.

The other example is Solomon's idolatry. What was it, says St. Austin, that made Solomon an idolater? Certainly the wisest of men could never be so stupid as to attach divinity to an idol, or think it useful to worship it. There must be then some other cause why he offered incense to them. Would you know what it was? It was love, as the Scripture positively declares in these words—" He loved a great many women that were strangers and gentiles, concerning whom God had given this commandment to the children of Israel: none of you shall marry any of these women, nor shall any of their people espouse your daughters; for certainly they will pervert you, and make you worship their gods. Solomon notwithstanding loved them most passionately, and in his old age his heart was turned away by them to adore their strange gods"—III. *Kings*, xi. 1, etc. Solomon did not obey God's orders, and therefore what God had foretold happened to him. For most of his concubines differing from each other in their way of worship, he ordered them to have particular idols set up that they might adore them, and he himself adored them and offered incense to them. "Not", says St. Austin, "that Solomon judged their idols worthy of adoration, but being besotted with love, he was afraid to offend those women, whom he was so passionately fond of as to idolize them in his heart".

The saints and masters of a spiritual life, taught by these two sad examples, and by many more of the like nature, advise us to stand continually upon our guard against this dangerous passion, and against all the occasions which may give birth to it. And let no one imagine, say they, that even the love which is most pure, and which is founded only on virtue and merit, is free from danger. For however pious the conversation may be—however likely to promote spiritual advancement,—yet there is ever cause to fear, and one cannot be too much on his guard. The reason is, because all holy doctors state, particularly St. Bonaventure, that spiritual love easily degenerates into that which is carnal and sensual. It is at first the best and purest wine. But it afterwards happens, according to the words of Isaias, " your wine is mixed with water" —*Isai.*, i. 22,—that they mix it with water, which destroys all its goodness. It is a great cordial of itself, yet it is often spoiled and adulterated by other mixtures, and thus it is that the Devil lays his baits to seduce us. In this he acts like the bridegroom of Cana in Galilee, who told his steward that waited at the marriage feast, "that it was the custom to serve in the best wine first, and after the guests were well warmed to bring in worse"—*John*, ii. 10. The Devil wishes to make those believe who are engaged in such friendship, that virtue is their only object, that piety is the sole cause of their correspondence, and that an advancement in good is their only motive for engaging in this particular familiarity. But when once the engagement is made, he discovers his malice and venom. All the fine things he showed them at first were but a bait to draw them into his snare. Nor does it weary him to keep a person long in this error; for he thinks not the time long which he devotes to this project, if he can at last but compass the end of his design, which is to change chaste and virtuous love into that of flesh and blood. How many, says St. Bonaventure, have begun their friendship under the appearance of piety, imagining that their only objects were the service of God and their own salvation! And perhaps this was really the case at first; yet afterwards this virtuous and holy friendship degenerated by little and little, and entertainments not altogether spiritual crept in, " and so what was begun spiritually unfortunately ended carnally"—*Gal.*, iii. 3.

Gerson relates a story of a holy man, no less commendable for his learning than virtue, who, instructing for some time a young woman of great sanctity, and having had many pious discourses with her, came at last to conceive such a violent affection for her, that he could not refrain from paying her very frequent and long visits, and had her, when absent, always in his thoughts. Though an affection of this nature could not be from God, yet as, according to himself, he had no bad intention (in which particular many are deluded and blinded), he was so far overseen, that he did not believe there was any harm at all or any illusion of the Devil in it. Nay, he persisted in this error, till being once obliged to take a long journey, he found by the great difficulty he felt in leaving her, that his kindness for her was not so spiritual as he imagined, and that had not God by this absence taken him from the occasion, he was on the point of falling into very great disorders. The same Gerson, speaking of the dangers and illusions of love, says, that everything which has the appearance of charity, is not charity; that all is not gold that glitters; and adds, that a holy man used to say that nothing caused so much diffidence and fear in him as love, even between persons of great sanctity and eminent virtue. And to this purpose he cites these words of the wise man, "There is a way that seems right to a man, and yet it leads to death"—*Prov.*, xvi. 25,—and such, says he, is the way we are speaking of.

CHAPTER VI.
Certain remedies against temptations to impurity.

IN the fourth treatise of the second part of this work, we have touched on several remedies against these temptations, but in this place we shall treat of them more at large. The first that presents itself is prayer, recommended to us by the saints as the most sovereign remedy against all sorts of temptations, and taught us also by the Son of God himself, when he gave this counsel and admonition to his apostles, "Watch and pray, that you enter not into temptation"—*Mat.*, xxvi. 41. Venerable Bede says, that as a noise and outcry makes thieves run away, and brings the neighbours to our aid, even so the voice of prayer makes the devils fly, and calls the saints and angels to our assistance. We read of St. Bernard, that an improper woman finding him all alone, and tempting him to commit sin, he found no better remedy to deliver himself from the danger than to cry out, thieves, thieves. Now, if the voice of one man in a fright is so powerful against thieves, what force must we not allow to earnest prayers against our invisible enemies, who would rob our souls of grace? And how can we but hope that they will soon betake themselves to flight, when once we begin to call upon God for help?

A frequent meditation on the passion, and putting ourselves in the wounds of our Saviour, is an admirable remedy against all suggestions to impurity. "There is no remedy so powerful", says St. Austin, "against the heat of concupiscence, as the remembrance of our Saviour's passion. In all my difficulties, I never found anything so efficacious as the wounds of Christ. In them I sleep secure; from them I derive new life"—*In Manuali*, c. 23. A grave doctor observes that the gospel, speaking of the wound in our Saviour's side, does not say that Christ was wounded in the side, but, "that a soldier opened his side with a lance"— *John*, xix. 34,—as if the holy Scripture would signify to us, that the way to Jesus' heart is open, and that we ought to retire thither, as "into the holes of a rock and caverns of a wall"— *Cant.*, ii. 14. St. Bernard proposes the same remedy to us in this manner: As soon as you feel any temptation of impurity, apply yourself to think of the passion of the Saviour of the world, and make the following act: " My God is nailed to a cross, and shall I admit of these most unlawful pleasures?" Thus the faithful Urias, when arrived from the army to give David an account of the siege of Rabba, would not, though greatly fatigued, sleep in his own house, but answered thus to David, when he asked the reason of it, "The ark of God, and the people of Israel and Juda, are still in the camp; Joab, my general, with a great many more of your servants, sleep upon the ground; and shall I go eat and drink, and sleep with my wife? I swear by your sacred life and my own, that I will never do it"—II. *Kings*, xi. 2. Let us imitate his zeal, and say as he did : Lord, you are fastened to a cross, to atone by your sufferings for man's sinful pleasures; I am resolved, therefore, not to give myself up to that pleasure which cost you so dear.

There are others who, when tempted, help themselves by remembering in general the four last things, as the wise man advises, " in all your actions, remember your last end, and you will never sin"—*Ecclus.*, vii. 40. Several also make use of the consideration of Hell in particular, and seriously weigh that saying of St. Gregory—Pleasure is momentary, but the punishment due to it is eternal. And without doubt, " to descend alive into Hell", by an act of faith, and to consider the torments there, which shall never have an end, but last as long as God shall be God, is a means very proper to prevent our falling into sin. There are others who find much comfort and assistance from the contemplation of eternal glory, by reflecting what folly and madness it is to lose that and God for all eternity, only for a moment's pleasure, and to neglect those things which God invites us to, and to which he has inseparably annexed such glorious rewards, in order to perform what the Devil solicits us to, and which will infallibly be punished by endless pains. Others find much profit from the consideration of death and the last judgment : all these considerations are very good, and every one would do well to make use of that which he finds to move him most. Sometimes one, sometimes another, will make a more lively impression upon us, so that it will be no small advantage to put them all in practice occasionally.

To make the sign of the cross upon our forehead and heart, and earnestly invoke the holy name of Jesus, is also a remedy no less profitable than comfortable. The effects of this have been wonderful, and we read in history of many miracles which God has wrought by this means. Devotion to the blessed Virgin is likewise most profitable in all our difficulties; and hence, all persons should practise this devotion, and fly to her with confidence in all their necessities. For it is impossible that she who carried the Eternal Mercy nine months in her bowels, should not be most merciful herself. She is the mother of mercy, the advocate of sinners, whom she loves most tenderly, knowing how much her dear Son loved them, and how much they cost Him. Nay, she knows, moreover, that sinners were the occasion of the Eternal Word's taking flesh upon him in her sacred womb, and of her becoming thereby the mother of God. For this reason her tenderness increases towards them, and she intercedes the more willingly for them with her Son, from whom she obtains whatsoever she pleases. For what is it that a son can refuse his mother, especially such a son to such a mother? This made St. Bernard cry out: "If there be one in the whole world, O sacred Virgin, that can say you failed to succour him after he called upon you in necessity, let him speak not of your mercy"—*Serm.* 4, *de Assumpt.* Now, if application to the blessed Virgin be very profitable in all troubles and temptations in general, it must certainly be much more in what relates to the virtue of chastity in particular. For she being herself most pure and immaculate, and a virgin by preëminence, is particularly inclined to show her care of those who call upon her in order to maintain their purity. Some doctors, speaking of the Baptist's extraordinary purity, which he always kept free from the least stain of sin, ascribes it to the visit our blessed Lady paid St. Elizabeth, and to her three months' stay with her. "This visit", says St. Ambrose, "related no less to his soul than to his body; for the blessed Virgin's acquaintance with her cousin Elizabeth, was not the only thing that kept her so long at Hebron, but the advantage so great a prophet was to reap from thence was partly the cause of her stay"—*Lib.* ii. *Sup. Luc.*, c. 9. For if, upon the first arrival, the Baptist was sanctified, and leaped for joy in his mother's womb; if upon the first salutation, St. Elizabeth was filled with the Holy Ghost, what benefit do you think, continues St. Ambrose, did three months' presence yield both to the mother and to the son? Father Avila says, that he himself has seen several wonderful effects of this devotion to our Lady in divers persons, who used to say some prayers in memory of that purity in which the blessed Virgin herself was conceived, and of that also with which she conceived and brought forth the Saviour of the world; for these persons have been freed by this devotion from filthy temptations which had a long time tormented them. The prayers which holy Church sings in honour of our Lady, are very proper for this effect:—

> O Virgin Mother, ever meek,
> In our behalf to Jesus speak,
> That from our hearts all sin effaced,
> We may through you be mild and chaste.
> *Post partam*, etc. *Virgo singularis*, etc.

Whilst we thus celebrate her virginity and spotless purity, we at the same time ask her to obtain purity of heart for us, that we may be the more pleasing both to herself and her blessed Son.

Devotion to the saints and their holy relics is another excellent remedy. Cæsarius relates an affair (*Lib.* 18, *Dial.*, c. 68), which he says he heard from the person to whom it happened, and who was a Cistercian monk, by name Bernard. This man, when a secular, being one day travelling, was attacked by some impure thoughts, and as he was not so careful then, he took no pains to banish them or resist the temptation. Upon this a reliquary, in which were some of the relics of St. John and St. Paul, and which he was used to carry always about his neck, began to strike him upon his breast, but not knowing what it could be, and searching no farther into the matter, he still entertained his bad thoughts till some other object he met having made the thoughts to cease, the reliquary also ceased striking him upon the breast. Soon after, the same temptation set upon him again, and the holy relics began to renew their strokes, as if warning him to banish these impure thoughts from his heart. Here he began to enter into himself, and with the assistance of God's grace he courageously overcame the temptation.

It is also a devotion no less commendable than powerful against unchaste thoughts, frequently to prostrate one's self before the blessed sacrament, and to beg God's grace to be able to overcome them. But above all, there is nothing contributes so much to the obtaining of this grace, as frequent communion, since our Saviour himself "has prepared that table against all those who persecute us"—*Ps.*, xxii. 6. And all saints and holy writers agree that the blessed sacrament is not only a great remedy against all temptations in general, but particularly sovereign against impurity; for it deadens the fuel of sin, checks the motions of concupiscence, and extinguishes the ardour of sensuality, as water extinguishes fire. And hence it is that St. Cyril, with some other holy fathers, as I have already observed elsewhere, apply that passage of Zacharias to this adorable sacrament of the altar, " wherein does its goodness and beauty consist, but in its being the bread of the elect and the wine that produceth virgins?"—*Zach.*, ix. 17.

CHAPTER VII.

That penance and mortification of our flesh is a very good remedy against all temptations to impurity.

"WE are", says St. Jerome, "to quench the fiery darts of the Devil by rigorous fasts and long watchings". Thus he did himself, thus did St. Hilarion, who, as the same saint writes of him, when he found himself troubled with any temptation of the flesh, was presently enraged against his body, and spoke thus to it: Wretch that thou art, I will soon put an end to thy rebellion; I will punish thee with hunger and thirst, lay many a heavy load upon thee, and by exposing thee to violent heats and colds, teach thee rather to think of necessities than of sensuality. The saints very earnestly recommend this remedy to us, some by their words, others by their example, to the end that the flesh may not rebel against the spirit.

We read in the Chronicles of St. Francis, that a secular asked a good religious, why St. John Baptist, having been sanctified in his mother's womb, should retire to the desert, and lead there such a penitential life as he did. The good religious answered him, by first asking this question,—pray why do we throw salt upon meat that is fresh and good? To keep it the better, and to hinder it from corruption, replied the other. The very same answer I give you, says the religious, concerning the Baptist; he made use of penance as of salt, to preserve his sanctity from the least corruption of sin, and as holy Church sings of him, "that the purity of his life might not be tarnished with the least breath". Now, if in time of peace, and when we have no temptation to fight against, it is very useful to exercise our bodies by penance and mortification, with how much more reason ought we do so in time of war, when encompassed with enemies on all sides? St. Thomas, following Aristotle's opinion, says that the word chastity is derived from "chastise", inasmuch as by chastising the body, we subdue the vice opposite to chastity; and also adds, that the vices of the flesh are like children, who must be whipped into their duty, since they cannot be led to it by reason.

But suppose we should by this ill treating of our body, by fastings and other austerities, prejudice our health, St. Jerome says, "it is better the body should be sick than the soul"; and that our legs should rather shiver and tremble with weakness, than that our chastity should stagger and be ready to fall. Notwithstanding this, discretion is to be used in this point. Mortification is to be measured by our strength, and regulated as the greatness of the temptation and danger shall require. When the temptation is weak, and scarcely dangerous, we need not employ all our forces against it. But if this intestine war be so violent as to threaten destruction to our chastity, then without question we are not to spare our body, but treat it as an enemy, and resolutely risk all to save our soul. Physicians say, "that violent distempers must have violent remedies". Now if this is done in the diseases of the body, surely there is more reason for doing it in the fevers and distempers of our soul, which are sometimes more violent, and always more dangerous, than those of our body.

Spiritual writers remark, that temptations have two sources and two causes. Sometimes they arise from the body itself, and by it are communicated to the soul, as it commonly happens in young people, and in such as live well and enjoy perfect health. In this case, the body is to be mortified and rudely dealt with, because it is the source of the evil. Sometimes also they proceed from the soul, by means of the Devil, and communicate themselves to the body, and this may be known by several marks. First, when we are more attacked by impure thoughts and images than by revolts of the flesh, or when we never have these revolts but subsequent to such thoughts, which sometimes are very lively even in the most mortified bodies. Thus St. Jerom, though his body was quite reduced by age and mortification, yet could not prevent himself from being present in idea at the balls and amusements of the Roman ladies. Besides, when these ideas occur at a time that we have not the least wish for them, and in a place where there are no causes of them—when they respect neither the time of prayer nor the sanctity of the place we are in—when they are so lively, so fantastical, that the like was never before heard of—when, in fine, we fancy that we hear uttered within ourselves, some words, which we would not upon any account utter; all this shows clearly, that what passes within us, does not proceed from ourselves, but that it is an effect of the persecution of the Devil, and that our flesh has no other share in it than that of being the theatre on which he wages this war against us. We must therefore make use on this occasion of remedies different from the former; and according to all holy men, one of the best is some laudable occupation, which, vigorously engaging the mind, effaces every filthy image that had been impressed thereon. It was with this view, St. Jerom, as he himself owns, applied himself to learn Hebrew, in which he became so great a proficient.

The same St. Jerom relates that a young Grecian, a religious in a monastery in Egypt, was much troubled with temptations of the flesh, and having in vain endeavoured by fastings and other austerities to overcome them, discovered at last the state of his soul to his superior, who having comforted him, took this expedient to cure him. He desired an ancient, grave, and severe monk to make it his business very frequently to contradict this young monk, and to chide and reprehend him very severely, and after this to come and complain as if the other had offended him. This senior seized every opportunity of quarrelling with the young man, and acquitted himself of his charge extremely well. Besides this, he would carry to the superior not only his own complaints, but also those of other religious, who failed not to say, according to the word given them, that the young monk was passionate; and the superior having always severely reprehended him, imposed some heavy penance on him, as if he had been really in fault. This happening every day, the young religious, extremely troubled to see himself thus roughly dealt with, and so many false testimonies daily raised against him, had recourse continually to Almighty God, and laying all his miseries before him, begged with tears that he would take him into his protection, since all the world had forsaken him. Notwithstanding this, all the religious still continued so to torment him, that there was no mischief done in the house which was not immediately laid to his charge, and that by two or three witnesses, so that he had every day new reprehensions and penances given him.

This having lasted about a year, one of the religious asked him how he found himself as to those temptations of the flesh which formerly used to be very irksome to him. "What!" says he, "it is scarce permitted me to live, and can you think my thoughts can be employed upon sinful pleasures? It is a great while since all those ideas have been effaced from my mind". It was thus the superior cured him, finding means to banish the old ideas, by introducing new ones, which were more troublesome but less dangerous. Here St. Jerom takes occasion to praise our living in communities; for had this young man, says he, been alone, who would have helped him to overcome this temptation? In other places he speaks of the advantages those religious who live together have above hermits, and adds these reasons why it was better to live under the obedience of a superior, "because here", says he, "you do not do your own will, you eat what is set before you, you take such clothes as are given you, you do the task that is set you, you go weary to bed, and are obliged to rise before you have slept enough. Thus, whilst obedience finds you continually engaged, bad thoughts will find no room in your heart, and you will not have time to think upon anything but what obedience appoints".

St. Francis said, he knew by experience that the devils fled from those that led severe and penitential lives; and on the contrary, that they willingly set upon those that pampered their flesh. And St. Athanasius writes that St. Anthony used to say to his monks, " Believe me, brethren, the Devil is afraid of the prayers of men, he dreads their watchings, fasts, and voluntary poverty". St. Ambrose applying to this subject these words of the Psalmist, " I have covered my soul with fasting, and my garment is haircloth"—*Ps.*, lxviii.,—says, that fasting and other rigours used on the body, are very good defensive weapons against the assaults of the Devil. Our Saviour taught us the same docrine, for having cast out the unclean spirit, which his disciples could not do, he said to them, "This kind of devil cannot be cast out, but by prayer and fasting"—*Mark*, ix. 29. You see how he joins fasting with prayer, as the most proper means to terrify the impure spirit. In the same manner, when we find ourselves pressed by temptations to impurity, it is not sufficient to fall immediately to our prayers, and there make acts and resolutions opposite to the temptation, but to this we must add mortification, or exercise some severity upon our flesh, yet so as that we do nothing in this kind without the direction of our confessor or superior.

A religious that was much troubled with such temptations as these, one day asking holy brother Giles how he might be freed from them, received from him this answer: Pray, brother, what would you do to a dog that is going to bite you? I would either take up a stick or a stone, says the other, and not cease beating and pelting him till I made him run away. Very well, replied the good brother, do the same to your flesh, which is always barking at you, and the temptation will soon fly from you. This kind of remedy is so efficacious, that the least pain or mortification you put yourself to, will suffice sometimes either to drive the temptation quite away, or at least to divert it. For example, you need do no more than hold your arms stretched out in form of a cross, kneel down, strike your breast, pinch yourself, give yourself a dozen strokes with a discipline, stand upon one leg, or the like.

It is said in the life of St. Andrew, that while he was at Corinth, an old man, by name Nicholas, came to him and told him that he had led a most dissolute life, and that very lately he went to an infamous public-house, with an intention to offend God; but, having the holy gospels about him, the courtesan to whom he paid his addresses, drove him rudely from her, and desired him not to come nigh her, for she saw something extraordinary in him which affrighted her very much. The old man added, that this accident made him enter into himself, and that now he was come to him for a remedy against his weakness and the vicious habit in which he had grown old. The saint, moved at his sad condition, betook himself to prayer, fasted five days together, beseeching God that he would pardon this poor man's sins, and make him chaste for the future; at the end of the five days which he had spent in continual prayer for this effect, he heard a voice from Heaven say to him: I grant your petition for the old man, but my will is at the same time, that, as you have fasted for him, so he fast also for himself, and afflict his body, if he desires to be saved. The apostle, in obedience to this voice, enjoined the old man to fast, and all the Christians to pray for him, who, returning home, distributed all his goods to the poor, macerated his body, and fasted six months upon bread and water. Having performed this penance, he died, and God revealed to St. Andrew, who at that time was not at Corinth, that he had shown him mercy.

We read in the Spiritual Meadow, that an hermit addressing himself to one of the old fathers of the desert, discovered to him how violently he was tormented by a thousand impure thoughts; and the old father saying, that he was never disquieted in that manner, this answer scandalized the hermit, who presently departed without saying a word more. But finding another of the ancient fathers, he spoke thus to him: I cannot but tell you what such a one said to me, which was, that he was never troubled with any impure thoughts, at which I cannot refrain from being scandalized: for I think this a thing impossible, and absolutely above the force of nature. Since so great a servant of God has said this, replied the other, without doubt he has his reasons for it; and therefore go back to him again, ask his pardon, and he will satisfy you in the matter. The young hermit followed his counsel, and meeting with the holy man, begged his pardon for his late rude departure, and desired at the same time to know how it was possible that he should never have been tormented with impure thoughts. The reason is, says the holy father, because, since I came to the desert, I have lived upon bread and water, nor did I ever drink or sleep any more than what was barely necessary to support nature, but never enough to satisfy its desires. Upon this account, God has been pleased, by a special privilege, to exempt me from those temptations which you feel so tormenting.

CHAPTER VIII.
Several other remedies against temptations to impurity.

ST. GREGORY says that temptations to impurity, and wicked thoughts which often torment men, are sometimes the effect of a wicked life, and remain as a punishment of those vicious habits, which they had before contracted. Wherefore this kind of fire is to be extinguished by tears, and by bitterly weeping and bemoaning our past follies. St. Bonaventure says, that it is a very good remedy against these temptations, to look upon them as a due chastisement for our past disorders; and by an humble and patient submission to them, to say with Joseph's brethren, "We deserve to suffer all this, because we have sinned against our brother"—*Gen.*, xlii. 21. God is moved with mercy, when man acknowledges that he deserves the punishment which the divine justice inflicts upon him, as the same father observes; and holy Scripture tells us, that the people of Israel made frequent use of this means to obtain their pardon from God. Another admirable means to obtain God's assistance in all our temptations, and particularly in impure ones, and to make us come off always conquerors, is to diffide in our own strength, and put all our confidence in God. I have already spoken of this, and I shall speak more hereafter, when I come to treat of the fear of God: so that at present it shall suffice to say that, generally speaking, humility is a sovereign antidote for all manner of temptations. The revelation which St. Anthony had, is well known. He one day saw in spirit the whole Earth covered with snares, and all of them were so dexterously laid, that being affrighted at the vision, he cried out, Lord, who can escape all these? And presently it was answered him, The humble of heart: be you therefore humble, and God will deliver you from those tempting snares of the flesh. "God has a particular care of little ones", says David: " I myself was humbled, and he delivered me"—*Ps.*, cxiv. 6. The highest mountains suffer most from storms; a tempestuous wind roots up the tallest oak; whilst the little shrub and the osier, by yielding and plying to the wind, resume their former attitude as soon as the violent blast is over.

According to this, one of the advantages we are to derive from these temptations, is to humble ourselves before God, acknowledge our misery and frailty, and to say to him: You see, O Lord, what I am: what can be expected from filthy clay but poisonous exhalations? Who can hope for anything else from an earth that you have cursed, but thorns and briars? It can produce nothing else, unless you cultivate it by your grace. Here is matter enough for our humiliation. If a poor coarse coat, which is an exterior thing, serves, as the saints take notice, to humble him that wears it, what must an infinity of shameful thoughts, which every moment pass through our hearts, wherein they make so much havoc, do to us? Holy brother Giles compared our flesh to a hog, that takes pleasure in wallowing continually in the mire, and to a beetle, that always lives in dirt. This consideration ought to prevail so far upon us, as to divert our attention from impure thoughts; and commonly it is better not to dwell on, or combat the objects which the temptation presents, but immediately to turn our eyes from them, and contemplating our own condition, say with an humble heart, certainly I am a very wicked creature, since so many bad thoughts as these come into and fill my mind; for by this we evade the stroke intended by the Devil, and so put him to confusion. It is also very profitable, when we are surprised with bad thoughts and evil motions, to conceive as much confusion for them as if we were really in fault, for hereby we shall be very far from consenting to them. The Devil, the first author of pride, cannot see so much humility without being in a fury. And you cannot vex him more, or sooner oblige him to leave you in peace, than by turning those means by which he designed to ruin you, to your own good and advantage. Moreover, this holy confusion is a sign that the will is very far from consenting to the sin, and consequently brings along with it great confidence and satisfaction.

It may be useful likewise, sometimes to say abusive words to the Devil. For example, to say to him, Get thee behind me, thou unclean spirit; vile wretch as thou art, hast thou lost all shame? Certainly thou art the filthiest of creatures, since thou presentest me with such filthy imaginations. For the Devil is so full of pride, that he will sooner quit the place than suffer such reproach and contempt. St. Gregory (*Lib.* 3, *Dial. c.* 4) relates that Dacius, a holy bishop of Milan, on his way to Constantinople, passed by Corinth, where he found no other lodging but one in a house which had been a long time deserted by reason of its being haunted with spirits. Here he and his retinue lodged. About midnight the devils, in the shape of divers kinds of beasts, began to make a terrible noise. Some of them roared like lions, others hissed like serpents, and others bellowed like bulls. The bishop, awakened by this noise, and looking upon them with scorn and indignation, spoke thus to them: Ye are come finely off indeed; ye who desire to be like God, have transformed yourselves into beasts, in whose shape ye best show what you are.

This railery, says St. Gregory, so confounded the devils, that they immediately disappeared, forsook the house, and never returned to it any more, so that it was inhabited again. St. Athanasius (*in Vita S. Anton., c.* 3) writes, that when St. Anthony was much troubled with temptations to impurity, a little filthy ugly black, that even turned his stomach, came one day and threw himself at his feet, saying: I have subdued many thousands, but you are the only person I cannot overcome. The saint asked him who he was; he answered, the spirit of fornication; very well, replied the saint, since thou art so despicable, I am resolved hereafter to contemn thee more than I have done yet; whereupon he disappeared. Our Saviour also, as St. Luke relates, called the spirit of fornication the unclean spirit, saying, " When the unclean spirit is gone out of a man"—*Luke*, xi. 24. And hence, to treat the Devil thus, and to despise him as he deserves, is the way to free ourselves from him. Not that it is always necessary to speak, or to discourse with him; no, it may be sufficient sometimes to show our contempt of him by any other exterior sign.

CHAPTER IX.

That the fear of God is the most sovereign remedy against temptations to impurity.

"WORK out your salvation with fear and trembling"—*Philip.*, ii. 12,—says the apostle. To live in fear, to diffide in ourselves, and to fix all our confidence in God alone, conduce very much to maintain a pure spirit, and to preserve ourselves in the grace of God. " I have found by experience", says St. Bernard, " that there is nothing more proper to obtain the grace of God, to preserve it when obtained, or to recover it when lost, than never to think or presume too much on ourselves, but always to walk before God in holy fear"—*in Cant. serm.* 54,—according to these words of Solomon, " happy is the man that is always fearful"— *Prov.*, xxviii. 14. On the contrary, too much self-confidence, and a want of this fear, has been the cause why several great saints have fallen. And therefore the Holy Ghost by way of advice tells us, " that a wise man always fears, and so avoids danger"—*Prov.*, xiv. 16. He that carries a precious liquor in a glass, will not take precautions to carry it safe if he does not know how brittle the glass is, and so upon the first occasion the glass will be broken and the liquor lost. But he who knows the nature of glass will use all possible precaution, and consequently the liquor will be much more secure in his hands than in the other's. The same thing happens to all men in respect of divine grace. "We carry that great treasure in earthen vessels"—II. *Cor.*, iv. 7,—which are easily broken, and so much the sooner, because sometimes we are driven to and fro, as in a crowd, and every moment very much shaken with the winds of temptation which the world raises against us. Those that are not sensible of the weakness and frailty of their nature, take no care of themselves, but perish by a supine security, into which they are lulled as it were asleep, by not knowing themselves. But those who know themselves well and walk in fear, are always upon their guard, and by this means are more secure; for if there be any security in this life, they must infallibly have it.

How comes it to pass, says St. Bernard, that some Christians, who lived very chaste in their youthful days, in the midst of all those violent temptations which that age is usually subject to, have fallen afterwards into the greatest vices of the flesh, and so desperately too, that they have even been astonished at themselves. The reason is this, they spent their youth in humility and in the fear of God, and then seeing themselves every moment in danger of falling, they continually had recourse to God, who never failed to succour them. But having lived long chaste, they hereupon grew proud, and when they presumed too much upon themselves God withdrew his hand which sustained them, so that being left to themselves, they followed the motion of their own weakness, which is to fall. St. Ambrose attributes the fall of several great men to the same cause, who, after having served God a long while, making his law their daily and nightly meditation, crucifying their flesh, restraining the heat of concupiscence, and suffering great afflictions and outrages with a generous patience, fell at last from the very top of a perfect and elevated state into an abyss of misery and disorder. They began at last, says he, to set too great a value upon their good works, and to presume too much upon their own strength, so that the Devil, who was not able heretofore to seduce them by all the imaginary baits and allurements which sensuality has, nor overcome them by the violence of persecution, has now undermined them by their own pride and presumption, and hereby insensibly wrought their ruin.

Holy Scripture and the works of the holy fathers furnish us with infinite examples of this kind. "I tremble", says St. Austin, "when I think of so many great men, whom we have seen and heard of, who, after their virtues had placed them amongst the stars and almost fixed their habitation there, have miserably fallen into most grievous sins, and died impenitent. We have seen, Lord, the great lights of your Church fall from Heaven, being pulled from thence by the infernal dragon; and on the contrary, some that lay as it were grovelling upon the ground, wonderfully elevated all at once on a sudden by the power of thy almighty hand"—*Solil.*, c. 19. How often have we seen those, who for a great while eat of the bread of angels at your table, fall afterwards to feed upon husks of swine! How many have we known that for many years lived pure and chaste, and afterwards plunged themselves into all the filthiness and beastliness of lust and uncleanness!

Who can read in Lipomanus—(*tom.* v.)—the unhappy fall of James the hermit, and not be seized with wonder and amazement? This man was threescore years old, forty of which he had spent in continual austerities; he was even famous for the many miracles he had wrought, and God had given him the power of casting out devils. Having one day cured a young woman who was possessed by the Devil, and finding that the persons who brought her to him were afraid to take her home with them, for fear the Devil should repossess her, he consented that she should stay some time with him. Now because he was too confident and presumed too much upon his own strength, God permitted him to fall into the sin of fornication with her. And as one sin ordinarily draws on another, fear of being discovered made him murder her and throw her body into a river. To conclude all, despairing of God's mercy, he left his solitary way of living, went into the world again, and gave himself over to all manner of wickedness, till at last entering into himself, he merited by a severe penance of ten years to be restored to the state and perfection from which he had fallen, and to be canonized for a saint after his death.

Who is it that is not likewise astonished at what happened to another hermit, of whom St. Anthony speaks in these terms: This very day, brethren, one of the greatest pillars of a religious life is fallen. Who is it that does not tremble to hear it? Who is he that dares confide in the holiness of his life or profession? Consider, says St. Jerom, that persons far more eminent for virtue than you are, and once great favourites of Heaven, have fallen. "You are not more holy than David, wiser than Solomon, nor stronger than Samson", and yet all these have fallen; one of the twelve apostles fell likewise, though fortified by the example, by the good instructions, and by the miracles of his Divine Master. Nicholas, who was chosen by the apostles to be one of the seven deacons, and upon whom the Holy Ghost descended as well as upon the other six, became not only a heretic, but the author of a new sect and a father of heretics. Who is there, continues St. Jerom, that can think himself secure from the malice of the old serpent, when he remembers how by pride "he drove Adam out of Paradise, who had care of that place", and was endowed with original justice? We cannot believe, says St. Austin, that ever man could have been deceived by the Devil, if he had not first left God by pride. It is a truth taught us in holy Scripture, and therefore not to be doubted of, that "pride goes before. humiliation; a haughtiness of mind is a forerunner of our ruin"—*Prov.*, xviii. 12,—" and the heart of man swells and grows big before a dejected submission".

If these examples do not move us, let us ascend to Heaven, and take a survey of the glory from which so many thousand angels fell by their pride and arrogance. "Behold! those who attend upon him are not stable; he has found his angels faulty; with how much more reason shall those that dwell in houses of clay, and have only earth for their foundation, become motheaten like cloth! From morning till night, they shall be cut down like grass that is mowed"—*Job*, iv. 18, etc. St. Gregory, in his morals upon Job, applies these words very happily to our present subject. If, says he, God found so little stability and permanency in the angelical nature--if he met with so much dross in such fine gold,—what will become of us who live in houses of clay, which may be destroyed in one moment, and which so easily run to decay of themselves? How can the soul that is penned up in a body, which breeds worms to its own destruction, be free from fear and solicitude? How can those presume upon themselves, who carry the source and origin of their own ruin about them? Job says, continues St. Gregory, "that they shall be consumed by worms", and that comparison is exact. For as moths, which destroy cloth, are bred in it; so our flesh, with which our soul is clothed, engenders a kind of worm, I mean, carnal concupiscence, which daily wars against us, and when it overcomes us, then we are properly consumed by the very worms which breed in our bodies. Besides, as moths spoil cloth, and eat it through without making any noise, so the worm of our depraved inclinations and concupiscence, "the fuel of sin", which we carry about us, destroys us so quietly and insensibly, that the evil is sometimes committed even before we perceive it; and if those pure spirits, that had no flesh about them, as we have, to engender corruption in them, did not persevere in good, which of us dare be so bold as to confide in our own strength, since he knows that he continually carries about him a sufficient cause of his ruin?

Let us learn from these sad examples to live in continual restraint and holy fear, and wo be to him that does not. We may very well at present mourn for him, for he certainly will fall. It is the holy Scripture, not I, that advances this truth. "If thou dost not live as it were fixed in the fear of God, thy house will soon be overturned"—*Eccl.*, xxvii. 4. That is, if you do not behave with a great deal of circumspection and fear—if you do not keep at a distance from danger by avoiding all occasions, by suddenly suppressing evil thoughts, and preparing against the day of temptation, you will infallibly soon fall into some disaster. Do not flatter yourself by thinking that you are not subject at present to such temptations; that motions to impurity make no impression upon you; and that, moreover, you think that frequent visits and conversations with people of the world are not at all dangerous for you, nor do you any hurt. Do not trust to this: it is an artifice of the Devil, who thus lulls you now into this false security, that he may the more easily surprise you hereafter, and cast you headlong into Hell when you least suspect him. It is, on the contrary, the opinion of holy men, that the more favour and grace you receive from God, so much the more you are obliged to stand upon your defence, for then it is that the Devil is most irritated and most active to destroy you. "He loves to feed upon choice food"—*Hab.*, i. 16,—says the prophet: he had rather, as you will see in those examples I will set down by and by, procure the fall of one of God's servants—of a religious person that aspires to perfection, than of a thousand others, who live in the disorders of the world. This made St. Jerom, in one of his epistles to the holy virgin Eustochium, admonish her not to neglect herself by relying too much upon the holiness of her state of life. "Your good resolutions", says he to her, "must not make you proud, but humble and diffident. You carry a great sum of gold about you: take care not to meet any highwaymen. This life is a race for all mankind; we run here to obtain a crown hereafter in the other world, and how can you hope for peace and quiet in a world which produces nothing but crosses and affliction?"—*Ep. ad Eust.*, c. i. There is nothing certain in this life; we are in a continual warfare, and therefore ought to be upon our guard day and night. We sail in a tempestuous sea, in a poor leaky vessel; the rocks threaten us on every side; and the Devil, who aims at nothing else but our destruction, never ceases to increase the storm, to overwhelm us thereby if he can. Hence it was that the apostle gave this precaution even to the virtuous, "Watch, ye just, and be upon your guard against sin, and he that thinks he stands firm, let him take care lest he fall"—I. *Cor.*, x. 2. Certainly if there be any means to prevent our ruin and to place us in a secure state, it must necessarily flow from a diffidence in ourselves and from the fear of God.

I have heard an affair of this kind, which happened about the beginning of our society, and I will tell it to you just as I heard it. When Mary, Infanta of Portugal, went into Spain to be married to the prince who was afterwards Philip the Second, king of Sapin, the king of Portugal appointed Father le Fevre and Father Araoz to go along with her to the court of Spain, from which time our fathers of the society obtained great reputation in that court. These two, though they were but young (for at that time there were few or none old in the society), heard the confessions of most of the women of quality. They led a life very angelical, and behaved themselves with so much prudence and moderation, that all were astonished to see such rare examples in so young men and in such dangerous occasions. The prince himself admired them also as much as his courtiers, and one day conversing with Father Araoz, he spoke thus to him: They say, father, that those of your society carry an herb about them which has virtue in it to preserve chastity: is it true? The father being a man of good parts, told him that it was certainly true. But what herb is it? replied the prince. The father answered: It is, may it please your royal highness, the fear of

God: this is the herb with which our society preserves itself pure and chaste—from hence proceeds what all the court wonders at, and it is what God has blessed us with. It is this fear of God that has virtue in it to drive away devils, as the liver of that fish had, which Tobias took with him when he travelled with the angel Raphael.

This may still be confirmed out of Scripture. "No evil shall happen to him that fears God, God will defend him in time of tribulation, and deliver him from evil"—*Ecclus.*, xxxiii. 1. "The fear of the Lord expels sin"—*Ecclus.*, i. 27. "By fearing the Lord we decline from evil"—*Prov.*, xvi. 6. This is the herb, therefore, we are always to carry about us as an antidote against the temptations of the flesh: and as long as we have not this holy fear before our eyes, our chastity can never be secure; it is by the fear of God that every one declines and avoids evil; nor can any virtue or sanctity be relied upon without it. Therefore the Holy Scripture, to show us that we are never to be without this holy fear, counsels us to "live in this fear, and grow old in it"—*Ecclus.*, ii. 6. For it is proper not only for beginners, but also for those who are well advanced in God's service; and the just themselves have reason to fear as well as sinners. These must fear, because they are fallen; and those must fear to prevent their fall. The remembrance of past falls should make sinners tremble, and the uncertainty of what is to come should make the just tremble. "Happy is the man that always lives in the fear of God"—*Prov.*, xxviii. 14.

CHAPTER X.

The advantages which flow from the fear of God.

THAT we may set a greater value on this wholesome fear, and even force ourselves more and more to preserve it in our hearts, I will touch on some of the benefits which it confers. First, it does not in the least destroy our confidence in God, nor abate our courage; but on the contrary, it strengthens and relieves us, and like true humility, makes us diffide in ourselves, by placing all our hopes in God alone. St. Gregory, upon these words of Job, "where is your fear, that gives you so much courage?"— *Job*, iv. 6,—explains this admirably well. Job had reason, says he, to join fear and valour together; for God's proceedings differ much from ours. With us, courage makes us stronger, and fear makes us weaker. But here courage makes us weaker, and fear stronger, according to the wise man, who says, "courage and confidence consist in the fear of God"—*Prov.*, xiv. 26. And the reason is this : he that truly fears God has nothing else to fear; all things else are too despicable and mean to be a subject of apprehension to him. "He that fears the Lord", says the Scripture, "shall not be afraid of anything else ; he fears nothing, because the Lord is his hope"—*Ecclus.*, xxxiv. 26. Fear in some sort subjects us to what we are afraid of, as to a thing that has power to hurt us: and he who fears God exceedingly, who esteems nothing but God, who reposes all his hope in him alone, knows not what it is to fear the world, tyrants, death, devils, not even Hell itself; for none of all these can hurt him, or discompose one hair of his head, without God's permission. The strength he feels in this holy disposition of mind, exceeds all the strength and power of mankind united together. For it is God that is our strength, according to these words of the Royal Prophet, "God is the strength of those that fear him"—*Ps.*, xxiv. 14.

Nor does this holy fear bring bitterness or trouble with it; it does not disturb the mind, nor prove the least inconvenience to it, but on the contrary fills it with joy and sweetness. The fear which some have of losing their honour or fortune, as also the servile fear of death and Hell, really afflicts and torments; but a filial fear, such as good children have of displeasing their father, imparts to the soul holy satisfaction, and softens the heart by means of the acts of the love of God which it continually produces. Dear Lord, never permit me to be separated from thee. Let me die a thousand times rather than once offend thee. "The fear of the Lord", says the Scripture, "is an accumulated glory and a most accomplished joy. The fear of God rejoices the heart, and brings pleasure, content, and long life with it. The man that fears God shall meet with blessings to the end of his life, and he shall be blessed and happy on his dying bed"— *Ecclus.*, i. 11, etc.

You see with what eloquence and variety of expression the wisest of men describes the pleasure and satisfaction which the fear of God brings with it. It does not make us tremble like slaves who dread chastisement, and thus the more we love God, the more we fear to offend him. The more a docile son loves his father, the more he endeavours to please him. And a good wife, the more kindness she has for her husband, the more careful she is not to give him the least cause of discontent.

In a word, all the praises and advantages which holy Scripture assigns the humble, it equally assigns to those who fear God, and this almost in the same terms. For if it says, that "God fixes his eyes upon the poor and humble"—*Isa.*, lxvi. 2,—it also says, that "the eyes of the Lord watch over those that fear him"—*Ecclus.*, xxxiv. 19. If it says, that "he exalts the humble and fills them with good things"—*Luke*, i. 53,—it also says, that "his mercy shines upon those that fear him, from generation to generation"—*Luke*, i. 50,—and that "those that fear him shall be great with him in everything"—*Judith*, xvi. 19. Nor do the saints attribute more to humility than to the fear of God. When they say, that humility is the guardian of other virtues, and that there can be no solid virtue without it, they say the same of fear, and call it with the prophet Isaias, "God's treasure"—*Is.*, xxxiii. 6. For in effect it preserves all other virtues, and is the source of grace. And they also add, that as a ship can never sail securely without ballast, because the least wind would overset her; so a soul can never sail prosperously through the sea of this world, unless ballasted with the fear of God, which is the only thing that can keep it steady amidst the tempestuous blasts of pride and prosperity. Let it be ever so richly laden with virtues and talents, if it wants this ballast of fear, it will be in very great danger of sinking. St. Gregory says, "that the weight of the fear of God is the anchor of our soul". St. Jerome makes "fear the preserver of virtues, and too great a presumption the highway to ruin". "Fear is the foundation of our salvation", according to Tertullian. "If we fear", says he, "we shall be cautious, and if cautious we shall be saved; for care and solicitude bring at last certain security".

To conclude, all that Solomon says of the excellency of wisdom, is ascribed by him to the fear of God, in these words: "The fear of God is true wisdom"—*Ecclus.*, i. 34. Job speaks in the same manner, saying, that "the fear of God is wisdom itself"—*Job*, xxviii. 28. So that you see whatever is said of wisdom, may be justly applied to this wholesome fear. Nay, it has something more in it than the other, for Solomon owns, that "the perfection of wisdom consists in the fear of God"—*Ecclus.*, i. 20. And in another place having cried out, "how great is he that has found wisdom and knowledge!" he presently adds, "he is not greater than he who fears God". The fear of God is above all things. Happy is the man whom God has blessed with this fear! To whom shall we compare him that posesses it in his heart?"—*Ecclus.*, xxv. 13, etc.

CHAPTER XI.

The preceding doctrine confirmed by examples.

IN the Spiritual Meadow,—*tom.*, ii., *Bibl. SS.*, *P. P.*,—it is recounted that an hermit of Thebais, who was the son of a heathen priest, related one day to several fathers of the same desert, that when young he used always to go along with his father to the temple, and see him offer sacrifice. But one day in particular, said he, having got privately into the temple, I saw the Devil seated upon a high throne, with the whole infernal court around him; and I saw moreover, that one of the principal devils approached and adored him. And Satan said to him, from whence come you? He answered, from such a province, where I have raised sedition, kindled war, put all to fire and sword, and now I come to give you an account of it. Satan asked him how much time he had spent in the performance of this enterprise; the other told him a month. Whereupon he judged him to have spent too much time in so small a matter, and therefore commanded him to be scourged most severely on the spot. After this another devil presented himself at his throne, and likewise adored; to him he put the same questions as to the former, viz., from whence he came, and what he had been doing. I am come from sea, says he, where I raised violent storms, in which many vessels and men were lost, and I am come to acquaint you of it. How much time have you employed in this? said Satan; twenty days replied the other; whereupon he was also condemned to the same punishment as the former, and for the same reason. A third then presented himself, to whom the same questions were put. This devil told him he came from such a city, where he had made several marriages, been the author of several quarrels, in which some were murdered, and amongst others even the bridegroom himself; and that in ten days he had done all this. Notwithstanding, he was likewise condemned as the others, for having done so little in so long a time as ten days. Lastly, in comes a fourth, who, having paid his adoration, was asked the same questions as the former; to which he thus replied: I am come from the desert, where, after having tempted an hermit these forty years in vain, I this very night have brought about my design, and made him commit a sin of the flesh. Upon these words the Prince of Darkness rose from his throne, embraced him, put a crown upon his head, made him sit down by him, and then highly commended this his action. When I saw this, says the hermit of Thebais, I concluded with myself that a solitary life had something very extraordinary in it, and that hermits very much excelled other men; and therefore, at that very time I resolved to quit my father's house and retire into the desert. Here you may observe, by the by, that the hermit's fall was the occasion why this young man set such a value upon a solitary life, and afterwards embraced it; whereas, now-a-days, the world views the failings of religious in such a light, that from hence they take occasion to condemn not only themselves but their institute also. St. Gregory has a story in his dialogues—*Lib.* iii., *Dial.*, c. 7,—much like this I have now related to you.

We read in the lives of the fathers, that a holy hermit being brought into a monastery where there were many religious, had a certain vision, in which he saw many devils who did nothing but pass and repass through all the apartments of the house. The angel that had conducted him thither, carried him also into a city not far from this monastery, where he was very much struck to see only one devil, and to see him sitting still at one of the gates, as if he had little or nothing to do. The hermit wondering at this difference, asked the angel the reason of it: he told him that in the city every one did what the Devil put him upon, so that one was sufficient to work mischief amongst the citizens; but in the monastery, all the religious used their best endeavours to resist temptations, and therefore a great number of devils was necessary to tempt and draw them into sin.

Palladius relates a strange story (*Pallad. in Hist. Lausiac.*, c. 44, *et Ruf. in Vit. S. Ægyp.*), which is also in the lives of the fathers. It is this: an hermit after a long practice of all sorts of mortification, when he was come to a high pitch in virtue, grew hereupon so proud that God permitted him to fall into a most dreadful sin. It was as follows: whilst this hermit was mightily puffed up, and swelled with a great opinion of his sanctity, the Devil appeared to him in the shape of a very handsome woman, who pretended she had lost her way in the desert. He received her into his cell, where he entertained her, and giving himself up to wicked desires, he put all things in readiness to accomplish them, when at the same instant this woman, with a horrid outcry, broke from his arms and disappeared. After this, different voices were heard in the air; some laughed at him, others insulted him with these bitter taunts: O brave hermit, you who were just now at Heaven's gates, are fallen as low as Hell; know henceforward that he that exalts himself shall be humbled. But this unhappy man did not stop here; for though he passed all that night and the following day in mourning and tears for his sin, yet despair at last so far overcame him, as to make him leave his solitude and return to the world, where he led a most lewd life, in all manner of debauchery.

The fall of that other hermit, whom we spoke of in the ninth chapter, is also very remarkable. His virtue was so admirable that even the wild beasts acknowledged it by obeying him; yet he fell, and it is probable St. Anthony foresaw his fall; for, one day speaking of him, he compared him to a rich vessel at sea, adding, God grant that he arrive safe to harbour; and soon after, the unhappy man struck upon a rock and was lost. He who before had commanded wild beasts, says St. John Climacus, is now become a prey to his own passions, more fierce and cruel than the wildest savage. He that fed upon the bread of angels, now lives upon filth and ordure. After his fall, whilst he was yet lamenting it, some other hermits came and visited him, and he conjured them to desire their father St. Anthony to obtain of God ten days of him to do farther penance. And now it was that the saint cried out, as we have already told you, This very day, brethren, one of the greatest pillars of religion is fallen. He said no more, being unwilling to particularize the fault, for he knew it was a sin of impurity. The hermit died five days after, leaving behind him a lively example of the frailty of those who depend too much upon their own strength, and an admirable lesson of humility for proud men.

Father Avila says, that a certain hermit to whom God had

revealed the great danger he was exposed to in this life, was interiorly so moved with it, that ever after he used to cover his face and head in such a manner that he could not see anything but the ground, nor would he speak to any one, but continually bemoaned the dangers of human life. Those who occasionally paid him a visit, were extremely surprised to find him in this condition; and when they asked him the reason of so sudden a change, and of such an extraordinary way of living, he would never answer more than this, Pray let me alone, for I am a man. Another saint deploring the unhappy condition of mankind, had a custom of crying out: Alas! O how unfortunate am I! since I am still capable of offending God mortally!

THE FIFTH TREATISE.

ON OBEDIENCE.

CHAPTER I.
Excellency of the virtue of obedience.

"Do you think that God would have you offer him victims and holocausts? No, he would rather have you obey his commands; because obedience is far better than victims, and it is better for you to comply with his will than to offer him the fat of rams"— I. *Kings*, xv. 22. This is what Samuel told Saul, when that prince had reserved the best and fairest flocks of the Amalecites for sacrifice, contrary to the express command God had given him, which was, totally to destroy the Amalecites and all that belonged to them. The holy fathers take occasion from this and several other passages of holy Scripture, which declare the excellence and merit of obedience, to bestow the highest praise on this virtue. St. Austin, in several passages of his works, asks, why God forbade Adam to eat of the tree of the knowledge of good and evil; and one of the reasons he gives is, that it was, "to teach man how great a good obedience is of itself, and how great an evil disobedience is"—*Lib.* i. *contr. adv. Leg. et Proph.* For it was not the fruit of the tree that wrought all those evils which followed from Adam's sin; because the tree had nothing that was bad in it, since God himself " saw all his works to be excellent and good"—*Gen.*, i. 31,—nor is it to be presumed that he would permit any evil thing to grow in Paradise. Disobedience therefore, and a breach of God's prohibition, was the cause of all the evil. And for this reason St. Austin says, that nothing shows the malice of disobedience more than the punishment inflicted upon Adam for eating the forbidden fruit, which was harmless and innocent in itself, independent of the prohibition. Let those who easily dispense with obedience in small matters learn from hence to see their error, and to correct it. For the sin does not arise from the nature of the thing, but from the disobedience, which always vitiates the act, let the thing be of great or small importance. St. Austin, giving another reason why God issued the prohibition to Adam, says, that since man was created to serve God, it was necessary to restrain him in some one particular, to make him sensible of his dependence upon a superior power, for otherwise he would not so easily have known it. And therefore God tried him by obedience, which was an act whereby he was not only to acknowledge his Creator, but also to merit, if he had pleased, an eternal union with him in the end. This holy father, after passing an high encomium on this virtue, concludes its commendation thus, that one of the reasons which moved the Son of God to take human nature upon him was to teach us obedience by his own example. Man, says he, was disobedient even to death, that is, death was the deserved punishment of his disobedience; and the Son of God made himself man, that he might be obedient even to death. Adam's disobedience shut Heaven's gates against us, Christ's obedience threw them open. "For, as by the disobedience of one man, many sinned; so, by the obedience of one, many were justified" —*Rom.*, v. 19. Nor can there be a greater argument of the merit or excellence of this virtue than the glorious reward which God has given to the sacred humility of his Son Jesus Christ, "who was obedient to death, even the death of the cross: for which", says St. Paul, "God has exalted him, and given him a name above all other names, the holy name of Jesus, at which all the powers of Heaven, Earth, and Hell do bend their knees" —*Philip.*, ii. 8, etc.

The holy fathers bestow the highest praises on this virtue; but I will here confine myself to one of the good qualities they assign it, and only treat of it as one of the chief virtues of a religious. St. Thomas, who usually adheres scrupulously to scholastic principles, asks, whether obedience be the chief and principal vow made in religion; and, having answered himself in the affirmative, he proves his assertion by these three following reasons, no less profitable than solid. The first is, that by the vow of obedience we offer more to God than by the other vows. By the vow of poverty we sacrifice our riches, by that of chastity our body, but by obedience we offer up our will and understanding, and entirely sacrifice the whole man to God, which, undoubtedly, is the noblest sacrifice of the three. St. Jerom, speaking of the difference "between sacrificing ourselves and sacrificing our riches" is of the same opinion, and says, "that a consummate virtue is not requisite to forsake our riches, since those who are only novices in perfection are capable of it: Antisthenes and other heathen philosophers have done it before us: but to sacrifice ourselves to God belongs peculiarly to Christians and apostolical men". Hence, St. Thomas remarks on this subject, that Christ, speaking to his disciples concerning the reward he had prepared for them, did not say, "ye that have left all", but "ye that have followed me"; for all perfection lies in following Christ. "Verily I say unto you, that you who have followed me shall sit upon twelve thrones"— *Mat.*, xix. 28. Now, the counsel of obedience is included in these words; for, as the holy doctor adds, obedience is nothing else than to follow the sentiments and will of another.

The second reason why obedience has the preference is, because it really includes the other virtues, and is not included in any. For, though a religious bind himself by the two distinct vows of poverty and chastity, yet both these obligations are contained in the vow of obedience, by which he is obliged in general to observe all that shall be commanded him. This truth is so evident, that the Benedictine and Carthusian monks make no other vow than that of obedience. "I promise obedience according to the rule", says the religious at his profession; and under these words the vows of chastity and poverty are comprised, according to the rules and practices of the order.

The third reason is this, the more a thing advances us to the end for which it was instituted, and the more it unites us to that end, the more perfect it is. Now, it is obedience which most unites religious with the end of their institution. For as, to make us attain the end for which our society has been instituted, it commands us to labour for our own and our neighbour's spiritual advancement, it commands us to give ourselves to prayer and mortification, to employ ourselves in hearing confessions, to preach the word of God, and exercise ourselves in all those functions which conduce to the helping our neighbours and saving their souls; in like manner, it prescribes to all other religious what they are to do, in order to attain the particular end of their institution; and by consequence the vow of obedience is more excellent and perfect than the other vows.

St. Thomas draws a conclusion from hence of very great consequence, viz., that the very essence and soul of a religious life consists chiefly in the vow of obedience. For suppose one should live in voluntary poverty and chastity, or even engage himself to such a life by vow, this would not make him a religious, nor would he be in the perfect state of religion, if he should not add the vow of obedience. Unless a man makes a vow of obedience, he cannot be a religious; it is obedience which makes religious, and places them in a religious state. St. Bonaventure is of the same opinion, and says, that the perfection of a religious man consists in denying his own will, and following the will of another; and that the vows of poverty and chastity, by which we renounce riches and sensual pleasures, are only helps to disengage us from temporals, and from the allurements of the flesh, that we may be in a better capacity to comply with our main obligation, which is that of obedience. And therefore he adds, that it will signify nothing to have renounced all the goods of fortune, unless we deny our own will also, and entirely submit to all the injunctions of holy obedience.

Surius, in the life of St. Fulgentius, who was first an abbot, and afterwards bishop, amongst many other remarkable things, related, that whenever he spoke of obedience, he always used to say, "that these were true religious, who, having mortified and broken their own wills, lived in a holy indifference to all things, and gave themselves totally into the hands of their superiors, by neither willing or not willing anything of themselves, but by following their abbot's counsel and commands in all things". Take notice that he does not fix religious perfection in austerity and mortification of the body, nor in continual labour, nor in profound learning, nor in good talents for preaching, but only in a submission of our will to our superiors, and in self-denial.

You may infer from what has been said, that obedience is the virtue which essentially constitutes religion and properly makes a religious. It is this that pleases God more than all the sacrifices we can make him; it is this that comprises not only poverty and chastity, but all other virtues also. For, admit that you be truly obedient, you cannot fail of being poor, chaste, humble, modest, patient, mortified, and in a word, master of all virtues. This is no exaggeration, it is plain truth. Virtuous habits are got by a frequent exercise of their particular acts, and this is the only way that God is pleased to bestow them upon us. Now, obedience gets us this frequent exercise: for all that our rule prescribes, or our superior commands, is an exercise of some virtue. Take obedience along with you for your guide, and embrace all the occasions which it shall present you, and you need do no more. Sometimes you will meet with an occasion to exercise your patience, sometimes humility, sometimes poverty, and at other times mortification, and now and then temperance and chastity; and thus, as you improve in obedience, so will you advance in all other virtues. This is the opinion of our holy founder, who, speaking to his children, says, according as obedience shall flourish amongst you, so all other virtues will equally flourish with it, and produce in your souls the fruits which I desire. All holy men agree in this one point, and for this reason call obedience the mother and source or origin of all other virtues. St. Austin calls it, "the greatest of virtues, and likewise the mother and source of all virtues". "This is the only virtue", says St. Gregory, "that plants other virtues in our mind, and preserves them after they are once planted". The same St. Gregory and St. Bernard, in their explanation of these words of the Proverbs, " the obedient man shall speak of victory"—*Prov.*, xxi. 28,—says, that an obedient man shall get not only one, but even many victories, and with them make himself master of all virtues.

If you therefore desire a short and easy way to make great progress in virtue in a little time, and thereby to attain great perfection, be obedient. "That is the way; you need only follow it without turning either to the right or left, and you shall soon come to the place you wish for"—*Isai.*, xxx. 21. St. Jerom speaking of obedience, says, " O great and abundant happiness! O extraordinary grace! For obedience is an epitome of all virtues, because it leads directly to Jesus Christ; and if we follow the way which it points out to us, we shall soon be perfect men".

St. John Climacus came one day to a monastery, in which he saw many venerable religious men, who were always ready upon the least sign given them, to do whatsoever was commanded them; and he says, that some of them had been enlisted under the standard of obedience for above fifty years. He asked them what benefit they had derived from this their submission: some of them answered, that they were hereby come to a most profound humility, and by that means had defeated the Devil in several dangerous attempts he had made upon them; others said, that it had taken from them all resentment of any injury or affront offered them. Thus we see how much obedience helps to acquire all other virtues. And therefore the ancient fathers of the desert looked upon an hermit's submissive obedience to his ghostly father as an infallible sign that he would one day become a perfect man.

St. Dorotheus tells us that his scholar Dositheus was of a good family and of a very delicate constitution, and that whilst he was in the world, he was struck with a lively apprehension of the judgment, and of the rigorous account he was one day to give of himself, God granting to him the request which the Royal Prophet made in these words, "pierce my flesh with a fear of thee; for I tremble at thy judgments"—*Ps.*, cxviii. 120. To be able to answer for himself on that great day he became a religious; but finding that his health would not permit him to rise at midnight to matins, nor eat the ordinary diet, nor comply with the ordinary observances of the community, he resolved to devote himself entirely to obedience, and to serve in the infirmary in the most low offices, and to do whatsoever was commanded him there, though ever so humiliating. Having done this for five years, he died of consumption, and God revealed to the abbot of the same monastery that Dositheus had merited as much as St. Paul and Anthony the hermits had done. When the other religious heard this, they began to murmur and complain, saying, Where is God's justice, if a man that never fasted, and that always eat of the best, be equal to us who perform all duties of religion, "and bear the heat and burden of the day"?—*Mat.*, xx. 12,—what are we the better for all our austerities? Our continual labour and pain signify nothing. Whilst they were thus complaining, God gave them to understand that they did not know the worth and excellence of obedience, and that it was of so high a value in his sight that Dositheus had merited more by it in a short time, than several of them had done by their long and rigid mortifications.

CHAPTER II.

Of the necessity of obedience.

SAINT JEROM exhorting all religious to be obedient to their superior, cites divers examples to prove the absolute necessity of obedience to one supreme head, in every condition or state of life. In civil government, says he, all are subject to kings, emperors, or their lieutenants and deputies. Romulus, to build Rome, slew his brother, and "founded the city in blood", to show us that two kings are things inconsistent in one kingdom. Jacob and Esau struggled in their mother's womb for primogeniture. In ecclesiastical government, all people obey the bishops in their respective dioceses, and the bishops themselves are subject to his holiness, who is the head of the Church, and Christ's vicar upon Earth. Nor is there any state of life whatsoever, where this subordination is not absolutely necessary. The greatest army submits to the authority of one general. One captain commands a man-of-war; there would be nothing but disorder and confusion on board a ship if every man were master; and God knows when she would get securely into the harbour, if every private seaman had full power to steer her as he pleased. Every family, every private house and poor cottage, has always one whom the rest obey, and indeed there is neither house, congregation, city, nor kingdom that can long subsist without it. "Every kingdom and house that is divided shall become desolate"—*Luke*, xi. 17. This order is not only practised amongst men, but even amongst the angels themselves, where one hierarchy is subordinate to another; nay, irrational creatures do likewise observe it. Bees have their king, and cranes in their flight form the letter Y, having always one to head them and command the rest. What more shall I say? adds this father. Do not the heavens themselves take their motion from the *primum mobile?* But not to trouble you with any more examples, all that I pretend to by those which I have already alleged, is only to make you sensible how beneficial it is to live under the authority of a superior and in the company of other servants of God, whose object is the same with yours, and who, by their example, may help and assist you very much to attain it the more easily.

Though St. Ignatius's intention is that all virtues should flourish in our society, yet he most particularly and frequently recommends to us obedience, hereby to signify that as other orders are distinguished, some by their extreme poverty, others by great austerities, others by choir-duties, and others by perpetual enclosure, so he desires that obedience should be our distinctive mark and character, as if all our advancement in virtue totally depended hereupon. The great end of our society is first to attend to our own perfection and salvation, and then to our neighbour's; and therefore we must always be in readiness to go to any part of the world where our superiors shall employ us in the salvation of souls. And for this reason the professed fathers of our society oblige themselves by a fourth vow, to go on the mission wheresoever his holiness the pope shall please to send them, whether it be amongst Catholics, heretics, or infidels, and this without their pleading any excuse to the contrary, or asking anything to maintain themselves on their journey. Nor must they be thus perfectly resigned and entirely obedient only to his holiness, but also to their other superiors, both as to their place of abode as well as employment, or whatever else they shall think fit to enjoin them. There is a great variety of employments in the society, and several offices and functions of all sorts, both high and low, which necessarily require a great stock of obedience in a man, in order to be equally disposed for all or any of them, according as superiors shall ordain. Here we may justly admire the wise conduct and great foresight which St. Ignatius had, when he desired that obedience should be the proper badge and peculiar mark of the society, since he certainly foresaw that we should be employed in many things no less difficult than painful to flesh and blood.

A father of our society said (and I wish we could all say the same), that he was not afraid of being commanded anything against his will, for he was still ready for whatever he was commanded. And it is a certain truth, that a religious man, who is thus resigned and totally indifferent as to any command, never troubles himself with what is assigned to him, nor wishes to be subjected rather to this than to that superior. For true obedience ought not to depend upon this or that person, or this or that thing commanded; for if it should, it would be but a weak and lame obedience, and bring great fear and apprehension along with it. "Have you a mind not to stand in fear of men in authority?" says the apostle. "Do well, and you shall be commended for it, but if you do ill, then you have reason to fear them"—*Rom.*, xiii. 3, 4. Highwaymen and others, that by their crimes deserve death, fear every moment to be seized upon, and tremble at the sight of a justice of peace. "Yet", as St. Chrysostom observes, "it is neither the prince nor the law of the land that fills them with these apprehensions, but they proceed from an ill conscience and their own wickedness". The same holds in religion, for the fear you have does not come from the superior's authority over you, but from the sense you have of your want of mortification and submission. If you therefore wish to live easy and void of this fear, be always ready to comply with obedience, and be still resigned to anything your superior shall enjoin you. He that shall do this, shall enjoy a perfect peace and quiet of mind, and religion shall be to him a Paradise upon Earth.

CHAPTER III.

Of the first degree of obedience.

ST. IGNATIUS, speaking of this virtue in the third part of his Constitutions, says, that it is much to our purpose, and very necessary for our spiritual advancement, to propose to ourselves a perfect and entire obedience; and afterwards, declaring in what this obedience consists, says, that we are not only to obey in the exterior, that is, in barely doing what is commanded us (which is the first degree of obedience), but we must also obey interiorly, by making the superior's will our own: and this conformity of our will is the second degree of obedience. But the saint not thinking this enough, bids us advance still farther, and conform our judgment also to our superior's, making his sentiments ours, and believing all to be good and just which he commands, in which consists the third degree of obedience. When our exterior actions, when our will and judgment all agree, and equally conform to what is commanded, then obedience is most perfect and entire; which it can never be, so long as any one of these three conditions is wanting.

To begin with the first degree: I say, that a great diligence and exactness is required in the performance of what obedience prescribes us. St. Basil says that we are to act in this, as a man that is extremely hungry does, in order to satiate his hunger, or as a man that is much in love with his life does, in things relating to the preservation of it. Nay, says the same saint, we ought to show far more earnestness and zeal than these do, since eternal life, which is the reward of our obedience, is infinitely more noble and excellent, than this present life is, which the others are so careful to preserve. St. Bernard gives us this description of an obedient man. " He does not know what it is to delay and put off the business till to-morrow; he is an enemy to all kinds of demurs;

he prevents his superior, and even gets the start of his commands. His eyes and ears are still open to the least sign given him; all his other senses and every part of him faithfully wait the motion of his superior. He does what he is bidden, goes where he is commanded, and is always ready to receive and execute every order of obedience"—*Serm. de Obed.*

Our holy founder, speaking of the punctuality with which we ought to obey, says, that when the clock strikes, or the superior commands, we must be as ready to obey as if Jesus Christ himself called upon us, and at that very instant lay by what we are doing, and even leave a letter of a word, which we have begun, unfinished. This rule doubly instructs us; first, to look upon the striking of the clock, or a word from our superior, as the real voice of God himself. To do this the better, we may piously consider and represent to ourselves the disposition of mind which the eastern sages had when they saw the star; and say with them, "This is the sign of the great king, let us go pay him homage, and offer gold, incense, and myrrh to him". This is the voice of God that calls upon us, let us make haste and obey it. Secondly, it instructs us to quit at that very moment the employployment we are about, and even leave a letter half formed. We cannot do better than to follow in this point the examples of some ancient fathers, whose obedience Cassian recommends to us. Speaking of what they did, he says, they were continually employed. One wrote books of devotion, another meditated, some translated spiritual books, others were employed in manual works. And they no sooner heard the clock strike, or the superior's call, but they even strove who should be first out of his cell; and their haste was so great, that he who was writing would not allow himself time to finish the letter he had begun. Thus you see how they preferred obedience before all other duties whatsoever, even their spiritual reading, prayer, meditation, and all other works of piety. Here you see what it was that made them such exact observers of obedience; you see here their punctuality and readiness, such as if God himself had given the word of command. St. Bennet recommends this kind of obedience very earnestly in his rule, and it is from him and other ancient fathers that our holy founder took his perfect model of obedience, as it is set down in his Constitutions.

God has been pleased to show by miracles how pleasing to him this exactness in obedience is. There was a good religious

(*S. Cath. de Sien. in suis Dial.*, c. lxv.) employed in copying out some written paper; he was no sooner set to it, and had made only one letter, but the clock struck: to comply with the call of obedience he left it in that manner, and when he returned found it all written in letters of gold"—*Hist. Ord. S. Fran.*, 6, p. 1. 7. c. xxxix. Our Saviour himself appeared once to another religious, in the shape of a little child, who was no sooner come, but the bell rung to vespers, with which call the religious complying, he left little Jesus all alone. At his return he found him still in his cell, to whom the Divine Infant spoke thus:—Your going was the cause of my stay; if you had staid, I should have gone away. Rusbrochius (*Tract de precip. quibusd. virt.*, c. ix. p. 243) tells us of another religious, who, being favoured with the like apparition, left the little Infant Jesus to comply with obedience, and, at his return to his cell, found him in the shape of a young man. Christ said to him, Behold how much I am grown since you left me, and so much I am also grown in your soul, upon the account of your punctual obedience. The Devil, on the contrary, is such an enemy to obedience, and so jealous of our spending any time in it, that when he cannot rob us of all, nor cheat us into a total disobedience, he endeavours to deprive us of some part of it, by making us less punctual and observant. For example, the bell that calls you up in the morning has rung, and you heard it, but the Devil strives to keep you still in your bed. When you are writing, the bell rings again to call you to some duty, and he endeavours to make you stay and finish the letter you had begun, and sometimes to write out the whole line, if not, to end the period; or to conclude your discourse, under pretence of not forgetting some fine thought that offers itself. He is always desirous to have the first fruit and flower of our actions; wherefore, on the contrary, we ought to make it our business to give them all to God, the blossom as well as the fruit; and thus they will be more acceptable to him. The first as well as the last part, nay, even the whole action, is to be given to God, without reserve, if we desire to make him such a present as may please him.

St. Ignatius would have this exterior obedience extend itself yet farther, and desires that we should not only obey the bell, or the superior's voice, with that exactness we have now spoken of, but also even the least sign or intimation of his will. Let every one, says this great doctor of obedience, make it his care and concern to signalize himself in the practice of obedience, and not only in things of pure obligation, but in others also, when he has only a hint of the superior's will, without an express order from him. "He that is truly obedient", says Albert the Great, "does not wait for a command, but, as soon as he judges that his superior would have it done, he immediately falls to work without any further orders. And he adds, that this was what our Saviour himself practised; for, knowing that it would be grateful to his Eternal Father if he should die for our salvation, he turned that knowledge into a command. Cassian, speaking of the ancient hermits, says, that their obedience was so zealous and exact, that they did not only obey the superior's voice, but even the least sign of his will, which made him think that they sometimes foresaw what was to be done; they frequently preventing their superior's command, and performing what he had only resolved on, but not declared to them. From hence St. Bernard took the description of an obedient man, which was cited above, where he says, "that he gets the start of a command, and even prevents his orders by a prompt obedience".

Our holy founder tells us of three sorts of obedience. The first is, when we comply with a precept of obedience, and this we are obliged to. The second is, when we do a thing for the least word's speaking. This obedience is more perfect than the other, for he that obeys at a word is certainly more humble and submissive than he that waits for a command in virtue of holy obedience. The third is, when we perform the superior's will upon the least sign of it being manifested, and without our being spoken to. The saint adds, that this last is the most perfect obedience of the three, and most grateful to God. A servant who upon the least hint given him sets himself to work, certainly pleases his master better than another that will do nothing without being desired; so in religion he that is ready to obey upon the least sign given him of his superior's will, is most agreeable to God and superiors. St. Thomas says, that our knowledge of the superior's will is a tacit order, and that our performance of it then is a proof of prompt obedience. This is the obedience we are to aim at; and the more so, because sometimes the superior will not lay an express command upon us, being desirous to treat us mildly, and not give us too great a mortification; or for fear we should not relish the command. So that, suppose you should know the superior to be thus inclined, you would do ill in not preventing him, and offering yourself to perform what he secretly wishes you should do. When God designed to send a messenger to the people of Israel, he spoke so that Isaias might understand his pleasure, " whom shall I send, or will go as from me?"—*Isa.*, vi. 8. The prophet took the hint immediately, and offered himself upon the spot; "here am I, Lord, please to send me". In the same manner, we ought to present ourselves to our superior, upon the least notice or signification of his will.

I could produce many examples, to show the readiness and exactness with which we ought to obey, but I will content myself with two. The first is that of Samuel, who in his youth waited upon the high priest Heli in the temple. The Scripture says, that one night, as he slept in the temple, where the ark of God was kept, the Lord called upon him, and he immediately got up and ran to Heli, saying, " You called upon me; here I am"—I. *Kings*, iii. 5, etc. But Heli told him, " that he did not call him, and bade him go to bed again". He did so, and was no sooner fallen asleep, but the Lord called him again. Up he got, went to Heli and said, " You called me; here I am". To whom Heli answered as before, " Child, I did not call thee, go and sleep". He obeyed, and God calling him the third time, he got up and went again to Heli, saying, as he had done before, " You called me; behold I am here". Upon this Heli understood that it was God who had called upon Samuel, and therefore bade him " go back and sleep, and if any one should call him again, to say, Speak, Lord, for thy servant hears". Samuel returned and lay down again, and God appearing to him, called twice upon him, to whom he answered in Heli's words, " Speak, Lord, for thy servant hears". Upon which God told him, that the punishment he had threatened Heli with should very suddenly be inflicted upon him. Now let us consider a little Samuel's very exact and ready obedience. Though Heli himself tells him he did not call him, and bade him go take his rest; yet for all this Samuel never thought of any other person's calling him there in the temple excepting the high priest; and therefore he got up three several times, and went to know his commands. Such ought to be our obedience towards our superiors. Our minds must, like his, be equally disposed at all times for anything which we think our superior would have us do.

The second example is that of Abraham, whose readiness to obey, when commanded by God to sacrifice his only son, is an admirable model of punctuality and obedience. Abraham " got up in the night"—*Gen.*, xxii. 3,—says the Scripture; he would not stay till it was daylight. Upon the receiving his orders, which were very severe for the father of an only son, he put himself in readiness to execute them without the least demur. The Scripture also observes, that he would not permit his servants to wait upon him at the place of sacrifice, but bade them stay for him at the foot of the hill: for no other end, without doubt, but that they might not hinder him from a punctual and faithful compliance with God's commandment.

CHAPTER IV.
Of the second degree of obedience.

THE second degree of obedience consists in an entire conformity of our will to that of our superior, by really making his will ours. And that is what no religious person can be ignorant of, since they are all received upon this condition. At their first coming this is proposed to them, and laid down as the first great principle they are to act by. And when they are desired to consider that they are come to religion, not to do their own, but another's will, they never fail to answer that they knew this very well beforehand. Now, the things had been told them exactly as they are, for it is most certain that it is obedience makes a religious. St. John Climacus calls " obedience the tomb of our will, wherein it lies dead, and from which humility rises again"—*Grad.*, iv. *art.* 3. For, certainly the very moment we enter into religion, we ought to think that our will dies to ourselves, and that henceforward we ought to live only to that of our superiors. St. Ignatius adds, that we must be always ready to execute our superior's orders, though ever so difficult and repugnant to nature. This he calls the proof of prompt obedience; for, as other saints observe, true obedience is best known in difficult commands. For obedience is not easily discerned when the thing commanded pleases, and is according to our inclination; which circumstance sometimes may prevail more upon us in order to a compliance, than a real submission to the will of God. But when the command is harsh and very repugnant, and we notwithstanding zealously embrace it, there is no doubt but that our motive is good, since we are assured we do not seek ourselves, or our own satisfaction by it, nor aim at anything but God and the fulfilling of his will. Hence we may deservedly commend those religious, who, mistrusting themselves and fearing to be surprised by self-love, are really troubled when they are put into an employment that naturally pleases them. They think that they shall find nothing here to do but to follow their own inclination, and that they consequently have no merit; and thus they remain uneasy, until they have acquainted their superior with their apprehensions and the cause of them. On the contrary, when they are commanded a thing to which they have an aversion, they are glad of it, being satisfied that they do not seek their own will, but God's. St. Gregory says, "that our will must have a part in the obedience, when the command is harsh and troublesome; but nothing at all, when it is easy and agreeable"—*Lib.* xxxv. *Moral.*, c. 10. For instance, our will ought to have nothing of its own when obedience lays an honourable command upon us; then we embrace the charge, purely because our superior commands, and because God will have it so. On the contrary, when we are appointed to do an action not only painful, but also mean and contemptible, then our will ought to have a larger share therein, by a ready compliance with it, and perform it with no less zeal than love. He that shall do thus in things to which he feels repugnance, will have no reason to distrust the motive of his obedience in those things to which he has an inclination. Whereas, he that does not obey as readily in mean and low offices, which he has an aversion to, as well as in others that are better, has reason to suspect that his obedience has more of that satisfaction which he finds in the latter, than of submission of his will to God. By this means we shall easily know whether we seek God or ourselves in what we do.

Hence it follows, that those who wish for such commands from their superior as they like themselves, who use little arts to make him condescend to their will, and who love to do nothing but what they find satisfaction in, are very ill disposed in order to obedience, or rather have no obedience at all. St. Ignatius says, that we are deluded and blinded by self-love, if we think we practise obedience, when we endeavour to incline our superior to assign us what we ourselves wish for; and he alleges these words of St. Bernard in proof of what he says: " He that either openly or covertly endeavours to have his superior command him what he has a mind to himself, is much deceived if he pretend to any merit from such obedience: for in this case he does not obey his superior, but his superior rather obeys him"—*Serm. de Trib. Ord. Eccles. ad Patr. in capitulo.* There is nothing more generally or more highly approved of in religion than this maxim; yet for all that, we must not pass it over too lightly, since it is at the same time one of the chief and principal points to be treated of in this matter. One of the things which a religious ought to fear most, is when he has an employment given him of his own seeking, or when he has made a difficulty to accept of another which they wished to assign him. For perhaps he may imagine himself afterwards to have done wonders, by the great pains he took in such employment, and to have merited much in the sight of God; yet he will find himself very much deceived, and that he has merited nothing towards eternity, because his own will and not God's prevailed in all he did. The children of Israel said thus to God, "Why hast thou not looked down from Heaven upon us, who have fasted? We have humbled ourselves before thee, O Lord, and thou seemest not to take notice of us". And he answered them, "because ye are glutted with your own will upon your fasting days"—*Isa.*, lviii. 3,—that is, because in your fasts you do nothing but what you will yourselves.

St. Bernard having applied these words of Isaias to the same purpose, adds, "that self-will must needs be a great evil, which renders even our good works so unprofitable and even of no service"—*Serm.* 71, *sup. Cant.* Speaking also of St. Paul's conversion, he treats this subject at large, and observes that the first thing St. Paul did or said, after the light from Heaven had opened the eyes of his soul, was to know God's pleasure in these words:—" Lord, what wouldst thou have me to do?"—*Acts*, ix. 6. This was a sign, says St. Bernard, of a true conversion, and an argument that he had for ever renounced this world, and was fully determined to follow Jesus Christ, by desiring to know, " what God would have him do".—A short sentence, but very comprehensive, pithy, expressive, full of energy, and worthy of all commendation! How few are there now-a-days, as St. Bernard complains, that aspire to this perfection in obedience! How few are to be found now, who, entirely renouncing their own will, wish never to do anything again of their own accord, and only desire with St. Paul, that God's will may be accomplished in them, saying, "Lord, what wouldst thou have me do?" Or with the prophet, "My heart is ready, O my God, my heart is ready"—*Psal.*, lvi. 8,—to do all you please to command me. But alas! the blind man in the gospel has more proselytes than St. Paul. The Saviour of the world asked the blind man, "what wouldst thou have me do to thee?"—*Luke*, xviii. 41. In which words we may admire the mercy of God, and his humility in forgetting his dignity, by stooping thus low to a poor man. Where was there ever a master that desired to be informed of the will of his slave, in order to execute it? "It is clear this man was blind, and wanted both reflection and fear, since he did not cry out hereupon: Far be such an action from me, O Lord! it is I that desire to know thy will and pleasure concerning me. It is not fit, O my God, that thou shouldst ask to know my will and to do it; it is my duty to inform myself of thine, and perform it, though with ever so much difficulty"—*Serm.* i. *de Convers. Apos. Pauli.* Here, says St. Bernard, you have a portrait of most religious of these days. They must, like this blind man, be asked, "what would you have me do to you?" The superior must continually employ his thoughts in finding out what every one will soonest obey in, and accommodate himself to every man's particular humour; whereas, on the contrary, they ought to know his will and to prevent it by obedience; since they are come to religion not to make the superior conform and submit to their desires by only commanding them what they please, but rather to live in an humble submission of mind, ready to perform the superior's will, without which there is neither obedience nor religion.

CHAPTER V.

Of the third degree of obedience.

THE third degree of obedience consists in a conformity of our judgment to that of our superior in such sort that, as our will must be one with his, so our judgment also ought to be the same; so that we ought to look upon all his commands as reasonable and just: and lastly, we must submit our understanding to his, as to the rule of our actions. To perceive the necessity of this third degree, you need only call to mind, what has already been said, namely, without this, obedience can never be perfect and entire. This doctrine is conformable to the opinion of holy men, who term obedience a perfect holocaust, in which the whole man, by the hands of those whom God has put in authority, is entirely offered up to God in the fire of charity. We find this difference in the old law, between a holocaust and other sacrifices:—in a sacrifice one part of the victim was burnt to God's honour, and another part was kept for the use of the priests and of such as served in the temple; but in a holocaust, the whole victim was burnt and totally consumed, without any reserve. In like manner, your obedience can never be a holocaust, unless you submit your understanding as well as your will; nor can it be entire or perfect as long as you fail to sacrifice your judgment, which is the noblest power of the soul. This made St. Ignatius say, that those who submit their will, but not their judgment, to the superior's orders, have only one foot in religion.

St. Bernard, in his first sermon upon St. Paul's conversion, is very copious in laying down and declaring what this obedience of the understanding ought to be; and for this effect, assigns it different qualities, which he applies according as different circumstances require. When St. Paul, struck with a light from Heaven, and seized with fear, cried out, "Lord, what wouldst thou have me do?" it was answered him, "go into the city, and there thou shalt receive thy orders"—*Acts*, ix. 7. You came to religion, says St. Bernard, to know what you are to do. It was for this end that divine Providence so disposed that you should be struck with a fear and dread of God's judgments, which created an earnest desire in you of serving him, and inspired you with a design of entering this holy city of religion, the school of virtue and piety. Here it is that you may learn his will and pleasure in all things. The Scripture adds, says St. Bernard, that St. Paul " saw nothing, though his eyes were open, when he entered the town, and that those who were with him led him by the hand"—*Acts*, ix. 8. " Here, brethren", continues the same saint, " you have a lively figure of a true conversion" and an exact model of religious obedience, which chiefly consists in seeing nothing, though your eyes be opened, and in not determining any thing by yourselves, but giving yourselves totally up into the hands of your superior, and letting him lead you where he pleases. Take care lest you see too clear, like Adam and Eve, whose eyes being opened as soon as they had sinned, saw themselves naked, and were ashamed. Some may ask me if they were not naked, or did not see clear before their fall. I answer in the affirmative; but they were not concerned about their being naked, because they lived in the purity and simplicity of original justice. Now, the purity and simplicity which they forfeited by disobedience, we should endeavour to acquire by our submission; so that we should never have our eyes open to see the faults of our neighbour, though they be ever so visible; and always have them shut in everything that relates to obedience.

St. John Climacus, speaking of the necessity of restraint in this point, says, " that we must behave ourselves, when we have thoughts and sentiments contrary to obedience, just as we would do in temptations against chastity or our holy faith; that is, not dwell upon them, but take occasion from them the more to abase and humble ourselves". St. Jerom, writing to a religious concerning his conduct in religion, recommends this submission of mind very particularly to him. Do not concern yourself, says he, in judging of the orders which your superior gives out, nor in examining the reason why they lay such commands upon you; it is your duty to obey and execute their orders, as Moses declares: " Hear, Israel, and be silent"—*Epist. ad Rustic. Monach.* St. Basil proposes to religious the example of an apprentice, whilst he learns his trade under his master, as a pattern of their obedience. He has his eyes continually upon his master, he obeys him in everything without contradicting, without interposing his judgment, or without ever inquiring the reason of this or that command, and by so doing, in a little time he becomes a master himself. Pythagoras' scholars had so much respect for him, that his bare authority was so convincing a reason to them, that all controversy was silenced by an "he said it". How much deference then ought religious to have for their superior, who is far above Pythagoras, and holds the place of Christ! Ought they not, when there is question of obedience, to think they have a sufficient reason to submit their judgments, and believe whatever is commanded them is most convenient for them?

Eusebius the historian tells us of a very good law amongst the Lacedemonians, which forbade all young people to meddle with the government of the commonwealth, or to examine whether their laws were good or bad, or to inquire into their inconveniencies; showing by this, that the veneration they had for their ancestors who had handed these laws down to them, sufficed to make them believe them as just and holy as if the gods themselves had made them. And in case any of the old men should judge anything to stand in need of reformation (because forms of government change frequently with the times), the law ordained that this proposal should only be made before the old senators, who were to be the only judges of it; thereby to take away all occasion of young men's losing their respect and veneration for the laws, which, should it once happen, might give a dangerous blow to their commonwealth. If these wise heathens wished all people to have respect and esteem for the laws of their forefathers, which were only grounded upon natural reason, and looked upon only as a means to preserve their government, with how much more reason ought we Christians and religious have the highest veneration and respect for the commands of our superior, which are not founded upon bare natural reason, but upon the light of faith and the holy Gospels! St. Ignatius, in the admirable letter which he wrote on obedience, proves clearly, that without this obedience of the understanding, the will can never perfectly or long obey, nor perform a command with that exact perfection which obedience requires. He also sets down several inconveniencies, which arise from a want of this obedience of our understanding and submission of our judgment.

CHAPTER VI.
Blind obedience.

OUR holy founder says, that as there are two ways in God's Church to salvation—one which relates to the keeping of the commandments, and which equally concerns all Christians; the other which regards religious in particular, viz., the practice of evangelical counsels, which are superadded to the commandments —so in like manner there are two sorts of obedience in religion. The one is general, common, and imperfect; the other is perfect, and shows the force and virtue of obedience, and teaches us how far a true religious may advance in perfection. The imperfect obedience, says this saint, has eyes to its own advantage; the perfect is blind, but in this blindness, wisdom and perfection are clearly perceived. The one discusses every command; the other obeys without reasoning upon any point. The first is always more inclined to one thing than another, and is never indifferent upon the matter; the second is like the tongue of a balance, which without leaning this or that way, is always equally disposed to the different things it may be commanded. The first complies exteriorly, by executing the orders given, but resists interiorly, whereby it disobeys, and consequently does not deserve the name of obedience. The second is not only content to do what is appointed, but even submits both will and understanding to that of the superior, always concluding that he has reason for what he does; nor does it seek out reasons to obey, nor so much as permit itself to be led by those which do occur. The bare consideration of the superior's command is the only motive why it obeys. This is properly the blind obedience which the saints and spiritual writers so constantly recommend to us, and of which they have left behind them so great examples in their own practice. When they call this obedience blind, they do not mean an indiscriminate submission to everything commanded, though the thing should even be criminal. This would be a very dangerous error, as St. Ignatius observes. Their meaning therefore is, that in all things, where there appears no sin, we ought not to discuss the case, but to obey with a holy simplicity of heart, concluding our superior's command to be conformable to the law of God, and making this command and obedience itself the sole motive and reason why we obey. Cassian calls this an obedience "without discussion or examination"—*Lib.* 4, *de Inst. Renunt.*, c. 10, 24,—for in effect we ought perform simply what is commanded us, and not exert ourselves to find out and examine the reasons thereof. St. John Climacus says in like manner, "that obedience is a movement of the will, without previous discourse or examination". He calls it also "a voluntary death, a life void of curiosity, and an entire renouncing of our own discernment"—*Grad.* 4, *art.* 3. St. Basil upon these words of Christ, "feed my sheep"—*John,* xxi. 17,—which were spoken to St. Peter, and in him to all ecclesiastical superiors, says, that as sheep follow their shepherd and are led by him to what place he pleases, so a religious ought to be guided by and follow his superior, by obeying him blindly, without reasoning on his orders.

St. Bernard says, "that perfect obedience, especially in beginners, ought not to ask, what? or wherefore? but endeavour to execute faithfully and submissively what is commanded"—*Ep. de Vit. Solit. ad. Frat. de Monte Dei.* "True obedience", says St. Gregory, "neither examines the superior's command, nor his intention therein; for he that has once given up himself entirely to the conduct of his superior, never finds greater satisfaction than in obeying his orders. He that knows how to obey well, does not know how to interpose his own judgment, since he knows obedience to be his greatest good"—*Lib.* 2, *Reg.*, c. 4. The questioning God's prohibition cost our first parents very dear. Their ruin and ours took its date from hence. By this the Devil wrought their fall. "Why", says he, "has God forbidden you to eat of all the fruit that grows in Paradise?" Eve answered him, "that thereby they might avoid death"—*Gen.*, iii. 1. For God, speaking of the tree of knowledge of good and evil, said expressly, "the day you eat of this fruit you shall die"—*Gen.*, ii. 17,—and yet Eve began to doubt of the meaning of God's threat. She imagined that it was only to affright them, which thought very much disposed her to be afterwards deceived. For the Devil laid hold upon this advantageous occasion, and said to them, "You shall not die, but thereby come to the knowledge of good and evil, and become like gods yourselves"—*Gen.*, iii. 4, 5. Thus he persuaded them that God had laid the prohibition upon them for fear they should eat and grow as wise as himself. Eve, carried away with a desire of being raised above her present condition, gave credit to the serpent, eat of the forbidden fruit, and made Adam eat with her. Here you see that our first parents, in consequence of their reasoning, disobeyed, and thereby incurred the death of their souls at the same moment, and made themselves subject also to the death of the body, and were for ever driven out of the garden of Eden. This stratagem of the Devil against our first parents succeeded then so well, that he has made use of it ever since against us their posterity. This made St. Paul, who knew the Devil's craft and cunning, forewarn us of it in these words, "I fear lest the serpent, who so artfully seduced Eve, should corrupt your minds also, and make you fall from that simplicity which Christ demands of you"—II. *Cor.*, xi. 3. Take care therefore that you be not deceived by this old serpent; apply yourself to what is commanded you, by executing it punctually, without examining the reasons or motives of it, and this prompt and blind obedience will serve you as an infallible rule in everything you do. It is of great importance in the beginning, says St. Bernard, to accustom ourselves to a blind obedience. " For it is morally impossible that a novice should long keep in his cell, or persevere in religion, if he follows the common rules of ordinary prudence, and if he desires to know the reason of everything commanded him". What therefore must he do— how must he behave himself? "Let him become a fool, that he may become wise; let all his discretion be to have none at all whilst he obeys; and let his wisdom and prudence never appear in matters of obedience. It belongs to the superior to examine and consider well of things, before he commands; but the subject's duty is to execute them with humility, confidence, and simplicity, when once commanded"—*Ep. ad. Frat. de Monte Dei*. In fine, the superior is to reason the case, and the subject is to obey.

The remarks which the apostle makes upon Abraham's blind obedience, in doing his duty by preparing all things to sacrifice his son Isaac, are very fit and proper for our present discourse. God had promised to multiply Abraham's posterity, like the stars of Heaven and the sands of the sea, and to make him the father of many nations. Now Abraham had only one son by Sarah, nor were there any hopes of having any more, by reason of their great age; and though he might have expected more children, yet this very promise was made to him only in behalf of Isaac, God telling him expressly, "Isaac shall raise posterity to thee"— *Gen.*, xxi. 12. Yet notwithstanding all this, when God commanded him to offer up Isaac to him as an holocaust, he made no delay, nor doubted in the least of God's fulfilling the promise made him, but put all things in readiness blindly to execute God's orders. He took his son, bound him, laid him upon the altar, and had his arm lifted up ready to sacrifice him. "He still hoped", says St. Paul, " even against hope, that he should yet be the father of many nations"—*Rom.*, iv. 18. Natural reason told him, that he had no more children when Isaac was once taken away; but supernatural hope vanquished this diffidence of nature, and Abraham, without relying upon probabilities, firmly believed that God would perform his promise, either by raising Isaac from the dead, or by some other way he did not know of. "Distrust did not stop him; because he was strengthened by faith, giving glory to God, and knowing most certainly that God was able to fulfil the promise he had made him"—*ibid.*, iv. 20, 21. God was so pleased with Abraham's obedience, that immediately upon it, he promised him that the Messias should descend lineally from him, and by that means his posterity should be as numerous as the stars, in these following words: "I have sworn by myself, that since thou hast done this action, and not spared thy only son for my sake, I will bless thee and multiply thy seed as the stars of Heaven and the sands of the sea-shore. Thy posterity shall be masters of their enemies' towns, and all nations shall be blessed in thy seed; because thou hast obeyed my voice"—*Gen.*, xii. 16, etc. Consider, says St. Jerom upon this passage, how much God was pleased with Abraham's blind obedience, since he rewarded it so generously, as, "for one son whom he would have sacrificed upon Earth, to promise him a progeny equal in number to the stars of Heaven". The ancient fathers set so great a value on this kind of obedience, and so constantly practised it, that whole volumes are full of the examples they have left behind them; and several of these examples were ratified from Heaven by miracles, to make us the more sensible of the merit of obedience, and to teach us how pleasing it is to Almighty God.

St. Ignatius, following these holy men, as well in their practice as doctrine, instructs us in our duty of obedience by things very obvious to sense, and makes use of the two following comparisons, no less profitable than proper for that end. All those, says he, that live under obedience, must know that they are to suffer themselves to be led and guided, as Divine Providence shall direct, by the hand of their superior, just as a dead corpse, which permits itself to be moved and carried where you please. St. Francis likewise made use of this comparison, and proposed it often to his religious, in the words of the apostle, "you are dead, and your life is hidden in God with Christ"—*Colos.*, iii. 3. And, indeed, a good religious ought to die to the world in this manner, since his entrance into religion is a civil death. Let us, therefore, die this happy death. A dead body sees not—it answers not—it complains not, nor has it any perception. Let us have no eyes to observe curiously our superior's actions; let us make no reply to the prescriptions of obedience; and, when we are commanded anything against our inclination, let us act as if we had no feeling. Linen that has been much used, and is almost worn out, commonly serves as a winding-sheet for the dead. A religious ought to wish to be treated in the same manner, no less in respect of his clothes than in everything else. He should wish to wear, for example, an old torn habit, and to have the worst and most ordinary things both in his cell and in the refectory. He that has not a will thus disposed, but frets and troubles himself when he meets with this kind of usage, is not truly dead to the world, as becomes one of his profession, but is totally a stranger to the spirit of mortification.

St. Ignatius says, moreover, and it is the second comparison he makes use of, that we must be in the hands of God and our superior like a staff which we take in our hand to walk with. A staff goes wherever you carry it; where you lay it down, there it stays; nor has it any other motion but what it receives from the hand that holds it. A religious ought to be the same —he must give himself up into the hands of his superior when put in this or that office; and whether it be honourable or mean, he must be content with it, and remain in it without showing any repugnance at all. If a staff should come once to make resistance, and carry itself to some other place than that in which you laid it, or if it should become rather inconvenient to you than serviceable, you would certainly throw it away. So, when you resist him who is to govern you, and when you show dislike of the place or employment he has put you in, or when there is any opposition in your actions, and in your will and judgment, to the intentions he has on you, it is certain that you rather inconvenience him than do him the service you owe him. If you persist in this spirit of indocility, you will soon be thought a burden to every superior you live with;

it will not be known how to deal with you, or how to derive advantage from you; and at last every one will be glad to be rid of you, so that you will be continually tossed from one house to another. There is no pain in carrying a staff in our hand, because it serves us for all uses we put it to; nor ought any subject to give pain or trouble to his superior, in whose hands he is, but, on the contrary, prove useful and agreeable to him, and give him occasion to say, as the centurion did: "I have soldiers under me, and I say to this, go, and he goes; and to another, come, and he comes; and to my servant, do this, and he does it".—*Mat.*, viii. 9.

St. Basil, treating of this subject, makes use of another comparison which is also very apposite. As a workman, says he, who is employed in a building, uses all the instruments of his art as he pleases, and never finds any of them disobedient to his hand, or resisting the motions he gives them, so a religious ought to be in the hand of a superior a useful instrument, which he may use as he pleases in a spiritual building; he is never to make resistance, but to do what is appointed him. Moreover, as the instrument does not choose its employment, so the religious ought never select any office, but leave that and himself also totally to the care of his superior. In fine, continues this saint, as an instrument does not act in the absence of its master, because it cannot move of itself, and has no other motion than what it receives from the artist who makes use of it, in like manner a religious ought to do nothing without orders from his superior, nor in the most trifling things dispose of himself even for one instant, but at all times and in everything follow the movements and impressions of his superior.

Such ought to be the obedience of religious; and I remember one of our fathers (P. Antone Araoz), who had been a long time superior amongst us, said on this subject, that for fifteen years together he never thought of giving a reason of his commands to any one of his subjects, thinking that if he had done otherwise he should have done them an injury. Then it was that they lived in such holy simplicity and profound resignation, that nobody interfered with or questioned the superior's orders, but as soon as the word of command was given, every one submitted his judgment so far to it, that he forthwith concluded the thing commanded not only just, but most suitable and best for him. We ought to propose this holy simplicity to ourselves; and, as the most ancient in religion are those who ought to give example to others, so it chiefly belongs to them to edify by their submission and obedience, for they must not think that their seniority authorizes them to examine or find fault with the orders of the superior.

It is related in the life of St. Ignatius, that he used frequently to say, when he was general of the society, that if his Holiness should command him to embark in the first vessel he found at Ostia, a port not far from Rome, and to put to sea without mast, sail, oar, helm, or any other thing necessary for a sea voyage or for the maintenance of life, he would immediately obey him, not only without uneasiness or repugnance, but with great interior satisfaction. A man of quality hearing him say this, was struck at it, and told him there would be no prudence in such an action. Prudence, replied the saint, is more necessary for him that commands, than for him who obeys in simplicity of heart.

CHAPTER VII.

Obedience in spiritual matters.

IT is not only in things which seem to bear relation to flesh and blood that we are to submit our judgment to that of our superior, but even in those also which have no relation at all to the body, but are altogether spiritual. Let no one think, that in these things he is more at liberty to swerve from the will and judgment of his superior, than in the others. On the contrary, submission and obedience of the understanding is far more necessary here; because spiritual things, being of their nature more elevated, the danger would be far greater, and the fall more disastrous, if we had no one to direct us. This is a truth so evident, that Cassian says the Devil makes use of nothing more to precipitate monks into sin, than to persuade them to contemn in spiritual matters the advice and counsel of the seniors, and to follow the dictates of their own understanding. The same author (*Cass. Coll.* ii. *c.* 5, *and seq*), and St. John Climacus cite examples of several hermits much given to prayer and spirituality, and advanced in years, who, trusting too much to their own reason, and becoming their own directors, were at last deceived by the Devil's illusions. The

Devil urged one of them to sacrifice his own son that lived in the same monastery with him. This poor man, imagining that he should hereby become another Abraham, would certainly have put it in execution, had not his son by seeing him prepare the cords and whet his knife, suspected his design, and fled from him. He suggested to another to throw himself from a precipice, and made him believe that he should obtain a crown of martyrdom by it, and go immediately to Heaven.

Cassian likewise cites the example of Heron the hermit, who lived in such retirement and abstinence, that upon Easter-day, when all the hermits used to dine together and have better fare than usual, he staid in his cell, and was abstemious to that degree, that he made no addition to his ordinary fare, which was only bread and water. This austere life made him so proud, and wedded him so much to his own opinion, that he persuaded himself that he was a great saint; that he had no more danger to apprehend in this life; and that if he should throw himself headlong into a well, the angels would bear him up and preserve him from being hurt. Full of this fancy, and not doubting but that God would work a miracle to make his virtue and merit known to the world, he threw himself one night into a deep well, out of which some of the brothers, who ran hither upon the noise of the fall, with great difficulty pulled him up half dead. Notwithstanding this, the illusions of the Devil had made so deep an impression upon him, that for the three days he lived after it, neither his own unhappy experience, nor all they could say to disabuse him and to make him repent, could efface this impression from his mind. This proves clearly how extremely dangerous it is even for persons advanced both in years and perfection, to rely too much upon their own judgment, and not to submit to those whom God has placed as guides over them. And therefore a holy man said with reason, that one that is too confident of himself needs not the Devil to tempt him, since he is become the greatest tempter and devil to himself.

St. Chrysostom tells us, that he who depends altogether upon his own judgment, though he be ever so well versed in spiritual matters, is in far greater danger of falling, than one who is a novice in a spiritual life, but who gives himself up to the conduct of another. He compares the first to a skilful pilot, who, trusting to his art and abilities, puts to sea in a ship that has neither sail nor oar; and the second to a passenger, who, being altogether unacquainted with sea affairs, embarks in a well-rigged vessel with an experienced master. Let none then deceive themselves by thinking that in spiritual affairs, for example, in the spiritual exercise, or the practice of penance and mortification, they can dispense with obedience, and guide themselves by their own reason. For, as Cassian justly observes, to transgress the superior's command through a desire of labouring, is no less a disobedience, than to transgress it through a desire of remaining idle. "Always remember this maxim", says St. Basil (*Exhort. ad Vit. Mon.*), " never to do anything contrary to the advice or without the knowledge of your superior; for these hidden doings are a kind of secret theft and sacrilege; they are also extremely prejudicial to you, nor can they ever turn to your profit. I admit that you look upon them to be good, but if so, why do you conceal them? Why do not you ask your superior's leave to do them? He wishes you as well as you do yourself; apply to him; he will not deny you, and then God will bless all your undertakings. Do not expose yourself for want of a little submission, to do that which is not only unprofitable, but also highly prejudicial to you: and take care that God say not to you, as he said once to his people by the prophet Isaias, offer me no more of your unprofitable sacrifices"—*Isai.*, i. 13.

We must never command evil to be done, say St. Gregory and St. Bernard; nor must we obey, when there is question of our committing sin. But when there is only question of omitting a good act, which obedience prohibits, we are obliged to submit to obedience. The tree which God prohibited Adam and Eve to eat of, was not bad in itself, but on the contrary very good and excellent; yet God, to give them an occasion to merit more by submission and obedience to their Creator, was pleased to forbid them the use of a thing which, abstracting from the prohibition, had nothing bad in it, and which, were it not for the prohibition, they could have eaten of very innocently. Now a superior sometimes does the same to his religious that are under his care; he forbids them things that are good of themselves, and he does this either because these things are not proper for them, or in order to try their submission and obedience.

St. Basil says that the perfection of obedience in inferiors shines less brightly in their abstaining from evil, than in their abstaining from good which they are forbidden to do. His reason is, because they have always an obligation of abstaining from evil, independent of any particular prohibition; but that it is only in virtue of a particular prohibition they abstain from what is good in itself; so that we may justly say, that their obedience appears far more in the latter, because there is nothing but obedience which restrains them. On the contrary, want of submission in things purely spiritual, shows more indocility and more attachment to self-will. For in other things, for example, in silence, modesty, temperance, and the like, satisfaction and pleasure may have a part in the disobedience; whereas in matters purely spiritual, and opposite to flesh and blood, nothing but a desire to do our own will, and a proud mind, can move us to disobey. So that, whatever comes from hence, even the things we undertake for our spiritual advancement and to render ourselves more pleasing to God, produce no other effect than to remove us farther from perfection, and to render us more displeasing to God and superiors. There is danger in riding a hard-mouthed horse; for, not feeling the bit, he cannot be mastered, and he may run away with the rider, and even throw him down a precipice. Hence, as a horse, to be good, must be soft-mouthed and yield to the curb, or to the least check of the bridle; in like manner, a religious ought to be flexible, complying, easy to be governed, never resisting the curb of obedience, but suffering himself to be guided as his superiors think proper.

We read in Ecclesiastical History (*Evag.* l. i. *Hist. Eccl.* c. 13, 14), that St. Simon Stylites chose for his retirement to live upon a pillar forty cubits high, and practised such penance there as the like had never been known before. He was continually exposed to all the inconvenience of heat and cold; he passed whole Lents without eating or drinking, and added so many other austerities to these, that some, thinking it impossible for a man to undergo such rigorous penances, doubted whether or not he were really a man. Several fathers of the desert hearing of this strange and new way of living, met to consult about it, and the result of their debate was to send a messenger to him in their names, who should say to him: What new kind of life is this that you lead? Why have you forsaken the high road marked out to us by so many saints, and taken this byeway which never man trod before you? The fathers of the desert, from whom I come, have met in full assembly about you, and command you to come down from your pillar, to live like them, and to distinguish yourself no longer by such singularities. This messenger had also in his commission, that, in case he should not obey these orders, he should be forced to a compliance; but if he should obey them, and be willing to leave his pillar, he should then declare to him, in their names, that they permitted him to live there, and to continue his new rigid way of living, because they were satisfied by this obedience that God had called him to it. He that had this charge given him, went to the saint, and delivered his orders. He had scarce finished these words, "the fathers of the desert have ordered you to come down from your pillar", but the saint put himself in a posture of descending and of obeying their orders. The messenger seeing this great obedience, put the second part of his commission in execution, and spoke thus to the servant of God: "Take courage, father, and continue this sort of life with the same generosity you have begun to embrace it; it is God has called you to it, your obedience declares it, and all the fathers of the desert are of this opinion". Let us take notice here, on the one hand, how readily Stylites obeys, how soon he abstained from a holy action, to which he really believed God had called him; and on the other, in what esteem the ancient fathers held obedience and submission, since they really believed that they needed no other proof of God's having called him; and on the contrary, they require no other sign but disobedience to their orders, to conclude that his vocation was not from Heaven.

Confessors and spiritual directors usually adopt the same method, in order to discern by what kind of spirit their penitents are led in those practices of devotion which they impose upon themselves. One, for example, has a great desire to communicate frequently, and his confessor will have him not do it so often. Another is much given to mortification, as fasting, disciplines, and hair-cloth; another will sleep upon the bare ground; another scarce allows himself any sleep at all; and so of the rest. Without doubt all these desires of penance and mortification are very commendable, and of the two extremes, that which is contrary to the inclinations of our nature, ought to be the less suspected, because there is always reason of distrust in those things which have an appearance of self-love in them. But the best and surest way of all is, to give an account of all your thoughts and actions to your superior or confessor, and act according to their advice; for it is most certain that by this means you will merit much more and please Almighty God far better. And let due attention be paid to this doctrine, as it is both holy and infallible. If, for example, a religious intends to impose some mortification upon himself, and if his superior, whom he has acquainted with it, forbids him to do it, I say, that by omitting it he shall be so far from losing the merit of the good action he intended to do, that he will even acquire additional merit in the sight of God. For he has merited by the good actions he had intended to do, because he had an efficacious will of doing them, and he has the merit of obedience, because it is through obedience he abstains from doing them. Nay, sometimes it may happen that this obedience may be far more meritorious than the good works themselves, upon account of the great resignation that is requisite, both to abstain from doing what we so earnestly desire, and to submit our will and judgment to that of our confessor or superior. This is what was revealed to St. Bridget in the following manner. This saint was used (*Lib*. 4, *Revel. S. Bri.*, c. 26) to practise great austerities, and her spiritual director at once curtailed several of those she practised, thinking fit to do so for the good of her health. She obeyed him in this, though with some difficulty, fearing lest it might retard her spiritual progress. Being once thus piously uneasy, the Blessed Virgin appeared to her, and said to her: Daughter, suppose two persons agree to fast one day out of devotion, and one of them that is his own master performs the fast, and has his reward for it, but the other living under obedience, does not fast that day, because his superior will not give him leave, certainly this last will receive a double reward; the one for his real design to fast, and the other for his submitting to obedience.

The heathens were no strangers to this sort of obedience, as we may infer from the esteem they held it in. Plutarch says, that Agesilaus, king of Lacedemon, having been successful in war in Asia, whereby he restored the Grecian cities to their ancient liberty, and being upon the point to carry his victorious arms into Persia, received orders from the ephori, or supreme magistrates, to return home; and that he instantly abandoned his enterprise, and put all things in readiness to obey these orders. And never, says he, did this prince acquire more glory than he did by setting this example of respect and obedience to his native country.

But why search abroad for examples, since we have some of this kind, and those the most admirable, set by members of our own society? Witness the opinion our holy founder had of St. Xaverius's obedience, when he resolved to call him from the Indies, where he laboured so profitably in the conversion of souls. St. Xaverius was at this time wonderfully successful in his evangelical expeditions. He had converted many thousands, and was on the point of gaining whole kingdoms to Jesus Christ. Notwithstanding all this, St. Ignatius having written a letter, and only subscribed it with a single I, to give him notice to return, he doubted not that upon the receipt of it he would leave his glorious enterprises, forsake the eastern world, and return forthwith to Rome, whither obedience called him. And had not God called him to Heaven to receive the recompense of his labours before that letter came to his hands, he would certainly have obeyed.

CHAPTER VIII.

What has been said in this treatise confirmed by several examples.

IT is related that abbot Nisteron, the day he became religious, spoke thus to himself: " Now I consider that myself and the ass of the monastery are but one. He carries the burden they lay upon him, be it light or heavy, without murmuring or making resistance. He suffers without resentment the blows they give him, as well as the contempt the world holds him in. He works continually, and yet is content to feed upon a little straw. Such ought to be the disposition of my mind: moreover, as a carrier's horse goes not out of the road when he pleases, nor lies down when he pleases, but obeys his master in everything, so a religious ought to submit to all the orders of his superior. And as the horse does not work, sleep, or eat, for his own convenience, but does all for his master's service, in like manner the labour, rest, sleep, yea every action, and even the life itself, of a religious, ought not to have for its end his own particular advantage, but the advantage of his order and the glory of God"— *Vit. Pat. Lib. de Humil., p.* 651. " I am", said the Royal Prophet to God, "as a beast of burden before thee, but yet I am always with thee"—*Ps.*, lxxii. 23. If you desire to be always with God, and labour profitably for your spiritual advancement in religion, strive to make yourself like a pack-horse, or a beast of burden, by submitting to all things which shall be required of you.

Surius, in the life of St. Melania, has the following example, and he says that he himself used frequently to tell it to his own Carthusians. A young man went into the desert, and finding there one of the ancient fathers, he begged of him to admit him as his disciple. The good old man being willing to show him what disposition of mind was required in order to have his petition granted, bade him go and beat a statue which stood hard by his cell. He did so. Upon which the old father asked him if the statue complained or resisted; to which he answered, no. The father then bade him go beat it again, and lay a heavy load upon it. After he had commanded him to do this three several times, he asked him again whether the statue had shown any sign of resentment or impatience. The young man told him that it did not, because it was a statue, and destitute of feeling. Hereupon the man of God says to him: If you can suffer to be treated by me as you have treated the statue, without murmur, complaint, or resistance, stay in God's name and be my disciple; but if you find yourself incapable of suffering all this, go back from whence you came, for you are not fit to be a religious.

We read that St. Gertrude lived under an abbess whose life was truly exemplary, but whose temper was disagreeable; and that one day as the saint was praying for the improvement of the abbess's temper, our Saviour spoke thus to her: Why do you ask that she should be freed from an imperfection which gives her such frequent occasions of humiliation in my sight, upon account of those failings which her warmth of temper and impatience cause in her? Besides, what merit would you have in obeying her, if she were of a sweeter temper? I permit this imperfection in your superior for the exercise and improvement of your obedience, and for her own merit.

Blosius (*Mon. Spir.*, c. 4) also relates of the same St. Gertrude something very like unto this. One day, says he, she offered up her prayers for a certain superior of a congregation, and begged earnestly of God that he would be pleased to free him from a fault he was very subject to. Whilst she was at her prayers our Saviour appeared unto her, and said : The same excess of goodness and mercy that moved me to institute that congregation, causes me to permit imperfections in those that govern it, thereby to increase the merit of those they have command over; for there is more virtue in submitting to the orders of a person whose faults we know, than to one whose faults we know not. When I permit superiors to have their failings, and to forget themselves sometimes by reason of temporal affairs, which they must be employed in, it is to the end they should from thence take occasion to humble themselves the more: and as subjects may increase in virtue by the defects of their superiors; even so the faults, as well as the virtues of inferiors, may serve sometimes to augment the merits of superiors. These words filled her with admiration, to see how God's infinite goodness and wisdom dispose all things for the advantage and good of his servants, and that even those defects he permits in them, should serve and help to render them more perfect.

St. Athanasius, in the life of St. Anthony, says, that the ancient hermits who consecrated themselves particularly to obedience, ordinarily sought for harsh superiors, who would treat them rudely, and never show approbation of anything they did for them; and the more disagreeable the superior's temper was, the more readily they obeyed him. The ordinary custom observed in those days amongst them was, that two solitaries should put themselves under the conduct and government of an ancient father as his scholars, and serve him in everything as a servant does his master; so that the authority a master has to correct and chastise his servant when he fails to do what is commanded him, the same the ancients had over their disciples when they failed in the most trifling affair. Nay, they more frequently treated their disciples very harshly, either out of natural severity or else to exercise their patience, as St. Pachomius did to his scholar Theodosius, to cure him of vain glory. And St. John Climacus says, that to suffer these hardships and injuries, was a trial which lasted till they were thirty years of age.

Cassian tells us (*Collat.*, xviii. *c.* 14) of a lady of Alexandria, who was so very desirous of sufferings, that not content with what God was pleased to inflict on her, she most earnestly sought after more occasions of suffering and of exercising her patience. As the Church of Alexandria maintained a great many poor widows in those days, this person of quality went to St. Athanasius, to request that one of them might live with her, for whom she would provide, and thereby impart so much ease to the Church. The holy bishop, highly approving of her intention, sent her a widow that was pious and sweetly tempered, whom she kept with her, and sometime took great care of her, even waiting upon her herself. But this poor woman being always praising the good lady, and thanking her every moment for her care and goodness, the lady addressed herself once more to St. Athanasius, and complained that she had asked a woman of him that might try her patience and give her an occasion of merit by serving her, and that he had not granted her request. The bishop not well understanding at first what she meant, thought that they had not executed his orders; but informing himself how the case stood, and finding they had given her a holy, sweet-tempered woman, he presently knew the reason of her complaint, and told her that he would take care to rectify the mistake. Whereupon he gave new orders that they choose out another, of a very sour and uneven temper; and one of that description, says Cassian, was easily found. In effect, they selected a testy, melancholy, stubborn, peevish, and prating old woman, and presented her to the lady, who carried her home with her, making it her business to show more humility and care to her than she had done to the other. As a recompense, she now meets with ingratitude, affronts, curses, and such like ill returns; for this cross woman always contradicted her, and reproached her every moment that she had brought her to her house, not to treat her kindly as she pretended, but to drive her to despair; nay, sometimes she was so very passionate that she was ready even to beat her. The good lady suffered all this without saying anything to her; nay, the worse she was treated, the more careful and ready she was to serve her, and finding great benefit to her soul from this continual exercise of patience and humility, she went to return her most humble thanks to St. Athanasius for having given her one that had so well tried her patience, and furnished her every day with new matter of merit. And this lady having lived some time in this charitable practice of mortification, died most happily in our Lord.

Abbot Pœmen, novice to Abbot Joseph, says, that this holy man used to send him every morning to a fig tree that belonged to the monastery, to take his breakfast of green figs, which was a very unusual thing, considering the rigorous abstinence these hermits professed. One day Abbot Joseph, according to his usual custom, bade him go to the fig tree, but it being Friday, he durst not eat, being afraid to break a fast so religiously observed by all the other hermits. However, this disobedience left a scruple of conscience behind, which made him go to his abbot, and say: Pardon me, dear father, and give me the liberty of asking a question. Whence comes it that, notwithstanding the strict abstinence we profess, you bid me every morning take my breakfast of green figs, and particularly upon a Friday too? I assure you that the shame of not fasting upon Friday, according to the general custom, would not permit me to eat any figs to-day; yet nevertheless I feel some remorse for not having obeyed your commands, since I am persuaded they are always just and reasonable. Son, says the good old man to him, the fathers of the desert do not at first command their religious things which seem feasible and reasonable, but, on the contrary, such as are odd and extravagant, for a trial of their submission and resignation; and when they once perceive that they comply without difficulty or reply, they never more put them upon such experiments, but employ them in what is really necessary, according to the custom of their order.

In the lives of the holy fathers we read of a certain vision which an old hermit had, in which he saw four distinct orders or ranks of the blessed in Heaven. The first order was of those who had been visited with long sickness, but bore it patiently, and blessed God for it. The second consisted of those who had served the sick in hospital, or received poor people and pilgrims, and had been employed in such like charitable offices. The third were those that had left all, and retired into the desert to pray, and to live in poverty, abstinence, and a mortification of their senses. But the fourth were those who, for the love of Jesus Christ, had dedicated themselves to obedience and totally subjected to the will of another. These last wore chains and collars of gold about their necks, and were far more bright and glorious than the others. The holy man, surprised to see this wonderful sight, asked why these that were last had a greater share of glory than either the hermits or the others had. It was answered, that the hermits and those others who had exercised acts of charity, followed their own will in what they did: whereas those who had devoted themselves to obedience had sacrificed their will to God, who esteems no sacrifice like that of the liberty of our will, man having nothing more noble or precious to offer him; and that those collars of gold were the reward due for their having yielded their necks to the yoke of obedience.

This story is much like that which is told of Abbot Pambo. There were four hermits of extraordinary virtue, who went one day to pay him a visit. The one afflicted his body with continual austerities; the other made profession of most rigid poverty; the third was daily employed in charitable offices towards his neighbour; the fourth was one who had lived in a most submissive obedience for two-and-twenty years. The holy abbot preferred the last before the other three, by reason, that in renouncing his own will he had made himself a slave to another man's; but the others had still followed their own will in the practice of their virtues. After this he added, that whosoever should follow this obedient man's example, and be constant in it to the last, might justly be styled a martyr.

CHAPTER IX.

Whence proceeds that opposition we find in our judgment to the orders of obedience.

THE arguments we oppose to obedience spring in general from our want of mortification; but it will be advanced by some one that this is saying nothing; for every one knows that the greater our mortification is, the greater is our simplicity in obeying: and it is the same as if a man should tell another, who inquired into the cause of pride, that it proceeded from a want of humility. To explain myself, then, I say, my meaning is, that our unmortified passions, our desire of conveniencies, our attachment to our own will, and a want of resignation to all the orders of obedience, is what urges us to search for arguments against obeying whenever the thing commanded does not please us. Hence let any one seriously reflect on himself—let him examine on what occasion there occur to him arguments and feelings contrary to religious obedience, and he will find that they come in crowds to him whenever he has repugnance to what is commanded; whenever he cannot attain the object of his desires; whenever he is touched in any sensible part: but when the command is easy and agreeable, then no argument occurs to us to prove it unreasonable: nay, we judge it to be a thing most fitting, and applaud the wisdom and prudence of those who issued it.

St. Jerom, writing upon these words—" Ephraim is become as a dove that is taken and that has no courage"—*Osee*, vii. 11,— asks himself the question, why Ephraim should be compared to a dove, rather than to any other bird. And answers, that all other birds expose their life to defend their young ones: when they see, for example, a bird of prey or a snake make towards their nest, they flutter about it and make the best defence they can; and when they are not able to prevent the ruin of their young ones, they mourn for them in plaintive notes. It is only the dove that uses no endeavours at all to save her young ones; "she shows no concern at them being taken away, nor does she endeavour to find them again". This is the reason why Ephraim is compared to a dove. Likewise, when our Saviour bade us imitate a dove, it was partly to teach us to show no resistance, to suffer without complaining, and to give no sign of grief, when we are deprived of our little ones; that is, of such things as we have the most attachment to. Thus you see how this opposition of our judgment to the orders of obedience proceeds from a want of mortification in us, and from the repugnance we find, when we are commanded what is not according to our will; and consequently the best remedy against this temptation, is to mortify our passions, to deny our will, and to be so, far resigned as to be really indifferent to whatsoever obedience shall command.

Hence you may learn why the fathers of the desert, those excellent spiritual men, exercised their scholars so much in obedience, by commanding them things in appearance unreasonable, to try their submission and habituate them to deny their own will, and never to interpose their own judgment in what related to obedience. Their commands, though they seemed strange and odd, were by them esteemed most rational, because the mortifying our passions and the annihilating our own will and judgment by such holy practices, is of far greater importance than all we can gain by adopting other methods. It is for your own gain and your advancement in virtue that your superior wishes you to annihilate your will and judgment; and, in doing so, instead of losing, you will gain most considerably. When one wishes to break a horse, he sometimes makes him walk, sometimes puts him in a gallop; now he drives him around a wide circle; again around a narrow one, in the midst of which he makes him turn on a sudden; sometimes he runs him full speed, and stops him in the middle of his career; and all this is done to accustom him to obey, and to break him of vicious tricks. It was for this reason that spiritual directors did the same to those that were under their tuition. St. Anthony made his disciple Paul first sew his habit, and afterwards rip up the seams—to make baskets of willows or palms, and then pull them in pieces. Others made their scholars draw water out of a well, and to throw it in again. And we read, that St. Francis commanded Brother Macè, his companion, to turn round in the highway, till he fell down through dizziness. He made all those that asked the habit of his order plant cabbage and lettuce with their roots upwards, and did all this for no other end than to try their obedience, and even to deprive them of their own will and judgment so far as that no trace of either should remain. I wish to God these practices were in use at this day more than they are; for if once inferiors could suffer without murmur to be commanded to undo what they had done well, they would not take it ill when reprehended for what they had done amiss.

But, since the mortification and resignation we speak of suppose a very rare and extraordinary perfection, which is not attained on a sudden, in waiting to attain it, we should endeavour to turn our want of mortification to our advantage by having a deep sense of it, and by attributing thereunto all the motions of our own will and judgment which are opposite to obedience. Thus we shall prevent its doing us any harm at all; for being once persuaded that the opposition we find comes from thence, we shall take little or no notice of it, and give no credit at all to it. One that knows himself to be really sick is satisfied that he must not have everything he desires; for example, that he must not drink as often as he is thirsty, and though bleeding be painful, and physic unpleasant, yet, for all that, he admits of both as good for him, because he does not listen at all to his own inclination or aversion, but wisely submits to the doctor, complies with all his prescriptions, and believes that everything he ordains tends to his good. His being convinced of his indisposition makes him diffide in himself, and give himself totally up to one that he knows can cure him. We are sick of self-love, and a thousand disordered passions; we desire what is bad for us; and nothing will relish or go down that is good for our distemper. This being the case, let us imitate a sick man who wishes to recover; let us distrust ourselves in everything, and rely on our superior, who is careful, when we are sick, to find out means for our recovery. Let us be persuaded that all his orders are discreet and rational, and that all our suggestions to the contrary are no other than the ravings of a distempered brain. By this means we shall not only receive no damage from the thoughts and arguments that occur to us against obedience, but even make our advantage of them, by conforming ourselves so much more to the practice of obedience. For then we will immediately reflect that we are indisposed, and have lost our taste, and that this is the reason why we have an aversion to what may be most useful to us, and that thus we need no other proof of a thing being to our advantage than the aversion you feel to it, and the difficulties which arise in your mind thereupon.

Nor is this an admirable remedy for the judgments only which regard obedience, but likewise for such as regard the neighbour. So that when your brother's temper or manner shocks you, you cannot do better than turn your thoughts against yourself, and lay your brother's fault at your own door, saying, certainly I deceive myself; it is my own vanity that urges me to judge thus rashly of others, and to desire that others should square their actions according to my judgment; this blindness to my failings, and this evil disposition of mine, makes me interpret good for evil, and take everything in the worst sense. The fault is not my brother's, but my own. In fine, it is an excellent remedy for any temptation whatsoever to know that it is a temptation. Hence, as when a sportsman set his nets, he does it as secretly as possible, and lets them scarce be seen; otherwise he would take neither bird nor beast in them: even so the Devil, when he tempts us, endeavours not to show the temptation as it is, but to give it the appearance of something reasonable. "He transforms himself sometimes into an angel of light"—II. *Cor.*, ii. 14,—and casts a mist before our eyes to make us believe his dark illusions to be God's inspirations. God deliver us from those temptations which are thus disguised under a colour of good. When you have a bad opinion of your brother, and at the same time are persuaded that it does not proceed from passion or any other temptation, and that it is the love of truth, not any private interest, that makes you speak, and that all the world, had they been in your place, would be of the same sentiments with you, it is then, I say, that the temptation is dangerous, and the remedy difficult to be found; for there is nothing more to be feared than evil when it is to be disguised under the appearance of good. When you are tempted openly you may adopt sufficient means to overcome it; but when you are set upon in the dark, and do not know that it is a temptation, but on the contrary, think it an effect of justice and reason, how will you be able to banish it? Or how will you defend yourself against an enemy you do not know, nay, whom you suppose to be your friend? A great servant of God used to say, that he was not afraid of the faults which he knew and detested in himself, but of those which he did not know, or at least excused, or made very little or no account of.

But to return to our subject: I say that as often as we find our judgment clash with obedience, we cannot have a better remedy than to turn this opposition against ourselves, and attribute it all to pride and an unmortified disposition of mind. We have but too much reason to do this, since we know that our flesh and sensual appetite never want a plausible excuse for what they like, and on the contrary, find a thousand inconveniences in what they dislike. We are not ignorant that passion and self-love make things appear to us otherwise than they are. For as one that is extremely thirsty fancies water to be the best thing in the world, because the circumstance he is in biasses his judgment; so those things which flatter a violent passion in a man, appear to him otherwise than what in reality they are, because he judges of them only by his present disposition of mind. Since then we know for certain that we are not quite disengaged from terrene affections, and that we are as yet much subject to our passions, the surest way is not to rely upon our own judgment, but to look upon it either as distempered and full of troubled notions, or else as an enemy against whom we ought to stand upon our defence.

Moreover we must not rest content when we do not give way to this opposition of our judgment to obedience, but endeavour to derive advantage from it by making it the occasion of our greater humiliation, and say, how can I be so proud or presume to prefer my own judgment to my superior's? Did I not come to religion to be every one's foot-stool? how dare I then lift up myself above him who is the head and superior of us all? I did not come hither to command, but I came to obey; not to govern, but to be governed; it is above my sphere to be judge of my superior, it belongs to him to be judge of me. This remedy may be very serviceable to us in all sorts of temptations, and there is no better way than this to turn them to our advantage; so that when pride or vanity fills their minds, we are to make the best use can be made of them, which is to humble ourselves in the sight of God. And as the Devil endeavours to poison our best actions with vain-glory, and make us proud even of an act of humility, so we must endeavour to turn his poison into an antidote, by making our pride the subject of our greater humiliation and debasement, saying, how can I, who am nothing but frailty and corruption, be proud? Is it possible that these things which ought to create shame and confusion in me, should puff me up and make me vain? How can I think of gaining men's esteem and praise, since I deserve nothing but their contempt? To know how to turn the Devil's arts, whereby he intends to ruin us, to our advantage, is an admirable counter-battery against all his attacks. It is then that with David we shall, "derive safety from our enemies, and from the hands of all those that hate us".

There are also several other ways to prevent us from listening to our own judgment, and to make us diffide in it upon all occasions. First, we must consider, that if it be a part of prudence not to trust our own judgment too far in anything we do, much more ought it to be so when our own interest is in question; it being a maxim in morality, that no man is a proper judge in his own cause. Self-love and passion, which blind us, usually affect our judgment in the things which immediately regard ourselves, and therefore it is neither convenient nor good to refer these matters to our own, but to our superior's judgment, and to believe his to be the best standard of reason and equity. Secondly, we must suppose that a subject sees no farther than what his private reason suggests, and that the superior sees this as well as he, and sees much farther than the subject's sight can reach to. So that if we take into consideration particular reasons, perhaps it would be better to act as you think; but if we cast our eyes upon the general motives and the common good, which the superior is guided by, then we shall find it much more expedient to obey his command. This great truth does not only hold in spiritual matters, but in all the rules of human prudence. For, certainly it is not only indiscretion, but even presumption, to judge positively of your superior's orders from one or two reasons which present themselves to your mind, without reflecting that he has examined the business as well as you, and that several reasons of great importance obliged him to overlook those very inconveniencies you boggle at. St. Austin, discoursing upon this subject, makes use of this very apposite comparison. He says that the soul animates the whole body, yet its chief functions are seated principally in the head, where the five senses are lodged; and that there is only the touch, which is common to the rest of the body. It is for this reason the head is elevated above the rest of the body, and that the rest of the body is subject to it, as to a superior, whose duty it is to direct it. Now, what the head is, in respect of the body, a superior is, in respect of his subjects. For he being the head, has all the five senses; but you being only part of the body which he is the head of, have only the sense of touching. You touch only one reason, and the superior touches them all. He sees, hears, and knows all that ought to be considered in the matter, and therefore it is very just that you should submit to the care and management of this your head. It is an ordinary saying, that an *ignoramus* is clearer-sighted in his own affairs, than a wise man in another's business. How much more insight, then, will a wise man have in his own concerns, than he that meddles with, and judges of them without knowing what they are? "Do not judge your judge", says Solomon, "because he judges aright"—*Eccl.*, viii. 17. Consider how great a folly it is to judge of any matter when you are ignorant of all its motives, circumstances, and dependencies, which you can never come to a knowledge of, nor is it perhaps fit that you should. What should still urge us to the submission of our judgment to that of our superior, is to consider that he has in view the general good of his house, whereas, you being only a private person, look no farther than yourself and your own particular conveniencies; and who is it that does not know that the public good is to be preferred to the private? We see even in the order of nature things which cease to act according to their particular inclination, and even use violence to themselves, "for the good of the whole", that is, as philosophers say, "for the perfection of the universe". Thus, water, in order to prevent a *vacuum*, which, it is said, nature abhors, when on a sudden you turn a bottle upside down, does not fall for some time, and even ascends till a sufficient quantity of air is entered. Individuals ought to copy the example set them by nature. They ought to divest themselves of particular inclinations, and where there is question of the public good, of which the superior is guardian, they ought to sacrifice to it their private interest. In fine, the experience we have, or at least ought to have, of ourselves, is a very proper means to prevent our giving credit to our own judgment. How many things have we believed, how many things have we given out for certain and infallible, which, when afterwards being disabused, we have found to be otherwise, and we have met with the confusion which rashness and too much credulity bring along with them. If another person should deceive us twice or thrice, we should never trust him more; why then do we still trust our own judgment, that has so frequently imposed upon us? This experience of man's ignorance, and his being too easily deceived by himself, is the reason why old men are slow and wary in deciding these very things which young men determine without the least hesitation.

CHAPTER X.

The explanation of St. Paul's three arguments for obedience.

"OBEY your superiors, and be subject to them; for they watch continually, being to give account for your souls; and obey them so that they may discharge their duty with joy, not sorrow; for that would do you no good"—*Heb.*, xiii. 17. These words contain the apostle's three arguments to persuade us to obey our superiors in all things: I mean in all things which are not sinful. For it is of things not sinful we have hitherto spoken, and shall speak of in what follows. As it is the Holy Ghost advances these reasons by the mouth of St. Paul, it is impossible but they must be good and profitable for us. The first argument is drawn from the circumstance that our superior "continually watches over us, as being to give an account of our souls". And, without doubt, this assurance of always doing well if we obey, is one of the greatest comforts and blessings of a religious life. The superior may be sometimes faulty in commanding this or that, but the subject can never be so in obeying, for God will only ask you if you have done what was commanded you, and if you can give a good account of yourself in this point, you may be sure of having done your duty. You will not be asked if what you had done was to the purpose, or the best thing you could undertake, since this does not belong to you; it is your superior must give an account thereof, and not you. As long as you comply with obedience, if anything be amiss, God takes it off from your account and places it to your superior's. It is for this reason that St. Jerom, speaking of the advantages of obedience, exclaimed: "O sovereign liberty! O happy and holy security, which renders us almost-impeccable"—*in Reg. Mon., c.* 6.

This assurance that we always do the will of God, is one of the greatest benefits enjoyed by us who are employed in charitable offices towards our neighbour. Though we had resolved to lead a good life in the world, yet we should still have been at a loss to determine whether taking pains for our neighbour's salvation or the bare attending to our own, would be more grateful to God. At present there is no doubt or difficulty in this case, because the institute of the society which God has called us unto, is to labour for the salvation of souls; and since we know that we execute God's orders by doing so, we must of necessity be very certain that our labours are grateful to him. Had you remained in the world, perhaps you would not have ventured to hear confessions; and in case you had, there would still have remained this doubt, whether you had followed God's call or your own choice in doing so, and whether in the end it would prove to your advantage or disadvantage. But now you hear confessions and exercise the other functions of the society, with an assurance that you thereby accomplish the will of God. For it is not you yourself but your superior that has engaged you in these duties; nor is it your part to judge whether you be fit for them or not. This is the duty of your superior, who has selected you, and who is obliged "to watch continually over you, since he must give an account of your soul".

St. John Climacus is of the same opinion, who speaking of obedience says, that it does excuse us before God. And it is certain, when Almighty God asks you why you did this or that, if you answer that you were commanded to do so by your superiors, you will need no other excuse or acquittal for so doing. The saint says again, that to obey is to sail in safety and to sleep during the passage. For as a passenger in a stout ship steered by an able pilot, has nothing to trouble his head with, but may sleep securely because the pilot is careful and vigilant; so a religious who lives under the yoke of obedience, goes to Heaven sleeping, that is, totally depending upon the conduct of his superiors, who are his pilots and who watch for him. And surely it is no trifle to be carried in the arms of another through all the difficulties and storms of this life; and this is the favour God vouchsafes to all those who live under obedience. It is the superior bears the whole burden; subjects need not concern themselves whether this or that be fittest to be done; they have nothing else to do than to live in repose and rely upon their superior who is their guide.

The advantage which religious feel in being thus delivered from the uneasiness and perplexity which seculars are liable to, and in knowing the infallible way to Heaven, has induced many devout persons to enlist themselves under obedience. For though they be ever so well employed in the world, they may still doubt whether God called them to those employments; because every man has not the same call, even to what is good, much less to an office so much above his abilities as is the care of souls. This made a grave doctor say, that had he rather pick straws out of obedience, than to do the greatest charity imaginable of his own choice; because in the first we are sure that we do God's will, but our own choice renders the second suspected. But obedience gives us this security and frees us from inquietude, not only in things that relate to our neighbour, but also in what concerns our own spiritual advancement. For suppose I were now in the world, and had a desire to serve God, I should perhaps often doubt whether I eat too much or too little; slept more or less than I ought; performed too great or too small penance; allowed too much or too little time to my prayers; and so of other things. Whereas in religion I am exempted from these inconveniencies; for here I only eat what they give me, sleep only as long as my rule permits, do what penance is appointed, and employ in prayer all the time my rule assigns me. All things are so well weighed and regulated by my superiors, that I cannot doubt of my accomplishing God's will as long as I observe obedience. But this is not all; the tranquillity of religion does not confine its charity to the soul; it goes farther, and extends its care to the body also; so that a religious needs not trouble himself about temporals, any more than he that embarks in a ship which is stored with provisions of every kind. The superior continually watches over both body and soul. He provides for our diet and clothing, that we may employ ourselves more freely in the service of God; and this is so great an advantage, that Cassian relates (*Collat.*, ix. *c.* 13) it engaged the abbot John, after twenty years' solitude, to put himself once more under the obedience of a superior. This holy man, having lived in a monastery thirty years, retired into the desert according to the practice of those days, where he lived twenty years, so much favoured with divine consolations, and so absorbed in contemplation, that he seemed almost to have lost the use of his senses, and frequently forgot to give his body some small refreshment. Yet neither these extraordinary favours which God did him, nor all the sweet raptures of a solitary contemplative life, could divert him, after twenty years spent in them, from resolving to return to his monastery and to live in community as he had done before under the yoke of obedience. He told his motive in these words: Though, says he, contemplation has more advantages in solitude than in a monastery, yet I find this inequality recompensed by the happiness we find in a monastery, of "not being solicitous about to-morrow"—*Mat.*, vi. 34. And indeed to be freed from all care of temporals, as religious are, must needs bring much peace and quiet along with it; and yet the certainty religious have of their actions being grateful to God, and that as long as they are obedient they cannot displease him, is incomparably a far greater happiness.

All religious have, like the children of Israel, a Moses that goes up to the mountain and declares the will of God to them. They have a prophet too like them to clear their doubts; so that whensoever they have any difficulty, they can say, as the Israelites said in the like occasion, " Let us go and consult him that sees" —I. *Kings*, ix. 9. They called their prophet "the man that sees", because he saw and knew the will of God, and then declared it to the people. In this we have the same advantage they had, and can say in all our doubts and difficulties, "let us consult him that sees"—let us address ourselves to him whom God has given us for our prophet—to him who holds the place of God himself, and can make known his will unto us. Nay, we may justly apply these words of Baruch to ourselves, "We Israelites are happy, because we know what pleases God"—

Baruch, iv. 4. For, pray tell me, whether every religious does not enjoy this happiness, since he assuredly knows what God requires of him, and what will render him more pleasing in his sight.

The second argument which the apostle makes use of to persuade us to obey superiors, is, "that they may discharge their duty with joy, and not with grief". St. Paul, sensible of the great charge which superiors have, does out of compassion recommend a prompt obedience to their orders, thereby to render their burden the lighter. Let us enter into this consideration with the apostle, and since those that are in superiority have already so great a load upon them as to render an account to God of both their own and our actions, let us not add to their load by our indocility. A superior is certainly to be pitied when he meets with stubborn persons, whom he cannot deal with as he pleases, nor command as he judges convenient, and when he must have his thoughts continually upon the rack to find out whether his command will be well received, or what reasons and difficulties they will allege for a dispensation, and what steps he must take to render his orders palatable. There is as much trouble in governing persons of this description as there is in making use of a sore leg or arm. For the pain of even moving the leg is sometimes so intense that we cannot advance one step, though it be ever so much to our advantage; and the pain of the arm is often so acute that we cannot so much as lift up our hand to our mouth to feed ourselves. The reason is, because they are so sore that you cannot use them without pain. It is the same with every religious, who is a member of the order to which God has called him; for the whole order, like the Church, is only one body. Now if there be any one member of this order indisposed, or stubborn and intractable, his superiors can never employ him without feeling pain themselves, though they have ever so much need of his service. For when a superior sees that a subject obeys with reluctance and discontent, he is so sensibly troubled at it that he dares not command this member, though the business be ever so pressing, and though great inconveniencies follow from its being neglected.

This consideration may be serviceable in order to undeceive those who fancy that it is a fine thing to be superior of a house, and to have so many spiritual children at a word of command. Rebecca longed very much to have children, and God complied with her desire; but when seized with the pangs of childbed, and feeling the twins dispute the right of primogeniture in her womb, she began to repent her longing, and say, "What necessity was there of my conceiving if this was to follow upon it?"—*Gen.*, xxv. 22. Superiors are much in the same situation. When they see their commands obeyed with reluctance—when their subjects reply, complain, and murmur, then it is that they feel the grief their spiritual children give them—then it is that they groan under their burden, and sigh that they are not so happy as to be in a post where they might have nothing else to do than obey the superior's orders; then they say, is this the advantage of superiority? Is this the satisfaction our spiritual children afford us? It is better to be without them than pay so dear for them. It is but those who have had experience that know the pain attached to superiority. It is an ordinary saying, that a good superior must first be a good subject, and no doubt he must have carried the yoke of obedience, that he may apply to himself these words of St. Paul: "We have a High Priest that can compassionate our infirmities; he himself has gone through all sorts of trials"—*Heb.*, iv. 15. I must needs add here, that I think with a great deal of reason, that as in order to know how to govern others, it is of great advantage to have had an experimental knowledge of obedience; in like manner, in order to know how to obey, it is very useful to have had an experimental knowledge of governing, and of the pain felt by a superior when his subjects do not obey freely. For, with this experimental knowledge, no man will give pain so acute to his superior. In order to gain this experience, it is not necessary to have been a superior, but it is sufficient to have been for a time entrusted with the command of another. How often then did you forbear to command for fear of being disobeyed! And how often has it happened that you yourself had rather have done the thing than command it to be done by another! It is easy to infer from hence how much a superior suffers when his subjects think his commands hard, and show their unwillingness in obeying them. A superior that is reduced to these straits would rather choose to do everything himself, if it were possible, than command anything; and for this reason he cannot but always groan under his burden. Nor is this his greatest trouble—their own frailty is his greatest affliction; for, being a father, he cannot but grieve to see these failings in his children. It touches him to the quick to see how little they relish mortification; to see their reluctance in accepting of lowly offices, which they should be ready to embrace upon all occasions; whereas, whenever they are offered them, they immediately reply, repine, excuse themselves, and find some inconvenience or other in what is commanded. Thomas à Kempis says, that a lukewarm religious is always indisposed to what he does not like, and never wants his pretences to be dispensed with in the things he has no mind to perform. We always want strength to do such things as we feel a repugnance to; but when they are according to our wishes, though ever so painful, they must be done. It is this made St. Chrysostom say, "that the force of the will must needs be great, since it enables us to do whatever is pleasing to us, and not to do whatever is displeasing".

There is no pain so sensible to superiors, nor any mortification so great, as when their subjects are thus indocile and unmortified. Obey them therefore submissively, do not give them this affliction, hinder them from groaning under their burden; "for after all this will do you no good"; and this is St. Paul's third reason or argument to exhort us to obedience. Consider that this indocile temper of yours can never turn to your advantage—that you will be the first to suffer by it, as all persons of a stubborn disposition have found to their cost; that you will one day groan under the burden as well as your superior; and that if you continue thus, your life will be very uneasy. Consider that you will be looked upon as a sick member, and one unfit for any service, a circumstance which certainly will not conduce to your salvation. Lastly, consider that your superiors, out of condescension to your humour, will let you do what you please, so that instead of doing God's will, you will do your own, than which nothing is more pernicious, or more to be dreaded by a religious, as has been already declared elsewhere.

CHAPTER XI.

That to look on your superior as on Jesus Christ himself, is an excellent means to obtain obedience in perfection.

ONE of the most proper, and indeed the chief means to acquire the perfection of obedience, is to behold God in your superior, and to make account that it is God who commands you, and that you obey him, not man. This is earnestly recommended to us by St. Paul in several of his epistles, but particularly in that which he wrote to the Ephesians, where he thus addressed himself to servants: "Servants, obey your masters with fear and respect, and with simplicity of heart, as you would obey Jesus Christ himself"—*Ephes.*, vi. 5. If St. Paul commands, says St. Basil on this passage, obedience to be paid to higher powers upon Earth as to Jesus Christ himself, and even to such of them as remained in sin and infidelity—if St. Peter would also have us obey "not only the best, but even the worst of masters"—I. *Pet.*, ii. 18,—with how much more reason ought religious obey their superiors, who desire nothing more of them than to accomplish the will of God! It is for this reason St. Paul subjoins: "You must not serve them only when their eyes are upon you, as if it were barely to please them, but, like servants of Jesus Christ, do the will of God, by serving them readily and cheerfully, as if it were Christ and not man yon were serving"—*Ephes.*, vi. 6, 7. We are not to regard *man* but *God* in the person of our superior, for we are not come to religion to serve man, but God; nor do we live with men, but God, since our life is crucified with Jesus Christ. "All that you do", says the same apostle, in another part, "do it with a good will, as if it were done for Christ, not men, being assured that he will reward you for it"—*Coloss.*, iii. 23, 24.

Our holy founder, resting on this apostolical doctrine, insists very much in his constitutions upon the same motive, and frequently recommends it to us. In one place he tells us that in order to give ourselves up totally to obedience we must of necessity look upon our superior, whosoever he be, as holding the place of Christ himself. In another place he tells us that it is very necessary to obey not only the general of the society, or particular superiors of houses, but also all those who derive authority under them; and that we must not regard the person of the superior whom we obey, but the person of Jesus Christ, for whose sake we obey, and to whom all the world owes homage and obedience. This furnishes him a secure and solid principle to enlarge on in the sixth part of his constitutions, where, treating expressly of obedience, he says, that if you desire to attain perfection in this virtue, "you must continually have before your eyes God himself, our Creator and Redeemer, for whose sake you obey". The following supposition will show the efficacy of this means. Should Jesus Christ himself appear, and in his own person lay a command upon you, how readily, how submissively, with what satisfaction would you obey him! You would not weigh or examine his orders, nor have the least doubt of the equity of them, but blindly execute them, because it is God that commands, it is God that will have you do it, and by consequence the best thing you can possibly do is to obey him. You would think yourself happy to be thus employed by Almighty God, and the command most difficult to be executed would be deemed the greatest favour. Now, this is exactly the means we propose. St. Basil lays down the same in his rule, and to raise in us a just esteem of it, he says thus: "Do not think that I presume of myself to make this comparison. No; I take it from our holy faith, and the authority of Christ himself, who says, he that hears you hears me, that is, he that obeys you, obeys me". All the holy fathers give the same interpretation of these words, and say, that they are to be understood not only of the apostles, but of all superiors and spiritual directors; and this doctrine was so generally received amongst the ancient fathers of the desert, that they looked upon the command of their superior to be the command of God himself. They did not, in the person of their superior, regard man, but God himself, whose place he held; and the same is expressly recommended to us by our Saviour, in these words: "The Scribes and Pharisees sit upon the chair of Moses; observe and do all they shall say to you, but do not do as they do"—*Mat.*, xxiii. 2.

All therefore that we have to consider when we obey, is the will of God; for whether it be declared to us by himself, by an angel, or by any one whomsoever, we are always obliged to a submission to his orders, let the instrument he uses to signify them to us be what it will. St. Bernard, discussing this subject, cites St. Bennet's words, which are the same in substance with those already mentioned. "The obedience", says he, "which we render a superior is paid to God, who says, he that hears you, hears me. So that whatever he who holds the place of God commands, supposing it to be not evidently contrary to God's will, is to be received by us as if it came from God himself. For it is the same thing to know his will either from his own, from an angel's, or from a man's mouth". St. Bernard also, in the same place, cites a maxim generally admitted by holy men. "Let it be God himself or his vicegerent that commands us anything, we must execute it with equal care, deference, and respect, so long as man commands nothing that is repugnant to the law of God". We must not for the future expect that God should work miracles for us, nor pretend that he should come in person to declare his will and pleasure—"he has already spoken to us by his Son"—*Heb.*, i. 2. "The only begotten Son, who is in the bosom of his Eternal Father, has told us what we are to do"—*John*, i. 18. He left Heaven and lived with us upon Earth, to instruct us when there was a necessity for it. But those days are past: God at present requires that we live and act by faith, and that those whom he has given us for superiors should be the interpreters of his will.

St. Austin says, that God intimated all this to us in the order he observed in converting Cornelius the centurion. This man was a heathen as to his religion, but otherwise, as we read in the Acts of the Apostles, a very good man, and a great almsgiver, and one that prayed very much. God, in order to convert him and instruct him in the Catholic faith, sent an angel to him with this message: "Cornelius, thy prayers and alms-deeds have ascended to the presence of God, and he is mindful of them; therefore despatch a servant to Joppa for one Simon surnamed Peter. He lives in the house of one Simon, a tanner, nigh the sea: he will instruct thee and tell thee what thou art to do"—*Acts*, x. 4, etc. Whence comes it, says St. Austin, that God did not appoint this same angel to instruct him? "Was it because the angel was not capable?—Without doubt he was able to do it". Notwithstanding, God would have him make his address to Peter. He would not undertake it himself, nor commission an angel to do it, but commits him to man's care, thereby to honour mankind, for whose sake he himself became man, and paid obedience to man, as the gospel states in these words, "and he was subject to them"—*Luke*, ii. 5. St. Bernard makes a similar remark upon St. Paul's conversion. Though Christ appeared to him, yet he would not declare his will himself, but remitted him to another, saying, "Go into the city, and there thou shalt be told what thou must do"—*Acts*, ix. 7. "How admirable is your wisdom, O God", says St. Bernard upon these words, "that so sweetly disposes all things to their end. You are pleased to send him whom you spoke to yourself, to a man for farther instructions, thereby to show the advantages derived from living in society. You send him to a man, to honour man the more, the better to show his authority, to make us respect him as your vicegerent, and to oblige us to receive the orders of our superiors as coming from yourself".

Nor is our present condition inferior to theirs, whom God has vouchsafed to speak to in person. On the contrary, as our faith is more meritorious when we believe what we do not see, than when we believe what we see, according to the words of our Saviour to St. Thomas: "Thou hast believed, Thomas, because thou hast seen. Blessed are those who have not seen, and yet have believed"—*John*, xx. 29. Even so, if we by way of faith look upon the command of a superior to be a declaration of God's will and orders, we in some manner merit more than if we paid our obedience to Christ himself in person. Holy doctors say the same of alms when given for the love of God; and does not Christ say in the gospel, "verily I say to ye that what ye have done to the least of these my brethren, ye have done it unto me"? —*Matthew*, xxv. 40. So that here Jesus Christ pledges himself to reward a charity done to a poor body, as much as if it were done to himself. Nay, there are some holy men who say, that he who gives an alms to the poor for Christ's sake, does more than if he bestowed it upon Christ himself. Just as when one receives an acquaintance of his friend, and entertains him hospitably for his friend's sake, he gives greater proof of friendship than if he paid all this civility to his friend himself, for it would be looked upon as due to the person and merit of his friend; but when he does to all that have any dependence upon him, or belong to him, as he would do to himself, he certainly gives a greater demonstration of his kindness, and this is what we do by an act of true obedience. Hence St. Bonaventure says, that it is a great act of obedience to obey God, when he himself commands us, but a far greater to obey man for God's sake. And the latter has often more merit, and consequently a greater reward annexed to it; because when we obey man for God's sake, we thereby more debase and humble ourselves, and show a greater denial of our own will by a perfect resignation of it to God's. Should God in person command you anything, your most ready compliance would not be wondered at; but should you for God's sake comply as readily with the command of a man like yourself, and submit your will and judgment to him with the same deference as to God, it would certainly be an act of greater merit and of greater value.

CHAPTER XII.

That to acquire this virtue, we must obey our superior as Christ himself.

To behold God in our superior is not only, as we have shown, a proper, but it is likewise a necessary means to acquire this virtue of obedience. For he that obeys, if he does not believe that it is God commands, and that it is God he obeys, will not only fail in the perfection of obedience, but even in the very essence of it. As this is of the utmost importance, I shall endeavour to place it in the clearest point of view. If you consider nothing but the bare man in your superior, you will find no more in him than in yourself, since you are no less a man than he: and though he be ever so learned, prudent, or holy, you will still say he is but man, and that his knowledge does not equally extend to all things, and that he may very well mistake in some one thing or other. Moreover, influenced by this consideration, you may think that, like other men, he has his particular inclinations, and that he did not look upon you with so favourable an eye as upon some other religious. But above all, if he commands you what is hard, painful, and contrary to your desires, self-love, that is always extremely ingenious, will most certainly furnish you with a thousand arguments to oppose him; and thus you will live uneasy, and will not entirely submit your will and judgment to his, because you will never want human reasons to oppose the human reasons which will not be in your favour. But if, instead of looking upon your superior as a man subject to error, you behold in him the person of Christ, who alone is sovereign wisdom, goodness, and charity, and who can neither deceive others, nor be deceived himself, then all your arguments are put down, for this reason, that the orders of Christ admit of no reply. It is this the Royal Prophet said—" I was dumb and opened not my mouth, because thou didst it"—*Ps.*, xxxviii. 10. How ready, how perfect would our obedience prove, were we but thus disposed like David! On hearing the superior's voice we would obey it as readily as if Christ spoke to us himself. Though we had begun to form a letter, we would leave it without finishing, and would deem ourselves to commit a great fault if we deferred our obedience even for a moment. How attentive, how careful would we be to comply with his commands by making his will ours!

In a word, there would be no difficulty which this consideration would not smooth.

By adhering to these principles a doubt in this matter may be easily solved. It may be asked why a religious, who has lived under obedience several years and daily practised it, has not acquired the habit of it, that is, the virtue itself in perfection, since both philosophers and divines agree that a virtuous habit is acquired by different acts and by a frequent exercise of the virtues. I answer, that a virtuous habit is acquired by frequent acts conformable to the virtue which is to be acquired; and to speak more like the schools, obedience is one of the branches of the virtue of religion, God and his divine worship being the object of it. Now the religious concerning whom the doubt was proposed, does not look totally to God in his superior when he performs an act of obedience, and consequently he does not obey purely to fulfil the will of God, but rather does it to content his superior, to be esteemed the more, to decline a penance or a chiding which would follow upon his disobedience, or perhaps because the command is to his fancy, or because his superior treats him well, or lastly, out of some other mean temporal motive. Hence his acts of obedience are not acts of religious obedience, since they want the very essence of it, and by consequence he neither has nor ever will acquire the habit of a religious obedience unless he change his way of acting. He may very well, indeed, acquire a sort of civil political obedience, such as soldiers pay their general, or seamen their captain, or such as is practised by any other body of men towards their head and ruler; but it will never be true religious obedience.

This made St. Ignatius say, that it is not because he is prudent or holy, or upon account of any other good quality in him, that we are to obey the superior, but only because he holds the place of God and is the representative of the Almighty. And the same doctor, speaking of obedience, says, if you turn away your eyes from this consideration, and fix them on motives barely human, it is impossible but *that* will utterly destroy religious obedience. For by this means there will not be in your obedience any act of religion, but you will do as seculars do when they follow the advice of any experienced person. This would be to live with men, not God, and instead of obeying the latter, to pay all your obedience to the former. The more willing you will be to attach yourself to human reason, the more you will shake off the spirit of God and of true obedience, and debase yourself beneath the yoke of men. The same saint adds, in his general examen, that we must not consider whether it be the superior or one in authority under him that commands, since we obey God, not them. He would also have us obey all under-officers with as much respect, readiness, and resignation, as the superior himself.

St. Francis truly attained this perfection when he said that amongst many other favours he had received this one from the hands of God, that he could as easily and readily obey the last novice in the convent that should be appointed his guardian, as any religious, however full of years, experience, and wisdom. He understood this great art of obedience admirably well, and therefore considered that it was God alone he obeyed in his superior. He said, moreover, that the obedience we pay to a superior who has not the qualities which command respect, is most perfect and of greatest merit. It is an ordinary saying amongst us, that he who obeys the lowest officer in the house, gives a greater testimony of his obedience, than if he obeyed father minister; and also in obeying father minister than father rector; and father rector than the provincial or general. The reason is, because the less the dignity is of the person we obey, the more pure is our obedience. For obedience to a general may be tainted by a consideration of the respect due to his person and place, or by a desire to gain his favour: whereas, the obedience paid a private religious can have no other motive than God. And our holy founder, in confirmation of what has been said, adds, that he who will not obey and submit to the lowest officer in the house, will never do it for those in higher authority, since true genuine obedience does not regard the person whom we obey, but God, for whose sake we are equally to obey all other persons in authority. Now he that observes this distinction of persons, and performs his obedience with respect to them, fails in the most essential point of this virtue. For did he obey for God's sake, he would as soon obey a low as a great officer, since they both equally derive their authority from God in what they command. And since he does not obey the one, it is a great sign that the obedience he pays the other does not terminate in God, but is grounded upon some human motive, which destroys the perfection of obedience, which a religious ought to aim at in all he does.

CHAPTER XIII.

Of other advantages which arise from obeying the superior as we would Christ himself.

THERE are several other considerable advantages in looking upon our superior as Christ himself, and obeying him as if Christ himself had commanded. The first is, that this very consideration will give us new strength, as also a firm hope of success in the performance of what is commanded us. There is this difference between God's and man's commands—that man oftentimes commands what we cannot perform, without giving us strength to execute it, whereas God never commands impossibilities, and always helps to the performance of his orders by the assistance of his divine grace. Now, in religion we stand in need of the encouragement which confidence in God brings along with it, upon account of several difficulties we meet with, and therefore nothing can be of greater advantage to us than to consider that it is God who commands us—that it is God has put us in this or that employment, and that he will infallibly give us such strength as shall be necessary to acquit ourselves well of it. It is one of the greatest comforts which missioners living in heretical or heathen countries can have, to consider amidst all their dangers and sufferings that they undergo all in obedience to God's commands, and therefore may say with the Psalmist, " Save me, O God, for I am thine"—*Ps.*, cxviii. 94. St. Chrysostom, upon these words of Christ to his disciples, " Behold it is I who send you"—*Luke*, x. 3,—says, that the Son of God declared hereby that, however weak his disciples were, however strong their enemies, however imminent their dangers, yet they ought not to lose courage, because they were going by his order. " It is I", says he, " who send you"; and this is as if he had said, do not be afraid, it is I that send you, I am able to rescue you from danger, and give you victory over all your enemies. This was the comfort the apostles had in the laborious conversion of the world, and we ought to have the like in all the employments and functions in which we are engaged by obedience, saying, it is God that sends me, it is God that commands me, he will give me strength and courage to perform his commands, and to execute his will. When God ordered Habacuc to take the dinner he had prepared for his harvest people and to carry it to Daniel, who was prisoner at Babylon in a lion's den, the prophet answered, "Lord, I never was at Babylon, nor do I know the lion's den; and immediately an angel took him up by the hair of his head, and carried him to Babylon, setting him at the mouth of the den"—*Dan.*, xiv. 34, 35. This shows us how ready and how willing God is to assist us in the execution of his commands.

By obeying our superior as if he were Jesus Christ, we live in a continual submission and resignation to the divine will, which is another of its benefits, and an admirable help to preserve ourselves in a constant and uninterrupted love of God, and in continual prayer. For, to produce continually acts of conformity to the will of God, and to place all our content and satisfaction in accomplishing it, must needs be a very profitable way of praying and an excellent manner of living constantly in God's presence.

Moreover, he that acts thus never troubles himself at what is commanded him, for he is only and always intent upon doing the will of God. All his time is taken up therein. This is the manna he lives upon, and in this alone he places all his joy and satisfaction.

Besides all this, how great is the peace and quiet he enjoys who sees God in the person of his superior, and looks upon himself as in the hands of God, who, he is confident, will take care of him? He can say with the prophet, "in this hope will I sleep and rest in peace"—*Ps.*, iv. 9. "It is God that takes care of me, I shall want for nothing"—*Ps.*, xxii. 1. I am in very good hands, and it is certain that nothing can happen to me which God wills not to happen, and which he does not design for my good.

Did we but once accustom ourselves to see God in our superior, and make account that we live with God, not men, we should find a great increase in virtue and in spiritual treasures. But it is not bare speculation will make us thus happy. One who had lived long in religion, said that he had lived therein above twenty years before he could comprehend what it was to obey his superior as Jesus Christ, or what it was to serve God, and not man, in his superior; and you perhaps think that you comprehend it perfectly by only hearing it spoken of. No; this speculation does not suffice; we must put our hand to work, and practise what I have said, and in the way I have described, if we desire to be perfect in obedience, and to enjoy all those blessings which are annexed thereunto.

CHAPTER XIV.

That God looks on disobedience and disrespect to a superior as an injury done to himself.

As when we obey a superior we obey God, whose representative and vicegerent the superior is, in like manner, when we fail to pay the respect and obedience we owe a superior, we fail at the same time in our duty and respect to God. The same reason proves both, and therefore the Saviour of the world, when he said, " He that hears you hears me", presently added, " He that despiseth you despiseth me"—*Luke*, x. 16. St. Paul, in his epistle to the Romans, says the same; for, having exhorted them to submit to higher powers, " because all power is from God", he draws this consequence, " therefore he that resists lawful power resists God"—*Rom.*, xiii. 1, 2. The authority of holy Scripture in several places confirms what I say. When the Israelites were in the desert of Sinai, fear to die of hunger made them repent that they had left Egypt, and caused them to murmur against Moses and Aaron, who had brought them from thence by God's orders; whereupon Moses and Aaron said to the children of Israel, " We have heard your murmuring against the Lord; for who are we, that ye murmur against us? Know ye not that your murmuring is not against us, but against God himself?"—*Exod.*, xvi. 6, etc. When the same people rejected Samuel, and wished to have a king like other nations, God said to Samuel, "They have cast me off, not you. They are unwilling I should reign over them". And in this sense they interpret these words of Isaias, " Do you think it nothing to trouble men, that you are also thus troublesome to my God?"—*Isa.*, xvii. 13. Do you think it a small matter to oppose those men whom God has appointed to govern you? Know that it is a heinous crime, for it is God you resist, it is God to whom you offer the injury.

In fact, the rigour with which God has punished all offences offered superiors proves how careful and tender he is of their authority, by making their interest his own. What a dreadful punishment followed the murmuring of Core, Dathan, and Abiron, against Moses and Aaron, whom they reproached with arrogating to themselves too much power and authority over the people! The earth opened and swallowed them alive, with all their riches and family; and fire from Heaven destroyed a hundred and fifty abettors of their rebellion. St. Thomas, treating this subject, observes, that God chastised those that murmured against their leaders far more rigorously than those who directly offended himself by worshipping the golden calf. For he only put part of the latter to the sword; but of the former he destroyed some by fire from Heaven, and the earth swallowed up the others alive; and this shows, says St. Thomas, how sensible God is of the injuries done to those who are in authority and who hold his place.

Hence you may infer why Samuel, in his speech to Saul, compares the sin of disobedience to idolatry. "To resist God's orders", says he, "is like the sin of witchcraft, and not to submit, is like the crime of idolatry"—*Kings*, xv. 23. St. Gregory and St. Bernard infer from these words that disobedience is a very enormous crime, since holy writ compares it to idolatry and magic. The reason they give to prove the comparison is drawn from the nature of idolatry and witchcraft, which rob God of the worship due to him in the same manner as disrespect and disobedience to a superior deprive him of the honour and deference due to the person who represents him. Besides, as by idolatry we adore an idol of wood or stone, instead of the true God to whom that adoration alone is due, so by the spirit of disobedience we stray from the true rule, which is God, and follow a deceitful one, which is that of our own judgment and of the maxims of the world.

But to resume our subject. The children of Israel murmured against Moses and Aaron, upon which God immediately sent serpents, which killed a great number of them. And at another time he almost cut off at once all this disobedient generation for murmuring against the same persons, upon the return of those who had been sent to view the land of promise. At Moses' intercession he granted a pardon to all except to those who had been the authors of the rebellion. "They were struck dead before the Lord"—*Num.*, xiv. 37,—as holy writ declares; and it is on this account that St. Paul, writing to the Corinthians, says, "Do not murmur as those did who were struck dead by the exterminating angel"—I. *Cor.*, x. 10. Was not Mary the sister of Moses likewise punished for speaking against her brother? She was upon the spot covered over with a filthy leprosy; nor would God remit her sin, or cure her disease, for all Moses could do or say, till she had been seven days outside the camp, and separated from the rest of the people. He who had restrained the arm of vengeance which had been raised to destroy an idolatrous generation, could not obtain pardon of his own sister's murmuring till she had done penance for it. St. Basil followed this example in chastising murmurers and detractors in his monasteries. He would have not only the persons themselves, but all that belonged to them, separated from the rest of the monks, nor would he permit them to work together. Just as, in time of contagion, they remove from the society of men not only the infected person, but, through fear of infection, cast away all his clothes and everything belonging to him; even so St. Basil would have all murmurers separated from the rest of the community. He would have nobody speak to them—nobody have any communication with them, either in eating, drinking, sleeping, working, or even in praying, in order that this great confusion might help to correct their fault, and cause an entire reformation in them.

Pope Nicholas the First, writing to the emperor Michael, who had defamed some bishops, relates what David did when flying from his persecutor Saul. He found him all alone in a cave, where, if he pleased, he could despatch him. Saul had frequently endeavoured to murder David, and at this very instant he was in search of him; yet David, though he had him now in a place where he could easily despatch him, would attempt nothing against him; for he thought that he should offend the Divine Majesty by laying violent hands upon the Lord's anointed, though at this time Saul was his mortal enemy and reprobated by Heaven; he contented himself with only cutting off a piece of his royal robe in secret, and for which even he was afterwards very much concerned. The Scripture says, " that he struck his breast for having cut away a piece of the hem of Saul's garment" —I. *Kings*, xxiv. 6. Learn hence, says this holy pope, how a Christian, who ought to see God in his bishops, should act. He is not so much as to touch the hem of their garment; and if at any time he chance, by negligence, human frailty, or passion, to cut off a piece from it, that is, if he should speak ill of them, he ought immediately, like David, enter into himself, and be sorry for having touched their reputation. We ought not employ the sword of the tongue-to cut in pieces the actions of superiors, however censurable they may appear, because they hold the place of God, who honours them with the title of gods, and forbids all people " to speak ill of the gods"—*Exod.*, xxii. 28.

Besides, we are to consider that, in detracting a superior, we not only offend God and injure the superior, but we likewise do great prejudice to the subjects; because this detraction lessens the esteem and affection his subjects had for him, and gives them an aversion to him. So that by this means their obedience grows cold, and they reap no profit from anything coming from him, which is properly to put a stop to all the spiritual good they might have acquired through him. We therefore ought to take all manner of care "that no root of bitterness", as St. Paul calls it, "spring up amongst us, to the prejudice of their souls"—*Heb.*, xii. 15. We can never be too careful in this point; for though the thing be light and trivial in itself which we say or do, yet we must reflect that it is a matter of no small importance to destroy in your brother's heart the esteem, confidence, and respect which he had for his superior. This, however, is the ordinary effect of all murmuring and detraction, and consequently it is our duty to take into consideration not only the malice of these sins in themselves, but likewise the evil effects they may produce.

CHAPTER XV.

That obedience does not hinder us from representing our difficulties to the superior: the manner of doing it.

To represent our difficulties to our superior is so far from being a sin, that on the contrary we are bound to do so; and he would do amiss that should fail in this particular, as we have a rule that expressly commands it. As too much solicitude concerning our body, says the rule, is not commendable, so a moderate care to preserve our health and strength, in order to do God service, is lawful and just, and all religious are bound thereunto. And hence, if any one finds his diet, clothing, lodging, or employment, prejudicial to his health, or judges something else to be necessary for it, he ought inform the superior or the person under whose care he is. St. Ignatius shows great wisdom in this rule; for, though it be true that all the care of our health and life depends chiefly on our superiors, yet, because they are not angels, nor can know our particular wants, nor have always our private necessities before their eyes, it is thought fit we should aid them in this point, by representing our necessities to them, in order to have them supplied. The principal thing is to represent them in a proper manner; for it is much to be feared that we be actuated by self-love, or guided too much by our own judgment. Hence St. Ignatius requires that, to be on our guard against ourselves on this occasion, we observe two things: the first is, to pray before we make the application, and if we then find it necessary, we are to make our application to him that is charged to provide for us. Yet we must not think that he would have us just kneel down to say an *Ave Maria*, and so go to our superior with our petition; but the prayer he speaks of is a serious recollection and strict examination whether your proposal be with a view to God's greater glory or rather to your own private interest. If, after this examination, you find that self-love is your motive, desist from your proposal; but if you seriously judge that you have no other motive than God's greater glory, you may confidently make it.

The second precaution which our holy founder gives, is totally to acquiesce in our superior's determination after we have represented our case to him, either by word of mouth or in writing for the better help of his memory; and whether he grants or denies his request, not to make any reply to his orders, or renew our instances either by ourselves or others, since we ought to be persuaded that whatever he ordains, after information given him, shall tend most to the service of God and to our spiritual advancement. We ought therefore so dispose ourselves, both before and after the proposal made, as to be equally ready, not only to obey what the superior shall ordain, but also to receive it with satisfaction, as being the most advantageous for us. This indifferency of mind towards the thing proposed, is of very great importance in this matter, since it makes a denial, as well as a grant, equally welcome to us, and easily shows whether we seek God or ourselves in our request. For, if we aim at nothing but God's great glory and the accomplishment of his divine will, we are sure to derive content and satisfaction from our superior's orders, since we can no longer doubt but that they are a declaration of God's will. On the other hand, if a refusal troubles us, and if we fret, it is a sign that we were not indifferent to the thing proposed, and that our private interest, not God's, lay at the bottom, since we are so uneasy at not having obtained our desires. So that the fruit we should endeavour to reap from the prayer we make antecedent to our proposal, ought to be to beg this entire resignation to the will of our superior concerning the thing proposed; and this is the best disposition of mind in the present circumstances, and makes us as glad of a denial as of a grant. It would also be very well to consider, after our superior has granted our request, whether a refusal of the same would have been as agreeable to us; and if we find that it would, we may look upon it as a very good sign, and we may hereupon assure ourselves that we shall fulfil God's will, not our own, in the performance of what we asked leave to do.

This presupposed, I assert that to represent our necessities to our superior with this indifference and resignation, is so far from being contrary to the perfection of obedience, that it is the most perfect and most mortified way of proceeding. And not to do it in a case of necessity, is not only an express disobedience to the rule above cited, but also a great want of interior mortification. You know, for example, that such or such a thing is injurious to you—that you stand in need of such thing—yet you remain silent, only thinking within yourself that if your wants are supplied by the superior, all is well, and if they are not supplied, all is equally well; and you think that these ideas spring from a desire of mortification and of suffering for God; but you must know that this is so far from springing from an humble, patient, and mortified spirit, that it is nothing else than self-love and a fear of suffering; for you look on your present condition as less painful than the bare representation of your necessities to your superior, solely lest he would think you too solicitous for yourself and too attentive to your private conveniencies. This sometimes also proceeds from your want of indifferency to the thing you propose, or because upon the like occasion you have met with a flat denial, which has made you resolve never to petition any more unless absolute necessity should oblige you. But pray, whence comes this resolution? Certainly from a want of indifferency towards the thing proposed, and also from a want of courage to bear a refusal; and for these reasons you are better pleased to keep your difficulties to yourself, and suffer them in private, than represent them to your superior. Consider, however, a moment, how far the Devil imposes upon us, and how violent our self-will is, which makes us better pleased to suffer because we wish to suffer, than to address ourselves to the superior merely through fear of being refused. Nay, if we consult even self-interest, we shall see that obstinacy of this kind betrays much folly. For, let us suppose the worst; let us suppose that the superior does not grant your request. Pray, tell me would it not better in this case that what you now suffer from attachment to your own will, you would then suffer out of obedience and a submission to the will of God? Besides this, you would have the merit of having complied with that rule which commands you to state your wants; and when you will have stated them, you need not apprehend the consequences; for, whatsoever should happen afterwards would not be ascribed to you, but to your superior, and to God himself, who directs you by your superior. It was to obviate these inconveniencies, and to remove the repugnance and bashfulness which we might feel in exposing our wants, that this rule was established. For, why should any one be afraid or blush to do what this rule prescribes him? Can the superior take it ill to see this rule kept? Does not the general custom in our order of representing our least difficulties to the superior, render this practice easy? Let not then your want of mortification make it hard and difficult.

But all the difficulty consists in making the proposal with indifferency and resignation; and as this is a matter of consequence, I will endeavour to enlarge upon it. When we have anything to propose, we must not prepossess our minds with the thought that the thing to be proposed is most convenient for us; for, if we be refused, this would certainly make us uneasy, but in making our proposal we must remain in a doubt, and await with indifference the resolution of the superior; and in this case, happen what will, we are sure to be at ease. When a scholar doubts upon a point of learning, he proposes his difficulty by way of doubt, and with deference as to his master's opinion upon it, and therefore abides by his decision. It is thus we ought to propose our difficulties to the superior, still doubting of the convenience of the thing demanded, and never determining to this or that side, till the superior has first explained himself. For then we must believe that his conclusion is most conducive to our welfare; we must under this impression abide by it, and receive it with joy. So that in the prayer we make before the proposal, we are not to examine whether our design conduces most to God's glory, but only whether it be convenient to acquaint the superior with it, and whether we seek God or ourselves in our request; as to the expediency or inexpediency of it, we are to suspend our judgment till the superior has determined.

Too great attention cannot be paid to this point; for on it depends not only our making the proposal in a proper manner, but also our receiving the superior's answer with satisfaction and quiet of mind. Now, as it is so ordinary a thing amongst us to have recourse to our superior upon the least occasion or necessity, it is of the utmost importance that we do it well; and religious discipline would receive a deep wound if we take it ill to be refused anything by our superiors—if we be troubled at it, and think that they have no kindness for us—if we censure them ourselves, and perhaps induce others to censure their moroseness, stiffness, and severity. Here we should consider, that if our natural parents, when we were under their power, refused us several things, and yet that we took it very well of them, and did not in consequence diminish our love and respect towards them, it is much more rational to act in the same manner towards our spiritual parents, especially since we have made profession of renouncing our own wills and of overcoming ourselves. Superiors heretofore used to train up their religious to this kind of mortification; and to make them the better able to support a denial, they would frequently refuse them such things as they might have granted them without the least inconvenience. And in those days the religious were so zealous for their spiritual advancement, that they were glad of such occasions of mortifying their wills. How comes it then to pass that we, when denied even those things that are really prejudicial to us, show ourselves hereupon uneasy, and complain of it? And what if this should be the reason why superiors sometimes, though much against their will, must grant what is prejudicial to us in order to avoid a greater evil? A true religious ought to dread and abhor a disorder of this nature, as we have already said elsewhere.

But that this manner of stating our wants may be the more perfect, we ought to have not only this interior resignation and indifference we have already spoken of, but also show it by our words and actions, which must accord to our thoughts and bear witness of our interior; and the more visible this accordance is, the more perfect the manner of stating our wants will be. But if we could so make our statement, that without giving room to the superior to find out our own inclinations, we would enable him to decide on what is most expedient for him to order, this mode of stating our wants would be the most perfect of all.

This may be made more clear by a rule regarding provincials, which says, that when the provincial wishes to consult the fathers of his province upon any matter, he must propose it in such manner as not to discover his own sentiments, lest the knowledge thereof should abridge their liberty and bring them over to his opinion. Thus subjects ought to represent their wants to a superior by using simple language, whereby he cannot at all discern their wishes, lest, knowing their frailty, he might be too condescending; in fine, we must use such words as may just suffice to declare our case, but leave him at liberty to ordain what he shall think most convenient, without having regard to our particular inclinations.

We have in holy Scripture two admirable examples of the conduct we ought to observe on this occasion. The first is set by our Blessed Lady when present with her Son at the marriage feast of Cana: she said, "They have no wine"—*John*, ii. 3. She does not say, Lord, supply this want, for you can do it, and prevent all confusion of the new married couple; no, she barely states their want. The second example is that of Mary and Martha, who, when their brother Lazarus was sick, sent an account thereof to the Saviour of the world. The sacred text mentions that they sent this message to him: "Lord, he whom thou lovest is sick"—*John*, xi. 3. " Observe", says St. Austin, " they do not bid him come, because to one that loves, a bare declaration is sufficient. They durst not say, come and cure him; nay, they durst not even so much as use the centurion's language, by saying, Lord, speak the word where you are, and it shall be done here. They only said: Lord, he whom thou lovest is fallen sick. For it is enough, O Lord, that thou knowest our wants, since thou never forsakest those who love thee". Thus we ought to propose our wants to our superior by plainly and simply representing them without manifesting our desires, which if we do, we may be assured that we do not seek ourselves in the proposal, and that the measures our superiors shall take will not spring from condescension.

St. Ignatius, speaking in his constitutions of those who find the air of the country they live in not to agree with them, takes express notice of this way of proposing it to the superior. He that finds himself in this condition, says he, must not ask to change air, or signify any desire of it, but must barely represent his indisposition, with the impossibility he is in of complying with the duties of religion, and then leave all the rest to the superior's care. This done, it belongs to the superior to judge whether it be more fitting for him to change air, in order to recover his his health, and thereby to become more capable of doing service to his order; or, whether it be better for this person in particular, in regard of his spiritual improvement and God's greater glory, to let him remain where he is, notwithstanding the small service he does; nay, though he should be altogether unserviceable and useless. If this be St. Ignatius's opinion in so considerable a business as that of our health, what would he say concerning a great many things of less moment? But because we cannot always conceal our inclinations in the proposal we make, there are some (and it is a very laudable custom) who, having represented their case very modestly and handsomely, earnestly desire the superior not to regard their particular inclination, and that he would set nothing before his eyes but God's greater honour and glory. These persons use all possible means to make him sensible that hereby he would show the greater charity towards them, and confer this comfortable blessing upon them of being sure to do entirely the will of God; whereas, should he out of too much compliance condescend to them, they would be extremely afflicted at it, and look upon themselves as not doing the will of God and of their superiors, but rather their own.

CHAPTER XVI.

Of too much solicitude for the things which relate to the body, and how necessary it is to avoid all singularity in this point.

THE same rule which recommends a moderate and reasonable care of our health, condemns our too much solicitude for it; and the latter shall be the subject of the following discourse, as we have sufficiently treated of the former. It is very hard to observe a medium in all things, but most of all in what concerns our body, since self-love, which is its agent-general, immediately turns physician. It says this is bad for the breast, that for the stomach, this offends the head, that is bad for the eyes; and thus under pretence of necessity, sensuality and squeamishness are insensibly introduced.

St. Bernard inveighs much against those who are too solicitous for their health, and who, under colour of preserving it, are very nice in their diet. These, says he, are Hippocrates' and Galen's scholars, not the disciples of Jesus Christ; for it is not in holy writ, but in books of medicine, they find the various properties they attribute to food. "All sorts of pulse", they say, "are windy; cheese lies heavy upon the stomach; milk does the head harm; pure water is very hurtful to the breast; colewort breeds melancholy humours; leeks beget choler; and fish taken out of stagnant or muddy water agrees not with my constitution. What a strange thing is this", St. Bernard goes on, "that our rivers, plantations, gardens, and cellars, can scarce provide you a dinner which you can eat! Consider that you are a religious, not a physician, and that there is question of your profession, not of your constitution". After this, he lays down four reasons which are very proper to persuade us to live up to the rules of the community, and to avoid all singularities. "First, have pity upon yourself", says the saint, "and consult your own quiet", for these singularities bring uneasiness with them, and expose you to it every moment. At one time you will fear that what you ask will not be given you, or that it will be given unwillingly; at another, you will be obliged to wait too long; and for the one time that your request will be granted, it will be rejected twenty times. In a word, no one knows all the inconveniencies which flow from hence, but those who have unfortunately experienced them; and it is a great ease to a man to be able to live like the rest of the religious. "Secondly, do not give those who serve thee so much trouble"; reflect that you make the refectorian, cook, and server at table, take a great deal of pains, and that they seem to have scarce any other employment than to wait upon you. "Thirdly, beware of giving too much trouble to the house"; consider that you increase it very much by your singularities. It is not very troublesome to prepare necessaries for the community at large; but, besides this, to be obliged to gratify your whims without necessity, is very troublesome and inconvenient. "In fine, be tender (I do not say) of your own conscience, but of your brother's". He sits by you, eats what is given him, whilst you scandalize him : through squeamishness you will not eat that with which he is contented. But suppose he should really believe that you do this out of necessity, you still give him occasion of murmuring, either because sufficient care is not taken of you, or because superiors fail in providing for you as they ought.

But some perhaps may quote these words of St. Paul to Timothy, and urge them in their own defence: "Drink no more water, but use a little wine, by reason of the weakness of your stomach and of your frequent infirmities"—I. *Tim.*, v. 23. To this, says St. Bernard, I answer, first, that it is not a rule which St. Paul makes for himself, but an advice he gives to another, and that it is not an indulgence which Timothy had previously sought for, but one which of his own accord the apostle granted him. But your case is not the same; you have petitioned to be treated better than others, and therefore I have reason to fear that under the colour of a reasonable care of your health, the prudence of the flesh has seduced you, and that sensuality has a great share in what you think to be pure necessity. Take notice, adds the same father, that St. Paul gives this counsel not to a simple religious, but to a holy bishop, upon whose health the good of the infant Church of Christ in a great degree depended. "Give me, however, one like Timothy, and I will treat him with pearls and liquid gold. But if you still insist upon this authority of the apostle, and will have it prevail, pray do not forget that St. Paul, when he advised Timothy the use of wine, prescribed a very small quantity of it".

Abstinence from wine was what St. Jerom first of all advised Eustochium to practise in order to preserve her chastity. "A spouse of Jesus Christ", says he, "ought to look upon wine as poison", and observe how well these words agree with St. Paul's, "there is luxury in wine"—*Eph.*, v. 18. "These are the first weapons the Devil uses against youth. The disquiet of avarice, the swelling of pride, and the charms of ambition are not so dangerous. Wine and youth doubly inflame our sensual appetite: why therefore do we cast oil upon a flame? What need of more fire to a body that already burns?" But to resume our present subject: I do not pretend to recommend anything to religious, which Saints Basil, Bernard, Bonaventure, and several other holy men have not already earnestly recommended, which is no more than to endeavour to live like the rest of the community in everything, and to avoid all singularities as much as we are able. Now, to engage us in this practice, one would think it were sufficient to consider how by this means we free not only ourselves from several vexations and uneasinesses, but also several others, as has been already proved. If, therefore, we consult nothing but our own interest and ease, we should do well to conform to the rules of the community, though some little inconvenience might arise from it, because the advantage we derive from these petty singularities is never so considerable as is our peace of mind. But what ought chiefly determine us in this matter is to reflect that we shall edify our brethren, content our superiors, and be the more pleasing to God. We ought to take particular notice of this, as it is a salutary doctrine, and the practice of it very holy; for to live up to the rigour and severity of our rule—to be contented with the common treatment—to seek no dispensation, to claim no privilege or distinction in anything, is one of the greatest sacrifices we can make to God in religion, and one of the mortifications best calculated to please him, to serve ourselves, and to edify our brethren. We have bound ourselves by our profession to a state of penance and to the practice of mortification; let, therefore, our exact performance of all the usual and ordinary duties of religion be the subject to exercise our penance and mortification upon. For whatever we shall be able to do besides, the saints and spiritual directors would have us so regulate it, that there remain with us sufficient strength to meet the principal mortifications of religion, which consist in these practices. It will be in vain for you to wear a hair-cloth and to afflict your body with long disciplines, for your superiors will make little or no account of either, so long as you are not content with what satisfies the community, or so long as you seek after distinction or delicacy in your lodging, clothes, or diet. Continue, therefore, to adopt those means of doing penance which your profession furnishes you with, for you are sure that *these* are permitted you, that there is nothing more agreeable in the sight of God, and that your superiors will rejoice at your practice of them. Besides, you need not be afraid of vain-glory in this point, for thus you will do penance without being taken notice of by the rest. This is to lead a life common and uniform in appearance, but in the sight of God it is a very distinguished life, which leads to the most solid piety and perfection.

On the contrary, exemptions and particular privileges, though under the most specious pretexts, do the greatest prejudice imaginable to religious communities. And the truth of this is so clear, that St. Bonaventure thinks them one of the chief causes of laxity in religious discipline. Though you have lived long in religion, says he, and done very great service in it, yet you cease not to do it an injury: those who entered it after you do not see your interior, nor consider how much you laboured before their admission. They consider only the example you give them in the observance of the rules, and hence they are always desirous that the seniors should lead the way, and that, as they have been the first received in religion, they should likewise be the first in the exact observance of its rules, in order to serve as guides to those whom the same zeal binds to the same duties. Whenever the contrary happens, they are either scandalized at the bad example of the seniors, or what is worse, follow their steps, and, like them, quickly relax. St. Ignatius, foreseeing the consequence of those particularities, and willing to obviate such inconveniencies as may arise from them, ordained that every one before his admission into the society should be asked "if he would be content to live like the rest of his brethren, without claiming the least exemption or privilege in anything whatsoever, but abandoning himself totally to the care and conduct of his superiors". Particularly, he would have this question put to such as are scholars, and who might one day fill the highest offices and be principal men in the society; for such persons seem to be the most ready to claim exemptions and privileges. They, however, are not aware that the least privilege they claim does a great deal of harm to religion; for another that thinks he has done as much as they, and stands in as great need of the like indulgence, will desire to be treated in the same manner. And perhaps another, who, though he has not done altogether so much as the former, may claim the same, and after him a third and fourth; and by this means religious discipline will be weakened and utterly destroyed. St. Bernard calls such men enemies to peace and union; and without doubt it would have been better if they never preached, wrote books, or performed anything extraordinary, than to have distinguished themselves from others by such privileges as these, for the harm they do this way is more than the good they do otherwise.

For this reason our holy founder forbids all such exemptions and particularities amongst us, nor will he have one that has been preacher, teacher of divinity, or superior, claim on that account any privilege; on the contrary, he wishes that we be fully persuaded that one of the greatest injuries which can be inflicted on the society, is to give cause to believe that for any reason whatsoever a claim would be made for indulgence, or for treatment different from that which others receive. It particularly behoves the seniors and the more learned to edify and instruct others; it is their duty to maintain and strengthen religious discipline by their example, "in conforming themselves to the most humble"—*Rom.*, xii. 16,—as the apostle says, and it is this seniority and learning ought to promote in religion.

CHAPTER XVII.

An objection answered.

THE care we think ourselves bound to take of our health being the most ordinary and the most just ground for claiming exemptions, it is plain that by answering this objection, we will answer the principal one which can be made to the preceding doctrine. We shall begin then by stating the doctrine of divines on this subject. It is universally asserted by them, and it is obvious to every one, that for a man to kill himself, or deliberately to drink poison to procure his death, being a great sin, is quite a different thing from his not taking pains to preserve health and prolong life; for not to take these pains is permitted. A man is not bound to use the most nourishing food and that which agrees best with his constitution, however assured he may be to improve his health and prolong his life thereby; nor is he bound to live in those places where the purest air is, with an equal assurance of better health and longer life. To hold the contrary opinion would be to condemn holy fast, abstinence, and all other austerities practised in the Church. Moreover, holy and learned men justly blame and disapprove in most persons, and particularly in religious, too great a solicitude for health. Nor is any one obliged in time of sickness to have recourse to the most able physicians, or to be at the expense of procuring extraordinary remedies to preserve life; on the contrary, all this is censurable in a religious who makes profession of poverty and humility. It is sufficient that, amid common and easily obtained remedies, we select the most proper; nor does God exact more, because life and health are only temporal and perishable blessings, and scarce deserve to be taken notice of when compared with the life and welfare of the soul. But it is not only lawful to abstain from extraordinary and costly remedies, but even to retrench something of the common practice. Hence it is that the servants of God frequently make this retrenchment in their eating, drinking, sleeping, and in everything which regards the body, though they know it may prejudice their health and shorten their days; and we are so far from blaming this their practice as unlawful, that we look upon it as a great perfection and an effect of sanctity in them. Again, as it is lawful to expose our own life to save our neighbours, or procure their salvation, as those really do who serve in time of the plague, so it is equally lawful to endanger our life and health by mortification in order to work out our own salvation. If, to enable ourselves to live comfortably and honourably, it is permitted us to cross the seas, and to make journeys into foreign countries, to the prejudice of our health and even at the risk of our lives, how much more ought we to think it not only lawful, but good and holy, to neglect our health and hazard our life that we may secure our salvation, by keeping our flesh subject to the spirit, by preventing its rebellion, and not suffering it to destroy the soul? This is what we call a penitential life; and if this practice be once abandoned we may bid adieu to most of the penances now in use in holy Church. Divines put the question, whether a servant of God who has a great pain, for example in his liver or stomach, or who has any other disease, can in conscience, as long as there is no danger of death, abstain from the use of all remedies in order to suffer his pains for the love of Christ. And they answer that without doubt he can, being warranted by the authority and example of St. Agatha. This holy virgin and martyr having her breasts cut off by command of the tyrant, and St. Peter appearing to her in the prison in the shape of a venerable old man, and proposing to cure her wounds, she refused, saying, " that she had never made use of any corporal remedies in all her life". They quote also the example of several other great servants of God, who, to mortify their flesh, to subject it entirely to the spirit, and in some sort to suffer with Christ and share in his dolours, have endured long and painful sickness without applying any remedy, and who by this means made great progress in virtue. To prove still more clearly that we are not to set so high value on health or life, and that we are not obliged to take so much care of both as some imagine, divines put the following case: Let it be supposed that a man will certainly die unless one of his legs or arms be cut off. It is asked, is this person obliged to suffer this painful operation? They answer in the negative; and in support of this decision they quote the answer of Marius, who having suffered several incisions, commanded the surgeons to give over, " for he would not buy his cure at so dear a rate". They hold likewise that we have no obligation to make use of remedies to prolong life, though we know our days will be shortened by not using them: for instance, should the physicians advise you to purge once a month, or prescribe you some other painful remedy or disgusting potion, you might abstain from taking them, though you were assured that thereby you would hasten your death ten years. They further add, that if a man were certain to shorten his days by drinking cool wines, yet he would not be obliged under pain of mortal sin to abstain from them. Now, to apply this to our subject: if men, barely to gratify their senses by drinking cool wines, or to please their palates with the richest dishes of meat, neglect their health and prefer these delights to the preservation of life, without being condemned for it, shall a religious, upon fancying this sort of victuals does him harm, or that the other is better for him, prefer the care of his health to the observance of his rule? But admit that it is not a "fancy" of his, but a real truth: let us put in one scale the necessity he has of taking this care of his health, and the advantage he can hope from it, which frequently is very uncertain; and in the other scale the trouble, uneasiness, and difficulty he will bring both upon himself and others, the scandal and other ill effects these particularities cause, and we shall easily see that the latter much outweigh the former. If worldly men, to satisfy their sensuality, do this every day, and perhaps you yourself heretofore have done the like upon the same principle, is it not just you should do it now in religion, thereby to keep your rule, conform to the community, and avoid giving scandal to your brethren by your being singular and nice in your palate?

Hence it undeniably follows that at least the consideration of our health does not oblige us to seek after particular conveniencies or extraordinary remedies. So that, though the treatment you receive either in sickness or health were still more painful, and even of prejudice to your health, you may be assured without a scruple, that you will do much better to suffer something to testify your love of God and expiate your sins, than to seek your ease and convenience, or complain that they do not take sufficient care of you, or feel as they ought for you. God Almighty does not wish to have us thus solicitous for our health, whereas he says, "He that will save his soul shall lose it, and he that shall lose it for my sake shall find it"—*Mat.*, xvi. 25. Hence St. Bernard says very justly, that Hippocrates teaches us how to preserve life, Epicurus how to spend it in pleasure and delight, and Jesus Christ how to lose it, to fly sensual delights, and to account everything in this world as nothing in comparison of our salvation. Choose now, says St. Bernard, which of these three you will have for your master. To this we may add what is known by daily experience, that those who are so exceedingly attentive to their health are commonly infirm, and often ruin their health by those very means they use to preserve it; whereas those who trust in God, who commit themselves to the protection of obedience, and endeavour to live like the rest of the house, are ordinarily fit for anything, and enjoy perfect health.

Cassian makes a very good remark upon this subject, and says, that there are some religious who seek after exemptions and privileges, not because they stand in need of them upon the account of their health, but because they wish to gratify their pride and vanity; or sometimes because they would be looked upon to be more than others; or, in fine, because they deem this distinction as due to their seniority and merit. Such religious, says the same author, never prove great spiritualists or proficients in virtue. For, we see that those ancient fathers who excelled in the observance of regular discipline, and whom we ought to imitate, have always made it their chief care to live up to the practice of their holy rule, and have been enemies to all singularity and distinction.

We do not, however, pretend by this to hinder any one from representing his necessities; for it is certain that all have not health and strength alike; and, therefore, in a considerable number there is always some one or other who stands in need of some particular assistance. Hence, no one is to put a sinister construction on what has been said, or thence take occasion to censure his brother; but, on the contrary, when he sees any one not complying with all the rules of the community, he ought immediately think that necessity obliges him to it, and thereupon charitably compassionate his infirmity. It sometimes happens, as St. Bernard observes, "that on seeing these distinctions we envy him whom we ought to sympathize with; and within ourselves we think that a happiness which he esteems a misery and a most painful necessity"—*Serm.* i. *de altit. et bassi. cord.* Now, as you would not envy the man whom severe illness urges to have recourse to extraordinary remedies, but, on the contrary, would pity him, even so, if you knew what pain your brother feels at not being able to conform to the practices of the rest of the religious, perhaps you would pity rather than envy him. You would think yourself obliged to return Almighty God thanks for your being able to live up to your institute, without being under the necessity of being indulged and exempted in point of sleep, diet, or any other particular. The same saint says, that whoever criticises on these little privileges some are forced to make use of, shows very clearly that his own thoughts are not in Heaven, and that he is addicted to softness and sensuality.

St. Bernard concludes his discourse in the following manner, and by the mercy of God I can do the same. I do not, dear brethren, says he, speak this by way of complaint of any one here present, but I thought it necessary to put you in mind of these things, because several of you have a tender and delicate constitution, which requires dispensation. I thank God, however, that many of you are so far above any meanness of sentiment, and so attentive to your own spiritual advancement, that without taking notice how your sick and infirm brethren are treated, you attend only to yourselves, continually complaining as if hitherto you had done nothing, and, according to St. Paul's commands, " esteeming every one your superior"—*Phil.*, ii. 3.

However, I must needs set down the excellent advice which St. Bernard subjoins in these words: Do not take notice of those who stand in need of dispensations, but have your eyes always upon such as are the most zealous and exact observers of religious discipline, and strive to imitate them. And he relates a passage which is adapted to this subject, and was much to his satisfaction, concerning one of his own religious, who came one morning very early to him, and, prostrating himself at his feet, said: "O father, I am altogether unworthy and wretched! Last night at matins I was thinking on the holiness of one of my brethren, and I find that he is master of at least thirty virtues to which I am a stranger". Such a thought as this is very profitable; and I desire, says the saint, that the fruit you reap from my sermon be to observe always what is good and excellent in others, and not their defects; but in yourselves, on the contrary, to look on some matter of humiliation and vileness, but never to cast your eyes on what might be an occasion of pride and vanity. For what avails it to you that you take more pains and suffer more rigid fasts than your brother, if he, at the same time be more patient, pious, humble, and more charitable than you are? "Observe rather what he has, and what you want, than what you have, and what he wants"; or, to express it better, "make it your chief study to know what is wanting to yourself in order to attain perfection". For by this means you will maintain humility and charity in your soul, and make great progress in the duties of religion.

CHAPTER XVIII.

The preceding doctrine confirmed by several examples.

WE read (*Hier. Plat.* l. 3. *de bono statu. Relig. c.* 26), that Rabaudus, a French prince, was called miraculously to religion, but this new way of living seemed at first so difficult and painful to him by reason of his former life, that his abbot, Porcarius, was obliged to order him at every meal something that was better than what the rest of the community had, yet this did not prevent him from becoming daily more and more delicate and infirm. One day when he ate in the refectory with the rest, who had but bread and beans for dinner, he saw two venerable old men, of whom one was bald, with two keys about his neck, and the other in the habit of a monk, with a crystal vase in his hand, walking round the refectory, and pouring out of the vase something on every monk's portion, but when they came to him they frowned upon him and gave him nothing. He ventured, however, to taste of his neighbour's portion to see what had been given him, and found that it was far more delicious than anything he had ever eaten in his whole life. The same vision happening thrice, he acquainted his abbot with it, and begged to know who these two old men were. The abbot presently perceiving the matter, told him that one of them was St. Peter, patron of their church, and the other St. Honorius, founder of the monastery; and having given his judgment upon the matter, added that his not living up to the rule like the rest, was the reason why they withheld from him what they gave the other monks. Upon this Rabaudus resolved to live up to the exactness of his rule in every point, and he found it far easier than he thought it had been. Not long after he saw the same two saints making their round, from whose hands he now shared equally with the rest, and this was an extraordinary comfort to him, and gave him new courage and resolution to support for the future all the austerities of his order.

Cæsarius relates (*Lib*. iii. *Dial*., *c*. 48) an example very like this of a Cistercian monk, who had indeed the name of a religious, but nothing more. This person, under pretence of having been a physician, was almost continually abroad, and appeared in the monastery only upon solemn festivals. When he was at matins with the rest upon one of the feasts of our Blessed Lady, he saw her enter the choir, bright and shining, and perceived she poured an Heavenly liquor into every monk's mouth, which gave them new force and vigour to sing the praises of God; but when it came to his turn to receive the same, she passed by without giving him any, telling him that the sweets of Heaven were not destined for him who thought of nothing but Earthly pleasures. This reproach so sensibly afflicted him, that, entering into himself, he instantly changed his life, and commenced a course of mortification, never afterwards going out without leave of his superior. The next feast of our Blessed Lady he had the comfort, that on coming again into the choir, she stopped before him, and thus spoke to him : Since you have amended your life, and preferred the sweets of Heaven before those of the Earth, I will regale you as I do the rest of your brethren : and he no sooner tasted of the liquor than he felt himself confirmed in the love of mortification, and in a contempt of the vanities of this world, this liquor being nothing else than the unction of devotion, which makes all things sweet and easy.

The same Cæsarius tells (*Lib*. iv. *Dial*., *c*. 80), of a clergyman who, after having lived in great delicacy, became a religious in the monastery of Clairvaux, where, finding nothing but very poor brown bread, he had scarce courage to look at it, and his stomach turned at the very thoughts of eating it. Our Blessed Saviour appeared one night to him and presented him a piece of the same bread, but he replying that it was impossible for him to eat it, our Saviour dipped it in the wound of his sacred side, and then commanded him to taste it. The religious obeyed, and found such an admirable taste in the bread, that from thenceforward, seasoning in a similar manner all the things he could not taste before, he found them most delicious.

The chronicles of the order of St. Francis, speaking (*P.* i. l. i. *c.* 58) of that famous assembly which was held in the open fields, and was called the *bulrush* chapter, because cells of rushes were made there for more than five thousand persons, observe that the spirit of fervour and penance reigned then so much in that order that it was necessary to curb and restrain it. Many of them wore iron girdles and pointed coats of mail next their skin, and thence contracted such diseases that thereby they were quite disabled, and could neither attend to their prayers nor do their order any service, and several of them died; so that St. Francis was obliged to command them under holy obedience, to bring all those pious instruments of mortification to him, which amounted to the number of five hundred. Whilst this extraordinary fervour lasted, and when they held this their general chapter, purely for the spiritual perfection and advancement of their order, it was revealed to St. Francis that eighteen thousand devils were assembled between *Portiuncula* and *Assisium* to consult and deliberate how to oppose the growth of his order, and that after several had given their opinions about it, one stood up and gave the following advice:—These people, says he, meaning St. Francis and the order he had founded, love this world so little and God so much, and are so much devoted to penance and prayer, that it is very difficult for us, or rather impossible, at present to prevail against them. Without giving ourselves any further trouble, then, I advise you to have patience till their founder is dead and their number increased; then we will introduce young men amongst them who shall have none of this zeal for perfection, and the old ones too, who shall be looking for respect, as also people of quality, who have been tenderly and delicately brought up, and learned men, whose pride shall be great, but their piety little. Nor will they fail to receive persons of this kind, as well to maintain the credit of this order as to augment their number. By this means we shall draw them to a love of the things of the world—to a love of learning, dignity, and human praise; and when once they are thus corrupted, we may freely take our revenge upon them. The whole assembly of devils approved of this advice and separated, already enjoying in idea the pleasure to be derived from this promised success.

THE SIXTH TREATISE.

ON THE OBSERVANCE OF RULES.

CHAPTER I.

Of the favours God has bestowed on religious, by guarding and fortifying them with rules.

ONE of the greatest favours which God has done to religious is the having fortified them with many rules and counsels, in order that they might be in greater security against the enemies of their salvation. Hence the saints compare, very justly, the evangelical counsels to the outworks of a city; for as a city is in a much better state of defence when it is encompassed by outworks and ramparts—because, should the enemy become masters of the outworks they are still checked by the ramparts—even so, those who are fortified with evangelical counsels are in a far better condition to resist the attacks of the Devil than seculars are. Now this is the advantage enjoyed by all religious in general, and, through the mercy of God, enjoyed by us in so particular a manner, that we may very justly apply to ourselves the words of Isaias, "The city of Sion is our fortress. The Lord has encompassed it with a wall and with a bulwark to defend it"—*Isa.*, xxvi. 1. He has first encompassed us with the rampart of his law and commandments, and he has added to this rampart the outworks of our rules and constitutions, that all the endeavours of our enemies, with whom we are always at war, may be able only to make some breach in the first fortification, and so the law of God remaining always entire, we may be secure from all their insults. It is a great favour that God has bestowed upon us, to have put us in such a state that the Devil can hope, even by his most violent attacks, to prevail no farther than to make us fail in our rules, the transgression of which amounts not to a venial sin, and that at present we have a greater scruple to violate any one of these rules, than perhaps, had we remained in the world, we would have had to commit great sins.

This shows the error of some weak religious, who, as soon as they happen to commit some faults against their rules and fall into some imperfections, imagine that it had been better for them to have remained in the world than to live in such a manner in religion. This is one of the most dangerous temptations that the Devil can make use of against us, because it regards a thing of so great importance, and so essential, as is our vocation. He desires nothing more than to keep us exposed in the world, beyond the precincts of our rules and evangelical counsels; because then undisturbed he would play his machines against the rampart of the law of God, and perhaps make us fall into some mortal sin. But here it is not so easy for him to compass what he aims at, on account of the outworks against which though he employs all his force, he cannot put us in danger of receiving any mortal wound in our soul, whatsoever disgusts he may give us in the observance of our rules, and whatsoever imperfections he may cause us to fall into. A single sin you would have committed in the world would have been far greater than all the faults you commit in religion; and therefore, how dissatisfied soever you may be with the little progress you think you make in virtue, yet assure yourself that you are in a better state in order to your salvation than you would have been in the world. This advantage is without doubt one of those which ought to enhance our esteem of a religious life; and this alone is so great a good that if we should derive no other from it but this, it would be highly estimable, and we should always have an infinity of thanks to render to God for having called us to it. Do you think it a small matter that, whilst others are in the field exposed to a thousand dangers, you are in a place of security only looking on; that, whilst others are in the midst of the sea, weather-beaten by winds and tempests, you are at repose in the haven; and that, whilst they are tossed and turmoiling themselves in the midst of the waves of Babylon, the torrent of which carries them away, you repose in peace and tranquillity upon the bank?

The rules of a religious life and the evangelical counsels have also this advantage, that they help us to observe the commandments; because the observance of them becomes very easy to him who aspires to the perfection of evangelical counsels; whereas, on the contrary, he who does not wish to aim at the perfection of the counsels, is scarcely faithful to the commandments. This is the sense which St. Thomas gives to these words of our Saviour in the gospel—" Verily I say unto you, that it is hard for a rich man to enter into the kingdom of Heaven"—

Matt., xix. 23. Do you know why it is so hard? says the holy doctor. It is because it is hard to observe the precepts that lead to this kingdom, unless we follow the counsels and renounce riches. The observance of the counsels, on the other hand, renders the observance of the commandments far more easy; because it is certain that to renounce, for example, all the goods of this Earth, and to be incapable of possessing anything as our own, prevents us very much from coveting to have the goods of our neighbour. It is certain that to pray to God for those that persecute us, to do good even to those from whom we have received evil, is to be very far from hating our enemies; and that never to swear, even when we affirm the truth, keeps us at the greatest distance from swearing falsely. And hence the saints remark, that the evangelical counsels and the rules of a religious life are so far from being a heavy burden, that they even console us, and assist us admirably to bear more easily the yoke of God's commandments.

St. Austin, speaking of the sweetness of the law of grace, explains it by two excellent comparisons. He compares it to the wings of a bird and to the wheels of a chariot. The wings, says he, are no burden to birds, on the contrary, they help to render them less heavy and even to make them fly; the wheels add no embarrassing weight to the chariot, but on the contrary, they afford great ease and help to the beasts that draw it, and without them they would not be able to draw half the weight they do. We can say the very same of evangelical counsels, upon which our rules are framed. So far from being a burden, they are wings that make us fly towards Heaven, they are wheels that help us to bear more easily the yoke of the law of God, whilst the people of the world, who have not the same advantages, bear it with a great deal of pain, groaning under the burden, and oftentimes even falling under it. All this ought to inspire us with deep sentiments of gratitude towards God, make us set an high value on our rules, and render us very fervent in the observance of them.

CHAPTER II.

That our perfection consists in the observance of our rules.

"OBSERVE my law and my counsel, and this shall be the salvation of thy soul and the sweetness of thy life"—*Prov.*, iii. 21, 22. It is thus the Holy Ghost by the mouth of the wise man exhorts us to an exact observance of God's law and counsels; and those words are very conformable to these of the Royal Prophet, "how pleasing, O Lord, are thy words! They are sweeter to my mouth than honey or the honey-comb"—*Ps.*, cxviii. 103. St. Jerom, writing to Helvidius in answer to twelve questions he had proposed him, of which the first was, what he ought to do to attain perfection, made the same answer that Jesus Christ did to the young man in the gospel, who cast himself at his feet, and asked him what he should do to gain eternal life. Our Saviour answered him, "If thou wouldst enter into life everlasting, observe the commandments"—*Matt.*, xix. 17,—and this man answering that he had observed them from his youth, "Jesus looked upon him", says the evangelist, "and loved him"—*Mark*, x. 21. And here, by the bye, we may take notice of what merit virtue and goodness is, whereas it draws the eyes of the Son of God upon us, and gains his very heart. But to come to our subject. "There is one thing you still want", says our Saviour, "go, sell all that which thou hast, and give to the poor, and thou shalt have treasure in Heaven, and then come and follow me"—*Mark*, x. 21. Behold here, says St. Jerom, what perfection precisely consists in, it consists in adding the evangelical counsels to the commandments.

Venerable Bede says, "that the second crown of gold which God commanded Moses to put upon the first"—*Exod.*, xxv. 25,— signifies the recompense of those who, not content with keeping the commandments of God, practise also the evangelical counsels. It is for this reason that Jesus Christ adds, "and thou shalt have treasure in Heaven"—*Mat.*, xix. 21; as if he would have said, thou shalt not only obtain everlasting life if thou practise those counsels I give thee, but thy recompense in Heaven shall thereby also become greater and more glorious. Thus "God has not only called us out of darkness to the admirable light of his glory"—I. *Pet.*, ii. 9,—as he has called all Christians, "and will not only transfer us to the kingdom of his beloved Son"—*Col.*,

i. 13,—but he desires to give us the first places therein. And it is upon this account he calls us to keep his evangelical counsels, in which consists the state [of perfection which all religious have embraced. It is therefore very just to endeavour on our part to correspond to so great a benefit, and we shall infallibly correspond to it if we take care to practise what our founder has commanded us when he says, let all those who enter into the society propose to themselves to observe entirely all the constitutions, all the rules, and all the practices therein observed; and by the mercy of God let them apply themselves with all their heart and with all their strength perfectly to observe them. Behold here in what our spiritual advancement and perfection consists: and we shall become perfect religious if we observe these with all the perfection that is required of us. Nay, even the name of religious seems to signify this obligation; for it signifies a man who is bound again; because in effect religious are not only bound by God's commandments, as all other Christians are, but also by the evangelical counsels, which are contained in each order. The obligation which they have to observe their rules is also signified by the name of regulars, which the Church gives them, which is a very honourable name, and which is also given them by the canon law; and we ourselves are called regular clerks by the Council of Trent and in the bulls of several Popes. Let us then endeavour worthily to correspond to our name, by rendering our lives conformable to it, and by becoming regular observers of our rules. St. Bernard, writing to some religious to exhort them to persevere in their fervour: "I beseech you, brethren", says he to them, "and earnestly conjure you to live after such a manner in our Lord, that you may be always careful to keep the rules of your order, and that they may keep and guard you". By this we see that if we take care to keep our rules, they will also keep us and maintain us in the perfection of our state.

The holy Scripture takes notice (*Judges*, xvi. 19), that the strength of Samson lay in his hair, and that as soon as it was cut off he lost all his strength, and was easily overcome and bound by the Philistines. This is an admirable figure of the state of a religious life, for as all the strength of Samson consisted in his hair, which he kept without cutting, being of the sect of the Nazareans, that is, of such as, having consecrated themselves to God, made profession to wear their hair without ever permitting it to be cut, even so all our perfection, and all other virtue, consists in keeping our rules; for though they appear to us to be of as light and small consequence as hair is, yet they are of great importance, by reason of the vow which we have made to God to observe them. Moreover, as from the very moment that Samson had his hair cut by the treachery of Dalila, to whom he had confided his secret, he lost with his hair all his strength, which God had been pleased to join to it; so, as soon as we shall fail to keep exactly our rules, we shall easily be overcome and bound by the Philistines, as Samson was, that is to say, we shall easily fall into the snares and come under the power of the devils our enemies.

CHAPTER III.

That though our rules do not oblige under pain of sin, yet we ought observe them exactly.

OUR rules and constitutions do not oblige us under pain of mortal sin, nor even of venial, no more than the commands of our superiors, unless, as our constitutions declare, they command on God's part, or by virtue of holy obedience. Yet we ought take most particular care not to violate them for this reason, which is a kind of temptation the Devil ordinarily makes use of to make us careless in breaking them; nor can we, for the aforesaid reason, be even less exact in the observance of them. Our holy founder, not wishing, on the one hand, to bind us so fast to them as that they would be an occasion of sin; and, on the other, wishing to make us observe them with all possible exactness and perfection, says, that for this purpose "the love of God must succeed in place of the fear of offending him; and that it must be the desire of our greater perfection, and of the greater glory of God, which will move us to act". He says also, in the beginning of our rules and constitutions, that the interior law of charity which the Holy Ghost has written in our hearts ought to move us to an exact observance of them, which is the same thing as the Son of God tells us in St. John, "If you love me, keep my commandments"—*John*, xiv. 15. It is sufficient for any one who loves, to know the will of the person he loves. It is sufficient for a well-educated child to know the will of his father, he needs not the motive of fear to make him obedient; and he who contemns the rules and breaks them, because they bind not under pain of sin and damnation, shows himself neither to be a well-educated child nor even a good servant. In proof of this, I ask, what opinion would you form of a servant who would never do anything his master commanded him, unless he commanded it with sword in hand and under pain of death? What opinion would you have of a woman that should tell her husband, I will be an honest woman, if you be not unfaithful to me; but if you be, I am resolved to do what I please, how angry soever you may be with me for it? Behold here the very thing those do who break their rules because they bind not under pain of sin and damnation, which in effect is properly to imitate slaves, who do nothing but through fear of being punished. "The wicked", as an ancient poet says, "abstain from sin from fear of being punished; but the good abstain from it for the love of virtue".

St. Gregory relates, that a holy religious, called Marsius, being retired in solitude to Mount Marisque, put a chain upon one of his feet, which he fastened to a rock, that he might go no farther than the length of his chain. St. Bennet, hearing this, sent one of his religious to him, to tell him, "if you be a servant of God, let not an iron chain, but the chain of Jesus Christ, hold you". And the holy man presently took off the chain from his foot, in obedience to what was commanded him, continuing, notwithstanding, to go no farther than when he was chained. Our holy founder also wishes to tie us to our rules, not with chains of iron, that is to say, with fear of sin and damnation, but with the chain of the love of Jesus Christ; and it is this which ought oblige us to be still more faithful to our duty, and to remain in greater restraint.

We must, moreover, take notice here of two things. The first is, that when any of our rules and constitutions contains anything which either regards the vows we have made, or which is forbidden by the law of God, then we are obliged to the observance of this rule, under pain of mortal sin, not by virtue of the rule, but by virtue of the vow we have made or of the law which God has established. The second thing we ought to take notice of is, that though our rule does not bind of itself under pain of sin, yet there may be a sin in breaking it, when we do it through negligence, laziness, contempt of the rule, or through some other motive of the same nature. St. Thomas has very well taken notice of this, when speaking of the rules of the order of St. Dominick, which of themselves do not bind, any more than our own do, under pain either of mortal or venial sin.

CHAPTER IV.

The levity of the matter commanded by the rule is no excuse for our violating it. This circumstance, on the contrary, renders us more inexcusable.

To make us neglect the observance of certain rules the Devil makes use of another stratagem, which is to persuade us that they are of no great importance, and that our perfection consists not in the observance of them; so that, with the assistance of our tepidity and negligence, he easily prompts us to transgress them. Now it is necessary to arm ourselves against this temptation, and for this purpose, I say, that the levity of the matter does not render the fault more excusable, but in some manner aggravates it. This is the doctrine of St. Austin, who, speaking of the disobedience of our first father, says, that as the obedience of Abraham was enhanced in proportion to the difficulty of the thing commanded, " so the disobedience of Adam was so much the more criminal, because there was no difficulty in doing what was required of him". For what excuse could be made for refusing to obey so easy a command as not to eat of the fruit of a single tree, since there were so many other trees of which he might freely eat, and which probably were much better? What would he have done then, if God had commanded him something very diffcult—if, for example, he had commanded him to sacrifice his wife, as he commanded Abraham to sacrifice his son? How could he ever prevail on himself to sacrifice her out of obedience, he who chose rather to disobey and displease God in eating the forbidden fruit, than to displease her? We can say, in like manner, that the facility of observing our rules renders the breaking of them more criminal and less excusable; and St. Bonaventure is of the same opinion, when he says, "the more easily a thing can be performed, the more guilty we are in not performing it". We might, perhaps, have some excuse were we to obey a very difficult command, but what excuse can we have when the thing required of us is so easy? Moreover, how can I believe that you would obey in hard things when you disobey in those that are most easy? It is to be believed that he who does not perform lesser things will never perform greater; and he, says St. Bernard, that cannot command his tongue or his appetite cannot be a good religious. This maxim was considered a first principle by the ancient fathers; and it is for this reason that they always began their exercises with abstinence; for he, say they, who cannot overcome himself in certain exterior things where the victory is more easy, how can he be able to overcome himself interiorly where the difficulty is far greater? How can he be able to defend himself against the malice of his invisible enemies, if he cannot even resist those he sees? This may help us to discern what is true and false in the desires we may sometimes have of doing great things for the love of God, such as to endure all sorts of pains and mortifications, and even to go and suffer martyrdom amongst infidels. For if amongst our brethren we are not able to bear a light mortification—if we break sometimes one rule, sometimes another, only to avoid the asking leave of a superior—what can be expected of us in difficult matters? "Many", says St. Bonaventure, "would wish to die with Jesus Christ, yet they would not endure a hard word for Jesus Christ. Now he who trembles at the noise of a leaf shaken by the wind, how will he have courage to await the blow of a sword ready to light upon him?" If a word said to us is able to trouble us and make us lose our repose, what will happen when persecutions shall be raised against us—when they will bring false witnesses to accuse us of things of very great moment, and when we shall perceive that all the world believes them? And hence the same saint exhorts us, " to accustom ourselves to suffer patiently even the least things, for he will never be able to overcome great ones who has not learned to surmount small difficulties".

Denis the Carthusian relates (*in Scal. Relig. art.* 16) that a novice who had great fervour in the beginning, afterwards, as it often happens, came to fall into great negligence and tepidity. All things at first seemed easy to him, but a little while after, all the exercises of mortification and humility became very heavy and painful, and amongst other things he could not suffer the outward coarse habit which the novices wore during their noviceship. One day as he slept he saw in his dream Jesus Christ, who was laden with a heavy cross, and who, by his efforts to get up a ladder which was very straight, exceedingly increased his pain. The novice, touched with compassion, presently offered himself to our Saviour to help him to carry his cross; but our Saviour, looking upon him with indignation, said to him: How dare you pretend to carry my cross, which is so heavy, since you feel it painful for love of me to carry even your habit, which weighs so little in comparison of my cross? At the same instant the vision diappeared, and the novice awoke very much confounded at this reproach, and at the same time fully resolved to suffer all things for Jesus Christ; so that ever after the coarse and contemptible habit, which he felt difficult to carry, became a subject of joy and contentment to him.

CHAPTER V.

How dangerous a thing it is to contemn our rules, though but in small things.

"HE who is faithful in little things, shall be also faithful in great ones; and he who offends in small things offends also in great ones"—*Luke*, xvi. 10. It being the ordinary practice of the Devil to urge us to a non-observance of our rules under pretence that the things they order are of small importance, and that our spiritual advancement does not depend upon them, I shall speak here of two remedies against this temptation. The first is to consider how dangerous it is to neglect small things; the second is to consider what advantage is derived from a diligent observance of them. Our Saviour takes notice of the one and the other in the words I have just now cited. With respect to the first, he says, that " he who is faithful in little things, will be faithful also in greater". The Holy Ghost had said the same of them before, "that he who contemns small things, will by little and little come to fall"—*Ecclus.*, xix. 1. We cannot doubt but that these sentences come from God; and therefore they ought to suffice to render us extremely careful in the observance of our rules, and hinder us from breaking them under pretence of the small importance of the things they prescribe. The prophet Jeremiah assures us that it was from small beginnings that God came to destroy Jerusalem. "Our Lord", says he, " proposed to cast down the walls of the daughter of Sion—he has taken his measures with his line, and has not ceased to endeavour its ruin.

All its outworks are entirely demolished, and its walls in like manner cast down"—*Thren.*, ii. 8. Behold here after what manner even the strongest places are taken; and it is according to this method that the devils endeavour to make themselves masters of the fortress of our soul. The rules, as I have already said, are the outworks, and serve for a defence to the law of God, which is the chief wall. So that if you look not well to these outworks and exterior fortifications, your invisible enemies will afterwards undermine your chief wall, and hereby become masters of your soul. " He that destroys the hedge shall be bitten by the serpent" —*Eccles.*, x. 8,—says the wise man. If you begin to destroy this hedge and this enclosure of your rules, if you once come to break it, the old serpent, which is the Devil, will not fail thereby to enter into your soul and to destroy you. " Why hast thou destroyed the dry wall that encompassed thy vineyard", says the prophet speaking to God, " and now all passengers make their vintage there"—*Ps.*, lxxix. 13. If you destroy this wall which encompasses the vineyard of our Lord, you can never hope to reap any fruit from the vineyard; it will be soon laid waste. But since this is a matter of great importance, and cannot be rendered too intelligible, let us lay aside these figures and metaphors, and speak more plainly. Would you know how that is to be understood which the Holy Ghost says to us, that " he who despises little things, by little and little will come to fall" ?— *Ecclus.*, xv. We ought to understand these words in the same sense that saints and divines do, who say that venial sin is a disposition to mortal. Venial sins, though ever so great in number, can never amount to one mortal sin, and cannot inflict death on a soul, or make it lose the grace of God; but they leave behind them in the soul a certain disposition to a slackness to devotion, and a love of ease and softness, which weakens it, and renders it more easy to be overcome upon the first occasion, and to fall into mortal sin. It is in this manner that, though the first discharge of cannon against a wall does not beat it down, yet it shakes it so that it disposes it to be easily beaten down by the subsequent discharges; and moreover, though the first drops of water which fall upon a stone are not able to make any impression upon it, yet they dispose it in such manner that those that follow actually make holes in it. " Water makes stones hollow", says Job, " and floods by little and little carry away the earth" —*Job*, xiv. 19. The effects of venial sin are the very same.

They insensibly carry us to lose the fear of offending God, and to act by other motives than by that of his love; and after this we are not far from doing what is directly contrary to it. He who makes no difficulty in telling a lie, and who gives himself the liberty of swearing without necessity, will soon come to swear to a lie or to what is doubtful, and thereby miserably fall into mortal sin. He who makes little or no scruple to detract in small things, will soon find occasion to detract in things of great importance, and will hereby be in danger of losing the grace of God. He who keeps not a custody over his eyes, and has not a particular care to reject bad thoughts when they come to him, is very near his fall. An occasion will happen in which his heart and desires will follow his thoughts and looks; and behold here again a miserable fall. It is just this—the Devil aims at engaging us to commit venial sins, thereby to precipitate us into those sins which give death to the soul.

It is the same with the contempt and breach of rules. These are the means the Devil makes use of to urge us by little and little to do worse things, and to make us at last fall into a precipice. In the beginning we shall have a very great scruple to break the least rule, but afterwards we shall have less; and in the end we shall come freely to break them without the least remorse of conscience. The same thing happens also in regard of prayer and other spiritual exercises, because they carry with them no stricter obligation than the rest. At one time we neglect to make them, at another we make them by halves and very negligently, without reaping any fruit from them; and at last we fall into such remissness, and into so great a negligence of them, that we come to lose the gust of spiritual things. It is from these kind of beginnings, which seem very inconsiderable, that the mortal falls of a religious proceed; and St. Austin very well takes notice, in regard to the reflection made by the evangelist, which was, that Magdalen, having poured out her ointment of great price upon the feet of the Son of God, Judas murmured at it, saying, "Why was not this perfume sold, and the money given to the poor?" for the Gospel says expressly, "that he said not this because he took any care of the poor, but because he was a thief, kept the purse, and had the dispensation of all that was given"—*John*, xii. 5, 6. He was displeased that Magdalen hereby took from him the occasion of robbing or taking away some of that money for which the perfume might have been sold;

and to compensate himself for this loss the miserable wretch resolved to sell his Master. Remark, says St. Austin, that it was not in selling our Saviour that Judas began to lose himself. The evil began long before—he had been a long time a thief, and his body only followed Jesus Christ, while his heart was far distant from him. When you perceive that any religious has grievously fallen, believe not that the evil began only then; for without doubt, long before his mind and heart were not in religion, he had no care of keeping his rules, and he made not prayer, or examen, or any other exercise of piety. Consider into what a precipice Judas is fallen for want of repressing the motions he had of covetousness of money; and let us learn never to relent even in the least things, lest weak and small beginnings cast us into terrible consequences. "Poverty and want go before his face"—*Job*, xli. 13,—says the Scripture; and one of the senses which is given to these words is, that remissness and tepidity are always forerunners of the Devil into a soul; it falls first into this spiritual want, which proceeds from a multitude of venial sins, and because it has deprived itself of those helps which it was wont to derive from prayer and spiritual exercises, it afterwards easily gives way to the attacks of the first great temptation which comes upon it. Let us beware then of being in the least degree negligent of our rules for fear of giving entrance unto the Devil; for as soon as we make no scruple of falling into deliberate imperfections and of committing venial sins, we are not far from committing mortal. "Learn, O Jerusalem", says our Saviour by the mouth of Jeremy, "learn lest my soul retire from thee, and that I render thee a desert and an uninhabitable land"—*Jerem.*, vi. 8. Learn, O religious souls, learn how to conform yourselves to the practice of religious discipline, and apply yourselves to an exact observance of your rules, lest God leave and abandon you, and that thereby you receive some dangerous fall.

CHAPTER VI.

The great advantages derived from an exact observance of rules even in the least things.

" WELL done, good and faithful servant; because thou hast been faithful in small things, I will give thee the administration of greater; enter into the joy of thy Lord"—*Mat.*, xxv. 21. The

Son of God points out in these words the recompense which is annexed to fidelity in little things; and to make us see more clearly the greatness of his recompense, he says not that the joy of the Lord shall enter into us, because our heart is too strait a vessel to contain it, but he says that we shall enter into the joy of the Lord, which marks the excess and abundance of this joy, and that we shall be altogether plunged therein. In another place he promises us "that they shall cast in our breasts good measure, a measure filled and heaped up so high as it shall even run over"—*Luke*, vi. 38. But let us consider a moment why he promises so great a recompense to those who shall be faithful in small things; it is because as a man behaves in little things, so he behaves in great ones, according to the words of the gospel, "he that is faithful in lesser, is also faithful in greater things"— *ibid.*, xvi. 10. Moreover, take notice that he says, not that he who is faithful in great things shall be so in little ones, but he converts the proposition; because in fact fidelity makes itself more known in little things than in great ones. Is it in his not defrauding his master of one or two hundred pounds that the fidelity of a steward appears? No; but it is in his not defrauding him of a single farthing. A good servant does not show himself so much in those great things which purely belong to his duty, as in certain little cares to which he is not obliged; and in fine, a son does not give so strong a proof of love and respect for his father by obeying him in matters of consequence, as he does by obeying him in the least thing, and by the lively care he takes to avoid everything which might in the least degree displease him. It is the same with a good religious. He displays his virtue less in hindering himself from falling into mortal sin, than in applying himself faithfully to perform those things which his rules and obedience prescribe, and it is for this reason that God treats persons of this description so liberally and bestows so many graces upon them. He is liberal towards them because they are liberal towards him, which is conformable to the words of St. James, "approach to God, and he will approach to you"— *James*, iv. 8,—and the more they approach to God and use this liberality towards him, the more he approaches to them, and the greater graces he heaps upon them. He who takes particular care to please God, not only in things of duty and of precept, but also in those which are of counsel, and who, not only in the greatest but even in the least things, always diligently applies himself to do what he believes is most conformable to God's will, is truly liberal to God, and God recompenses him by the like liberality. The persons who serve God in this manner are those whom he makes his favourites; it is upon them he showers down his graces and blessings in greater abundance than upon others, and in a word, these are the persons who ordinarily distinguish themselves from others by their virtue and perfection. I have known some religious amongst us who by this means have become great and admirable men in spirituality; and I have heard of others who, though very much advanced in age, yet were so faithful in the observance of even the least rules, that they became an example to all their brethren, and at the same time gave them a great confusion. But it is not to be wondered at that these are the beloved favourites of God; for we see even in the world that the domestics who do that only which they think pleasing to their master, and who with cheerfulness perform the lowest as well as the highest duties in his service, are those upon whom he bestows choicest benefits. It is the same in the house of God. Those who stoop to everything—who make little of themselves—those who pay lively attention to the least things which regard the glory and service of God, are the dearly beloved favourites of the Almighty. It is to them he opens the treasures of his blessings and graces, and it is of them he properly says, " Permit these little ones to come unto me, and do not hinder them, for to them the kingdom of Heaven belongs"—*Mat.*, xix. 14. On the contrary, those that affect to be distinguished from others—who believe their seniority in religion gives them right to dispense with themselves in the observance of the common rules, and to look upon little things as employments fit only for novices, disdaining to stoop to them themselves—those God humbles and rejects, according to the words of David: "If I thought not humbly of myself, but proudly elevated my mind, treat me, O Lord, as a nurse treats her infant when she weans it from her breast"—*Ps.*, cxxx. 2. What ought a nurse to do that weans her child? She carries him no longer in her arms, and not only ceases to give him suck, but even rubs her breast with some bitter thing, that he may there find bitterness where he before was accustomed to find so much sweetness. Behold the curse which David gave both to himself and to all those who would appear great, and are ashamed of being little. He begs that God would reject them, that he would deprive them of his consolations, and that he would change into bitterness all that spiritual sweetness with which he was wont to favour them.

St. Jerom, who knew perfectly well what the sentiments of a true servant of God ought to be, says, "that he who is entirely devoted to Jesus Christ, is no less exact in the performance of small things, than of great ones, knowing that he must render an account for even on unprofitable word". He knows that from little defects we fall by little and by little into great ones, and it is very certain that he who is faithful in little things will be rewarded by a great abundance of God's favours, and therefore he is exceedingly exact in doing small things, and neglects not one of them, how little soever it may appear. St. Basil recommends to us the like practice: "Endeavour", he says, "to attain the most elevated virtues; yet notwithstanding neglect not the least, and think no fault little, though it should appear to you smaller than even a mite".

CHAPTER VII.

The preceding doctrine confirmed by examples.

WE read in the fourth book of Kings that Naaman, general of the army of the king of Syria, was afflicted with a leprosy, and having heard that the prophet Eliseus, who was in Samaria, infallibly cured it, he went upon this account to the king of Israel with letters of recommendation from the king his master. Eliseus knowing the cause of his coming, desired his servant to meet him; and Naaman being come to his gate with a great retinue, the prophet bid him say to him: "Go and wash yourself seven times in the river Jordan, and your body shall receive perfect health, and you shall be quite cured". Naaman received the message with indignation, and returned, saying: "I thought he would have come out to meet me, and that, standing, he would have invoked the name of his God upon me, and that he would have touched with his hand the affected parts, and would have cured me in this manner. Are not Abana and Pharpar, which pass by Damascus, better rivers than those of the land of Israel? Might I not rather have washed myself in them, and thereby have been cured?" However, his followers seeing him return very angry, said to him, "My lord, had the prophet commanded you anything that had been very hard, without doubt you would and ought have done it: with how far greater reason therefore ought you to obey him in what he tells you: wash yourself, and you shall be cured". This reasoning of theirs made such an impression upon him, that he went to Jordan, washed himself there seven times, "and his flesh", says the Scripture, "became like the flesh of a young child, and he was entirely cured"—IV. *Kings*, v. 10, etc. You see that his cure was annexed to what appeared to him to be very frivolous and of little or no importance; and it is often the same in respect to the soul and to our making a progress in virtue. For it is just that our spiritual perfection should consist in those small things which are prescribed by our rules. Do we not see that the perfection of an engraven plate consists in certain points and strokes which are scarcely perceptible? In order to acquire spiritual perfection, after which you ought to aspire, were you commanded to do something very hard, "without doubt you ought to do it": with how far greater reason, therefore, ought you to do what is prescribed you for this end, since there is question only of the easiest things in the world, which carry no difficulty at all with them? It ought not, then, to be a subject or occasion of remissness to us to see that what our rules prescribe is so inconsiderable and so easy in itself; but, on the contrary, nothing ought more strongly excite us to a perfect observance of them, than to see that our perfection is annexed to such small things as we can so easily perform.

The history of the illustrious persons of the Cistercian order observes, that there was a rule in that order which required that all the religious at the end of every meal should gather together all the crumbs of bread which were before them, and either eat them or put them upon a plate. One day a religious, who was a great observer of the rules, having gathered into his hand all the crumbs that were before him, it happened that he was so engaged in attending to the reading, that whilst he held them the knock was given to rise from table. Coming again to himself he was at a loss to know what to do, because he was not permitted to eat them, nor could he put them upon his plate, which was already taken away. In fine, he imagined that he could not repair his fault better than by going and declaring it to his superior, and by demanding a penance for it; and in effect he did so with very great marks of sorrow and confusion as soon as grace was ended. The superior, after having reprehended him for his negligence, asked him what he had done with the crumbs. The religious answered that he had them still in his hand, and when he opened it to show them, he found that instead of crumbs they were become very fine pearls. The author observes in this place, that God by this miracle deigned to show how pleasing to him the fervour of zealous religious is, who, not content with a careful observance of the more important rules, apply themselves also to an exact observance even of the least. Surius relates that the same thing happened to St. Eude before he was abbot, and says that out of humility he related it as if it had happened to another, yet notwithstanding it was for St. Eude himself that God was pleased to work this miracle.

Cæsarius relates (*Lib.* iv. *Dial.*, c. 15) that in the time of Frederick the First, emperor of Germany, there happened to become vacant an imperial abbey which the emperors were accustomed to dispose of. The religious having proposed two of their subjects that the emperor might choose which of them he pleased, one of them, in order to obtain the preference, offered great sums of money, which the emperor took, and promised to choose him. However, being afterwards informed that the other religious was a very holy man, and a great observer of religious discipline, he changed his resolution, and as he sought for some expedient to free himself from the engagement he had made, and to elect the more worthy, one of his followers said to him: Sire, I have heard that these religious have a rule which orders that every one should carry a sewing needle about him: when therefore you shall be present at their chapter, find some pretext to ask him whom you wish to exclude to lend you his needle, and as he is no strict observer of his rules, it is very probable he will not have one, and it will be a sufficient reason to exclude him to have detected him in such a fault. This counsel was followed, and it was found that this religious had no needle about him, so that the emperor, applying to the other, asked him for his. The holy man instantly presented it to him. You are a good religious, says the emperor, and deserve to be abbot; I had resolved to prefer your competitor before you, but he has shown himself unworthy of the dignity by not observing his rule, and it is very easy to judge that he who is negligent in little and easy things, will be far more in those that are very hard and essential; afterwards he declared that he chose the other for abbot; and so the one was punished for his little care in observing his rules, and the other was recompensed for his faithful observance of them.

The same Cæsarius relates that a woman of quality, resolving to become religious, made a great feast for all her relations and friends upon the day she was to enter into religion, and invited the superior of the monastery wherein she was to take the habit. They served in flesh for the seculars, but fish for the religious and his companion, because the rule and custom of their order permitted them not to eat flesh. The religious, however, tempted at the sight thereof, and desirous to show he was not scrupulous in small matters, took a bit of roast meat to eat it, but he had no sooner put it into his mouth, than it stuck so fast in his throat that he could nether swallow it nor get it up again. Whilst he was in this condition, and his eyes were already rolling in his head, his companion gave him a blow upon the back with his fist, which made him cast up the piece of meat, which had like to have choked him; and the whole company easily conceived that the extremity to which they had seen this religious reduced was a punishment of his disobedience and of his neglect of his rule. We read also in the order of St. Dominick (*Lib.* i. *c.* 60) that this saint being at Boulogne, the Devil on a sudden seized upon a lay brother, and began to torment him in so strange a manner, that the religious who were going to rest awoke at the noise, and ran to help him. The saint commanded them to go with him to the church, whither ten religious were scarce able to carry him. It happened also, that as soon as he was entered, with one puff he blew out all the lamps. So that the religious, not being able to see anything, they left him there. The Devil began again to torment him anew, and to bruise him with many blows. Then the saint commanded him, in the name of Jesus Christ, to tell the reason for which he possessed this brother, and why he so cruelly tormented him. The Devil answered, it was because he had drunk over night, without having asked leave, and without having made the sign of the cross upon it, according to the rules and practice of the order. But it having begun to ring matins, I can stay here no longer, says the Devil, for behold the brothers are rising to go sing the praises of God; and, having said this, he left the poor man so bruised and broken in pieces, that it was two days before he was able in any manner to move himself. St. Gregory (*Lib.* i. *Dial.*, *c.* 4) relates almost the same example of a religious woman, who, having neglected to make the sign of the cross before she eat a salad of lettuce, was presently possessed by the Devil.

CHAPTER VIII.

Some other causes of the non-observance of rules.—The remedy that may be applied thereunto.

As it is sometimes through a kind of timidity and reserve that we fail to observe our rules, or, to say better, as it is through a spirit of immortification, and because we have not strength to overcome the repugnance we have to go and ask permission of our superior for a small matter, it is fit that we provide for this difficulty. I do not require of you to abstain from eating, drinking, or speaking; nor would I hinder you from receiving what is offered you: the only thing I desire is, that you would do all with leave, for since you may do it with the blessing of God and with the good will of your superiors, why do you desire to do it otherwise? But you will say, must I every moment then importune my superior about mere trifles, which would tend only to hinder him from his business and to give him trouble? Behold here precisely the abuse I wish to correct, and the error I would disabuse you of. Superiors are so far from being displeased when one goes to ask leave for anything, that they are very much pleased thereat. It is their business to hearken to you at all times; and religion, which is a mother that seeks your advantage, and that knows of how great merit obedience is in God's sight, has so great a desire that you should be very obedient, and should do nothing without leave, that to facilitate the means thereof, it keeps one or two superiors in every house, whose office it is to give you leave as often as you ask it. Since, therefore, they know that they are established for this end, they will take as much care not to be angry when you have recourse to them, as a merchant or tradesman would when you go to him for anything belonging to his trade, or to buy any merchandise of him; and if you harbour any other thought than this of your superiors, it is wronging them and thinking that they do not their duty.

Moreover, why should a superior be troubled, that you should ask leave for a thing which he knows you cannot do without?

Should you go to him to entertain him with frivolous, idle, and superfluous discourse, you might have reason to fear the importuning him; but to go to him, when by your rules you are obliged to do so, is to do him a pleasure, because he ought to be glad to see that those under his charge keep an exact account of even the least things. What troubles and displeases him is the liberty which some take, in dispensing with the rules and in doing things without leave, as if they had no superior to go to; which is as if they made no account at all of their rules, and looked upon them as nothing. Behold here what we ought to avoid, that we may give no trouble to our superiors.

From hence we may draw this consequence, that as in regard to the things in which our hands are tied by the rules, and to do which we have not permission, we ought feel no difficulty to ask it; even so, we ought freely to tell our brother, who is instructed as well as ourselves in the rules, that we have not the permission. This advertisement is of great importance; because a great many easily permit themselves rather to break their rules, than to mortify themselves by declaring that they have no leave either to speak or to receive what their brother would give them. They pretend sometimes to excuse themselves, by saying that it is because they have no wish to mortify their brother that they violate a rule, and that they dared not tell him that they had not permission. But this is to have a bad opinion of your brother, and to believe him so little faithful in the observance of his rules as to imagine that you would hereby mortify him. Your exactness would rather have edified him; and that which he did was perhaps to try you, and to see your fidelity in the observance of your rules. You are a religious, and therefore ought to glory in and not be ashamed of the performance of the duties of your profession. Wherefore observe punctually your rule, and your brethren will be so far from having anything to say against you, that they will esteem you the more for it.

Some others, to excuse the liberty they take in breaking their rules, say, they do it not to appear scrupulous, which is also a very bad excuse. For to be an exact observer of one's rules, is not to appear scrupulous. It only makes a person appear truly religious. What a strange thing, then, would it be, should this give an occasion of shame! One of the abuses that is in the world is, that as soon as a secular gives himself to piety, frequents the sacraments, lives in retirement, he is presently exposed to the scoffs and railleries of seculars; and from hence it happens that many dare not make open profession of piety, being like in this to the Jew who went to find out our Saviour by night, not daring to go to him in the day-time. But it is not the same in religion, and God preserve us from such a misfortune as this would be! We have the advantage to live here amongst persons who make profession of piety and aspire to perfection; and he who makes the greatest progress in virtue, is he who is most esteemed. But notwithstanding, if it should happen that for this reason any one should receive contradiction from one of his brethren, yet a religious who ought to be firm and unshaken in the love of God, should not, upon this account, neglect at any time to aspire to perfection, or be ashamed to appear the disciple of Jesus Christ. "For he who shall be ashamed of me and my words", says our Saviour, "the Son of man will be ashamed of him and disown him when he shall come in his own majesty, and in that of his Father and of the holy angels"—*Luke*, ix. 26. If a man had taken one of his servants to follow him, and this servant, out of a foolish vanity, and that he might not seem to belong to his master, should affect to keep at a great distance from him when he went into the city, would not he deserve to be turned away? A religious who is ashamed to pass for a servant of Jesus Christ, and who for this reason omits to observe his rules, ought justly apprehend the like treatment. But in order to disabuse ourselves still more of this awkward bashfulness, we must fix this truth deep in our minds, that when we are careful and punctual in observing our rules, seculars themselves are no less edified at us than our brethren are. If you are, for example, in conversation with him when the bell rings, you would please him more by telling him civilly that obedience calls you away, and that therefore you are obliged to quit him, than by all you could have been able to say to him had you still remained with him; and the more aged and dignified the person is that you treat in this manner, the more he will be edified at it. We ought not therefore imagine, that to bind ourselves to an exact observance of our rules, or to say we have not this or that leave, is any offence against civility, or looked upon as scrupulosity; for there is no religious or secular that can find anything blame-worthy herein; but on the contrary, they will hereby be the more edified. If the thing in question were something extraordinary, or if you were not obliged to do it by your rules, you might perhaps have some reason not to do it for fear of appearing too singular and to pass for an hypocrite; but here the question is about your ordinary duty and the obligations of your profession. Moreover, if you permit yourself once to neglect your rules, it is to open a gap to do the same at another time in a matter of greater consequence; and on the other hand, if you make it appear that you are bound to an exact observance of your rules, you will thereby remove occasions of breaking them afterwards, and will obtain much quiet and repose. There is still another advantage herein, which is, that besides the good you do to yourself, you do also a very great kindness to your brother; for perhaps he did not think at all of the rule, and you, by your example, make him think of it, which is the best kind of advertisement you could give him.

The history of the Jeromites makes mention (*Luke*, xxviii.), of a certain religious who was a great observer of silence, and who had hereby gained the esteem and veneration of every one. A person of quality having heard him much spoken of, wished very much to see him and have some discourse with him, and one day having met him as he went to his little garden, he followed and called after him to oblige him to stay. The holy man, however, did not wait for him nor make him any answer, till being both entered into his garden, he cast himself at his feet, and then putting his hands before his face he spoke thus to him: Perhaps, sir, you know not that I cannot speak without leave of my superior; and after these words he prostrated himself again upon the earth and said not a word more; so that the secular, who would not importune him any longer, left him, and as the history remarks, returned home more edified at the silence of this religious than he should have been had he had ever so long a conversation with him.

The same history speaks (chap. xxi.) of another holy religious who kept silence so exactly in all the places where it was forbidden to speak, for example, in the church and cloister, that in them he never spoke to any one, nor even answered any one that spoke to him. It one day happened that king Henry walking in the cloister of the monastery where this religious was, perceived him pass by, and esteeming him very much by reason of his sanctity, he called him to entertain himself with him. But the servant of God would neither stop nor answer till he was out of the cloister, and then the king asked him why he did not sooner answer him. Sire, replied the holy man, it is not permitted to any of the religious to speak in the cloister, and therefore I did not answer your majesty till I was out of it. And the history takes notice that this prince was extremely edified at his answer.

CHAPTER IX.

Some other means which may contribute to an exact observance of our rules.

THERE are still other means which may extremely help to make us careful in the observance of our rules. The first of these is the good example and edification we are obliged to give, according to the words of the apostle, "let us take care to do well, not only before God, but also before men"—*Rom.*, xii. 17. It is not sufficient for you to be good only upon your own account; you ought moreover to apply yourself to edify the neighbour by your good example: "You ought to let your light so shine before men, that they may see your good works and glorify your Father which is in Heaven"—*Mat.*, v. 16. When we see a tree full of blossoms, or extremely charged with fruit, we bless God for it. We ought in like manner by the fruits of a holy and exemplary life move men to praise God; we ought to be an example to all, but particularly to our brethren with whom we live, and this is of indispensable obligation. For good example and edification consist not only in our not falling into great faults, but also in carefully avoiding to fall even into the least, and in showing by our conduct that we are extremely attached to the least duties of our profession, and that we have a very great esteem of the least things that regard it. He who distinguishes himself most in this is he who most of all edifies others; and the more considerable one is in religion, either for age or learning, the more ought he attend to the least things which may be of edification to his brethren; "Let him who is greatest among you", says the Son of God, " become as the least, and he who presides as he who serves" —*Luke*, xxii. 26. It is thus that the most ancient in religion ought to make themselves known to be so, by being more humble and more mortified than others, and by an exact observance of their rules, and those who do this are truly the pillars of religion. They are those that make piety and religious discipline flourish therein, and the words of the Apocalypse may with justice be applied to them: "I will make him a pillar in the temple of my God"—*Apoc.*, iii. 12. And these others also of Jeremiah, "I have to-day established thee to be as a pillar of iron and as a wall of brass"—*Jerem.*, i. 18. On the contrary, there cannot be a greater prejudice done a religious community than to give ill example in it, and the more remarkable he is that gives it, either for his age, learning, or any other quality, the greater will be the prejudice; because example, which has a great power over men in all things, as experience teaches us, has still greater to urge us to what is evil. For if your brother sees that you observe not the rules, and that you neglect little things, you especially who are a senior and who ought to give example to others, what will he do, considering the great inclination which nature gives him for liberty, and the repugnance and aversion which all the world has to anything that causes subjection or brings constraint along with it? When he sees such a path beaten, and such a gate as this opened by you, can he forbear from following you? Perhaps he only waited for some one to lead the way, and to banish that shame he had left in him. Your conduct does this and destroys him; it introduces the neglect of religious discipline; and therefore you will have a great account to render to God, not only for your own faults, but also for the faults of others, because you are the cause of them by your bad example. This consideration ought to be sufficient to move you to an exact observance of your rules, and to hinder you from ever doing anything which may be of disedification to your brethren.

The second means to make the observance of rules remain always in vigour, is very familiar and very easy amongst us; and St. Ignatius teaches it in the same rules. Let every one, says he, from time to time beg of the superior to give him some penance for his non-performance of his rules, and by this let him show the care he has of advancing in God's service. We ought to have so great an esteem of our rules, that if we happen to break any one, it should not be sufficient to have only an interior regret thereof, but we ought also to testify an exterior sorrow by some penance; and it is only in this manner we can completely repair the breach of our rules, and maintain them in such force and vigour as if they had never been broken. The "law", as divines and lawyers say, "is then in as great force and vigorous observance as if it had been but newly made, when care is taken to punish him that breaks it". To make it appear as if it were in its first vigour, it is not required that nobody break it, but it is sufficient that he who breaks it should be punished; but when one freely breaks the law without punishment, and without the magistrate's being at all concerned for it, it is a sign, say they, that it is not then in its vigour, and that the law has no longer any force, and that a contrary practice, " or the disuse of it has abrogated it". The same thing may be said of the rules. When in any religious order there is no fault committed against the rules, which is not presently followed with a penance, we may then say that observance of rules is in its vigour. But when on the one hand there are frequent violations, and on the other no punishment, it is true to say that the rules are no longer observed; and in a little time after it will be asserted that the rules have no longer any force, and that the contrary usage has abolished them, because they have been contemned even in the sight and with the knowledge of superiors, without their doing their duty to put a stop hereunto, or without their having imposed any penance upon the offenders.

Since then it is the duty of superiors to take care that the rules be observed, and that they are bound to see them maintained in vigour, they are also bound to impose a penance when any one fails to observe them; so that when a superior gives you a penance upon this account, or reprehends you for it, it is not that he is angry with you, or that he esteems you the less, for he knows that we are all of us men, and it is not strange that we should fail in the observance of one or two rules, but it is because he wishes to do his duty, which obliges him to take care that the rules be observed. But if when any of them are broken, he should dissemble without being at all in pain, and without imposing any penance for it, this would show that he had but little esteem of them, and hereby he would render himself guilty of a great fault, and concur in abolishing the rule and religious discipline. It is in this different mode of governing consists, according to St. Bonaventure, the difference between the religious orders which maintain the fervour of their institution, and those that are relaxed. For this difference is not occasioned by sin being committed in the one and not in the other: this would be impossible, "for all of us offend in many things"—*James*, iii. 2,—as St. James the apostle says, but it is occasioned by the violation of the rules being punished in the one and not in the other.

Now, St. Ignatius recommends to us all to assist our superiors in doing what they are bound to do by their office, and it is on this account he says that every subject should from time to time beg of the superior to inflict penance for having failed in the observance of the rules. For it would be a great trouble to the superior should he be obliged continually to perform the office of serjeant or spy with regard to those that break the rules, and for every fault to impose penance upon them. This would be a thing impossible, and though he could do it, yet it would be far from that spirit of sweetness with which the society is governed. It is your duty, therefore, to take care to discover your faults to your superior, and to go to him to ask penance for them, and you ought never permit that he should be sooner informed of them by another than by yourself. Because it is your business, it is more your interest than of any one else to do it, and all the advantage comes to yourself. Take notice, moreover, that the reason why St. Ignatius would have us act in this manner is, that we may show what care we take to advance God's service. So that when we fail in observing the rules, and take care to go ask for penance, we show also that we take care of our spiritual advancement; as, on the contrary, when we break them, without troubling ourselves to ask penance for it, we show that we neglect it exceedingly. We perceive also that when we are exact in this practice, and when the penances and mortifications upon this account become frequent, the spirit of fervour and zeal is far more flourishing amongst all the religious, and their edification is much greater.

It is in this practice consists the second means we have proposed to make the observance of rules be always maintained in vigour amongst us. I do not say that we can be able absolutely to hinder the rule from ever being broken, for to do this we should be angels and not men. We shall very often, without doubt, break them; and who is he, let him be ever so just, that happens not to commit some venial sins? "For there is no man who does not sin"—III. *Kings*, viii. 46. But what I ask is only this, that when you have broken your rules, you show some regret for having done so, and manifest thereby that you are truly religious, that you esteem them, and that you have a great desire to observe them. Go at least presently to acknowledge your fault; for by a small penance you will completely repair it, and you will not only repair it, but you will thereby gain more than you have lost, and the Devil hereby, instead of rejoicing for having made you commit it, will feel great confusion and despair on seeing that you know how to gain by your losses. It was a truth which he himself was constrained one day to confess to St. Dominick, when this saint forced him to follow him into all the different places of his monastery, to know of him the different temptations he made use of in each place against his religious. For, coming to the chapter-house, which is the place they were wont to declare their faults in, and to receive reprehensions and penances for them: it is here, says the Devil, that I lose all I have gained, either in the dormitory or refectory, and in all other places. This kind of reparation is, moreover, very full and entire, because, by this means, the fault committed against the rules is no less wholly repaired in the sight of men than it is in the sight of God. You fail, for example, to ring the bell precisely at the hour, or to be punctually present at any hour with the rest of the community. These are public faults which are perceived by all the world, and will also be repaired before them all, at the sight of the public penance you do for them. But if, after having seen the fault, they had not seen the penance, they would have reason to say, that the house was come to such a pitch that no value is set on exact observance, and that all things were performed in it with more or less imperfection, and without being in the least troubled thereat.

We must withal observe, that though in the society penances are more ordinarily asked than given, and though this practice is very reasonable, yet care must be taken that the custom of giving penances be not quite abolished, according to the rule, which says, that the superior ought to impose some penance for the greater spiritual advancement of every one. For, if it should happen that no more penances should be given than are asked, it would follow that all the superior should otherwise give would become more heavy and troublesome, and those upon whom they were imposed would receive them with too much trouble and disquiet, which would be of great prejudice to religious discipline, and of very great disedification. Wherefore, care ought to be taken that this custom be observed, and generally practised towards all persons, because there will be always subject enough for it; and if there should be none, yet does not our holy founder say, that we ought to be disposed to receive and fulfil very willingly all those penances which shall be imposed, even when there should be no fault committed for which they were given? It is certainly in this that true virtue and the spirit of humility shine most conspicuous, and it is this manifests the desire we have to advance in perfection. "For what glory is it", says St. Peter, "if, when you have sinned, you suffer yourself to be ill treated? But if, when you have done well, you suffer with patience, you will gain great merit before God" —I. *Peter*, ii. 20.

It will also contribute much towards the exact observance of our rules, to practise what is prescribed in the last rule of the summary and in the last of the common rules, which is, to take care to imprint them deep in our minds, and to read them for this end, or to get them read to us, once a month. Many are not content with hearing them read in the refectory, but add every day to their spiritual reading three or four rules; so that every month they read them over at their leisure; and this, without doubt, is an excellent custom and a very good spiritual lecture. It is also an excellent means, for the same end, to make our particular examen upon the observance of our rules, not of all of them in general, but of those in particular which we find ourselves most subject to fail in, examining them one after another, and also examining ourselves upon all those that regard our particular employment, and this kind of examen cannot but be very advantageous and profitable.

THE SEVENTH TREATISE.

ON THE FIDELITY WHICH ALL OUGHT TO HAVE IN LAYING OPEN THE BOTTOM OF THEIR HEART AND CONSCIENCE TO THEIR SUPERIORS AND GHOSTLY FATHERS.

CHAPTER I.

How necessary it is to make ourselves known to superiors exactly as we are.

CASSIAN says, that the first thing the ancient fathers proposed to those who began to serve God was, that they should take great care presently to discover to their superiors whatsoever temptations or bad thoughts they had, or, in fine, whatsoever passed within themselves. And it was this, says he, that these men of God looked upon as a kind of first principle amongst them, and as the base and foundation of the whole spiritual building. "A religious", says the great St. Anthony, "should not, if possible, make one step, or drink one drop of water in his cell, without immediately declaring it to his superior, that there may be no irregularity even in his least actions, but that all things may be rectified by the spirit of obedience"—*in Vit. Patr.*, part 2, §. 104. St. John Climacus says, that he found in a very regular and holy monastery, several religious who carried a little book at their girdle, in which they daily wrote all their thoughts, to give an account of them to their superior, who had obliged them thereunto. St. Basil, St. Jerom, St. Ambrose, and St. Bernard, expressly prescribed the same thing; and it is this which St. Ignatius, resting upon their authority and the examples of the ancient fathers, in like manner recommends to us, even in the gravest terms we can find in his whole constitutions. "After", says he, "having well examined this thing before God, it seemed to me in the presence of his divine majesty, that it was very much to the purpose that all religious should make themselves perfectly known to their superiors"—*Exam.*, §. 34. He was not wont to speak in this manner in other matters how important soever; and yet he does not content himself with this, but goes still farther, proving by solid reasons the advantage and necessity of this practice.

The first reason he gives is, that by this means it will be more easy for superiors to direct those under their charge, and in effect it belongs to the superior to take care of them. His office obliges him to it, and it is for this reason that he was made superior. Now, how shall he be able to do this if he does not know you, and if you do not discover yourself unto him? "He that hides his crimes", says the wise man, "can never be well directed"— *Prov.*, xxviii. 13. A sick man can never be cured, if he discovers not his disease to the physician. "For the physician", says St. Jerom, "cures not that which he does not know". You must therefore entirely discover your sickness to the physician, and if you have many diseases you must discover them all. For if you hide one of them, the physician may, perhaps, give you such remedy as will make worse the disease which you concealed, and perhaps will not help that you discovered. We know that what is good for the liver, is not good for the spleen; wherefore all is to be told, that the remedies may be so prepared, that what relieves you on one side may not hurt you on the other. The same reason ought oblige us to discover in the same manner all the infirmities of our soul unto our superior, who is our spiritual physician. It contributes much to the cure of a patient to know perfectly his constitution and various complaints. For then it is easy to find the true cause of the disease, and to apply apposite remedies thereunto. It is for this reason that princes have always a physician to accompany them, not indeed to tell them constantly what they are to eat, and what they are to abstain from, as such never-ending prescriptions would be very unpleasant; but it is, that being present whilst they eat, and at the greatest part of their exercises, and seeing what does them hurt or good, the physician may be able to know their constitution, and upon this knowledge to regulate the quality of the remedies necessary to be given them when they shall fall sick. Now, our holy founder wishes us to enjoy the same advantage. He wishes us to have always our spiritual physicians with us, to the end that they may know the interior disposition of our souls, and also our strength and weakness, and thereby be the better able to conduct us. The government established in the society entirely regards the spirit and the interior; it is not a government of fear or punishment, and therefore superiors are seldom wont to proceed by the way of juridical informations or accusations therein. They have nothing else in view than the salvation and advancement of your soul. They wish to cure it of all infirmities, but you must assist them yourself to make this cure, by discovering all things to your superior, who is your spiritual physician, and who holds God's place. But if you do not this, you will remain exposed to very great dangers, and will tempt God, who desires to conduct you by putting a man in his own place, and consequently would have you discover your interior to this man. For as it is impossible, morally speaking, that this man should lead and conduct you well, if he does not know you, and that he cannot know you but by yourself, it is certain that you tempt God as often as you will not submit to this practice.

The second reason St. Ignatius rests on, and which is only an extension of the first, is, that the more perfect knowledge superiors shall have of the interior of their subjects, the more they will be able to preserve them from the inconveniencies into which they may cause them to fall, if, through want of knowing their temptations, inclinations, strength, and weakness, they should place them in certain offices and engage them in certain employments prejudicial to them. Above all, says he, since according to our institution we ought always to be ready to go to any part of the world whither it shall please the pope or our superiors to send us, "it imports not only much, but even very much", in order to succeed well in the choice to be made in missions of this kind, that the superiors should have an entire knowledge of the inclinations and temptations of all those under his charge, and that he should know to what faults or sins they are most subject, that by this means he may conduct each religious in the way most convenient for him, and that he do not command anything above his strength, or lay a burden on any one who is not rationally supposed to be able to carry it. One of the things which contribute to render the interior government of the society sweet, easy, and comfortable, is the knowledge it has of all the subjects that compose it, of their different talents, of their good and bad qualities, of the things for which they are fit and not fit. For by this means they know what is to be done to each person in particular, and how he ought to be employed, and will not command anything beyond his power to perform, or expose him to the danger of falling under too heavy a burden, but conformably to the words of the gospel, they will distribute employments and labours " according to each one's strength"—*Mat.*, xxv. 15.

The third reason why it exceedingly behoves superiors to know their religious thoroughly is, says St. Ignatius, that by this means they consult the interest of the whole society, whose welfare they are to have in view as well as yours. For when you discover to them the bottom of your soul, they can, without exposing your honour, or putting you in any danger or hazard, consult the general good of the whole society; but if you should not do this, it may happen that they would give you an employment wherein you would risk your salvation, and wherein your honour and that of the whole society, which depends upon yours, would be exposed to very great danger.

It is good to remark, by the bye, how conformable to the end of its institution those means are which the society makes use of to procure the advancement of each religious. Were it according to our institute to live shut up in our cells, and not to go out of them but to the choir or refectory, it would not be so necessary that our superiors should have so complete a knowledge of our consciences. But since amongst us subjects are put into so many different employments, that the care of several things of importance is often entrusted to them, and that they are sent to all parts of the world, amongst infidels and heretics, and sometimes alone and for a very long time, it is therefore necessary that superiors should know all of them perfectly well, that they may not expose them to dangerous occasions, nor expose the honour of the society with them. It likewise very much imports all religious, for the discharge and security of their own consciences, to let the superior see the bottom of their souls, otherwise they will render themselves accountable for all the misfortunes that may happen, since it is certain that had they made known their weakness as they ought to have done, and their want of the spiritual strength required, superiors would have taken care not to have exposed them to occasions so full of danger. The poor, says Plutarch, who wish to appear rich, soon render themselves more poor than they were, and in a short time effect their own ruin; for on account of their wish to imitate rich persons, they incur greater expenses than their state can bear. We may say the same thing of those that are poor in virtue, and have not a great stock of humility. If a religious who is in this condition should hide his poverty, and pass for being rich in spiritual goods, he will become still more poor, and perhaps will bring on his utter ruin, because they will treat him as a man filled with the treasures of grace, and upon this account expose him to dangerous occasions, for which he will not have a sufficient stock of virtue. And it was because he would not discover himself entirely to his superior that he has brought all these miseries upon himself. So that if we look only upon our own security and the discharge of our conscience, and that we may have nothing to reproach ourselves with, we must be glad to discover ourselves to our superiors, to be such as in reality we are, and thus we shall avoid those inconveniencies I have just now spoke of, and shall by this means draw upon ourselves the blessing and help of God in all the occasions in which it shall please obedience to engage us.

A religious who has thus discovered all his imperfections and infirmities to his superior, and is afterwards sent on some mission, or given some employment, ought to be in great quiet and repose of mind, and have a great confidence that God will happily extricate him from all the dangers he may meet with therein. It is not I, O Lord, may he say, who put myself into this office or into that employment; I represented my own incapacity and the little spiritual strength I had to acquit myself herein as I ought; it was yourself deigned to place me in it, and it is you who are to supply what is wanting to me to succeed therein. With what a plenitude of confidence may not he also say these words of St Austin—" Give me, O Lord, means to perform what thou commandest, and command me what thou wilt". It justly seems to him that God in these circumstances is obliged to grant him all the graces he shall stand in need of in the employment in which he has engaged him. But he that will not make himself known, and who neglects to discover his temptations and weaknesses, for fear he should not be put into such an employment as he desires, or should be taken out of that which pleases him—what comfort can he have, since it is not God that has called him to this function, and it is no longer obedience that engages him therein? For though his superior has placed him there, yet it was out of ignorance; and ignorance, as philosophers say, renders our actions involuntary, and consequently it was not the will of his superior, but his own, that established him therein. It is he that installed himself and introduced himself into this employment of his own accord; he was neither called nor sent to it, but entered into it by stealth; and therefore we can justly apply to him what our Lord says by the mouth of the prophet Jeremias—" I did not send them to act as prophets; they went of their own accord as if they had been sent. I said nothing to them, and yet they prophesied"—*Jer.*, xxiii. 21. Can we after this be astonished, if such persons as these do not succeed? For though they should in some measure do so, yet they have great reason to live in fear. Moreover, let them not think that they have satisfied their conscience or their duty by begging of their superior not to engage them in such or such an employment, representing to him in a general manner that they have not sufficient virtue and capacity to acquit themselves of it. This is not sufficient, since they ought, as I shall show hereafter, have more particularly explained themselves; for the superior attributes these general expressions to their humility, and even the greatest saints are wont to excuse themselves in this manner.

All the considerations I have here set down influenced St. Ignatius so powerfully, and induced him to think this practice of so great importance to the general good of the society, that in his constitutions he frequently recommends the adoption of it. His mind was so engaged with it, that in one place, after he had said that a religious ought not keep his door, or his coffer, or any- thing else locked, he added, " no not even his own conscience", though it should seem *that* was not a proper place to speak of it. The same spirit caused him to say in another place, that religious ought to have nothing hid from their superiors, neither without nor within—in a word, it is a thing he esteems so necessary, that he insists upon it both " opportunely and importunely", as St. Paul says, and frequently endeavours to revive in us the memory thereof upon all occasions.

In the fifth general congregation, when they came to examine what were the most essential things in our constitutions, it was said that they were those which were contained in the *formulæ* of our institute, which was presented to Julius III., and which were approved and confirmed by him and his successors. It was moreover said, that they included in this number all those things, without which the former could not *at all* subsist, or could not subsist without very great difficulty ; and in the list of the latter was placed the obligation of rendering an account of conscience to superiors. It was judged therefore that it was an essential rule, without which the society could not be preserved; and to say this is to leave nothing more to be said. Some historians have observed in regard of certain religious orders, that so far as this holy practice is observed, so far the purity of religious discipline is maintained in them; and experience likewise teaches us that the non-observance of this rule is ordinarily the gate through which a religious enters into the high way of perdition. He begins by little and little to fall into remissness and tepidity—he neglects to resist some bad inclinations—he either leaves off, or performs very ill his spiritual exercises—he then falls into one fault, and from that into another. Yet instead of discovering the wound, he endeavours to hide it; thus it augments and corrupts; and a wound, which would have been easily cured in the beginning, afterwards becomes incurable. In a word, the spiritual edifice falls to the ground, because not having repaired it for a long time, they permitted it to run to ruin of itself. St. Dorotheus knew very well the cause of this evil. Some, says he, are wont to say that such a thing is the cause of the fall of this religious; another, they say, went out for such a reason; it is his disposition caused another to quit the monastery; it was his parents influenced such a man to go out; and I answer, it was nothing of this, but it was because he concealed from his spiritual father the beginnings of his temptations, and because he would not discover to him the bottom of his heart.

CHAPTER II.

That great comfort and repose of mind is produced by keeping nothing hid from our superior or ghostly father: of several other advantages derived from this practice.

ST. AMBROSE, St. Austin, and St. Bernard say, that one of the greatest comforts a man can have in this life, is to have a faithful friend, in whose bosom we can securely repose whatsoever gives him any trouble, and in general all the secrets of his heart. "A faithful friend", says the wise man, "is a remedy against all the evils of this life"—*Ecclus.*, vi. 16. And St. Austin says, there is nothing equal to a friend, who can comfort us in our afflictions, give us counsel in our doubts, rejoice with us in our prosperity, and relieve us in our necessities. "Whoever has found such a one", says the wise man, "has found a treasure"—

Ecclus., vi. 14. But shall I call it only a treasure? "There is nothing", adds he, "comparable to a faithful friend, the excellency of whose fidelity exceeds all the gold and silver in the world"—*Ecclus.*, vi. 15. Now this advantage, which is above all the riches of the Earth, God has bestowed upon the society, by giving each of us a friend of this nature in the person of our superior, who is at once our spiritual father, our master, our physician, our brother, and our mother, and who has greater tenderness for us than a mother can have for her child, for our superior makes our business his own. Endeavour then to avail yourself of such a friend in faithfully laying open your heart unto him, according to the counsel of the wise man—"If thou seest a prudent man, have recourse to him, and let thy feet wear out the steps of his gates"—*Ecclus.*, vi. 36. Communicate to him all your affairs and all your thoughts, and you will find in him all the comfort, all the counsel, and all the aid you stand in need of. As it is a very great ease to the minds of all persons to have given a good account of their disease to the physician who is in care of them, so it is a great satisfaction to the afflicted to be able freely to discover their pains to him from whom they expect comfort and assistance.

One of the means pointed out by moral philosophy for finding comfort in affliction is to discover our pain to some person or other. St. Thomas proposes this when speaking of sadness; and the reason he gives for it is, that when we wish to keep all our grief within ourselves, it draws our attention more violently to it, and thereby the sense of our grief becomes more lively, whereas when we discover it, it becomes less, because then our attention is divided and our heart is eased by dilating itself. Experience daily teaches us this truth; for do we not daily meet with people who tell us they find ease in relating their afflictions? The holy abbot Nilus, disciple of St. Chrysostom, says, that this remedy was very much in use amongst the ancient fathers, who made use of the following comparison the better to authorise its practice: Have you not taken notice, say they, that when the clouds are full of water, they are black and obscure, and the more water falls from them, and the more they discharge themselves, the clearer also they become? The same also happens in those disquiets of mind and temptations which a religious suffers. The more he keeps them to himself, the more pensive, troubled, and melancholy he is. But when he frees himself from them by discovering them to his superior, he feels, according to the measure that he discovers them, the black vapours of sadness and disquiet to be dissipated; and in fine, in freeing himself from that which put him into so melancholy a humour, he resumes his former joy and tranquillity.

St. Dorotheus relates of himself, that when he had given an account of the state of his soul to his ghostly father, he felt within himself such peace of mind that sometimes he was afraid it was a bad sign; "because", as the Scripture says, "we must enter into the kingdom of Heaven by many tribulations"—*Acts*, xiv. 21,—and finding nothing but joy and sweetness, he feared that he had reason to doubt whether he were in the right way to Heaven. But he was relieved from his anxiety by the abbot John, whom he consulted in this affair, and who told him that the peace and interior satisfaction he enjoyed was promised to those that hide nothing from their ghostly father.

This point is of so great importance that St. Ignatius, not content with earnestly recommending it to us, as I have already said, expressed his wish that superiors should accustom themselves to speak often to their religious; because, besides many other good effects produced by such conversation, it would give their subjects confidence to accost them more freely and to open their hearts unto them. Moreover, for the greater satisfaction of all his religious, he ordered that in every college of his society there should be a prefect of spiritual things, to whom each one for his comfort and direction of conscience might address himself in his necessities. We see, says Cassian, that human sciences, having in view no other object than temporal advantages, and in which nothing but sensible and palpable things are treated of, can never be well understood if we put not ourselves under some master to learn them. How then can any one imagine that there is no necessity of a master in the science of salvation and of spiritual advancement, since it is so hidden and spiritual a science, that the means of obtaining it are not exposed to corporal eyes, and that even those of our soul cannot discover them without great purity of heart? In other sciences we risk only some temporal advantage if we succeed not therein, and it is a thing that otherwise may be easily repaired, but here salvation or damnation depends upon the good or bad success. Here we are not to fight against visible but invisible enemies— not against one or two, but against legions of devils, who cease neither day nor night to make war upon us. And hence, continues Cassian, we cannot do better than to have recourse to our ghostly fathers, by discovering to them whatsoever passes in our souls, that they may assist and conduct us by their counsels.

But, setting all this apart, the very subjects for which we usually address ourselves to the prefect of spiritual things show of how great profit it is that in each house there should be one to whom we may have recourse. For when we address ourselves to him it is to give him an account, for example, how we make our prayer, the method we observe in it, the fruit we reap from it, and with what care we observe the additions and other rules prescribed about prayer. It is to consult him about the subject we should choose for our particular examen, and about the number of faults we have set down therein—the difference we find between the number we have marked in the morning and that of the afternoon; it is to inform him of our spiritual reading and of the profit we make thereby; and, in fine, it is to discover to him the temptations we have, and how we behave therein, the penances, the public or private mortifications we practise, and how we behave with respect to obedience, resignation, humility, observance of rules, and all other things of the like nature. And our knowing that we must give this account, is a means without doubt to help us to keep ourselves in a better disposition to give a good one. It is certain also that the esteem which we perceive is had of anything, ordinarily moves us to make a greater account of it; and consequently when I perceive that I must be asked and examined on matters, they become more considerable to me, which is the reason that if I have once committed a fault herein, I take care not to commit the like for the future. Moreover, according to the opinion of saints and divines, as confession is a great bridle to hinder men from falling into sin, so it is a great bridle to a religious person to hinder him from falling into many faults and imperfections, to reflect upon the obligation of his giving an account of them to his ghostly father. This advantage of confession has been moreover so apparent even to heretics themselves, that perceiving that in those places in Germany which had left it off, they were all filled with disorder, and that no one was in security, they begged of Charles the Fifth that he would issue an edict to oblige all to go to confession. The emperor could not but smile at this petition, yet remarked at the same time the necessity people had of confession, and the ignorance of those who had recourse to him upon this subject, as if it had been in his power to make a law about this matter.

But to continue the comparison I have before mentioned, it is certain that frequent confession is the best means we can furnish a Christian with in order to save his soul. For besides the grace which is annexed to this sacrament, and the remission of sins obtained thereby, it is certain that it comprehends all the remedies and all the counsels of a Christian life. Hence, when we would move a worldly person to take care of his spiritual advancement, we counsel him to say his beads often, to hear mass every day, to hear the word of God, to examine his conscience, to practise penance, and to let no day pass without doing some one or other of these things; but to affix the seal to all, we propose to him to go often to confession, and to an able confessor; and we believe that hereby we have given him all spiritual remedies together, and that we have said all that can be said, and all that is necessary for him to be told; for if he does what we have counselled him, his confessor will not fail every eighth or fifteenth day, or at least every month, to furnish him with several spiritual remedies which we shall either not be able to give him, or at least not be able to persuade him to practise on a sudden, and he will also take care to exact an account of the use he makes of his counsels; it is this good confessors ought to perform; they ought always take care that their penitents continually increase in virtue. And it is for this reason that masters of a spiritual life counsel to have always one constant and fixed confessor; because, to confess this day to one, and to-morrow to another, is not the way to make progress in perfection. Now, as all the remedies of a Christian life are comprised in confession, so all the means that can be given to a religious for his spiritual advancement, are comprised in the obligation of rendering an account of his conscience, because the superior or the prefect of spirit, who is appointed to hear you, sees thereby the profit you make in prayer, examens, and spiritual reading. He sees how you resist temptations, how you overcome your passions and bad habits; he sees how you are disposed to the observing of silence, humility, and resignation, and whether you advance or recede in virtue, and regulates his remedies and instructions according to the necessity you are in and to the disposition of your soul, reprehending you for your defects in your duties, and encouraging you in the performance of them. When all this is done with a due spirit of sweetness and charity, and as it is effectually practised amongst us, and when you perceive that they seek nothing herein but your good and spiritual advancement, it is impossible but this means should be of wonderful profit and advantage.

CHAPTER III.

To lay open our hearts to our superior or ghostly father, is a most excellent remedy against temptations.

I HAVE already said that it was the general opinion of all the saints, and a sort of first principle amongst the ancient fathers, that all temptations ought to be discovered to superiors, and St. Ignatius recommends it to us in his constitutions. But that this truth may be more deeply imprinted in our heart, let us reflect a moment on the reason why all so strongly insist upon this point. The reason, says Cassian, is, that the Devil cannot deceive you by his craft as he does an ignorant man, if you know how to have recourse to the experience and wisdom of your spiritual father, and if you guide yourself by his knowledge. For then he will not have to contend with a new and inexperienced, but with an old soldier, who has been brought up all his life in this spiritual warfare; because, whatever experience or abilities your spiritual father has, he communicates to you as soon as you entirely subject yourself to his direction. And it is after this manner, says he, that we gain the true spirit of discretion and prudence, on which St. Anthony set so high value. For one day, says Cassian, when this great saint was in conference with other holy fathers of the desert, they disputed which virtue was most conducive to perfection. One said it was chastity, because it kept sensuality subject to reason; another said it was justice; and, in a word, every one gave his opinion of what he thought best. When St. Anthony had heard them all, he decided the question, telling them that the most necessary virtues to acquire perfection, and which contributed most to it, were discretion and prudence; because, if these two do not regulate all the actions of virtue we perform, they are not properly acts of virtue, nor can they be pleasing to God. Now, would you know, adds Cassian, a short and easy means to acquire this virtue? Communicate all your thoughts to your superior, and guide yourself in all things by his advice, and by this means all the prudence of your superior will pass into yourself. St. Bernard affirms this in express terms:, "Because the spirit of discretion", says he, "is a thing rarely found in the world, therefore make obedience supply the defect of this virtue in you; so that you do nothing, either small or great, but what is commanded you, nor after any other manner than you are commanded to perform it, and you will supply the defect of that experience you stand so much in need of"—*Serm.* iv. *de Circumcis.*

It is upon this account that the saints earnestly recommend unto us presently to discover our temptations, and it is for the same reason that the Devil, who desires nothing more than to destroy us, hinders us as much as he can from declaring them. St. Dorotheus says, that nothing pleases the Devil more than to meet with one that will not discover his temptations; for then, since he fights with him hand to hand, he is sure of the victory, according to the words of Scripture, "Wo to him who is alone; because, if he comes to fall, there is no one to help him up"— *Eccl.*, iv. 10. On the contrary, adds the saint, there is nothing the Devil fears so much, and which gives him so much pain, as to see himself discovered. For then he loses all courage and hopes of gaining the victory, and therefore betakes himself to flight. St. Ignatius, the better to elucidate this matter, makes use of the following comparison: he says, that when the Devil tempts us, he deals with us as a man does who solicits to evil a young woman who has prudent parents, or a married woman who has an honest man to her husband. The first thing this young man does is to hinder the young woman from saying anything to her father or mother, or the wife to her husband, and fears nothing more than to be discovered, because then all hopes of effecting his wicked designs are lost; whereas, so long as they keep it secret, he thinks he has still ground to hope. It is thus, continues our holy founder, that when the Devil would deceive any one, the first thing he does is to hinder him from discovering his temptations to any body; because, as long as they are concealed, he is as it were sure to overcome and to obtain what he desires. But, on the contrary, what he apprehends most from those he tempts is their going presently and discovering the temptations to their superior or confessor. For since it is rather by craft than force that he defeats us, he looks upon himself as overcome as soon as he sees his craft discovered. "Whosoever does ill", says the evangelist, "hates the light"—*John*, iii. 20. And, moreover, it is proper to those who make it their business to deceive others to dread the light more than anything else, and to avoid it as much as they can.

St. Dorotheus relates (*in Vitis Patr. de S. Mach.* 26) on this head what happened to St. Macarius, and which helps much to our purpose. He says, that this saint, who had been a disciple of the great St. Anthony, and to whom God had given a great power over the spirits of darkness, asked a Devil one day what success he had with the hermits. The Devil answered that he succeeded very ill, because he could suggest nothing to them but they presently discovered to their superior. "But there is, notwithstanding, one of your brethren", adds he, " who is very much my friend, and whom I turn like a top which way I please"; and being hereupon constrained to it by the power of God, he declared the hermit's name. St. Macarius went presently to find him out; and, understanding by the conversation he had with him, that he discovered not his temptations to his ghostly father, and that he conducted himself only by his own lights, he exhorted him to do so no more for the future, nor to confide hereafter to his own judgment. The hermit received this advice with very great submission, and profited so well by it, that a little while after, the saint asking the Devil how it went with his friend the hermit, he is no more my friend, says he, in a rage and despair, he is become my mortal enemy. And here it is to be observed, says St. Dorotheus, that all the hermits who lived under St. Macarius were tempted; but because they took care to give an account of all their temptations to their spiritual father, and governed themselves by his advice, the Devil tempted them in vain; for he could effect nothing against any of them, but only against him who, relying upon his own judgment, would not discover his interior to his ghostly father, and yet, as soon as he did so, the Devil had no more power over him. Cassian says, that he who is not reserved with his ghostly father is entirely secure from all the snares and surprises of the Devil; and he applies to this subject these words of the wise man: "If thou discoverest his secrets, thou wilt no longer follow him"—*Eccl.*, xxvii. 19; and these others also, "if the serpent bites thee without noise"—*Eccl.*, x. 11. God preserve you, says he, from being bitten by a silent serpent; for, whilst he hisses and makes a noise so that the enchanter can hear him, there is some remedy to be hoped for; but God grant the old serpent, the Devil, does not silently bite you, for so long as your ghostly father hears him, he will be able to enchant him with the words of holy Scripture, and thereby preserve you from every danger.

But there is still another advantage, which is, that this recourse to our ghostly father in time of temptations is so pleasing to God, that oftentimes by this submission alone and by this sign only of humility, without even receiving any counsel or answer from him to whom we address ourselves, we shall free ourselves from the temptation that molests us. This is the opinion of Cassian, who says, "the suggestions of the Devil are no longer hurtful to us than whilst we hide them; for as soon as we come to discover them they lose all their force, and before the prudence of our superior has decided anything, the infernal serpent is constrained, by virtue of this humility and sincerity, to quit the obscurity in which he had hid himself, and to retire with shame. Just as when there is a serpent or adder under a stone, you make him fly as soon as you lift the stone up; so the Devil, who is the father of darkness and cannot endure light, flies away as soon as you expose him to the sight of others"— *Collot.* ii. *Ab. Moys.*, c. 10. Add to this, that as he is the father of pride, he cannot bear to have his weakness and want of power known; and, therefore, as soon as he is discovered, he shamefully flies away.

Moreover, we may here make a reflection that is very applicable to our subject. If the diseases of the body could be cured by barely discovering them to the physician, what care should we not take to give him an account even of the least infirmity we suffer! But this, which cannot happen in corporal diseases, happens and is daily experienced in those of the soul; because, as I have already said, as soon as we discover them to our superior, and even before he has said anything about what we propose to him, we are delivered from the temptation. Nay, give me leave to say yet more, we often find this effect even by the resolution only of discovering it to our ghostly father. For, going to give him an account of it even before you can get to his chamber door, you will find that God has dispersed the cloud, delivered you from the temptation, and restored peace and tranquillity to your soul.

We have an example of this in the lives of the fathers of the desert. An hermit had fasted above a year together to obtain light and direction from God about a doubt he had, and offered continually his prayers to God for this end; but at last perceiving that he received no light at all herein, he resolved to go and consult another hermit that lived in the same desert. He was scarce gone out of his cell to execute his design, but an angel appeared to him and clearly solved his difficulty, and added that he had merited this grace rather by his humility and submission, than by his fasts and prayers. The gospel also furnishes us with an example of the same nature, in the person of the ten lepers who came to Jesus Christ, crying out, "Master, have mercy upon us! Go", says our Saviour, "and show yourself to the priest, and it happened", says the evangelist, "that whilst they were upon their way they were all cured"— *Luke*, xvii. 13. God is so satisfied with our submission to those who hold his place, that he even declares it by miracles. It may likewise happen, that even by threatening the Devil that you will discover those temptations he torments you with, you may make him afraid, and oblige him to leave you in peace; so that it is always very good in these occasions to act like little children, who, when you do them any hurt, threaten to tell their father.

CHAPTER IV.

That we ought not neglect to discover our temptations to our ghostly father under pretence that we already know the remedies he will counsel us to make use of.

BUT some one may say, I have so often heard of remedies against temptations, and I have read so many spiritual books on the subject, that I already know every answer which can be given me by the superior or ghostly father; what need then have I to address myself to him? Let us take care not to be carried away with this temptation; and the more knowledge we conceive ourselves to have, the more should we be on our guard in this matter. St. Dorotheus was very much tormented with this temptation, but he knew how to deliver himself from it. He says that when he went to discover his temptation to his superior, this thought presently came to his mind, why should you lose so much time to no purpose? You may be assured he will give you such and such an answer, and tell you nothing but what you know already; why then go to importune him? Then I was moved to anger against the temptation, continues he, and also against myself, and said—"Wo be to thee, Satan! Wo be to thy wit and judgment: wo be to thy prudence and knowledge" —*Doroth.*, *Serm.* viii. And without hearkening any longer to the temptation, I went presently to give an account to my superior of all that passed within me. When I came to him he answered the very same things that I before thought of, and I felt something within me which said to me with some disquiet and trouble: Aye, did I not tell you what answer he would give, and that it was not at all necessary to go to him? But I presently answered: Now I am assured that what I before thought of was good, and that it came from God, which I had to doubt of when I was alone, and when it came only from myself. It was thus he freed himself from the temptation, never failing to address himself to his superior; and we ought to do the very same, without trusting to our own judgment, because it is certain that no one is a good judge in his own cause. But if this be true when we are not attacked by any temptation, what will it be when temptation hinders us from forming a right judgment of things, and even shuts our eyes according to the words of the prophet, "My iniquities have seized upon me, and I am able to see nothing"—*Ps.*, xxxix. 13. One knows not then what is most convenient for him, or, if he knows, he is not in a condition to profit thereby, and to put it in practice, because the temptation disquiets and even blinds him, whereas one word that the superior shall say to him will work a greater effect upon him than all he can say to himself.

St. Austin relates on this head a passage which is somewhat singular and pleasant. He says that a certain man finding himself oppressed by a distemper, sent for a physician who gave him a remedy that presently cured him. The same distemper attacking him some days after, he would needs use the same remedy which had done him so much good before, and having remembered the *recipe*, he did not send for the doctor. The remedy, however, gave him no ease, whereat being very much surprised, he sent for the physician, told him what had happened, and asked him the reason why the remedy which he gave him did him so much good the first time, and the second did him none at all. It was, answered the physician, smiling, because I did not give it to you myself. Now let us apply this to our subject. The spiritual remedy that you have heard of, and that you know very well, will do you no good, because it is not your spiritual physician that gives it you. The remedy given by the hand of the physician who observes times and circumstances, has a better effect than when it is taken in another manner or by one's own prescription. It is the same with the remedies relating to the soul. The water of the river Damas was very good, and perhaps better than that of Jordan; yet it was not the water of Damas, but that of Jordan that cured Naaman of his leprosy, when Eliseus commanded him to wash himself therein. The assistance of God is joined to what your superior directs and to the remedies he gives, because the superior holds the place of God; and thus a simple and easy remedy which the superior shall give, will do you more good than all others you shall make use of.

CHAPTER V.

That we must never omit discovering anything to our ghostly father under pretence that it is inconsiderable.

THE Devil makes use of another means to hinder us from having recourse to our superior or confessor, which is to represent unto us that the thing in question is of no moment, that it is not necessary to go to him about trifles, and that one ought to be ashamed to importune him to no purpose for things of no importance. To this I answer, first, that he who aspires to perfection ought not to wait till there is a question of an important or necessary matter; but he ought always propose to himself that which is better and more perfect; and therefore how trivial soever the thing may seem to be, it is always good not to neglect it, but to give an account of it to his superior, because it is properly herein he shows that he aspires to perfection. In effect, one thing which edifies extremely, is to have recourse to our superior in the smallest matters, and the more aged or learned a person is, the more he will edify his brethren by this submission, because this is to make ourselves little and to become children again for the love of Jesus Christ.

I answer, in the second place, that those things are not always inconsiderable which appear so to you. But it is the shame and repugnance you have to speak of them, that furnishes you with reasons to make you believe them such, and to persuade you that they are not worth speaking of. It is thus that when we are ashamed to confess anything, the Devil presently makes use of this criminal bashfulness, to persuade us that what we are ashamed to speak of is not in reality a mortal sin, and that therefore we are not obliged to accuse ourselves of it. How many has he abused in this manner, by hindering them from confessing those things they were obliged to confess, and hereby causing them to make sacrilegious confessions and communions! The very repugnance we feel to discover anything to our superior ought to be sufficient to make us suspect the reasons we believe we have for not discovering it, and ought fully convince us that we ought to speak of it. Cassian says, "that there needs no other reason to show us that a thing is bad in itself, than the desire we have not to speak of it, which is a pure temptation of the Devil"—*Cass. de Inst. Renunt.*, *lib.* 4. And he adds that this was the opinion of the ancient fathers, who held it for an infallible mark that the thought came from the Devil when one had a shame to discover it unto his superior. " All iniquity", says the prophet, " stops its mouth"—*Ps.*, cvi. 42, — and " whomsoever does ill", says our Saviour, " hates the light"— *John*, iii. 20; wherefore as often as we seek to hide anything from the knowledge of our superior, there is reason to suspect that it is not good.

In the third place, how trivial soever the thing may be, yet it becomes considerable as soon as we hide it, and therefore it is good to declare it in the beginning, that we may soon apply a remedy thereunto; for it is easier to do so then than it will be afterwards. St. John Climacus says, that as the eggs which the hen sits on, or which are hid under the dunghill, by little and little come to have life and afterwards are hatched, so the bad thoughts that we hide in our hearts, without being willing to discover them to him who may hinder their progress, ordinarily produce very bad effects.

Another means which the Devil makes use of in order to hinder some from addressing themselves to their superior, is to make them believe that they will give him too much trouble; but it is a great error to entertain this thought. For it is the duty of your superior to hearken to you at all times, and it is in this that the principal care of his charge consists. You do him wrong, then, to think he imagines himself importuned by that which is one of his chief obligations. On the contrary, he is very well pleased to be employed in so essential a thing, upon which, as I have already said, depends the spiritual advancement of all religious.

Cassian relates a thing to our purpose that happened to Serapion the abbot, in his youth, and which he was wont to relate to his religious to excite them to give an account of all things to their superior. When I was yet only a novice, says the abbot, I was tempted with gluttony, so that I thought I could never be able to satisfy myself, insomuch that every day, after I had dined with the abbot Theonas, my superior, I secretly took a loaf as I rose from table, and I eat it at night without his knowledge. However, though gluttony had such power over me, yet I had no sooner eaten my loaf but remorse of conscience seized me, and the grief I then felt for my fault surpassed very much the pleasure that I had in satisfying my appetite. The temptation, nevertheless, had such an ascendancy, that the next day I returned to steal another loaf and eat it in private as before, without daring to discover my temptation to my superior, till at length it pleased God to deliver me from it in the manner that I shall now tell you. Some hermits came to see the abbot Theonas, and entertaining themselves as they were wont to do after dinner in pious and spiritual discourses on God, it happened that this holy man in answering their questions spoke of gluttony, and of the power temptations get over us when they are kept secret. My cónscience at the time gave me a thousand reproaches, and I thought that all he said was addressed to myself, and imagined that, without doubt, God had revealed my temptation and my fault unto him; so that being at once touched and astonished at his words, I began bitterly to lament within myself. Afterwards sorrow for my fault increasing in my heart, I could no longer restrain myself, but giving way to tears and lamentations, I cast myself at the holy abbot's feet, and showing him the loaf I had stolen that very day, I publicly declared to him the fault I daily fell into, begging of him to pardon me and to impose some penance on me for it. The holy old man began then to comfort me, and said to me: Child, take courage: this heroic action you have now performed by publicly declaring your fault before the whole world, has for ever delivered you from this troublesome temptation. And you have to-day gained a greater victory over the Devil than that he had before gained over you; nor do I doubt but that God permitted that this temptation should have so much power over you because you kept it secret. Be therefore assured that since you have declared it, the infernal serpent will not for the future be able to do you hurt, but will fly far from you, because he cannot endure the light. The holy old man had scarce ended his words, when on a sudden a kind of inflamed vapour came out of my breast, which filled the cell with an insupportable stench; and then the holy man turning towards me: You see, dear child, says he, how God deigns by effects to confirm my words, because you see yourself that the merit of discovering your fault has cast out the Devil, who cannot bear to be exposed to the light, or to have his craft discovered; wherefore, fear not that he will ever come back to torment you for the future. What this holy old man foretold me I found true; for I was never after afterwards disquieted with this temptation, nor ever anything like it entered more into my thoughts"—*Cass. Coll.* ii. *Ab. Moys.*, c. 11.

CHAPTER VI.

A solution of the difficulties which might hinder us from giving an exact account of our interior.

I HAVE already said of how great importance and necessity it is to keep nothing hid from our superior; but the corruption of our own nature and the malice of the Devil are so great, that the things most necessary for our spiritual advancement, are ordinarily those to which we feel greatest repugnance, or in which he endeavours to cause us to meet with the greatest obstacles. It is very proper, then, that we endeavour to apply a remedy to this inconvenience, and in a matter of so great importance, it will be doing not a little if we find out the means of removing the difficulties and smoothing the way. Moreover, though this is addressed particularly to religious, yet every one may make an application of it to himself, because it is a doctrine which regards every man in general; and Gerson, as we shall afterwards see, speaking of confession, treats of manifestation of conscience for all sorts of persons.

As we are naturally enemies of labour and pain, and because the subject we treat of ordinarily appears to us very painful and troublesome, I will begin by showing, that without comparison there is far greater pain in being reserved towards our superior, than in keeping nothing hid from him. And let this be taken due notice of; for it is one of the best reasons to urge against those who love themselves so well, that they dare not embrace virtue and perfection on account of the difficulties met therein. I grant it is painful and mortifying to declare all our temptations, inclinations, and defects, to our superior; but at the same time I also affirm and maintain, that to hide them is far more painful. Daily experience proves this; and all those who never concealed anything from their superior can bear testimony of it. What trouble, what remorse, what disquiet do we not feel, when we will not make our interior known! "The iniquity of Ephraim is, as it were, tied up in a sack; his sin is hid, the pains of child-birth will come on him"—*Osee*, xiii. 12, 13. In the doubt and uncertainty we are, whether or not we should discover ourselves, we are always as it were in the pains of child-birth. Now we wish to say all, now we repent to have wished so; afterwards we go to our superior's door to lay open our hearts unto him; then on a sudden we return without daring to do it. "The children are just ready to be born, but their mothers have not strength to bring them forth"—*Isa.*, xxxvii. 3. We were upon the point of discovering and bringing to light our thought and temptation, which is the fruit and child of the father of darkness, and we had not strength to deliver ourselves of it, and in this manner we remain always in the pains of child-birth. Nay, even these pains augment, the longer we defer to discover our hidden imperfections, for the more we hide them the greater will be our pain and shame afterwards in declaring them. We are then angry with ourselves for not having done it sooner, and that which then gives us the greatest pain is to think thus with ourselves: How is it possible to go now to my superior after I have let so much time pass? Were it a thing to begin again, I would not fail to give him an account thereof, but with what face can I now appear before him? What will he say to me for having concealed myself so long from him? He will say that I have no confidence in him, because I did not presently manifest myself to him. To conclude, so long as we shall defer laying open our hearts to our ghostly father, we shall never find any quiet of mind, but shall always be exposed to the reproaches and remorses of conscience for having failed in a thing of so great importance; whereas, from the moment we had discovered them, we should have had none of these disquiets, but the trouble and interior agitation would have presently ceased, and we should have enjoyed a perfect peace and tranquillity.

It is the same in order to this, that it is in order to confession. For then, when out of shame we dare not accuse ourselves of some sin, we feel no peace within ourselves, but are in continual disquiet and anguish of heart. But as soon as we have confessed our sin, we presently find ourselves content and at ease—we seem as if we had cast off a heavy burden, under which we were ready to fall. "The wounds which are not open", says St. Gregory, " cause greater pain than others, by reason of the inflammation caused by the matter that is within, but as soon as they are opened, the matter and corruption go out, and the pain diminishes"—*L.* iii. *Past. Adm.*, 15. It is almost the self-same thing when we come from accusing ourselves of our sins, or from declaring our temptations and weakness. For as the saint adds, "confession of sins, what is it else, but the opening of a wound or imposthume?" We may also compare this state to a man whose stomach is overcharged with meat and bad humours, and who has a continual inclination to vomit; he suffers cruelly till he casts up what he had in his stomach, but as soon as he has done so he suffers no more, but feels himself entirely at ease. What I have said clearly shows that to hide what passes within us is a greater pain than we can have in declaring it, for one is presently freed from it by a little shame and mortification that passes in a moment, and afterwards we remain in profound peace and tranquillity. We may therefore very well say to those who, in order to spare themselves a little pain and trouble, hide their interior from their spiritual father, that it is for this reason they ought not to do so, for so long as they shall persist in hiding it, they will be consumed with irksomeness and be even eaten up with disquiet, according to the words of the Royal Prophet, "rottenness has pierced even to the marrow of my bones because I held my peace"—*Ps.*, xxxi. 3;—but as soon as they have laid open their heart, they will feel themselves at ease and find themselves comforted.

CHAPTER VII.

An answer to the principal difficulty which usually hinders us from freely discovering ourselves to our superior.

ONE of the chief difficulties that hinders religious persons from discovering themselves to their superior, if I may not say better, the greatest of all, is that they imagine they shall be dishonoured by it, and lose the good repute and esteem they had before gained; for after that the superior will always have his eye upon them, trust them no more, and have no farther kindness for them. Behold here the pretext the Devil makes use of to abuse them, and to hinder them from discovering their interior, or at least from making a full discovery thereof. But if, on the contrary, I can evidently prove that this is a false imagination, and that his esteem and amity for them will be augmented when they lay open entirely their hearts, and that it will be lost when they do the contrary, I hope the obstacle will be quite removed and the difficulty entirely taken away. Now, it is this which, by the assistance of God's grace, I undertake at present to prove, and shall make it appear that things are not so as the Devil represents them in order to seduce us: and in this he does but what he does in all other temptations, and what we may expect from the father of lies. I say then, that there is nothing which disgraces a religious so much with his superior, as his taking care to hide himself from him, that this is the means to make him be looked upon as a dissembler, and that no other fault does him more prejudice than this in his superior's esteem. For after all, one fault is but one fault; but they easily suspect that he whom they think a dissembler and insincere, is guilty of many. He is a dark man, say they, and how do I know, since he has not discovered to me such a thing that I have found out, whether he has not still other things which he does not discover to me? This thing alone lessens his reputation more with his superior than any other fault he can be guilty of. On the contrary, when we have no reserve towards our superior, and we discover to him all our temptations, inclinations, and defects, so far from lessening ourselves with him, we hereby gain greater esteem from him, because we pass for humble, mortified, and sincere persons, and to be truly in the interior what we appear to be outwardly.

But let us go farther, and ascend even to the fountain-head, since we treat here of a most essential and important point. I say, first, that a religious cannot make use of a better means to cause himself to be beloved by his superior, than to lay open his heart entirely unto him, without ever having anything hid from him; and the reason of this is, that nothing moves more to love than to be loved. Hence it is that St. John, to excite us to love God, represents to us, "that God loved us first"—I. *John*, iv. 10. But one of the things in which a religious can most show his love to his superior, is by laying open to him the bottom of his heart, and having no reserve at all towards him. For his friendship is very great who keeps nothing secret or hid from his friend; wherefore our Saviour, explaining to his disciples the parable of the seed, "To you", says he, "is given a special privilege, thoroughly to know the mysteries of the kingdom of God, but to others they are hid under parables"—*Luke*, viii. 10. And in the sermon at the last supper: "As for you", says he to his apostles, "I have called you friends, because I have discovered to you all that I learned from my Father"—*John*, xv. 15. When therefore the superior perceives that a religious entirely opens his heart unto him, he knows hereby that the religious loves him in effect, and looks upon him as his father, and as one who is in the place of God, because he confides all things to him, and wholly gives himself up into his hands, and this obliges him to love him so much the more, and to take greater care of him. But if, on the contrary, he perceives that you are reserved towards him, and instead of openly declaring all things to him, you speak to him in an obscure manner, so that, hearing you, he may not understand you, this is to give him a bad impression in your regard, and to oblige him to love you so much the less; because your diffidence and reservedness are sufficient marks that you have not the sentiments of esteem and affection which you ought to have for your father, and that you do not treat him as such, which is apt to give him less kindness, at least, if not an aversion for you. For how would you have him love you as his son, if you do not love him as your father? Love him, therefore, as you ought to love a father, by confiding in him, and entirely opening your heart unto him, and he will love you also as a son ought to be loved. I shall also make appear in the following treatise, that superiors ought to behave towards their inferiors in the like manner. For when a superior speaks to one of his religious with a free and open heart, and says to him, take care of yourself; you have such and such a fault—such a complaint is made of you—you neglect such a duty; endeavour to correct yourself. The religious loves him then so much the more because he perceives that this springs from the true affection he has for him. But when the superior treats him in a different manner, and instead of speaking to him with charity and confidence about what was faulty in him, he shows a sort of duplicity, and says one thing whilst he thinks another—this is not a cordial way of proceeding, it is full of dissimulation. When, therefore, there shall be great sincerity and openness of heart on both sides, then there will be true friendship between superiors and subjects, and a true union of hearts, and all things will go well; but when there will be no openness of heart, there will be no true friendship, but only such exterior expressions thereof as civility requires.

Hence it also follows, that there is no reason at all to fear the loss of the esteem of our superior, which ordinarily gives us the greatest pain herein, since friendship is always accompanied with esteem. For the will does not move us to love till the understanding proposes how much the object deserves to be loved. But besides this reason in general, let us descend to particulars; it is very certain that, how great soever the temptations of a religious are, his superior, for this reason, cannot have the less esteem of him; because those that serve God and give themselves entirely to spiritual things are the most subject to temptations. Others very often even know not what it is to be tempted, or do not perceive it when they are so, and of themselves they are but too much carried to sin, so that the Devil has no need to take the pains to tempt them. No; but it is those that apply themselves to God's service and aspire to perfection he turns his arms against; and this made the wise man say, "My son, applying thyself to the service of God, prepare thy soul for temptation"—*Eccl.*, xii. 1.

Moreover, there are some persons who form such a strange and shameful idea of their temptation, that, unable to believe that any one ever had the like, they do not declare it to their superior for fear of astonishing him. And this happens chiefly to novices or young religious, who, having very little experience in matters of temptation, look upon that which is ordinary and very common as a thing very strange and new. But be assured you can tell nothing to your confessor that will seem extraordinary to him; many others besides you have told him the same thing, and perhaps he himself will have experienced the like temptation. The wise man says, "there is nothing new under Heaven" —*Eccl.*, i. 10. Do not believe, then, that it is anything new because it never happened to you before.

Another reason which ought to hinder us from believing that by declaring our faults and imperfections to our superior we shall be the less esteemed by him, is, that all men are subject to fall. We are formed of the same frail matter, and have been all taken out of the same mass; and therefore the superior, who knows by his own the frailty of his subjects, is not easily astonished when they discover their thoughts and imperfections to him. Gerson, desirous to withdraw his young religious from a fault they often fell into, which was through a criminal shame to hide their faults from their ghostly father, said thus to them: Do you believe that by knowing your sins and weaknesses I esteem you the less? No such thing. I even love you so much the more because of the confidence you have placed in me in discovering to me things you would not discover to your own father. God is my witness, adds he, with how much tenderness my heart is touched, when any one discovers to me his weaknesses, and the greater and more shameful I find them to be, the greater is the tenderness and compassion I feel for him. The humility that a religious testifies, when of himself he freely owns his fault, and the desire he hereby shows of the health of his soul and of his spiritual advancement, touch superiors in so particular a manner that they even carry them in their bowels. When a mere stranger addresses himself to us, and relates to us his pains and afflictions, we presently conceive an affection for him, we feel ourselves moved to assist him, and we endeavour to comfort him in the best manner we are able. What sentiments then ought we not to have for the children of Jesus Christ! It is, without doubt, a thing of very great importance that all religious should be thoroughly persuaded that by discovering their faults to their spiritual father, they do not in the least cool his affection for them, but that, on the contrary, they very much increase it. And hence, when they shall be fully convinced of this truth, they will not easily give ear to what the Devil shall suggest to the contrary, thereby to withdraw them from so essential an obligation.

To confirm the more what I have already said, we must take notice, that it is a great shame before God and man to do ill, and to persist therein with a determined will; but to detest sin, to repent of it, to have confusion and sorrow for it, and to accuse ourselves of it, is what is very pleasing in his sight, and therefore ought to be thought so by those who are in his place. Divines treat this question—whether at the day of judgment the sins of the saints and blessed souls shall be made public as well as those of the damned. And they differ in their opinions therein; but what may be held for certain in this point, and what makes for our subject, is this, that should it happen that they will be exposed to the knowledge of the whole world, it shall not be to the shame and confusion of the saints who have committed them, but for their honour and glory, because the penance they shall have done for them will at the same time also appear before the eyes of the whole world. It is this which God at present does in regard of very many saints. For when they speak in the pulpit of the irregular life of St. Mary Magdalen, and when even upon her festival we read in the Church the gospel in which she is called a sinner; and when mention is made of the adultery of David, of the infidelity of St. Peter, and of the persecution of St. Paul against the Church of God, all that is said of the sins of those great saints turns to their praise; because the rigorous penances they did for them has increased the glory of our Lord, "who draws honey out of a rock, and oil out of the hardest stone"—*Deut.*, xxxii. 13. Masters of a spiritual life usually elucidate this point by a very just comparison. A man, say they, got made for himself a fine suit of clothes which fitted him very well. They are torn, however, by some accident or other, and behold them to all appearance spoiled; but he causes the rent to be drawn up, and covers it with gold lace or very fine embroidery, and by this means his suit becomes far more rich and magnificent than it was at first. If the sins of the blessed must appear at the day of judgment, it will be in this manner; they will be seen so well expiated that they will rather be to them a subject of glory than of confusion. The rent their sins had made in the robe of the Lamb shall be well drawn up and so richly covered over that it will serve for a greater ornament unto them. The same thing may be said of a religious who ingenuously discovers his wounds to his superior to be healed by him, and expresses a true sorrow for his faults. The discovery he makes of his infirmities and weaknesses does not diminish the esteem and affection which the superior had before for him, but on the contrary increases it. "For there is a confusion", says the wise man, "that carries sin along with it, and there is a confusion which causes glory and esteem"—*Eccl.*, iv. 25. The confusion and shame which urge us not to discover our faults, cast us into sin and disorder; but the confusion which we have for our faults when we declare them, attracts the esteem of men and the blessing of God to us.

It is related in the life of St. Ignatius, that having to no purpose tried all ways imaginable to gain unto God a religious of a very irregular life, he at last went and made his confession to him. After he had confessed the faults he had committed since his last confession, he told him that with his leave he had a great mind to confess the chief sins of his life past, and then he began to confess and to accuse himself of the weakness and irregularities of his youth, with so deep sorrow and such abundance of tears, that on a sudden the heart of his confessor was touched and entirely changed; for hereupon he felt so great a horror for his past disorders, and such sentiments of love and respect for St. Ignatius, whom he before hated, that he chose him for his director, made the spiritual exercises under him, and by an entire change of his life, edified all those that had before known him. This clearly shows how much they are deceived who are afraid of being lessened in the esteem of their superior by an humble confession of their faults. For what renders us more pleasing and considerable in God's sight, cannot do us any prejudice with those who are his ministers and who regulate themselves by his example.

From whence I may draw the following consequence, which deserves to be taken notice of, and which is but too true, namely, that when we show ourselves dark and reserved, and give not any account of conscience to our superior, it is a sign we have no mind to correct ourselves nor to cast off our bad habits. For do you not perceive very well, that if you had a sincere sorrow for your faults, and had made a firm resolution to be more faithful to your duties hereafter, you would do yourself no prejudice in the opinion of your superior by opening yourself unto him, because the declaration you shall make of your faults will be accompanied with such true repentance as will give him a very good opinion of you? It is not, therefore, the rendering an account of conscience to our superiors, but rather the withholding from them the knowledge they would thereby have had of us, that lessens us in their esteem; because, by the last they perceive that we think not at all of correcting or amending our faults.

CHAPTER VIII.
Another answer to the aforesaid difficulty.

THERE is still another manner of answering the difficulty which relates to the fear we may have of losing the esteem of our superior: which is, that if we truly have the spirit of humility, we ought to rejoice at being known to be as weak as we are; and therefore we need no other reason than this to move us to declare our defects and bad inclinations to our superior. For true humility not only makes us know and despise ourselves, but it also makes us be glad to be known and despised by others. It is true that the obligation of giving an account of conscience was established amongst us for other ends; but though there should be no other advantage to be derived from it than that of exercising ourselves in the practice of humility, this alone ought to be sufficient to engage us punctually to satisfy this obligation. And if we have not those sentiments of humility which we ought to have, but, on the contrary, desire to be esteemed, and to be promoted to the most considerable employments, I do not at all wonder that upon this account we let ourselves be seduced by those vain fears which pride and ambition are wont to suggest, and that we think thus within ourselves: if my defects come to be known to my superiors, they will have no more consideration for me, and will never advance me to any extraordinary employments, but I shall always remain in contempt and oblivion. Many great servants of God have attributed to themselves not only defects, but even considerable sins, for fear that any one should cast their eyes upon them to raise them to any great dignities in the Church; but he who, on the contrary, endeavours to hide his true faults that others may have a better opinion of him than he deserves, and consequently advance him to great employments, is far from resembling those I speak of, and clearly manifests that he has in his heart no feeling at all of humility.

We ought, moreover, take notice here of what is very essential, and what I have already touched upon elsewhere, which is, that the practices of humility and mortification, or of any other virtue whatsoever, to which a religious ought most apply himself, are those in which he cannot fail, without neglecting his rules at the same time; because it is in the exact observance of our rules that our spiritual advancement and perfection consist. But if we have not sufficient humility to perform the exercises of humility and mortification to which they oblige us, we may be confident that we have no humility. For of what use are humility and mortification, if, to spare ourselves a little shame, and not to expose ourselves to have a little less esteem, we tread under foot so essential a rule as that is, which obliges us to discover the very bottom of our hearts to our superior? We ought, on the contrary, if we had true humility and true sorrow for our defects, willingly submit ourselves to this shame in satisfaction for them; and it would be so far from hindering us to lay open our consciences to our superior, that it would even move us thereunto. The example of the great Theodosius deserves in this to be imitated by all the world. Rufinus, endeavouring to dissuade him from going to the church because St. Ambrose waited there with a resolution to hinder him from entering, he answered with a humility worthy a true Christian: For this very reason I will go thither, that the holy bishop may reproach me in such manner as I deserve. When the Devil would hinder you from addressing yourself to your superior or confessor, you must do this. You must answer him with resolution and courage: I will go to him, that he may reproach me as I deserve; I will go to him, that I may have the confusion of being known to be such as I am, and that this confusion may help me in some measure to expiate my sins. Behold here with what spirit of humility we ought to declare our defects; behold here an excellent mark that we are truly sorry for having committed them. But when we are more sensible to the shame of discovering them to a man, than to the sorrow for having offended God by them, we are far from those sentiments of humility which we ought to have; and if one of our rules says that we ought continually desire to see ourselves charged with injuries, affronts, false accusations, and all sorts of ignominies, in case God should not thereby be offended, with how far greater reason ought we desire to be contemned when we have given cause, and when the thing in question is to perform an act of religion, and to pay an act of obedience to one of the most important rules we have?

These considerations which I have now touched on should suffice to persuade us to keep nothing hid from our superior. But still to render the thing more sensible and palpable, and that it may not seem that we would not establish anything except on reasons drawn from spirituality, we pursued another line in the preceding chapter. We there made it appear that we not only do ourselves no prejudice in the esteem of the superior by discovering ourselves to him, but on the contrary, we thereby gain his esteem and affection, and that those expose themselves to lose it who adopt the contrary method; and now we shall add one thing more which necessarily follows from all we have already said upon this subject. It is this, that when you render a faithful account of your interior, the superior places great confidence in you, and with reason; because he knows you to the bottom, and is assured that as soon as any new thing shall pass within you, you will not fail to address yourself to him. But when you discover yourself only by halves, which he may easily find out, he can no longer place confidence in you, because he knows not what you have in the bottom of your heart, so that he is necessitated to watch you and to have his eyes continually upon you.

Moreover, this should be taken particular notice of, because a contrary procedure may give occasion on both sides to a great deal of disquiet and bitterness, which would not happen had you observed unlimited candour and openness towards the superior. Experience daily teaches that this candour helps exceedingly to reconcile minds, and to destroy many imaginations and suspicions which one may have of another, either superiors of inferiors, or inferiors of superiors. The same happens here as it does in certain objects, which seem frightful when they are but half seen, either by night or afar off. For when you have courage to approach them, you will find that what appeared a phantom was perhaps only a branch of a tree, or some other thing like it. You have certain imaginations and diffidences that make you apprehend your superior. Go to him, take courage to inform yourself and to open your heart to him, and you will find all your imaginations and diffidences very ill grounded. Seneca, speaking of the resolution with which we ought to push ourselves forward to great actions, says very well, that if we had but the courage to undertake them, we should find them less difficult than we had figured them to ourselves; and in fine, that "we want not courage because the things are hard, but they are hard because we want courage". Upon this occasion also he makes use of the comparison we have just related; and citing Virgil, who calls these phantoms and night-shades "dreadful figures to be looked upon", takes notice, that he does not call them dreadful or terrible in effect, but terrible only in appearance, to show that all this appearance has nothing in itself that is dreadful or terrible; we need but approach it, and thereby we shall be convinced that it is nothing. It is the same of those suspicions and imaginations we just now spoke of.

CHAPTER IX.

That we are under great obligations to God for having rendered this account of conscience amongst us so easy: the cause of this facility.

CERTAINLY we have great reason to give thanks to God for the practice he has established amongst us of entirely discovering our conscience to our superior, and for the sweet and easy manner in which we acquit ourselves of a thing which in itself is far harder than all other penances and exterior mortifications whatsoever. We may easily judge of this difficulty by that which is found in the sacrament of penance, which all Christians, generally speaking, feel to be more distressing than all the rest of their obligations. To render the pain of confession more supportable, it was found necessary to oblige the confessor by the divine law, even under pain of sacrilege, to keep it an inviolable secret, and yet confession ceases not to give such pain to many people in the world, that rather than confess their sins they choose to deliver themselves up to everything that is most terrible in remorse of conscience and in the dread of futurity—nay, to all that is most pungent in the eternal pains of Hell! Now, what you do, when you discover the bottom of your soul to your superior, is still something more than what is practised in confession; because we not only declare to him our sins, and all that which is matter of confession, but discover also many other things, and oftentimes such weaknesses as we have a greater repugnance to make known, or to accuse ourselves of, than of our sins themselves; and what is still more, all this is done out of confession. That a thing then which is of itself so hard, and at the same time so profitable and useful, should become, by the mercy of God, so sweet and easy, is a favour for which we can never give him sufficient thanks.

But let us see what is the cause that this practice is so easy amongst us. The first and chief cause is the grace of the religion to which we have been called; because God, as I have said elsewhere, gives to each religious order those particular helps that are necessary, to the end for which he has instituted it; and it is this which I call the grace of religion. Since therefore we are obliged by our institute to be always ready to go to any part of the world where obedience shall employ us for the help of souls, and to converse with all sorts of people, that the superior may not be deceived in the choice of those subjects he shall make use of for this effect, it is necessary that he should have an entire knowledge of us, which he can never have, if we ourselves do not entirely discover ourselves to him. From hence also it happens, that though this manifestation of conscience be a thing very painful of itself, and very troublesome, yet God, by a particular help of his grace, renders it very easy and comfortable.

The second reason of the sweetness and facility we find in it is, the manner wherein superiors treat such as address themselves to them for this end. They receive them as their children, with the tenderness and kindness of a father; so that their sole occupation seems to be to give them comfort; and, without doubt, it is of very great importance that they do so, and that the subjects be firmly persuaded that as often as they shall have recourse to them, they shall thus be treated with bounty and sweetness. For this being so, they will address themselves to them with all kind of confidence; whereas, if they apprehend to meet with harshness from them, this apprehension might discourage them. But they may be assured they will always receive kind treatment. For to this superiors are bound by their office; and if they neglect it, they will violate one of their principal obligations.

St. Bernard, upon these words of the Canticles, "we will rejoice and exult in thee, remembering thy breasts, which are more excellent than wine"—*Cant.*, i. 3,—gives a very profitable advice to superiors, touching the conduct they ought to observe towards their inferiors. "Let superiors", says he, "who always seek to make themselves feared by those that are under their charge, and seldom make themselves pleasing or profitable to them, hearken to this. Come hither and learn instruction, ye that judge the Earth, learn here that you ought to become like mothers, and not masters, to your inferiors—study to make yourselves beloved rather than feared; and if it is necessary sometimes to use severity, let it be the severity of a father, and not of a tyrant. Show yourselves mothers in your tenderness, and fathers in your correction; render yourselves affable; lay aside what may appear austerity; be not forward in chastising; reach out your helping hand to those in necessity; be filled with the sentiments and affection of a mother, and not puffed up with the tumours of pride and the authority of command"—*Serm*, xxiii. *in Cant*. The same saint recites upon this subject the words of the Apostle:—" My brethren, if any one falls into any defect, ye that are spiritual, reprehend him with the spirit of sweetness, each one making reflection upon himself lest he himself come also to be tempted"—*Gal*., vi. 1. And these others of Ezechiel, " the wicked man shall die in his iniquity, but I will require of thee an account of his blood"— *Ezech*., iii. 18. Wo be to the superiors, adds he, who receive not their subjects with sweetness when they address themselves to them in their temptations and weaknesses! Wo be to them who reject or check them, and show not the bowels of a father towards them. For if any one comes to grow worse by your harshness, as it often happens, and thereby comes to perish, God will require an account of his soul of you! Hence, though the superior should have regard only to himself, yet he ought to apply himself to perform his duty well, that you may do yours in like manner, and that he may not make himself accountable for your faults.

Thirdly, what renders this practice easy amongst us is its frequent and general use; so that we may avail ourselves of a consideration like to that St. Austin made use of when the difficulty of observing chastity opposed in his mind the design he had of turning to God. He says that he then represented continency to himself under the figure of a venerable matron, who, surrounded by many chaste persons of every sex, age, and quality, showed them to him, mocking him, and saying thus to him: Are you not able to do this, which so many persons practise? Or do you believe that what they are able to do, they do by their own strength, and not rather by his, who is all-powerful? And he assures us that this consideration helped exceedingly to give him courage. Do you the same in order to the manifestation of conscience which you ought to make to your superior; and when the Devil shall represent it to you as difficult, say you to yourself: What then! am not I able to do what others do ? Must I dispense with myself in doing what so many other religious, who are more learned, more elderly, more prudent and more enlightened than myself, daily practise? This consideration will readily remove all difficulties. It will not only hinder us from feeling pain while we practise things, but it will make us feel pain at our not practising them; for we will find it shameful and disedifying not to do what every one else is in the habit of doing. Hence we ought all of us endeavour to maintain in force and vigour so holy a practice as this is, that the example of some may encourage others; and in particular, as those that are more ancient in religion, and more advanced in knowledge, are capable of doing much hurt or good by their discourse or example; so it is chiefly their duty to endeavour by these two means to maintain practices of this sort, because all take notice of what they say and what they approve, and ordinarily regulate themselves by their example. I add that it very much imports each one in particular to exercise himself in this manifestation of conscience; because hereby the practice will become easy, whereas if he does not exercise himself therein, in a short time he will find it very hard. It is this which happens in regard of other exercises of humility and mortification, and even in regard of confession, which ordinarily gives great pain to those who confess but once a-year, and, on the contrary, gives great comfort and sweetness to those that confess often.

One thing which likewise contributes very much to render this practice easy, is to know that in giving an account to our superior, or prefect of spirit, of our consciences, we give it not to a judge from whom we apprehend punishment, but to a father from whom we expect comfort and consolation, and in whose good counsel we hope to find a remedy for our disease. Hence, whatever we can declare in this manner, we run no risk of punishment any more than we do by what we declare in confession; because these two tribunals are of the same nature, and what is practised in the one is consequently practised in the other.

In fine, what extremely facilitates manifestation of conscience, and what confirms very much all I have said, is that our superior is expressly obliged by our constitutions to keep in inviolable secrecy whatsoever is said to him. You may be therefore assured that what you shall say to your superior, in giving an account of your conscience, will remain in his own breast without any one else ever knowing it, and without your ever receiving any prejudice thereby. Besides, though they are already obliged, under pain of mortal sin, to keep a secret of this nature, yet Father General Aquaviva has taken care, by his most wise and most severe regulations, still more to oblige them to secrecy in this point; for he orders that a superior who shall violate this secret, shall be rigorously punished and deposed from his office; and he not only desires that all the religious be advertised of this order, but that they should also know that there is a precise order for the punctual execution thereof against any person whomsoever. Just as, in order to remove the difficulty which people felt in confessing, it was necessary to oblige confessors by all ways imaginable religiously to keep the secret thereof, even so, that we might have no difficulty to discover our conscience to our superior, Father Aquaviva judged that he could not take too many precautions to prevent superiors from revealing what was confided to them in this manner. I know not, says he, if anything could ever happen more prejudicial than this to the society, which proposes to draw its subjects to perfection rather by the interior way of spirit than by that of exterior penances and mortifications. And by these his words it is easy for superiors to judge what prejudice they will do their order, if ever they permit anything to escape their lips of what has been declared to them in manifestation of conscience.

CHAPTER X.

In what manner we are to render an account of conscience.

"POUR out your heart as water in the presence of the Lord"— *Lam.*, ii. 19,—says the prophet Jeremias; and these words explain admirably well in what manner we ought to pour out our hearts into the bosom of our superiors. It ought to be as if we poured out a pitcher of water. When we pour oil out of any vessel, there always rests something in the bottom; and when it is wine or vinegar we pour out, the vessel retains at least the smell thereof; but if we empty a pitcher of water there remains neither smell nor anything in the bottom; it has no more smell or taste than if nothing had been in it. It is in this manner you must pour out your heart in giving an account of your conscience; you must do it so as nothing may remain behind—no, not the least scent of anything whatsoever.

Since this point is of very great importance, and one of the chief means we have for the spiritual advancement of our souls, our holy founder requires, that besides the accounts of conscience we render all the year long, we should be particularly obliged to render one every six months, which should comprise that whole time; and that this should always be done before the renovation of vows. And it is in this manner that it has been always practised in the society, and from the time of the fourth general congregation there is a rule made to this effect, which is inserted amongst the common rules. As St. Ignatius requires at the time of renovation, besides the frequent confessions which are made before, that we should then make a general confession from the time of the last renovation; so he desires that, besides the accounts of conscience which we render from time to time, we give then a general account from the last six months. He thought he could not give a better means than this for the renovation and the regeneration of the interior man. And Father Aquaviva, moved by the same spirit, earnestly recommends the same means in his instruction to the visitors. "If subjects", says he, "give an account of their conscience as they ought to do, and superiors on their part receive as they ought the account given them by their subjects, this will, without doubt, be of great efficacy to renew in us a spiritual life and to contribute to our spiritual progress". These words agree admirably well with what St. Basil says, "that if subjects have a desire to make any considerable progress in virtue and to attain perfection, they ought to keep nothing hid from their superiors; because, by an entire manifestation of ourselves, it will happen that they will confirm us in what is good, and will suggest convenient remedies for what is bad within us; and so by means of this reciprocal communication we shall by little and little attain perfection". As when water is very clear we see the least gravel or sand in the bottom, so our manifestation ought to be so clear that our superior may be able to see even the least defects and imperfections which are in the bottom of our soul.

We have a very good instruction on this head which may help very much to render things more easy; and I must remark thereon, that of the two chief parts it contains, the first, which is as a preface and introduction, is the most considerable; because it contains in substance the whole fortieth rule of the summary of the constitutions, in which the obligation of rendering an account of conscience, and the manner of doing it, are fully set down. First, each religious is exhorted in this preface to consider in what manner St. Ignatius speaks of this obligation in the constitutions; and it is then added: Let all religious, either in confession or otherwise, as they shall choose and may be most to their comfort, take care entirely to discover the bottom of their soul, without keeping anything to themselves, in which they have offended God, from the last six months that they gave an account of their conscience; or at least let them make known the faults to which they are most subject. Now, I affirm it is in this that all which is of greatest importance in this matter consists, and that he who shall fail in what is set down in this first part would not give a good account of his conscience, though he should afterwards observe whatsoever is set down in the second, which contains fourteen points.

It is not necessary to run over them all to prove this truth; it suffices to take only one of the chief: let us take, for example, the third, which is to give an account of our temptations and bad inclinations. One of the chief things whereof we are to give an account, says the rule, is our temptations; how we resist them; what we do to resist them; and the facility or difficulty we feel in overcoming them; and so in the same manner in regard of our passions and bad inclinations. Behold here all that is contained in the third point, and all that there is upon this subject in all the second part of this instruction. Now, in order to render a good account of our conscience, and to make known the state of our soul to our spiritual father concerning the point we just now spoke of, I ask, is it enough to tell him all our temptations and all the bad inclinations we find within ourselves? I answer no, by no means; for we ought also render an account of all our falls, if we have fallen. For it is quite a different thing to say I am naturally prone to pride, and to say that I am so naturally given to it that I did such and such a thing purely to gain esteem; and I endeavoured to dispense with myself in doing such a thing I was commanded to do, because I felt a difficulty therein, not that it was very hard of itself, but because it hurt my vanity. There is also a great difference between saying, I am choleric and impatient; and I was so choleric and impatient that I fell into a passion, and did or said what might scandalize my brethren. In fine, there is a great difference between saying, I have had temptations against purity, and, I have dwelled on them or given consent to them. There is a far different judgment to be formed between him who consents to a temptation and him who resists it with courage; and the remedies that are to be prescribed or employed for the cure of the one, are far different from those that are to be made use of to fortify the other. For as when a physician treats a patient that is sick of a fever, it is necessary he should know whether the sick person be naturally strong and robust, or delicate or feeble, because the fever is differently to be treated, according to the difference of constitutions; so it imports very much that your spiritual physician should know your interior strength and weakness, that he may know how to treat you and prescribe fit remedies for you. Hence, it is not sufficient that you render an account only of your temptations and bad inclinations, unless you also give an account of your falls in them; because it is according as you have fallen or resisted them that he judges of your strength and weakness; and this is the reason that in the forty-first of the summary, where it treats of this matter, it is expressly said that we must discover to our superiors not only our temptations, but also our neglects and falls.

Now the same thing is not only mentioned in the preface of the instruction I speak of, which has in express terms that we must entirely discover to our superiors the bottom of our soul, without hiding anything in which we have offended God, or at least that we ought to make known the faults to which we are most subject. There is nothing said of it in the fourteen following points; so that if we should stick only to what they prescribe, it would be to reduce one of the most important and considerable rules that we have to a pure formality and ceremony. This observation may be of use to all in general, because it shows how they must give an account of conscience to their ghostly father.

To render this account still more clear and comprehensive, we must not be content with declaring our faults in general, but must specify them in particular, because it is hereby only that we can make ourselves clearly known, and this is also a very good advice for what regards confession. For as you ought not content yourself with saying in your confession, I have let myself be carried away by thoughts against purity, but you ought to discover how far you let yourself be carried; and though the things of which you accuse yourself should be only venial sins, which are not necessary matter of confession, yet, notwithstanding, since you confess them, as it is fit you should, it is not sufficient to express them in general terms, which always hides some of the fault, but to specify them in particular, which is the means of making the grievousness of the sin more clearly appear. In proof of this, is it not certain that it does not at all make known our fault, to accuse ourselves in general to have let slip some words of impatience and passion, when the words are such that by telling them it makes the fault appear far greater? Is it not also very true that when one has so failed in obedience as to have hereby disedified, we must not be content with saying, I have failed in obedience, but that the fault ought to be specified in such a manner as to make the quality plainly appear, and to convey a more distinct knowledge thereof? I say the same of the account of conscience we ought to render to our superiors. We must not render it in a general manner, nor make use of ambiguous terms, but we must express ourselves clearly, fully, and sincerely, without omitting anything that may serve to make known the state of our soul, without hiding anything from view, and without leaving the least folding of the heart unexposed. It is in these foldings that ordinarily the dust sticks; and "God would", says St. Paul," make himself a church that should be full of glory, where there should not be the least spot or wrinkle, nor anything like it, but that it should be holy and immaculate"—*Ephes.*, v. 27. We must, according to these words, have no folding in our soul, but all must be as smooth, plain, and clear as a mirror.

St. Ignatius requires this entire and exact account of conscience of each religious when he enters into the society, and will have him at that time discover not only his bad inclinations and sins to which he is then most subject, but also the bad inclinations which he has heretofore had, the sins into which he has oftenest fallen, and the vices which heretofore caused the greatest disorders in the soul. To inform a physician very well, and to make him be able to form a right judgment of our disease, and to apply such remedies as in curing one distemper may not occasion another, we must give him an account not only of the distemper we have at present, but of all those to which we have been subject at other times. It is the same here. If you wish to have your spiritual physician well informed of your interior state, you must give him a faithful account not only of the bad habits and inclinations you have at present, but also of all your past disorders, because they help to make him know the cause and even the source of your distemper. It is for this reason that we ordinarily counsel him who wishes to make a general confession, to make choice for this end of the confessor he designs constantly to confess to; and the reason of this is, that the confessor may have a more perfect knowledge of the soul of his penitent, and may labour more profitably in the direction thereof. For oftentimes impure temptations with which we are tormented, and the rebellion of the flesh against the spirit, are the remains and consequences of past irregularities and the punishment of that licentious life we have heretofore led; and therefore, however retired we live, sometimes, in punishment of our bad habits, to which heretofore we have abandoned ourselves, it will happen that we shall be tormented by these rebellious and involuntary motions. As to this point all that we have to do is to humble ourselves before God, taking this occasion to enter into lively sentiments of sorrow and confusion, not only in regard of what is present, but also of what is past, and thus we shall receive no prejudice from such impure motions as the force of temptation shall excite in us.

Lastly, we must remark that to render an account of conscience, and to make a general confession, are quite distinct things amongst us, as may be seen by the different rules we have concerning these two obligations, and by the end and matter of each one, which are also very different. However, it is very certain that every one has liberty to render an account of conscience either in or out of confession as he pleases and as he shall believe it will be most for his comfort, and our constitutions declare the same in express terms. But it is very good to reflect on one thing which Father Aquaviva says upon this subject in his instruction to visitors, which I shall set down here word for word by reason of the great importance of the matter. After having pointed out the difference that is between the account of conscience and confession, and after having said that each one may, if he pleases, give an account of conscience in confession, he adds: "Since, therefore, we ought not constrain our religious to give an account of conscience out of confession, because the constitutions leave an entire liberty herein for each one's particular comfort, yet we ought to praise those who, excepting the things that belong properly to confession, and which they may afterwards discover to their superior in confession, give an account of their conscience out of confession, and who let themselves be seen to the bottom, that the superior, not being constrained in any respect whatsoever, may freely make use of this knowledge for the advantage of their direction and the greater glory of God". It is better, therefore, to give an account of conscience out of confession, whereby we testify to have greater confidence in our superior; just as a man who puts many precious stones into the hand of his friend to keep, testifies a greater confidence than if he had given them locked up in a strong box.

CHAPTER XI.

An answer to several difficulties resulting from what has been said in the preceding chapters.

FROM all that has been said, there arise some difficulties which may present themselves to our mind, and therefore we must endeavour to remove them. The first is, that, on the one hand, we have said that it is better to give account of conscience out of confession, and again we have observed that we must not only declare our temptations and bad inclinations, but also our falls, if any such occurred, and that without this we do not render a good account of conscience. Now I ask, if it happened (which may the Lord in his mercy prevent) that a religious, by giving way to temptation, should fall into some grievous and shameful sin, it is possible that the rule should oblige him to give an account of it to his superior out of confession? This indeed would be very severe, and generally speaking, very few would be able to submit to it. To this I answer, that the intention of the rule and of our founder is not that in this case we declare our sin out of confession; on the contrary, it is chiefly to take away this restraint that the rule of which I have spoken establishes the alternative of accusing ourselves of our sins, either in or out of confession, according as we shall desire. The rules of the provincial expressly contain the same thing. For, after having said that when any religious has given an account of his conscience, the superior may ask him what questions he shall judge fit, they presently add, " with the reserve, however, that out of confession they put no question on matters which it would be very shameful to acknowledge. When the things are of such a nature that it appears we dare not mention them out of confession", we shall then do a great deal better to keep them for the tribunal of confession; and not only the superior or spiritual father ought never to ask any question of it about these things, but even they ought never suffer any one to speak to them on such subjects. Chaste ears ought not to hear such things out of confession, and therefore it is good to reserve for confession all that we may have to say upon this matter. It is what Father-general Aquaviva wishes to admonish us of by the words set down in the preceding chapter; for in saying that it is better to give account of conscience out of confession, he excepts such things as properly regard confession.

The second difficulty is of greater importance than the first. We have said, on the one hand, and St. Ignatius in his constitutions expressly says the same, that one of the reasons why we are obliged to give an account of conscience is, that superiors knowing perfectly well those under their charge, may be the better able to provide for the good of each religious in particular and the advantage of the society in general. We have also said elsewhere that the same constitutions permit each one to give an account of conscience in the tribunal of confession; so that in appearance it may be objected that the general government of the society is founded on knowledge acquired in confession. And in effect, some persons not well understanding the manner that the society governs itself herein, have been struck very forcibly by this objection. To answer it I say, first, that the society is so far from regulating its conduct by the confessions of its religious, that even Father-general Aquaviva, perceiving that some divines held that a confessor, without violating the seal of confession, might make use of what was revealed to him in confession in certain cases, rejects this opinion in his ordinances, and very severely forbids either to teach or follow it. Nay, he even commands all the confessors of the society, that with respect to things revealed to them in confession, they always act as if they had never come to their knowledge; and this is entirely conformable to a decree issued by Clement the Eighth four years after, upon the same matter, and of which Father Francis Suarez and many others make mention. But the society observes more strict measures than these; for it orders all superiors carefully to keep secret all those things

25 B

that shall be said to them in giving an account of conscience. Now if it wishes us to have so great circumspection in the things heard *out of* the tribunal of confession, what reserve ought they not exact in such things as belong to it, what care ought it not take to hinder confession from becoming odious, and a sacrilege from being committed against the inviolability of the seal!

I answer in the second place, that there is no inconvenience at all in making use of confession for the interior government of souls. On the contrary, it is one of the greatest advantages derivable from it. For, as the penitent discovers then all the wounds and infirmities of his soul, the spiritual physician, who is the confessor, is better able to judge of the remedies which are proper for him, and of the conduct he ought to make him observe for the future. This truth is so evident, that Pope Alexander the Third, speaking of certain habitual sinners, who, even in the tribunal of confession, declare that they cannot hinder themselves from falling back into the like disorders, and who consequently are incapable of absolution, because they have not a true desire to renounce sin, orders confessors to hear their confessions, that they may have an opportunity of giving them some good counsel for their direction and salvation. He exhorts even the sinners who are in this bad disposition, not to neglect confession, though absolution ought to be refused them, and counsels them to confess all the sins and disorders of their life, and also that bad disposition they then go with to confession. He commands ghostly fathers also to receive and hear them with kindness and sweetness; to give them afterwards good counsel and wholesome instructions, because it will perhaps happen that by little and little their hearts coming to be touched, they will quit the occasions; and, in fine, that by means of this practice of humility, and of such good works as their confessor shall recommend to them, God will open their eyes and move them entirely to renounce sin and to make a good confession. Wherefore it is not a new institution, but a very ancient and approved practice of the Church, to make use of confession as a very proper means to lead souls the better into the way of salvation.

We read in the life of St. Ignatius, that the first fathers of the society having unanimously chosen him general in two successive assemblies, he for a long time refused to accept it, as judging himself incapable of that charge. Yet they pressed him on all sides, signifying to him that to persist in refusing it was to resist the will of God, as appeared sufficiently by their unanimous suffrages. But notwithstanding all they could say, they could not obtain his consent; so that it was necessary to make use of an expedient which he himself proposed, and which I here set down. I will put, says he, this affair entirely into the hands of my ghostly father; I will declare to him all the sins that I ever committed, all the bad habits and inclinations to which I am subject, and lastly, all my weaknesses and infirmities, both corporal and spiritual, as well past as present; and if after this, he commands or counsels me in the name of Jesus Christ, to charge myself with so heavy a burden, I will obey without reply. He did as he said; he entered for some days into a retreat, at the end of which he made a general confession to a holy religious of the order of St. Francis, a Father Theophilus, of whom he asked, after he had ended it, whether or not he should accept of the election that was made of him: and the answer being given him that he ought to accept it, and that otherwise he would resist the Holy Ghost, he made no longer any difficulty to submit thereunto. Now, I ask whether any one can be so malicious as to find anything in this to reproach the conduct of St. Ignatius, and to suspect it of hypocrisy? I certainly believe that nobody can speak of it without praising it as in effect it deserves, and as it is praised by all that write his life. But our Saviour, who made use of this means to conduct our founder and our head, taught him to put the same in practice for our whole body, and therefore the custom of declaring to our superior, in or out of confession, all our vicious inclinations, faults, and imperfections, is a means given us by God, that the superior may be the better able to conduct us in the way of perfection, to which we make profession to aspire.

This being so, I say, that in what regards the exterior and politic government of the society, we can by no means make use of confession; but as to what regards the interior and spiritual conduct of souls, it is very proper, and even very necessary, to make use of it in the manner I have set down. Do not we also see, that it is a very common practice throughout the whole Church, that when we have any doubt or difficulty concerning our interior conduct, we address ourselves to a prudent and learned confessor, and confer with him about it, either in or out of confession, that we may receive his advice and counsel? Now this was precisely the intent of St. Ignatius, when he left it to the choice of his religious to give an account of their conscience, either in or out of confession. It is not therefore in consequence of the knowledge they derive from confessions, they make or appoint rectors, or receive persons to profession, or provide for all the offices of the society; for it would be very ill done to make use of it in this manner, as it would be also very ill to harbour such an opinion as this of superiors.

It is, however, very essential and of great importance to observe here, that a religious may find himself in such a disposition, and so many circumstances may occur, that his confessor should oblige him in conscience, and under pain of sin, to go and desire his superior not to put him in such an employment, or not to send him on such a mission, or to take him from such an occasion: declaring to him at the same time the danger he may thereby be exposed to by reason of his weakness. What better or more convenient means can be given to a religious in such an occasion as this, than to oblige him to lay open his conscience to his superior? for then the superior will have it in his power to remove him from this occasion without affecting his honour, and the superior will be hindered from exposing him to such dangers as may be above his strength, and at the same time secure both his honour and conscience. It likewise sometimes happens, that we are not certain whether we shall expose ourselves to danger or not; but yet we are afraid and doubt of it, and then nothing is of greater ease to our mind, and of greater comfort, than to propose our doubts and difficulties to our superior, and to put ourselves entirely into his hands. For if, after this, he engages you in any employment which you should apprehend to be dangerous to your salvation, the danger will no longer bear upon yourself as it would have done had you said nothing, but will entirely bear upon your superior; and God, who perceives that you have done as much as you could on your part, will lend you his assistance, and give you strength to acquit yourself well of what is commanded you.

In the third place, I further answer that, although the rule permits us to give an account of conscience in confession, it is still better, as I have already said, to give it out of confession; and that as amongst us each of us knows it is better to make this use of it, so each of us also, generally speaking, embraces that which is the best, and consequently we ought not to suspect that the government of superiors is grounded upon what has been revealed to them in confession, because it is ordinarily out of confession that we give an account of conscience. But suppose that one would not give an account of conscience but in confession, can we imagine that there should be any religious so great an enemy to perfection, as not to be glad, when he has said anything in confession to the superior, that the superior should make use thereof to remove him from the occasion of falling into sin, and to lead him more securely into the way of salvation? For, provided the superior acts with necessary prudence and circumspection, and that nothing can happen which is not for the good of the religious, and that nobody can thereby know the faults into which he has fallen, it is certain that the religious gains very much hereby. As, however, all the subjects of the society freely give an account of conscience out of confession, that the superior being no ways constrained by respect for confession, may more freely make use of the knowledge they give of themselves for their spiritual advancement and salvation, it is also true, that even for the spiritual and interior conduct of souls, it is not practised in the society to make use of confession, though they may lawfully and piously do so, but that ordinarily for this effect they make use of what they know out of confession.

St. Bonaventure teaches the same doctrine that we hold; and says, that it is of great importance the superior should know the conscience of those under his charge, as also their inclinations and habits, and the extent of their spiritual and corporal strength, that he may the better know how to govern them, and, as all persons are not equally fit for all things, so he may better distribute the burdens of religion according to each one's capacity. He relates upon this subject these words of holy Scripture: "Aaron and his children shall enter into the sanctuary, and they shall have the disposing and ordering of what every one ought to do, and shall distribute to each one the charge he ought to bear"—*Num.*, iv. 19. And he says that Aaron and his children are superiors, and it is their office to penetrate the interior of those under their charge, that, perfectly knowing them, they may make a just distribution of the employments and offices of religion, and give " to each one according to his ability"—*Mat.*, xxv. 15.

THE EIGHTH TREATISE.

ON FRATERNAL CORRECTION.

CHAPTER I.

That correction is a mark of charity: how useful it is.

ST. BERNARD says, that when God chastises us, it is a mark that he loves us as his children; and the holy Scripture abounds in proofs of this truth. "The Lord chastises whom he loves", says the wise man, "and takes pleasure in him as a father does in his son"—*Prov.*, iii. 12. The Son of God also, by the mouth of St. John, says, "that he reprehends and chastises those whom he loves"—*Apoc.*, iii. 19. And St. Paul teaches us the same thing, when he says, "The Lord chastises him whom he loves, and scourges every son he receives; for what son is there whom his father does not chastise?"—*Heb.*, xii. 6 and 7. It is for this reason that all the saints hold for certain, that one of the greatest favours God bestows upon a soul that falls into sin, is presently to chastise him by remorse of conscience. It is therefore a mark that God loves you, and that you are of the number of his elect; because he does not quite forsake you, but, on the contrary, invites and calls you at the very time you forsake him. But when a sin is not followed, either by remorse of conscience, or some other chastisement, it is, say they, a very great mark that God is extremely provoked, as this is one of the greatest chastisements with which he punishes sinners in this life. The same St. Bernard upon this subject alleges these words of Ezechiel, "My indignation shall cease against thee, and my zeal shall be taken away, and I will acquiesce and be angry no more"—*Ezech.*, xvi. 42; and these other words of Isaias, "I have sworn that I will be no more angry with thee, and will not reprehend thee any more"—*Isai.*, liv. 9. "Take notice", says he, "that God is never more angry than when he appears not to be so. If his zeal has then forsaken you, believe that his love has done so too, for you are certainly unworthy of his love, if he judges you not worthy of his chastisements, which are the favours he bestows upon those he loves"—*Bern. serm.* viii. *Cant.* But as the chastisements of God are a mark of his love towards us, so it is a mark also of the paternal love that superiors bear towards their subjects, when they reprehend them for their faults, and advertise them of them, that they may correct them. " An open reprehension is better than a hidden love"—*Prov.* xxvii. 5,—says the wise man. And in effect the charity and affection which they have interiorly for you is very good, but it is only good for him who loves you, and it is very prejudicial to you, if he does not give you some proof of it. This is what causes that earnestness in your superior when he charitably admonishes you of some fault, which you yourself either do not perceive, or else do not look upon as a fault. For hereby he loves you with profit and advantage to yourself, and loves you with the love of a father, who desires nothing more than the advantage of his children; because, had he not the true feelings of a father for you, he would not reprehend you for your faults. It is in this manner that, when a father detects his son in a fault, he reprehends and chastises him, because he is his son, and because he loves him as his son, and would fain see him accomplished in all perfections. But if the same person surprises another child in the same fault, he says nothing to him, and is not uneasy about him because he is not his son. Let his father, says he, look to him and correct him—it belongs not to me to give myself pain about what does not at all concern me.

Moreover, when the superior reprehends you for your faults, he shows not only that he loves you as his son, but is also persuaded of your affection for him, and that you are likewise persuaded of his, and of the zeal he has for your good. Nay, even hereby he signifies to you that he has a good opinion of your virtue; because if he did not believe you had sufficient humility to receive in good part his advice and correction, he would have abstained from saying anything to you. On the contrary, when he is not so free with you, but keeps certain measures, and says nothing to you of your faults, or of what was told him of you, it is because either he loves you not as a child, or believes you love him not as your father, or because he thinks you have not sufficient humility to make you profit by his admonitions and reprehensions; and in a word, it is always either want of love or want of esteem. It may happen, it is true, that externally he will show both the one and the other for you, whilst he will have neither in effect, but only a feigned esteem and affection. For what signify these exterior appearances of esteem and good-will of the superior, if in the bottom he has so bad an opinion of you as that he dares not take upon him to admonish you of your faults? It is acting a double part, to testify exteriorly sentiments different from our interior sentiments; and it is thus people of the world behave, because they dare not freely tell one another what they think, for it will often happen that they will praise and flatter you, to make you believe they have an esteem for you, and yet they have quite different sentiments in their hearts. "Their words", says the prophet, "are sweet like oil, yet they carry darts along with them; their mouths give a blessing to those whom they curse in their heart; they are deceitful in their discourse, and the poison of asps is under their lips"—*Ps.*, liv. 22, etc. We ought to be far from such proceedings as these; the charity we make profession of requires a sincere and open manner, and admits not of such dissimulation. What! I have defects which perhaps I do not perceive, or that seem to me not to be so, and yet the superior, who sees them, and knows that my brethren are scandalized at them, does not admonish me of them. This would be to have no charity at all. If you wore your cloak with the wrong side out, or if your face were besmeared, is it not certain that it would be a great charity to tell you of it, and you would not only thank him who did so, but on the contrary, you would take it ill if any one saw it and would not tell you of it? We ought with a great deal more reason have the same sentiments in regard of those faults which blemish the virtue of our soul, and which scandalize our brethren. And it is a great advantage for us, that there is any one who has the care with charity to admonish us of them; because the love which we bear to ourselves, and which blinds us, is the occasion that we perceive not our faults, or that we know them not to be what they are. As the tenderness which a mother has for a child makes her believe it handsome and beautiful, though it be in itself ugly and deformed; so the dangerous tenderness we have for ourselves makes even our defects appear to us as good qualities, and we always set them out in the best colours. Hence philosophers say very justly, that a man is not a good judge in what regards himself; for if the law has a suspicion of a judge who is a friend to one of the parties, how much more ought the love which we have for ourselves render us suspected to ourselves in our own cause! A third person, who is not prejudiced in our regard, perceives our faults more clearly, and is far more capable of judging of them, than we ourselves are. Moreover, as the common saying is, "two persons see more than one". Plutarch says, that we ought to give money for an enemy, because it is but our enemies that tell us truth; for from our friends we must expect nothing else but praises and flatteries. They will tell you that nothing can be added to your good qualities, though perhaps they find not so much as one in you; there is no language more common in the world than this, and God grant it be not introduced amongst us. Nay, what is still very bad, our vanity and weakness cause us to listen with pleasure to these sorts of flatteries, and even to believe them, instead of doing as the Royal Prophet did, who said, "The just shall reprehend me with charity, and give me a severe correction, but the perfumed oil of a sinner shall not anoint my head"— *Ps.*, cxl. 5. St. Austin says, that by the perfumed oil of a sinner flattery is to be understood, and that the prophet hereby signifies to us that he detests it, and that he had rather charitably and sincerely be reprehended by a virtuous man, than be loaded with praises and flatteries from the wicked. They serve, says he, for nothing else but to increase our folly and error, according to the words of Isaias: "My people, those who call ye blessed, deceive ye"—*Isa.*, iii. 12. And on the contrary, those that severely reprehend us do us a great deal of good, according to these other words of the wise man: "The wounds that are made by one who loves, are far better than the deceitful kisses of him that hates us"—*Prov.*, xxvii. 6. "And it is better to be reprehended by a wise man, than to be deceived by the flattery of fools"—*Eccl.*, vii. 6. What gives us pain for a short time is what cures us; whereas we become but so much the harder to be cured when we are too much flattered; for then we imagine that there is nothing that deserves reprehension in us, and therefore we never think of correcting ourselves.

Diogenes said, that we stand in need either of a good friend that will admonish us of our faults, or of a bad enemy that will reproach us of them; because the admonitions of the one and the reproaches of the other may help to correct us. The second means is but too much in use in the world, where ordinarily only hatred and enmity speak sincerely of other's faults, and where truth is only to be heard from the mouths of enemies. But in religion it is neither through hatred nor jealousy, nor through malice nor ill will, that they tell us of our faults, and it is only out of goodness, out of charity, and out of a desire of our salvation. It will therefore be our own fault, if we who have them do not make very great profit by them, having in the person of our superior a true and faithful friend, who charitably admonishes us of our faults; and, without doubt, we ought to believe ourselves happy when he reprehends us, because without that we should perhaps never be able to perceive our faults, nor consequently ever think of correcting them.

CHAPTER II.

That it is pride which hinders us from receiving corrections so well as we ought.

WHAT chiefly shows the pride of man is the repugnance he feels to be reprehended for his faults. "Who", says St. Austin, "can find out a man that wishes to be reprehended? And where is the wise man to be found, of whom it is said in the ninth chapter of the Proverbs, reprehend the wise man and he will love thee?" —*Prov.*, ix. 8. He truly deserves the name of a wise man, because he gratefully acknowledges, as he ought to do, so great a benefit as that of correction is; but where is such a one to be found? "And who is he, that we may give him such praises as are due to him?"—*Eccl.*, xxxi. 9. We are so puffed up with pride, says St. Gregory, and this vice is so rooted in us, that we cannot bear to be told of our faults, because we imagine that what they say to us lessens the good opinion the world has of us, and renders us less esteemed. And then we are very sensible to the least things affecting our honour, we presently take fire as soon as we believe it wounded, and instead of thanking those that reprehend us for our faults, we look upon their admonitions as injuries and as a kind of persecution. And in effect there are some people who, when care is taken to tell them of their faults, presently think themselves persecuted, and that it is done from some kind of aversion to them; nay, some are also to be found, continues this father, who, though of their own accord they frequently accuse themselves of their faults, yet, if any one happens to reprehend them, or accuse them of them, are presently moved and excuse themselves, because they cannot endure to be less esteemed than they think they deserve. Such as these are not truly humble, and speak not of their faults with the spirit of truth. For if they were truly humble, and believed what they said of themselves, they would not be angry that others said the same, and would not take so much pains as they do to excuse and defend themselves. True humility consists in the knowledge and contempt of ourselves, and in being glad that others also should know us and contemn us; and such persons as these, says St. Gregory, make it clearly appear that it is not that they may be contemned that they speak ill of themselves, but that they may pass for just and humble persons, because, as the Scripture says, "the just man is the first who accuses himself"—*Prov.*, xviii. 17. You would therefore gain esteem, and pass for one that is humble; and you speak ill of yourself, because you think this is a means to obtain what you aim at. But at the same time, because you do not believe that the evil that another says of you can help you thereunto, but on the contrary, as you imagine that it may destroy the good opinion that people may have of you, therefore you cannot suffer from another that which you say of yourself. All this proceeds from pride and vanity, and hence it often happens, though we see what they say is true, and that they have reason to reprehend us, yet we fail not to suffer the reprehension very impatiently, and to be displeased at it.

How then can we say any longer, "reprehend the wise man and he will love you"?—*Prov.*, ix. 8. For where are these wise men to be found that desire to be reprehended, and are pleased with those that tell them of their faults? No; but we are forced to say, what the same Solomon said in another place, "Take care of reprehending a scoffer for fear he hate you"— *Prov.*, ix. 8. This is the recompense that the world ordinarily gives to those that give good advice. "For a wicked man loves not him who reprehends him, and has no conversation with those that are wise"—*Prov.*, xv. 12, —or that are able to admonish him of his faults. In fine, it is an old saying, "that truth begets hatred"—*Ter. in Andr.*,—and speaking truth procures enemies. The saints compare these sorts of people to fools and mad-men, who cannot endure the sight of their physician, and refuse all sorts of remedies, because they feel them painful, and do not believe themselves sick. This comparison is taken from the Holy Ghost, who says, "that he who hates reprehension is mad"—*Prov.*, xii. 1. And in effect he wants not only humility, but he wants judgment and common sense; and, in a word, he is either a fool or a madman, because he refuses those wholesome remedies that are given him, and because he hides himself from his physician, who would cure him.

CHAPTER III.

Of the inconveniences resulting from not receiving correction in good part.

PRIDE and folly, of which I have just spoken, are grown to such an excess, and all the world knows it so well, that there is scarce one at present to be found who will admonish his brethren of their faults; because there is scarce any one that is willing to make himself hated, or, as the common proverb says, to give money to purchase ill-will. But proud men gain hereby only what they deserve. For what is it that a sick person deserves who will not permit himself to be treated? Why, he deserves to be forsaken and alone to die; and what else does that man also deserve who will not permit himself to be reprehended, and who receives in bad part all the charitable admonitions that are given him? "He that hates correction", says the wise man, "shall die, and he who hates discipline despises his own soul"— *Prov.*, xv. 10 and 32. He deserves, without doubt, not to be admonished, nor to be reprehended for anything, and that his defects should daily increase, that they come to be known to all the world, and that all the world may divert themselves with them without any one's having the charity to speak to him of them. It is this which ordinarily happens to those that find difficulty in being reprehended; and what greater punishment can such a man receive than to be left in his pride and obstinacy? "We have taken care of Babylon, and she is not cured; let us forsake her"—*Jerem.*, li. 9. He that will not make use of the remedies that are given him deserves to be forsaken. If we find a vineyard incapable of bringing forth grapes, we cease to dress and prune it. In like manner, when we cease to reprehend a person who takes it in ill part, we abandon him as being incapable of correction.

St. Francis Borgia, speaking of the inconvenience of not receiving correction in good part, says, that there are two very considerable inconveniences into either of which a person must infallibly fall. For either the correction will be entirely abandoned, as it is very distressing to be giving remedies to reluctant patients, and in this case the defects will take root; or, if the correction is continued, but taken ill, then the house will be presently filled with gall and bitterness by such indocile beings, who take that for an injury which they ought to receive as a favour, and who, converting wholesome remedies into poison, will be offended and exasperated at the very thing for which they ought to feel themselves eternally obliged. This methinks ought very much afflict those to whom no reprehension is given. For they ought to reflect upon themselves and say, "Is it not because I am like a sick person that is given over by the physician—is it not because I have received in bad part what has been said to me, that I am no longer spoken to?" The same saint afterwards recommends to us, in the same place, the spirit of sweetness, simplicity, and charity, that was practised in the beginning of our institution, and which caused that correction was so far from being an occasion of scandal and bitterness to those that were told of their faults, that it was a subject of edification and thanksgiving.

A grave doctor, speaking of those who wish not to be reprehended, compares them to the Devil, because they are as incorrigible as he is, and says, that one of the things that distinguish a sinner from the Devil is, that the sinner is capable of correction whilst he lives, whereas the Devil is eternally incapable of it. He applies to this subject these words of Ecclesiasticus, "He who hates correction is of the race of the sinner, that is to say, of the Devil, who figuratively is called the sinner"—*Ecclus.*, xxi. 7. As, then, the impression made by the foot is like to the foot, so he who hates correction is like to the Devil, because he renders himself as incorrigible as he is, and shuts the gate against one of the best means he can have to correct himself. St. Basil says, "that he who does this is a most dangerous companion, because his example makes others hate correction, and thereby diverts them from their enterprise, which is to labour continually in the amendment of their life". For which reason he orders that these indocile and incorrigible spirits should be separated from the rest of the community, lest they should communicate their disease to their brethren.

CHAPTER IV.

Of how great importance it is to receive correction well.

ONE of the best counsels that can be given upon this matter is that which Galen gives, who, not content with writing many prescriptions and aphorisms for the cure of the diseases of the body, has composed a book on the knowledge and cure of the diseases of the soul. He says that he who wishes to correct himself and make progress in virtue, ought to find out some prudent man that may admonish him of his faults; and that when he has found out such a one, he should earnestly conjure him to admonish him of whatsoever he shall observe to be amiss in him, promising him to be thankful to him during his whole life for it, as for the greatest mark of affection he can receive from him, and moreover assuring him, that inasmuch as the soul is more valuable than the body, by so much his obligation to him will be greater than if he had cured him of some very desperate sickness. But if he to whom you shall address yourself, adds he, and who has taken upon him to admonish you of your faults, should let pass some days without saying anything to you, go and make your complaint to him, and conjure him again more earnestly than you did the first time, that he would be mindful of his promise, and that he would admonish you of your faults as soon as you shall have committed any. If he answers that he remembers his promise, but that he has had no occasion of performing it, because either you have done nothing amiss, or not done anything that stood in need of admonition, beware of believing him, or of imagining that he wanted matter, but believe that his silence proceeds from one of three causes that I shall here set down: First, from negligence, and because he has not attended to your defects or to what he has promised, there being very few persons that will take pains in this manner to render others more wise. Secondly, because, if he has taken notice of any fault in you, he has not had the courage to tell it you, or because he would not put himself in danger of losing your friendship thereby, knowing very well that most commonly all that is gained by speaking truth is to procure hatred to one's self. Or lastly, because he has perceived that sometimes it has happened you have not received in good part the admonitions given you, and therefore, whatsoever you shall be able to say to him, he gives more credit to your deeds than words, and cannot persuade himself that you desire in good earnest he should admonish you of your defects. Observe, moreover, says he, that though the faults they reprehend you for do not appear to you to be so great, yet you must by no means defend them nor excuse yourself. First, because another ordinarily sees our faults better than we ourselves, and therefore can judge better of them than we can. And in the second place, though they should be deceived, yet what they tell you may always serve to make you pay greater attention to your conduct, and also to avoid with all care for the future the giving any occasion to suspect anything of that kind in you.

Behold here all that Galen says upon this subject, and we have need to put all in practice if we can but find out any one that will willingly take upon him the care of admonishing us of our faults. For it is not an easy matter; and every man may judge of it, not only by the disquiet correction may give himself when he receives it, but also by what he feels when he is obliged to give it to another, and when the superior orders him to admonish any one of his faults. It is certainly one of the things that gives the greatest pain to a superior, to have to do with religious who have not the spirit of humility and docility to receive correction in good part. For as, on the one hand, he is obliged to give it, and on the other, apprehends they will not receive it well, gives it with that fear and trembling which those have who perform a difficult and dangerous operation, and often he is ignorant whether he should speak or not. Sometimes he thinks he ought to do it, but not without taking the best time for it, and seasoning the reprehension with something that makes it less bitter; and sometimes he finds those to whom he ought to give it so little disposed to receive it well, that he thinks it better to say nothing, though with the hazard of seeing them still persevere in their defects. And this because he fears that his admonitions will do them hurt instead of good, and will serve only to embitter their minds against him, and perhaps be the occasion that for the future they will perform their duty far worse. The sun softens wax, but hardens dirt; and when plants have taken deep root, water, air, and sun help very much to make them spring up; but when they are not well rooted, the same things make them either rot or else dry up. It is in this manner that correction softens the hearts of those who are truly humble from a knowledge of themselves, whereas in those whose humility is not deeply rooted in the knowledge of their own baseness and nothingness, it produces only dryness and hardness of heart. Wherefore superiors often abstain from reprehending those in whom they perceive this bad disposition, because they perceive their distemper grows worse by these remedies; for, turning the best things into poison, they take that for an aversion and cruelty, which is an effect of friendship and of zeal for their salvation, and certainly persons of this description deserve to be left to themselves.

If you desire therefore not to be abandoned as a person sick of an incurable disease, and as one of an incorrigible spirit, you must receive in good part whatsoever is said to you. "It is an excellent thing to be reprehended", says the wise man, "and to manifest a sorrow for our fault"—*Ecclus.*, xx. 4. But even though you should not have committed the fault of which you are admonished, or that it should not be so great as it was made, or that the thing were otherwise than it was represented, yet you ought not neglect receiving the reprehension with a great deal of good will towards him that gives it, and to tell him that you will in future take more care thereof, and that he has done you a very sensible pleasure, because hereby you will encourage him to do the like again. But if you should begin to excuse and defend yourself, all that you would gain hereby would be that, at another time, and perhaps in an occasion wherein you would have greater need of this admonition, he will say nothing to you. The first thing that some people do when you reprehend them for a fault, is presently to excuse themselves; and when they perceive that they cannot entirely defend themselves, they seek out reasons and colours to make their fault appear less, and this is the true way to hinder any one from giving them any admonition for the future. For when one perceives he can never make you acknowledge the faults he tells you of, and that you find out excuses for everything, he resolves never to admonish you any more; and so, besides your giving scandal, all you gain by your justifications and excuses is to hinder him from ever more taking upon him to give you profitable advice upon any occasion.

It is looked upon as a very great defect even in superiors, not to receive the advices and counsels that are given them; insomuch that it is ordinarily said that a man of limited talents, but who knows his own defects and will hearken to counsel, is far more fit for government than another who has more extensive talents, but who is so full of self-conceit, and thinks himself so versed in all things, that he takes it ill to be admonished, or to have counsel given him. The Holy Scripture abounds in passages confirming the truth of what I here say: "Have you not seen", says Solomon, "one who thinks himself a very able man? There is more to be hoped for from a fool than from him. The carriage of a fool appears very good in his own own eyes; but a wise man hearkens to counsel. I am wisdom that make my abode in counsel. Where there is a great deal of good counsel, there salvation is to be found"—*Prov.*, xi. 14. St. James also takes notice, that to be tractable, and to let one's self be persuaded, is one of the conditions and qualities of wisdom: "Wisdom that comes from on high", says he, "is, in the first place, bashfulness; and afterwards it is a friend of peace—it is modest, tractable, and easily carried to God"—*James*, iii. 17. But if in superiors it is a laudable thing willingly to hear the advice and counsels that are given them; and if, on the contrary, it is so much to be blamed in them not to do so, with how far greater reason ought subjects to be blamed who cannot suffer with patience the reprehensions of their superiors! This alone should oblige us to receive correction with docility and sweetness. But that we may more willingly on our part be moved thereunto, it is good here to remark, that when we receive correction as we ought, and the superior is convinced thereof, he is not so much in pain for the faults we fall into, because, as he perceives the disease, so he perceives also the remedy. But when his correction is not well received, he feels great difficulty, because he finds the door shut against the only remedy; and this is one of the greatest troubles superiors meet. It is good then to testify in particular to our superior that we have a great desire to be reprehended for faults, and for this end to beg of him to watch our conduct with the eyes of a father, without taking notice of any impatience that we may at any time have shown, if while he corrected us we received not his reprehension with such submission as we ought. Moreover, it is not sufficient to have once made this petition to him, as a thing said out of custom, but often to reiterate the same even with great instance. For be assured that you cannot do too much to persuade and move him to acquit himself well upon your account of a thing that is so disagreeable and so hard in itself. And hence, though in all other occurrences we ought to be pleased when they believe us full of imperfections, yet herein we ought to take care to give no occasion to our superior to believe us so untractable and immortified as not to receive his correction in good part, but ought to make it our chief endeavour to persuade him of the contrary, for fear he should not give himself the pain and trouble of reprehending us, and that hereby we come to be deprived of the chief means we have for our spiritual advancement.

As a sick person who has a great desire to be cured, says St. Basil, willingly submits to the physician's orders, and "how difficult and sharp soever the remedies are", he takes it not ill, and suspects no bad intention therein; so a man who has a great desire to correct himself must willingly receive such admonitions as are given him, and never permit himself to think that it is out of ill will and aversion that they find fault with him. If, then, the interest and love of our health, adds the same saint, makes us willingly take very bitter medicines—if for this reason we permit the physician and surgeon to cut and sear us as they think fit, and if we even thank them for it as for a special favour, is it not very just that for our own salvation, and for the good of our whole order, we should submit in the like manner to correction, how hard and harsh soever it may appear in itself, and what repugnance soever we have thereunto?

CHAPTER V.

What has been said in the foregoing chapter confirmed by examples.

ST. CHRYSOSTOM, willing to move us to receive correction in good part, and to profit by the admonitions that are given us, cites the example of Moses, who being himself very wise and very much enlightened, and being moreover chosen by God to be the leader of his people and the instrument whereby he wrought many wonders, failed not to receive in good part the advice of Jethro, his father-in-law, who counselled him to make choice of some persons to assist him in the government of the people and in the administration of justice. "You do not well", says Jethro to him, seeing him do all things himself, "to consume yourself with imprudent labour; what you undertake is above your strength, and you can never be able alone to sustain it"—*Exod.*, xviii. 17, 18. And the same father hereupon takes notice, that Moses took a great deal of care not to act like those who, even when the counsel that is given them appears good, are angry with those that give it, as being displeased that any one less able than themselves should take upon them to counsel them, but he received this counsel with great submission, and put it presently into practice.

St. Cyprian and St. Austin propose also the example of St. Peter, when St. Paul reprehended him for having wished to subject to the law of circumcision those amongst the gentiles who were converted to the faith. Take notice, say they, that St. Peter presumed not upon himself, nor would he take upon him to decide the question, though he was head of the Church, and though his opinion should prevail over that of the rest. Take notice also, that he contemned not St. Paul, as having been a little before a persecutor of the Church of God, and was not angry or troubled at being reprehended by him, but took his counsel very well, and presently yielded to truth and reason.

It is also an example worthy to be remembered and taken notice of, which the great Theodosius gave, in receiving with submission and humility the corrections and checks of St. Ambrose. For whether or not this holy bishop did then excommunicate him, and forbid him to enter into the Church, by reason of the massacre which he had made of all the people of Thessalonica, or whether it was that being then placed within the rails or precincts of the choir, after he had made his offering at the altar, the same saint sent to him to bid him retire into the nave or body of the Church, because it belonged only to priests to be in the place where he was, and that the purple did not raise emperors to the dignity of the priesthood. Ecclesiastical history relates these two examples at length, and says, that it is hard to decide whether the constancy and courage of the bishop, or the obedience and humility of so powerful an emperor, ought to be more admired and praised.

We read in the life of the same St. Ambrose, that he thanked those that admonished him of his faults, and received their advice as a signal favour. The history of the order of the Cistercian monks makes mention of a religious of Clarevallis, that received any correction given him with so much gratitude, that as often as he was reprehended for any fault, he said a *Pater Noster* for him that reprehended him. And in the same place it is observed, that from that time, this custom has always been practised in this monastery, and observed as an inviolable law.

St. Arsenius was in very great reputation for sanctity amongst the hermits of his time, and had been before highly esteemed in the court of the Emperor Theodosius, who made him governor of his children Arcadius and Honorius, who were also emperors after the death of their father. As his sanctity had not entirely destroyed all the bad habits he had contracted whilst he lived at court, there still remained some slight defects in him, which were remains of the court life he had led for many years; and among other habits, he was wont to sit with his legs across, whilst he was at conference with the other hermits. This posture seemed to all very indecent and immodest, and they wished to admonish him of it; but no one being willing to undertake it, because they had a repugnance to reprehend a person of his consideration for what seemed so simple and trivial a fault, they consulted on the best means of making him correct this bad habit; and the abbot pastor, who was a very holy and ingenious man, proposed to them a very easy and proper expedient. The first time that we meet together, says he, I will put myself in the same posture with Arsenius, and you shall publicly reprehend me for it; whereupon I will presently put myself in a more modest posture, and so he will be sufficiently advertised hereof. All the fathers approved of this expedient, and the first time they met at a spiritual conference, the abbot pastor failed not to put himself in the same posture with St. Arsenius. The fathers presently admonished him thereof, as of a thing that was against modesty and good manners; he instantly put himself in a more becoming posture; and St. Arsenius presently understanding and taking this as an admonition given to himself, without taking notice of anything, by little and little set down his legs, and never after fell into the like fault. This example shows us two things; first, how troublesome and hard a task it is to reprehend others; and secondly, that every one ought to take to himself such reprehensions as are publicly given to his brethren.

CHAPTER VI.

Of the rule that obliges us presently to discover to our superior the faults of our brethren.

THE ninth rule of the summary of our constitutions, says, that for our greater spiritual advancement, but more especially for our greater humiliation, we ought to be content that all our faults and imperfections, and even whatsoever we have done that is known out of confession, should be discovered to our superiors. Here it will be much to the purpose, for the better establishing what has been already said upon this matter, to know that not only all our constitutions have been approved of and confirmed by the Apostolical See, and that Gregory the Thirteenth, in the Bull whereby he approves them, has expressly put this clause, "out of my own proper motion", but that this very rule which I just now cited, has also been particularly approved of, even by a particular sentence and decree, after its having been called in question, which renders it more authentic. I shall here set down how the thing happened:—A priest who had been of our society, and who had been dismissed as one of a turbulent spirit, caused to be printed one part of the sum of Cardinal Toletus, and joined a chapter thereunto, in which he said, that in a certain order, for which otherwise he had a great deal of respect, by reason of the many learned men that were in it, there was a certain rule which obliged all the religious, that as soon as they knew any fault of their brethren, they should immediately advertise the superior thereof, without saying anything to the person that had committed it; and he added, that great inconveniencies might spring from this rule, and that it was quite contrary to the gospel. Father Everardus Mercurianus, who was the general of the society, complained to the Pope of this calumny; and the Pope desiring to see the book and the rule, and being informed after what manner it was practised in the society, did not only declare that it was not contrary to the gospel, but that it was so far from deserving any just censure, that it truly contained evangelical perfection; and moreover ordained, that that part of the book in which it was so injuriously spoken of, should be forbidden, as afterwards it was by Cardinal Sirlet, by virtue of the power which the office of inquisitor-general gave him.

Although this rule has been hereby sufficiently justified, I shall endeavour to prove, first, how important and necessary this rule is; and secondly, how just and reasonable it is; and in this I shall not rest upon the subtleties of the schools, but will endeavour to give palpable and convincing reasons for it. As to the first point—*i. e.*, the importance and necessity of this rule—this may be seen by recurring to the very important rule of giving an account of conscience to our superior, of which I have spoken elsewhere. For all the reasons which our holy founder alleges in his constitutions, to show of how great importance and necessity it is to give an account of conscience to our superior, concur to prove the importance and necessity of the rule of which I now speak. I have already treated these reasons very fully, but they may be reduced to two: the first is, that superiors may the better know how they ought to govern each religious, and the second, that the general superior may the better provide for the good of the whole society in general. Now, it is for these very reasons that St. Ignatius judged fit that our superiors should be advertised of our faults and defects by any one that should know them out of confession. And he would by this precaution be assured of a thing that was of so great consequence both for your own good and for the good of the whole society, that in case you should neglect your duty, your brother might on this occasion do what you ought to have done yourself, had you been faithful in the observance of your rules. He does it only to pay your debt, and all is done for your greater good and for the better good of religion, and that superiors, for want of knowing the strength and capacity of each, may not expose any one to the danger of ruining himself.

Now as to what belongs to the second point, which regards the justice and equity of this rule, it may be maintained by many reasons and authorities, of which the first is, that the same thing is practised in the most ancient religious orders. It is in use no less in the order of St. Francis than in ours, that when any one knows a fault of his brother, he goes presently to advertise the superior thereof, without saying anything beforehand to the person that committed it. One of the books of this order, entitled "Serenity of Conscience", expressly takes notice of this practice in the hundred and fortieth question. And in other general statutes of the order, entitled those of "Barcelona", because they were made in a general chapter held there in the year one thousand four hundred and fifty-one, it is expressly said, that when the religious shall be out of their monasteries, they must, at their return home, make known to their superior all things of consequence that happened to their brethren abroad; and whosoever shall fail to do this shall be punished by fasting on bread and water, or by such other penance as the superior shall think fit to impose upon him. The same thing is also ordained by the statutes that were made at the commencement of this order, in the fifth general chapter; and it was confirmed in that also which was held when St. Bonaventure was general, where it was resolved that the contrary opinion should be banished the whole order as an enemy to religious discipline, and that he that should teach it should have all his books taken from him, be deprived of active and passive voice, and even be put in prison.

But farther, to show how ancient this doctrine is, and how it has been approved of by those who have embraced angelical perfection, I will here set down an ancient decree, made by the abbots Stephen and Paul, and related in these terms by the abbot Smaragdus, "If any sees or hears another do or say anything that is not of edification, and does not presently tell it to the superior, let him know that he foments the sin, and that he entirely renders himself as guilty thereof as he that committed it, and that, in a word, he is a cruel enemy both of his own soul and of his also whose defects he endeavours to hide. But if any one", says another decree, afterwards set down by Smaragdus, "should know that one of his brethren, finding a monastic life too hard, should have a design to run away, and does not go presently to discover it, let him not doubt but that he is in part the cause of his brother's perdition, and is to be separated from the conversation of his brethren till he that is run away be brought back". Here then we perceive that this rule is no new thing, nor in use only in our society, but was an ancient practice and observed in other orders. Moreover this custom is founded upon the end of the precept of fraternal correction, *i. e.*, the amendment of our brother, which, as it is ordinarily hoped, we may more easily compass rather by means of his superior than of any other particular person.

The reason that justifies this rule, and makes it appear to be neither so hard nor so rigorous as some imagine, is, that all it ordains and all that is practised amongst us upon this subject, is to tell the fault of our brother to our superior as to a spiritual father; that by reprehending him for it with the charity and tenderness of a father, he may by this means hinder him who was ready to fall, from doing so; or if he be already fallen, will presently help him up again. It is in this sense that the twentieth of the common rules says, that he who shall know any considerable fault of his brother, ought to advertise the superior thereof, that he may by his prudence and fatherly care procure a convenient remedy. So that when one discovers his brother's fault to his superior, he does not do it as to a severe judge that has a right to punish him for it, but as to a father, who cannot do but what is best for him, and to whom it belongs to apply a remedy, and to avoid such inconveniencies as might happen if nothing were known of it and if no step were taken on it.

Father Natalis, a man very distinguished both for his piety and learning, adds in the third place a very good reason: We see, says he, that both in the ecclesiastical and secular government, when they are about to seek out any person for an employment, they are wont to make secret inquiries into the life of those who aspire to it; yet this is not done with a design to punish any one whom they shall find to have deserved punishment, but only because they wish to be very well informed of those whom they trust with such offices of authority, in which the good of their order in general, or the spiritual good of particular persons, is concerned. Now, all subjects of the society may be chosen for missions, which is one of the ends for which it was instituted, and which requires persons of very solid virtue, and not such weak and frail ones as by their fault would ruin the good reputation of the society. So that the superior has consequently right to inform himself, and to desire to be informed, even of the most secret things, and even to establish a rule thereupon, that the light he shall thereby receive may better help him to know those subjects he should make choice of, and hinder him from being deceived in a thing of so great importance, both to the good of particular persons, and to that of the whole society in general.

In the fourth place, to show how much this rule is founded upon reason, let us put into the scales, on the one side, the prejudice you receive by having your fault told to your superior as to a father; and in the other, the inconvenience of its not being told, either by ourselves or others, and see which is of greater weight. All the prejudice it can do us is reduced to the little confusion we receive, and the little esteem that we think we lose; but the inconvenience that may happen by not having your fault discovered to your superior, either by yourself or another, is far greater. For the superiors, through want of a knowledge thereof, can apply no remedy to it, and a distemper to which no remedy is applied, ordinarily augments, and easily communicates itself to others. Moreover, this would afterwards infallibly turn to your own shame and confusion, and to the discredit of your order; because, "there is nothing hid which is not revealed"—*Luke*, xii. 2. Sooner or later, by one means or other, all things come to light, and a distemper, which at first might easily have been cured, if it had been then told the superior as it should have been, cannot afterwards be cured without applying fire and lance. All this, without doubt, brings along with it far more prejudice than the little confusion you would have undergone, or the little esteem you think you should have lost, by the discovery of your fault to your superior. Wherefore I say, that nothing is done against charity by discovering the fault of our brother to the superior, but that we are even obliged in charity to do so, and that we ought to have a great scruple not to do it. For this omission may sometimes happen to be a mortal sin—not by virtue of the rule—because our rules, as I have already said, oblige not under pain of mortal sin, but by virtue of the importance of the matter, and because of the great inconveniencies which may result from it, wherefore we render ourselves culpable, when we might have remedied and prevented them by giving notice in due time to our superior, which we neglected to do, and which we are obliged to perform.

St. Basil says upon this subject, "that to conceal the sin of our brother from our superior, is to accelerate the death of a sick person, and to push a man down a precipice, who is already running to it himself". For a sin which is concealed, is like an imposthume or gangrene, which daily augments, and at last gets to the heart, and brings death along with it. Hence, as it is to render great service to a man, to lance or cut the imposthume or gangrene, what pain soever the operation should give him; and on the contrary, as it would not be the part of a friend, out of compassion to hinder such an operation, though ever so painful —so, it is not to exercise the office of a friend, to hide from your superior the fault of your brother; but on the contrary, it is to contribute to his death, not to discover his infirmity to a physician able to cure it. "Do not think", says St. Austin, treating on this matter, "that it is any hurt to reveal the fault of your brother. There is far more in letting him perish by your silence, whom you might have cured by discovering his fault. For if your brother had any dangerous infirmity which he would keep secret, fearing the pain of incision, would it not be a great cruelty in you to say nothing of it, and a great charity to speak of it? With how far greater reason ought you then to discover this spiritual wound, which he has a mind to hide, which may occasion the death of his soul?"

The silence, therefore, which some observe from motives of honour and friendship, as they erroneously pretend, is a thing quite contrary to the duty and obligation of charity. They imagine that it is friendship and a point of honour to hide the faults of another from the superior, and therefore they feel great repugnance to mention them, because they fear they shall upon this account be less esteemed; and therefore, as they say, they will not at all interfere in carrying reports to the superior, as they wish not to hurt any one, or lessen his esteem with his superior. This is not the spirit of religion, and far less that of the society. They are worldly maxims, and such precautions as these are very dangerous for any one to have in religion. For it is not to carry stories about, nor to hurt your brother, that you discover his faults; it is, on the contrary, to do him good, and not to discover them is both to do him and religion a prejudice. Where have you learnt that, not to displease a particular person, you may neglect the fidelity you owe to a whole body? To whom have you a greater obligation,—to your whole order or to a particular religious? It is very ill to hide the faults of another; it is as if one had intelligence, or were partakers with him that committed them; and it is for this reason that one ought to be ashamed of not being faithful to religion and of not observing its rules. "Wherefore", St. Basil concludes, "let there be no one that helps to hide the faults of another, lest, instead of showing his affection to his brother, he procure his death". Hide not the disease of your brother, but discover it to the physicians before it becomes incurable, and before he is forced to suffer both fire and the lance; and this will be to perform the office of a true friend to your brother: for by this means you will save him; and, had you done otherwise, you would have been the cause of his perdition.

All these, and many other reasons which are adduced both by saints as well as divines, are sufficient to prove that this rule is both just and holy, even though a religious, in making his profession, should not expressly renounce, as we do, to the right he may have against this rule; because, in effect, there is no order in which they do not in this manner renounce to it. But we have, moreover, a reason which is peculiar to ourselves, namely, that when any one wishes to be received amongst us, the rules are given him, and a summary of the constitutions which he ought to observe, in which the rule we speak of is contained, and it is asked of him whether he be content to submit to these rules. This rule also is particularly specified unto him, and his express consent is again asked; and during the two years of his noviceship, before he can be received to his vows, every six months the same proposition is made to him. But there is still yet more, the master of novices is obliged, by a particular rule, to advertise the novices of those things which may afterwards give them any pain, amongst which this is particularly set down for one, and in effect he never fails to advertise them of it; and what removes all doubts on this matter, they answer according to the terms of the rule, that they voluntarily submit hereunto for their greater spiritual advancement, and that they may have greater occasion to humble and debase themselves. For it is very certain that there is nobody who may not, at his entrance into religion, renounce his own right upon account of greater perfection, and give his consent that, without being advertised, his faults may directly be discovered to his superior. For every man is master of his own reputation, and it is lawful for him, for his greater good, to be content to lose it, either with his superior or with any one else, so there be no particular circumstance that obliges him not to permit himself to lose it, as in effect there is not in the matter of which we speak. For as every religious may lawfully discover his sins to his superior, how great or secret soever they be, so he may lawfully give permission to another to do the same. And this is what all the religious of the society do by the express consent and approbation they give to this rule, as I have already said, and whereby they do nothing else than renounce the right they might have to the contrary. For if any one should reveal to me in confession, under the promise of secrecy, some great sin which he may have committed, and should afterwards give his consent that for the better judging what remedy he ought to apply thereunto, I might consult and advise with my superior about it, it is certain that by the consent he gave he renounced the right he had to hinder me from discovering his fault to any one, and, at the same time, I have gained a right to discover it to my superior to have his advice. Moreover, the novices see this rule practised for two years before they make their vows, which is sufficient to give them occasion to suppose, that when they afterwards make them, they tacitly renounce the right they may have against this rule, though they say not in express terms that they renounce thereunto. It is as a Carthusian does, when he makes his profession, who knows, that in the order to which he engages himself, perpetual abstinence is observed, which is never broken, upon any account whatsoever; and therefore by engaging himself he renounces the natural right he has to preserve his life by eating flesh, though he renounces it not in express terms, yet this right of his is much to be preferred before that of our preserving reputation. It is also in the same manner, that he who takes holy orders renounces the right of marriage, and remains strictly obliged to observe chastity all his life long, though he make no vow of chastity. Moreover, St. Francis Borgia being general, and being consulted about this matter by some provincial congregations of Spain, answered, that those who entered into the society were judged to have renounced all the right they might have had against this rule. It is moreover certain, both by the tenor of our bulls and by the privilege which the general of the society has, to declare the true sense of our constitutions, that we give up our right. To conclude, this rule having been afterwards discussed also in the sixth general congregation, all things were decided therein in the same manner; and a general congregation of the society, as it is noted in the same place, has authority from the Holy See to decide all doubts which may arise concerning the rules of our institute. It was also declared in the sixth general congregation, that these words of the rule, "by any one whomsoever that has had a knowledge of them out of confession", ought not to be understood, but of the faults which another has notice of, and not of those which may have been told him in secret by any one by way of asking his counsel and advice.

All the difficulties that may arise about this matter are hereby entirely taken away, and hereby all subjects of complaint cease, it being an undoubted maxim of the law, "that no injury is done to him who knows and consents to it". You were informed of this rule when you were first received, and then you signified that you were content to submit thereunto; if you are angry afterwards, that your faults are told to the superior, be angry, not with the rule that ordains it, nor with your brother that observes the rule, but with yourself, who ought now be more confirmed in the spirit of mortification and humility than you were in the beginning, and yet you are far less, because you are not now in the same disposition you were then in. It is from this the pain that this rule gives to any one proceeds, and our holy founder also knowing very well that pride and want of mortification were the only things that could render it troublesome, tells us that the spirit of humility and the desire of greater perfection ought to be the foundation thereof. If then we have this spirit and this desire, we shall be glad when they come to know our defects, that they may esteem us the less; and with how far greater reason ought we be glad that they are known, that hereby we may be reprehended and corrected for them! He that has not sufficient humility to desire his fault should be known upon this account, has scarce the spirit either of humility or of mortification.

CHAPTER VII.

Some important admonitions concerning this matter.

FROM all I have said, several good admonitions and advices may be gathered, no less for him that receives than for him that gives correction. And to speak first of him that receives it, it is certainly very ill done when one has been reprehended for any fault by the superior, to go and seek out how and by whom he came to the knowledge thereof, or to torment himself to know whether nothing more was told to him, or whether they have not exaggerated the fault, and in fine, to go and make complaints and inquiries in all directions, because, perhaps, he who related it may have done it in a more disadvantageous manner than he should have done. To do this is to commit a greater fault than the first, and very often we thereby more lessen our esteem and give greater scandal to our brethren than by the fault itself. They know very well that you are a man, and that you have your faults, but perceiving you are so sensible to a thing of this nature, they have but a worse opinion of you; because herein you show a great deal of pride, and give them occasion to think that you are not in pain about correcting your faults, but only how to hide them and to gain esteem by your exterior behaviour. " He who stiffly defends and excuses his fault", says St. Bernard, " when he is known to have committed it, how will he be able humbly to discover to his superior the secret faults into which he falls, and the bad thoughts of his heart, which are only known to himself?" He who is truly humble, and thinks of himself as he ought, does not wonder at what is said of him, nor of the faults he is accused of, because he still knows greater faults in himself, and thinks they have said too little in comparison of what they should have said of him. Self-love, with which you are blinded, makes you think the fault far less than it is, and even sometimes it makes you believe that it is no fault at all; but a third person, who sees the fault with disinterested eyes, as it is in itself, sees it after another manner than you do. But let us put the case that it appeared to him greater than it was in effect, and that for this reason he too much exaggerated it: do you not call to mind that when you were received to religion you were asked whether you were content to suffer, for the love of God, injuries, affronts, and false accusations, and that you answered you were content? How comes it then to pass that you have so soon forgot your promise, and how come you at present to repent yourself of it? You ought rejoice that your brother, believing he spoke truth, should have exaggerated your fault beyond what it deserved; and though he should not have done it innocently, but with a bad intention, yet you still ought to mind none but yourself, and be glad he has given you an occasion of greater humiliation and of imitating more perfectly Jesus Christ. With how far greater reason, then, are you obliged to be glad that he has innocently given you this occasion, as he thought what he said had been true! We gain a great deal more both in the sight of God and man when we do this, whereas, when we are too sensible to it, we lose on all sides whilst we think we gain.

But the fault would be still greater, if, coming to know by whom it was discovered, we should go to reproach the person for either having said it, or for having said more than was true, and afterwards show any coldness towards him, or let him know you retain any resentment thereof. He who truly desires to correct himself, and to aspire to perfection, would wish to have the eyes of the world upon him to make him more easily compass the end he proposes. "Oh! that I had", says St. Bernard, "a hundred pastors to take care of me; for the greater the number is, the greater security I find myself in. What a folly is it to make no difficulty to charge one's self with the cure of an infinity of souls, and to be angry when any one takes care of ours? For my own part I am more afraid of the teeth of the wolf than of a sheep-hook". Now, as to our brethren's faults, which we are to give notice of, we must, in the first place, know that they ought to be told to our superior in secret, that he as a good father may procure a remedy, and hinder the inconveniences that might otherwise happen thereby. Moreover, great care is to be taken herein, lest it should happen that, instead of telling the fault of our brother to our superior, who ought to go and remedy it, we should go and tell it to another, who has no right to know, nor has any care or inspection over him; for this would be very ill done, because it would be to fall into the sin of detraction.

In the second place we must, as the rule says, act with all possible "affection and charity". These are the terms with which Pope Gregory the Thirteenth was very well satisfied when he took the pains himself to examine our rules; and whoever wishes to do his duty herein ought to take great care that he acts not out of passion or envy, or that he permits himself to be carried away with an indiscreet zeal by presently going to make a report which he has but indirectly, and which is not as yet well digested. He ought also abstain from exaggerating things; such as of a fly making an elephant, and of a particular fault making a general destruction of all discipline. And, in fine, he ought avoid proposing his suspicions and mere imaginations as certainties and real truths; for there is reason to make a great scruple of this, and this indiscretion is oftentimes the cause of many disorders.

In the third place, it is to be observed, that though our brother likes not to be corrected for his faults, yet one ought not neglect to advertise the superior of them, and to do our duty, though he does not perform his. St. Austin, speaking of those that receive not correction in good part, says they are like frantic persons, who will hear nothing either of physic or physician. What, then, says he, ought to be done with such indocile spirits? Ought they be quite abandoned, and no care at all taken of their cure? No such thing; "for a madman has no wish to be bound, and he who is in a lethargy would not be awaked; and yet charity neglects not to persist in binding the one, and in waking the other, and in loving them both; and though both of them are herewith offended, yet both of them are beloved. Pain is caused to both, and disquiet also, so long as they are indisposed, which displeases them; but as soon as they are cured they perceive the favour that was done them, and are extremely pleased therewith". We must hope it will be the same with our brother; for though he is angry at present that he is reprehended, yet the time will come, when, entering into himself and considering the things as in God's sight, he will acknowledge his fault, and be sensibly obliged for the charity you have done him. If men, says the same father, neglect not to take a great deal of pains, and sometimes even expose themselves to great dangers, to cure beasts "who have no understanding"—*Ps.*, xxxi. 9,—and from whom they can hope for no thanks, with how far greater reason ought we labour for the cure and correction of our brother, that he may not eternally perish? He is endowed with reason, and he may one day come to be sensible of the greatness of the favour you have done him. "For he who reprehends another", says the wise man, "will afterwards be in greater esteem with him than he who deceives him by flatteries"—*Prov.*, xxviii. 23. St. Basil applies to this subject the words of St. Paul to the Corinthians, " who is there from whom I receive the greatest joy, but from him to whom I have given sorrow?"—II. *Cor.*, ii. 2. The pain and trouble that correction gives you is what gives me joy, because I know that you receive profit thereby. "For true sadness, according to God, produces a solid and wholesome penance; and even that which has afflicted you according to God, how great a solicitude has it caused in you!"—II. *Cor.*, vii. 10, 11. But you will say there are some persons to whom corrections and admonitions do no good at all. St. Austin answers very well to this objection : " Alas!" says he, " must we abstain entirely from medicine because some diseases are incurable?" No certainly; we ought not then abstain from the correction of our brethren, because some of them make not good use of it. It is a duty of physicians, both of soul and body, presently to employ all their care and art for the cure of sick persons, and never to abandon them, but always to give them some remedy or other.

Now, as to the manner of correcting, St. Basil says that he who does it ought to imitate physicians, who are never angry with their patients, but regard only their distemper, and endeavour all they can by remedies to resist and cure it. He therefore who reprehends another ought never be angry with him who has offended; he must only apply himself to retrench whatsoever is bad in him; he ought to do, continues the father, as a physician would that treats his own child for a very painful wound. With what niceness and circumspection does he dress it. One may perceive that he feels the pain of his son as if it were his own. Thus a superior ought to do in regard of those he corrects. He is their father, they are his children; he ought to reprehend them as the apostle did, "with the spirit of meekness"—*Gal.*, vi. 1. "He that would kill a man", says St. Austin, "cares not which way he does it; but he who desires to cure one, is obliged, in making incisions, to take care how he makes them". The superior who proposes to himself the cure of his brother by correction, and not to do him any hurt, ought to have the same regard and circumspection; and this is a thing of very great importance, and which the saints recommend very much unto us. Let him, say they, who reprehends another, take care of showing the least passion or anger; for he will thereby lose all the fruit he would otherwise have been able to produce—he will not cure the distemper, but rather make it worse. And they quote on this subject the words of the apostle, "reprehending with meekness those that resist truth"—II. *Tim.*, i. 25. For though the ordinary translation says, "with modesty", yet both signify the same thing; for to reprehend with modesty, one must do it without anger or passion. To conclude, we must so season correction, that he to whom it is given may be persuaded that whatever is said to him springs from an excess of affection and charity, and from an ardent desire of seeing him perfect. For when it is taken in this manner, it never fails to become profitable.

END OF VOLUME THIRD.

www.ingramcontent.com/pod-product-compliance
Lightning Source LLC
Chambersburg PA
CBHW022116290426
44112CB00008B/700